John Bankhead Magruder

SOUTHERN BIOGRAPHY SERIES

BERTRAM WYATT-BROWN, SERIES EDITOR

John Bankhead Magruder

★ A MILITARY REAPPRAISAL ★

THOMAS M. SETTLES

GENEALOGY BY KIMBERLY C. CAMPBELL

LOUISIANA STATE UNIVERSITY PRESS ⚜ BATON ROUGE

Published by Louisiana State University Press
Copyright © 2009 by Louisiana State University Press
All rights reserved
Manufactured in the United States of America
First printing

Designer: Barbara Neely Bourgoyne
Typefaces: Minion Pro, text; Onyx BT and Engravers Gothic, display
Printer and binder: Thomson-Shore, Inc.

Title page image of Magruder is reproduced courtesy of the Central Rappahannock Heritage
Center, Fredericksburg, Virginia.

LIBRARY OF CONGRESS CATALOGING-IN-PUBLICATION DATA
Settles, Thomas Michael, 1944–
    John Bankhead Magruder : a military reappraisal / Thomas M. Settles ; genealogy by
Kimberly C. Campbell.
        p. cm. — (Southern biography series)
    Includes bibliographical references and index.
    ISBN 978-0-8071-3391-0 (cloth : alk. paper) 1. Magruder, John Bankhead, 1807–1871. 2.
Magruder, John Bankhead, 1807–1871—Military leadership. 3. Generals—Confederate States
of America—Biography. 4. Confederate States of America. Army—Biography. 5. United
States—History—Civil War, 1861–1865—Artillery operations, Confederate. 6. United States—
History—Civil War, 1861–1865—Campaigns. 7. Texas—History—Civil War, 1861–1865. 8.
Soldiers—United States—Biography. 9. United States. Army—Biography. I. Campbell,
Kimberly Curtis. II. Title.

    E467.1.M36S48 2009
    973.7′82092—dc22
    [B]

                                                                2008034611

CONTENTS

PREFACE   vii

1   Every Inch a Soldier   1

2   Opportunity in Mexico   38

3   Between the Wars   79

4   Protecting the Approach to Richmond   118

5   Magruder Defends, Johnston Retreats   158

6   "In Obedience to Your Orders, Twice Repeated"   195

7   High Tide, Low Tide, in Texas   242

8   Postwar Odyssey   281

BIBLIOGRAPHY   307

INDEX   327

Photographs follow page 194.

PREFACE

Years ago, Pulitzer Prize–winning author John Alexander Carroll remarked that Douglas Southall Freeman had a curious bias against General John Bankhead Magruder. Moreover, Carroll, who for many years had been Freeman's full-time associate, suggested that a carefully researched study of Magruder might significantly improve the general's standing in history. When I showed an interest in undertaking the suggested study, Carroll referred me to Thomas Robson Hay, who had been researching Magruder since the early 1950s. Hay, winner of the American Historical Association's Robert M. Johnston Military History prize for his study *Hood's Tennessee Campaign,* was one of Freeman's closest friends in the history community, yet the two scholars viewed Magruder differently, Hay being much more positive about the general than Freeman. By the early 1970s, some twenty years after Freeman's death, Hay had become convinced that of all of the major figures of the Civil War era, John Magruder was perhaps the least understood. This, Hay believed, was largely because Magruder left no diary, no completed memoirs, no will, not even a family Bible. There are no birth records, no family records, and very few surviving personal papers. All of Magruder's personal papers were destroyed in a San Francisco fire in 1850, and he kept no papers thereafter. Given the dearth of personal correspondence and official legal papers, it is not surprising that much of what has been written about Magruder is incorrect.

Historians are even misinformed about the name by which Magruder was commonly addressed. When he accepted his appointment to the United States Military Academy, Magruder signed the letter "John B. Magruder." Afterward, however, he always signed his correspondence "J. Bankhead

Magruder." Thus, many have inferred that he used the name "Bankhead." For example, George Shackleford, in his biography of George Wythe Randolph states that friends and family customarily called Magruder "Bankhead." Yet this is not the case. Thorough research has uncovered numerous direct quotes from both close friends and family members of Magruder. They always referred to him as "John."

Other significant factual inaccuracies can be found in such standard reference works as the *Dictionary of American Biography* (*DAB*), which reports Magruder's date of birth as August 15, 1810, yet both John Magruder and his father stated that the birth date was May 1, 1807. The *DAB* records Magruder's place of birth as Winchester, Virginia, but he was actually born in Port Royal, Virginia, near Fredericksburg. And it erroneously declares that Magruder never married, when, in fact, he was married for almost forty years to Esther Henrietta von Kapff, who bore him three children: Isabella, Katherine Elizabeth, and Henry.

Freeman repeated several of these factual errors in both *R. E. Lee* and *Lee's Lieutenants*. More important, he glossed over mistakes that Lee and Stonewall Jackson made during the Seven Days' battles, deflecting the blame to others, including Magruder. Robert H. Chilton, Lee's chief of staff, likewise sought to direct blame for the quasi-failure of the Seven Days' campaign away from Lee and himself by charging Magruder with incompetence. Jefferson Davis allowed Magruder to counter Chilton's allegations with a formal written response. When submitted, the response satisfied Davis and quieted Chilton. Interestingly enough, it did not satisfy Freeman, who charged that the report was entirely self-serving. This he declared without ever knowing what the charges were to which Magruder was responding or even who authored them. Freeman, in fact, incorrectly surmised that the accuser was D. H. Hill. Assuming there to be a conflict between Magruder and Hill and that Magruder's response was directed against Hill, Freeman in *Lee's Lieutenants* criticized Magruder in support of Hill in a controversy that never existed. Hill never accused Magruder of anything, and Magruder's response was, of course, directed against Chilton, not Hill. In all of Freeman's fine works, this is the only instance of which I am aware that he based an argument on facts that were supposed rather than real. Had Freeman understood that Magruder's defense was written in response to a vicious personal attack by Chilton rather than as a discourse against Hill or as an elaborate justification of his own actions during the Seven Days' battles, he no doubt would have viewed Magruder in a much more favorable light.

Tom Hay knew what Freeman did not, having discovered Chilton's charges in the National Archives. And with all of the evidence before him, Hay concluded that John Magruder was unjustly blamed for mistakes that were more attributable to Stonewall Jackson, Robert Chilton, and Benjamin Huger. Regrettably, Tom Hay died before publishing his Magruder biography. Thus, historians who have subsequently written on Prince John were unaware of his findings. They have all used Freeman's skewed understanding of Magruder as their starting point and have consequently been entirely too negative toward the general. Under the circumstances, it is not surprising that Magruder's reputation has suffered. After conducting over thirty years of my own painstaking research, however, I have come to the conclusion that Hay's more positive assessment is the more historically correct.

I have endeavored to produce a work that rests upon an unshakable foundation of credible sources in order to provide readers with a complete and accurate portrayal of John Bankhead Magruder. In pursuit of that goal, numerous important factual errors previously made regarding Magruder are addressed and corrected. Painstaking genealogical research also uncovers a significant amount of new material on the Magruder and von Kapff families. Other research produces the heretofore untold final chapter on Prince John Magruder from the time of his death until he was memorialized by the citizens of Galveston in a splendid ceremony nearly a quarter-century later. And finally, the book addresses several areas of controversy, such as Magruder's alleged drinking problem and his relations with his family, in which earlier, incorrect conclusions have been drawn, preventing a proper understanding of Magruder the man and his place in history.

Because my study is revisionist in nature, I have always known that it would be received with some skepticism. In anticipation thereof, long before submitting the manuscript for publication, I had my own readers carefully evaluate the document in its entirety. The late Frank Vandiver was particularly helpful with Magruder's Civil War service in Virginia. Edward Cotham Jr. offered advice on the entire manuscript but focused his attention on Magruder's activities in Texas, which is his area of expertise. And Leonard Riedel Jr. of the Blue and Gray Education Society provided factual data and encouragement during the early years of this project. I am also deeply indebted to Kimberly Campbell of Bowling Green, Virginia, who provided invaluable assistance with the Magruder family background. Campbell is a professional genealogist whose husband, Ray, is the circuit court clerk for Caroline County, Virginia, the county in which Magruder was born and raised until he departed for college. By meticulously researching old Caroline County records and genealogical resources in nearby Maryland, she has discovered a wealth of important new information on John Magruder's date and place of birth, family background, and upbringing, all of which has until now been the subject of mere speculation. Credit Kim Campbell for all of the extraordinary research, plus the writing in the early part of the book on the Magruder family history.

This biographical endeavor would never have been possible without the scholarly assistance of Tom Hay, Frank Vandiver, Ed Cotham, and Kim Campbell, as well as the encouragement that I received from Jack Carroll and Len Riedel. I will always be grateful to them for their numerous contributions. I will also be eternally appreciative of the many years that Diane Thomas Roth spent by my side as typist, editor, critic, and friend. However, I absolve all of these talented people of responsibility for any shortcomings that the completed work may have. The final responsibility is mine and mine alone.

I submitted the Magruder study to the Louisiana State University Press because of the excellent reputation of the Southern Biography Series and because LSU is one of the few university presses remaining that places the referencing notes on the page of the citation rather than burying them at the conclusion of each chapter or at the end of the book. This is very important to me because my study invites historical scrutiny. I fully expect readers to encounter information and conclusions that run contrary to that which they had previously understood about Magruder. I want them to be able, at a glance, to see the source of the information so that they can conduct their own scholarly investigations and form their own opinions based on documentable facts. The facts, I believe, will reshape opinions that have been based on that which historian Justin H. Smith, nearly one hundred years ago, disdainfully termed "traditional prejudices and misinformation."

It has long been held, for instance, that Magruder took credit for the opening victory of the Civil War at Big Bethel when the credit should have gone to others. Historians who have promoted this notion did so based on the assertion by D. H. Hill's biographer, Hal Bridges, that while Magruder commanded the Confederate force at Bethel, he gave few battle orders and allowed Hill to manage most of the fighting. This was Bridges's conclusion after reading the writings of one of Hill's North Carolinians who carelessly bragged in the battle's aftermath that Hill and his men deserved full credit for the victory. Yet if Bridges and the more recent writers who shared his view had read D. H. Hill's detailed, official report of the battle, it would have become obvious that Magruder superintended the fighting for the Confederates. Hill, in fact, cited four occasions when Magruder rushed troops to assist at critical points when the Confederate line began to falter. Four! If those who have written inaccurately about Big Bethel exhibited an imperfect understanding of the battle because they failed to read Hill's report, their research is inadequate. If they read Hill's report but chose to ignore it, they are lacking in objectivity. Either way, their negative conclusions precluded Magruder's receiving the credit that he rightfully deserved for leading his men to victory.

John Bankhead Magruder possessed great talent and exceptional intelligence, yet he was far from perfect. He was nearly expelled from West Point during his First Class Year, when he came dangerously close to exceeding the maximum allowable number of demerits. He showed no aptitude for business and through his own financial mismanagement was constantly in debt. And he often disagreed with superiors, including Roger Jones, Joseph E. Johnston, Gustavus W. Smith, and Judah P. Benjamin. Magruder was headstrong, egotistical, vain, and occasionally ill-tempered; plus, he certainly enjoyed the high life. Adjutant General Roger Jones, who was well aware of Magruder's social proclivities, viewed Prince John as an unconventional player in a profession that demanded strict adherence to conformity. Jones failed to acknowledge Magruder's talents or service because he simply could not fathom how one could be such a maverick in private life yet a professional in his military service. To Jones and others Magruder was an anomaly, impossible either to comprehend or to appreciate.

In the end, John Magruder's own friends and contemporaries understood him best. Among them was fellow Caroline County native General Dabney H. Maury, who founded the Southern Historical Society in 1868. Maury paid fitting tribute to Prince John when he wrote: "Magruder was so brilliant and gallant in social life that his remarkable talents were not appreciated. He received less credit for his remarkable genius for war than he deserved. I wish I could do justice to a man so brilliant, so brave, and so devoted to Virginia."

It is my sincere hope that this work does justice to that man.

John Bankhead Magruder

1

EVERY INCH A SOLDIER

The *New York Herald,* on February 20, 1871, portrayed John Bankhead Magruder as the "aristocrat of aristocrats in the old army."[1] His modest military salary invariably lagged behind the cost of his spectacular social escapades, yet somehow he was always sufficiently ingenious to overcome his want of financial liquidity. In the end, a lack of funds would prove to be no more of a handicap on the social circuit than a lack of manpower on the Virginia Peninsula or a lack of firepower on the coast of Texas during the Civil War. Whether fighting or entertaining, Magruder had a magical ability to deceive others about the extent of his resources. It was a talent that would serve him well throughout his life.

John Magruder spent nearly all of his adult years in military service. Educated and trained to arms, he read voraciously and studied military science religiously long after graduating from West Point in 1830. Twice prior to the Civil War he traveled to Europe to observe Continental armies in battle. Magruder knew all of the maxims of warfare but was flexible enough to know when to deviate from them. He was a perfectionist. He planned his battles as meticulously as he planned his parties, and he was usually in the center of the action in both. Yet although he played important roles in two major American wars, disagreement remains regarding his effectiveness in them. Author David H. Strother judged that Magruder's genius in executing grand maneuvers was "Napoleonic,"[2] and Union general Edward R. S. Canby

---

1. *New York Herald,* February 20, 1871.

2. D. H. Strother, "Personal Recollections of the War," *Harper's Magazine* 33 (October 1866): 549.

called Magruder "the greatest strategist on American soil."[3] On the other hand, Colonel Robert H. Chilton, Lee's chief of staff, charged that he was "utterly incompetent."[4] Because the assessments are so varied, John Magruder remains one of the least understood of the major figures of the American Civil War.

Interestingly, while contemporaries and modern scholars alike disagree on Magruder's military standing, there is universal agreement on his standing in society. His intellectual versatility, graceful speech, impeccable dress, and courtly manners were legendary. In society Magruder had no peer. He was, according to Douglas Southall Freeman, a *bon vivant par excellence*.[5]

John Bankhead Magruder was born in Port Royal, Caroline County, Virginia, on May 1, 1807.[6] His father, Thomas Magruder, had emigrated to northern

---

3. Horace Bell, *On the Old West Coast*, ed. Lanier Bartlett (New York: William Morrow, 1930), 152.

4. Chilton to Cooper, July 11, 1862, Board of Proceedings in the Case of Colonel Robert H. Chilton, Confederate States Army, War Department Collection of Confederate Records, National Archives.

5. Douglas Southall Freeman, *Lee's Lieutenants: A Study in Command*, 3 vols. (New York: Charles Scribner's Sons, 1942), 1:15.

6. When Magruder matriculated at the University of Virginia, he reported his birthday as May 1, 1807, and when he entered West Point, he gave his age as nineteen years and two months, which confirms the May 1807 date of birth. Years later his father also reported the May 1, 1807, birth date when, in a deposition in a case involving family inheritance, he listed the birth dates of each of the ten Magruder children. Most encyclopedias, however, including the *Dictionary of American Biography*, erroneously record John Magruder's birth date as August 15, 1810. Beside the error in date of birth, there are two additional inaccuracies: Magruder's place of birth and the statement that he never married. When Thomas Magruder married Elizabeth Bankhead of Port Royal, Va., they eventually settled in her town of residence. Port Royal is located on the Rappahannock River in Caroline County, Va. Those reporting Magruder's place of birth have confused Port Royal with Front Royal, a small town near Winchester, Va., and consequently, Magruder's birthplace is usually given as Winchester. Birth records are not available at either location, but Magruder in his own hand repeatedly referred to Caroline County as the county of his nativity, and his obituary in the *New York Times*, February 20, 1871, reported he was "born at Port Royal, Caroline County, Virginia." Additionally, George Fitzhugh (1806–81), a Port Royal neighbor, states, "Those excellent officers, Captain George Magruder of the Navy and Colonel John Magruder of the Army, both natives of Port Royal," in an undated article written for *DeBow's Review* in the George H. S. King Papers, Virginia Historical Society, Richmond. And, finally, there can be no mistake about the marriage. On May 18, 1831, John Magruder wed Henrietta von Kapff, daughter of Bernard Johann and Hettie Henrietta von Kapff, of Baltimore. Marriage notices were printed in the *Baltimore American*, May 19, 1831; *Baltimore Gazette*, May 19, 1831; *Baltimore Republican and Commercial Advertiser*, May 20, 1831; and the Fredericksburg, Va., *Political Arena*, May 27, 1831.

Virginia from his home in Montgomery County, Maryland, and earned his living as a part-time lawyer, grocer, postmaster, and tavern keeper,[7] before settling upon a career in law. He practiced at the old Chancery Court in Fredericksburg and eventually won a "high reputation" in the profession as a contemporary of Isaac Williams, Carter Stevenson, General John Minor, and the venerable John Tayloe Lomax, "illustrious lawyers of that day, whose legal and forensic abilities adorn the history of the Virginia bar."[8]

The Magruders, Pendletons, Taylors, Turners, Corbins, Hoomeses, Dickersons, and others were the gentlemen farmers of Caroline. They usually lived on large estates and "were noted for their profuse living and lavish hospitality." Community social life revolved around an unending cycle of dinners, parties, and balls. Well-to-do parents prepared their children for future prominent roles in society by teaching the social graces and stressing the importance of such hallowed southern precepts as loyalty, integrity, dignity, responsibility, and honor. Parents also made sure their children were well versed in the classics and other works of literature, from which young readers learned lessons of chivalrous devotion to duty, patriotism, and valor. Outside of the home, however, the men of Caroline, when in the company of friends, participated in less laudable activities—cockfighting, hunting, horseracing, target shooting, informal political debating, card playing, and convivial drinking. These activities usually transpired in Bowling Green, the county seat and "rendezvous of many wild young men, whose reckless pursuit of pleasure often carried them into lamentable excesses."[9] As a boy, John Magruder witnessed this merrymaking. While growing into adulthood, he embraced southern values, learned courtly manners, and polished his social skills. He acquired a taste for classical literature, fine spirits and cuisine, and grand entertaining. And as a climax, in later years he became the centerpiece of society.

7. *Virginia Herald*, April 26, 1792; January 13, 1797; Ralph Emmett Fall, *Hidden Village, Port Royal, Virginia, 1744-1981* (Verona, Va.: McClure Printing Co., 1982), 97, 353–54, 359, 362. Thomas Magruder was a grocer in Fredericksburg and Port Royal, postmaster of Port Royal, and co-manager with Leonard George of Fox's Tavern in Port Royal, at the same time that he conducted his part-time law practice.

8. "Sketch of the Life and Public Services of Major General J. Bankhead Magruder," *Houston Telegraph*, December 24, 1862; "Gen. John Bankhead Magruder," *Richmond Whig*, July 4, 1861; in the Caroline County Order Book, 1822–24, inside front cover on one of the unnumbered pages, is a list of the attorneys practicing before the court: (1) John Tayloe Lomax (2) Carter L. Stevenson (3) Thomas Magruder (4) Garrit Minor . . . and (26) John Minor. Issac Williams was not listed.

9. Susan P. Lee, *Memoirs of William Nelson Pendleton* (Philadelphia: J. B. Lippincott, 1893), 23–25.

John Bankhead Magruder's family history begins with Alexander Magruder,[10] who had been a supporter of Charles I in his losing effort against the forces of Oliver Cromwell in the English Civil War. After the decisive Battle of Worcester in 1651, the Roundheads deported many Royalists to the British American colonies. Alexander Magruder, John's great-great-great-grandfather, was one of the deportees. He settled in what is now Prince George's County, Maryland. By the time he died, in 1676/77, he had amassed 2,400 acres of real property, including the plantations Alexander's Hope, Anchovie Hills, Craig Night, and Good Luck. In his will he divided the property among his six children, James, Samuel, John, Alexander, Nathaniel, and Elizabeth.[11]

Samuel Magruder, John B. Magruder's great-great-grandfather, inherited the plantation Good Luck. Samuel married Sarah, believed to be the daughter of Ninean Beall of Calvert County, Maryland, although no documentary evidence has yet been found.[12] They had eleven children, Ninean, John, James, William, Alexander, Nathaniel, Elizabeth, Sarah, Verlinda, Mary, and Elinor. Samuel Magruder died in 1711 and his wife, Sarah, in 1734, both leaving wills.[13]

John Bankhead Magruder's direct ancestor was William. He married Mary Frazer, and they had children Thomas, George Frazer, Basil, Ann, Susanna, Barbara, Elizabeth, and Verlinda. The family lived on Turkey Cocke Branch Plantation, a 193-acre tract in Prince George's County, which William had inherited from his father. William Magruder died testate in 1765, as had his wife, Mary (Frazer) Magruder, in 1774. They left Turkey Cocke Branch Plantation to "their unmarried daughters." George Frazer Magruder, John's grandfather, was left with a paltry twenty shillings and a mourning ring.[14]

---

10. The American family surname Magruder was originally MacGregor in Scotland. By an act of the Privy Council of Scotland dated April 3, 1603, however, all MacGregors were forced to take new surnames "on pain of death." Many of the Magruders and MacGregors today are members of the American Clan Gregor Society. Egbert Watson Magruder, ed., *Yearbook of the American Clan Gregor Society, 1913* (Richmond, Va.: Ware and Duke Printers, 1914) has excellent information on the family history.

11. Effie Gwynn Bowie, *Across the Years in Prince George's County* (Richmond, Va.: Garrett and Massie, 1947), 534–36; Will for Alexander Magruder, Prince George's County, Md., Wills. All Maryland records can be found in the Maryland State Archives, Annapolis.

12. This is probably due to the loss by fire of the Calvert County, Md., records.

13. Wills for Samuel Magruder and Sarah Magruder, Prince George's County, Md., Wills, in the Maryland State Archives.

14. Bowie, *Across the Years in Prince George's County*, 538; Wills for William Magruder and Mary Magruder, Prince George's County, Md., Wills, in the Maryland State Archives.

George married Eleanor Bowie, daughter of James Bowie and his wife, Martha. They lived for a time at Blue Plains in Prince George's County but later moved to Montgomery County. At the time that his will was written, George Frazer Magruder listed Montgomery County as his residence, although he died in Frederick County, Maryland, where his will was probated on January 27, 1801. He named six children in his will: William, Allen, Thomas, Dennis, Amelia, and Julia. All of the children except William were listed in the final accounting that was recorded on September 5, 1803. Division was "agreeable to [the] will," and each of the five legatees received seventy-two pounds, nineteen shillings, and four pence.[15]

By the time Thomas Magruder, John's father, claimed his inheritance, he had been living in northern Virginia for over a decade. On June 22, 1797, he married nineteen-year-old Elizabeth Bankhead, the eldest daughter of the late James Bankhead of Westmoreland County and Christian Miller Bankhead of Port Royal.[16] Over the next twenty-odd years Elizabeth gave birth to ten children: Eliza, George, Isabella, James, John, William, Allan, Juliana, Janetta, and Frederick.[17] After spending the first two years of their marriage

15. Will for George Frazer Magruder with Executor's Final Accounting, Benjamin Murdock, acting executor, Frederick County, Md., Wills, in the Maryland State Archives.

16. Fredericksburg, Va., Circuit Court Clerk's Auxiliary Office, suits styled *Magruder v. Miller,* ended year, 1818, and *Bankhead and Gray v. Miller's Executors,* ended year, 1823, Deposition of Christian (Miller) Bankhead, mother of Elizabeth (Bankhead) Magruder, in a dispute over inheritance. After James Bankhead died in Westmoreland County in 1785, Christian moved back to Port Royal, the town of her birth.

17. When Congressman Robert S. Garnett recommended John Bankhead Magruder for an appointment to the U.S. Military Academy, he mentioned in his February 4, 1821, letter to the secretary of war that there were ten Magruder children. Contrariwise, both of the genealogists who have subsequently researched the Magruder/Bankhead families, the Reverend Horace Edwin Hayden and Mrs. J. E. Warren, have written that there were eight children, four boys and four girls. Hayden and Warren have the same eight children listed in their genealogical studies, but they disagree on the order of issue.

Genealogist Kimberly C. Campbell of Bowling Green, Va., has resolved the conflict in favor of Congressman Garnett. In a deposition given by Thomas Magruder on September 8–9, 1845, in a chancery suit styled *Magruder v. Anderson,* Thomas Magruder lists the names of all ten of his children, with dates of birth and death. Campbell's research has at long last definitively solved three historical mysteries, which heretofore had been the subjects of mere speculation: (1) there were ten children, six boys and four girls. Neither Hayden nor Warren was aware of sons James and Frederick; (2) the order of issue has been correctly established; and (3) John Bankhead's birthday has been confirmed as May 1, 1807.

The Magruder children are: (1) Eliza B., born March 26, 1798 (married John L. Pendleton, a lawyer and clerk of court for Caroline County, Va.); (2) George Allan, born June 26, 1800

in Alexandria, Virginia, Thomas, Elizabeth, and their firstborn child, Eliza, relocated to Port Royal and lived in the household of James Miller, the grandfather of Thomas's wife.[18] Caroline County Personal Property Tax Lists, 1794–1811, show Thomas Magruder owning virtually no property until after the final accounting of his father's estate in Maryland in 1803.[19] However, the 1810 census for Caroline County lists him as the owner of thirteen slaves,[20] and in 1817 he purchased the former home of Dr. John Bankhead and the ac-

---

(George A. Magruder entered the U.S. Navy in 1817, attaining the rank of captain; at the beginning of the Civil War he was chief of the Bureau of Ordnance and Hydrography of the Navy Department but resigned from the service on April 22, 1861; he married Maria Margaretta Swan); (3) Isabella, born October 6, 1802 (married George Pendleton Turner and was living with her family, including Thomas, her father, at Aberfoyle until her death in 1859); (4) James, born December 26, 1804, and died January 28, 1822, at the age of seventeen (this is the only existing record of him); (5) John Bankhead, born May 1, 1807; (6) William B., born May 25, 1809, and died September 10, 1833, at the age of twenty-four years (in her research Mrs. J. E. Warren states incorrectly that he died in infancy; his obituary was printed in the *Richmond Whig* on September 24, 1833); (7) Allan Bowie, born September 6, 1811 (Allan Bowie Magruder was a lawyer admitted to the bar of Albermarle County, Va., in 1838, Confederate officer, and writer; he was probably named for his father's brother, Allan B. Magruder); (8) Juliana, born January 21, 1814 (never married; was possibly named for her father's sister, Julia Magruder Brashear); (9) Janetta, born March 26, 1817 (married Major Robert Poore, who was later killed at Gettysburg); and (10) Frederick, born in 1819 or 1820 and lived only a few months (there is no other existing record for this child). See Robert S. Garnett to secretary of war, February 4, 1821, National Archives; Rev. Horace Edwin Hayden, *Virginia Genealogies: A Genealogy of the Glassell Family of Scotland and Virginia, also of the Families of Ball, Brown, Bryan, Conway, Daniel, Ewell, Holladay, Lewis, Littlepage, Moncure, Peyton, Robinson, Scott, Taylor, Wallace, and Others, of Virginia and Maryland* (Baltimore: Genealogical Publishing Co., 1973), 448; Mrs. J. E. Warren, "Bankhead Family," *William and Mary Quarterly* 9, ser. 2 (1929): 305–7; and Caroline County, Va., Circuit Court Record Room, file drawer marked "Ended Papers: 1848–1849," suit styled *Magruder v. Anderson,* Deposition of Thomas Magruder, September 8–9, 1845. (The only birth date that cannot be discerned from the *Magruder v. Anderson* document is that of George Allan Magruder, as the month of his birth has been written over. Fortunately, the National Archives has George Allan Magruder's February 3, 1817, letter accepting his commission as a midshipman in the U.S. Navy. At the bottom of the letter Thomas Magruder certifies that his son "was born in the town of Port Royal, Va., on the 26th day of June, 1800.")

18. Fredericksburg, Va., Circuit Court Clerk's Auxiliary Office, suits styled *Bankhead and Gray v. Miller's Executors,* ended year, 1823; and *Bankhead v. Miller,* ended year, 1818.

19. Caroline County Personal Property Tax Lists, 1794–1811, Library of Virginia, Archives Division, Richmond.

20. Report of the U.S. Census Bureau, 1810, for Caroline County, Va.; Caroline County Personal Property Tax Lists, 1794–1811, Library of Virginia, Archives Division, Richmond.

companying two acres of land.[21] Unfortunately, Thomas Magruder failed in his role as the family provider. By 1820 he owned no slaves,[22] and his homestead was sold at public auction in 1825.[23] He never again owned real property in his name, and later court records indicate that he was constantly in debt, including to his own sons. Thomas was eventually reduced to living on his wife's property, Aberfoyle, in Caroline County with his daughter Isabella Turner and her family, while Elizabeth lived with son Allan and his family in Albermarle County.[24]

Thomas Magruder, even with his faults, had a profound impact upon John's life, as demonstrated by an unusual number of parallels. Each was involved in one or more duels, despite the fact that dueling was illegal. Both married wealthy heiresses who later lived apart from their husbands. Both Thomas and John enjoyed the high life; however, neither man had any discernible aptitude for business or financial management. Consequently, they were often in debt. It is entirely possible that their elaborate social displays may have been compensation for feelings of social and/or financial inadequacy due to the reduced circumstances of their immediate families while relatives around them enjoyed great wealth and possessed vast landholdings. Regardless of the reason, neither Magruder ever allowed a shortage of funds to curtail his social endeavors. They spent whatever money they had, and if it was not enough, they borrowed. And they did so without hesitation or reservation.

The principal difference between father and son was in their chosen professions. Thomas was a practitioner of the law; John became a military man. It was from the Bankhead side of the family that young John first acquired

21. Fall, *Hidden Village: Port Royal, Virginia, 1744–1981*, 140; Caroline County, Va., Land Tax List, 1817–26, two acres of land owned by Thomas Magruder from Mutual Assurance Society, Policy No. 797. Thomas Magruder's insurance policy on the home bought from John Bankhead, dated March 1817. Microfilm copies located at Central Rappahannock Regional Library, Virginiana Room, Fredericksburg, Va.

22. Report of the U.S. Census Bureau, 1820, for Caroline County, Va.

23. Fall, *Hidden Village: Port Royal, Virginia, 1744–1981*, 140.

24. Elizabeth Magruder died August 19, 1849, and is buried in Maplewood Cemetery, Charlottesville, Va. There is no record, however, of Thomas Magruder's death date or place of burial. No obituary can be located. No will, administration bond, or inventory is extant in the records. The 1850 Census for Caroline County placed Magruder at Aberfoyle with his daughter Isabella and her family, but he was not listed as residing in Caroline County or any other in the state of Virginia in the 1860 census. In all probability Thomas Magruder had died by this time and was buried with his daughter at Aberfoyle.

an interest in soldiering. He no doubt listened to the many exciting military stories about his late grandfather Colonel James Bankhead, who had served as an officer in the Revolutionary War, and the personal reminiscences of Bankhead's son, James, John's uncle, who was adjutant-general of the State of Virginia during the War of 1812 and later a brigadier general in the regular army during the war with Mexico. When John showed more of an interest in a military rather than a legal career, his uncle encouraged him to pursue an appointment to the United States Military Academy. Colonel Bankhead, Colonel Constant Freeman, Thomas Magruder, and Virginia congressman Robert S. Garnett wrote letters of recommendation,[25] and on February 25, 1825, Magruder was notified of his appointment by Secretary of War John C. Calhoun.[26] His class would not report until July 1, 1826, but his education continued uninterrupted after the completion of his studies at the Rappahannock Academy.[27]

On September 6, 1825, John entered the first class of the University of Virginia.[28] He was one of 123 students who came from such conspicuous Virginia families as Ambler, Bolling, Brockenbrough, Carter, Cary, Cocke, Eyre, Fairfax, Harrison, Hubard, Lee, Magruder, Marshall, Mason, Meriwether, Nelson, Page, Peyton, Preston, Randolph, Saunders, Selden, Scott, Slaughter, Spotswood, Stuart, Tayloe, Tazewell, Wallace, Watkins, Wellford, Wickham, and Yates. "To call the roll of their names," wrote Philip Alexander Bruce, who wrote the magnificent history of the University of Virginia, "is to call the roll of families who have deeply stamped their virtues and their talents

25. Thomas Magruder to secretary of war, January 13, 1821; Garnett to secretary of war, February 4, 1821; and Freeman to secretary of war, March 3, 1821. Hereafter cited as Magruder's USMA File, National Archives. Colonel Bankhead's letter of recommendation was not included in Magruder's File, but Garnett referred to it in his letter.

26. Calhoun to Magruder, February 25, 1825. Magruder actually received the appointment from Robert S. Garnett, the congressman from his district and father of General Robert S. Garnett, a brigadier general in the Confederate army, who was killed in action at Carrick's Ford, Va., on July 13, 1861. Magruder accepted his appointment in a letter to the secretary of war (James Barbour) dated March 11, 1825, Magruder's USMA File, National Archives. Magruder's letter of acceptance is the earliest in his autograph now extant.

27. Thomas Magruder was a trustee of the academy for many years. Rappahannock Academy Minutes, Caroline County, Va., 1810–22, part of the Robb-Bernard Papers, Swem Library, College of William and Mary, Williamsburg, Va.; Fall, *Hidden Village, Port Royal, Virginia, 1744–1981*, 290–92.

28. Matriculation Register of the University of Virginia, Alderman Library, University of Virginia.

upon every aspect of the State's history during the long interval . . . that followed the Revolution and preceded the War of Secession."[29]

The quality of the student body was indicative of the high opinion that the citizens of Virginia had of their new university. From the outset the school enjoyed an excellent reputation, if for no other reason than by association. James Madison was its rector, James Monroe a member of its Board of Visitors, and Thomas Jefferson its principal patron and benefactor. Furthermore, the faculty was carefully selected, and several of its members—including George Blaettermann, modern languages; Thomas Hewett Key and John P. Emmet, mathematics; George Long, ancient languages; and George Tucker, ethics—had been attracted to the university from Europe.[30]

There existed on the campus a bias against foreigners, however, which led to an unfortunate student riot. It appears that Key and Long were at the center of the controversy. On the night of September 30, 1825, a large bottle "filled with a foul liquid" was thrown through Long's window, and the following evening a group of students, disguised with masks, gathered on the lawn and began chanting, "Down with the foreign professors." Doctor Emmet and Professor Tucker emerged from the gathering and seized the sheet-clad leader of the demonstration, causing an instantaneous reaction from the crowd. One unidentified student threw a brick at Emmet, and another assailed Tucker with a cane. The demonstration quickly became a riot, and the two professors were fortunate to escape the angry, cursing mob.[31]

Instead of apologizing for their actions, sixty-five students, including Magruder, signed a petition sharply criticizing Emmet and Tucker for attacking the student leader. Key and Long tendered their resignations immediately thereafter. "We have lost all confidence in the signers of this remonstrance," they said, "and we cannot and will not meet them again." The other faculty members drew up a supporting resolution in which they threatened to resign en masse unless the Board of Visitors adopted an effective system of police and discipline. As the board was in session at Monticello, the riot became the object of their immediate attention. Jefferson declared it to be

29. Philip Alexander Bruce, *History of the University of Virginia, 1819–1919*, 4 vols. (New York: Macmillan, 1920), 2:68–69, 71n; "Magruder-Ewell Camp," Benjamin Stoddert Ewell Papers, Library of Congress. Ewell judged that Magruder's forefathers "were among the best of the people in Virginia."

30. Bruce, *History of the University of Virginia, 1819–1919*, 1:334–76.

31. Ibid., 2:298–99. Bruce's account of the riot, though excellent in detail, is slanted in favor of Key, Long, Emmet, and Tucker—the "foreign professors."

"one of the most painful events in [his] life," and he called for an investigation and immediate disciplinary action.[32]

Magruder appears not to have participated in the riot, though he was
probably an interested spectator. Nevertheless, because he signed the student
petition, he was called before the faculty investigating board on October
5, 1825. The board concluded that Magruder was "without any evil design"
and that he had "made no noise." But given that he had been "walking with"
Wilson Miles Carey, the ringleader, Magruder was reprimanded, while Carey
and two others were expelled.[33] After the riot John became a more conscientious student, studying, ironically, mathematics under Professor Key, who
had withdrawn his hasty resignation, and modern languages under Professor
Blaetterman.[34] When his year in waiting came to a close, Magruder, on May
11, 1826, formally requested permission to leave the university.[35] Shortly afterward, he returned home to Caroline County, where he visited briefly, then
said his good-byes and departed for the U.S. Military Academy at West Point,
New York. Young Magruder may well have traveled north with his boyhood
friend, Caroline County neighbor and fellow West Point appointee, William
Nelson Pendleton. If so, Pendleton's daughter and early biographer, Susan
P. Lee, reported that the week long journey took the travelers "by stage to
the Potomac, up that river by steamboat to Washington, on to Baltimore by
stage, and across the Chesapeake by boat to Frenchtown. From there to New
Castle, Delaware, [they] again took the stage. A steamboat carried [them] up
the Delaware to Trenton. Jersey was crossed by stage and canal to Amboy,
from which point steamboats ran daily to New York, a city of less than two
hundred thousand inhabitants."[36] From New York, Magruder and Pendleton
most likely boarded the Hudson River steamer for the final sixty-mile jaunt
upriver to West Point. Upon disembarking, they were taken by the officer in
charge from the steamboat wharf, along with all other arriving candidates
for admission, straightaway to their quarters at the academy.[37]

32. Ibid., 144–45, 299–301.

33. October 5–6, 1825, entries in vol. 1, Faculty Records, 1825–26, University of Virginia, Alderman Library, University of Virginia.

34. Matriculation Register of the University of Virginia.

35. May 11, 1826, entry in vol. 1, Faculty Records, 1825–26, University of Virginia.

36. Lee, *Memoirs of William Nelson Pendleton,* 26.

37. "Cadet Life before the Mexican War," Bulletin No. 1, Library, U.S. Military Academy (New
York: U.S. Military Academy Printing Office, 1945), 6.

John was nineteen years of age when he officially entered West Point on July 1, 1826.[38] By that time he had developed into a handsome, broad-shouldered young man over six feet in height. His only physical impairment was a slight lisp, but it apparently did not bother him because he talked incessantly. Magruder easily passed his preliminary examinations and signed the cadet oath,[39] which bound him to the regulations of the academy and to the U.S. Army for a period of five years.[40] Each cadet then purchased the required toilet articles and uniforms.[41] In addition to the regulation grays, the cadets bought a formal dress uniform consisting of white or blue trousers (depending upon the season), a blue fatigue jacket, and an impressive black leather cap that was bell crowned, seven inches high, with a polished leather visor, a diamond-shaped yellow plate, and an eight-inch black plume for dress parade.[42] John was particularly fond of the dress uniform and always dressed immaculately, stood erect, and appeared every inch a soldier.[43] When Benjamin Stoddert Ewell first saw the "much esteemed and respected" Magruder in 1828, he called him "one of the most soldierly looking men in the Corps."[44]

Magruder was a cadet during the academy's golden age. The superintendent was Colonel Sylvanus Thayer, who, since his arrival at West Point

38. George Washington Cullum, *Biographical Register of the Officers and Graduates of the U.S. Military Academy at West Point, New York, from Its Establishment, March 16, 1802, to the Army Reorganization of 1866–67,* 2 vols. (New York: D. Van Nostrand, 1868), 1:367.

39. The entrance examinations are briefly described in *The Centennial of the United States Military Academy at West Point, New York,* 2 vols. (Washington, D.C.: Government Printing Office, 1904), 1:229. Hereafter cited as *USMA Centennial.*

40. An example of the cadet oath that Magruder signed can be found in Douglas Southall Freeman, *R. E. Lee,* 4 vols. (New York: Charles Scribner's Sons, 1934), 1:51.

41. Among the required toilet articles were a looking-glass, washstand and basin, pitcher, tin pail, broom, clothes brush, hairbrush, toothbrush, and candlestick. "Regulations of the United States Military Academy at West Point—Extract from the General Regulations of the Army—Article 78," *American State Papers, Military Affairs,* 7 vols. (Washington, D.C.: Gales and Seaton, 1832–61), 2:654. Hereafter cited as "USMA Regulations," *American State Papers, Military Affairs.*

42. For a description of the various uniforms and a complete listing of the required clothing, see ibid., 653–54. Changes in the cadet uniform can be noted in *USMA Centennial,* 1:508–14.

43. "Recollections of Cadet Life," *Army and Navy Journal* 4 (August 1867): 794. The author, an "old friend and classmate" of Magruder, termed him "a first rate soldier" and "perhaps the most elegant and distinguished cadet at the academy." The author was probably Lloyd J. Beall, one of Magruder's roommates.

44. "Magruder-Ewell Camp," Benjamin Stoddert Ewell Papers.

in 1817, had brought order and efficiency out of the confusion that had disgraced the previous administration of Captain Alden Partridge.[45] Colonel Thayer was a disciplinarian. He even maintained a network of spies to ensure the enforcement of academy regulations.[46] He also insisted upon excellence in curriculum and instruction. The course of study Thayer outlined remains for the most part in place today, the methods and techniques he introduced are essentially the same, his disciplinary measures have remained largely intact, and his aims and goals are those of the present West Point. Thayer was in fact the "father of the Military Academy."[47]

The commandant of cadets was Major William Jenkins Worth, under whom Magruder would later serve in Mexico. Major Worth was a tall, handsome, skilled horseman as well as a conscientious instructor. Although he demanded much of the cadets, he imparted to them a sense of pride and military bearing that would remain paramount with them long after the conclusion of their West Point years.[48] Major Worth left the academy on January 1, 1829, but his successor, Captain Ethan Allen Hitchcock, maintained the same rigid standards and accomplished similar results.

Under the rules of the corps the best cadets of good standing acted as officers. Corporals were chosen from the third class; sergeants were chosen from the second class; and the lieutenants, captains, and the cadet adjutant were chosen from the first class.[49] Magruder was appointed third corporal of the 2nd Company during the first term of his Third Class Year, June–December 1827; second corporal of the 3rd Company during the second term of his Third Class Year; January–June 1828; sergeant of the 1st Company during his Second Class Year, June 1828–June 1829; and the captain of the 1st Company during his First Class Year, June 1829–June 1830.[50]

During his First Class Year, when commanding the Cadet Battalion, Magruder called upon Cadet Private Augustus Albert Allen to close up ranks.

45. Charles P. Roland, *Albert Sidney Johnston: Soldier of Three Republics* (Austin: University of Texas Press, 1964), 13.

46. Oliver E. Wood, ed., *The West Point Scrap Book: A Collection of Stories, Songs and Legends of the United States Military Academy* (New York: D. Van Nostrand, 1871), 31–33.

47. Stephen E. Ambrose, *Duty, Honor, Country: A History of West Point* (Baltimore: Johns Hopkins Press, 1966), 63. A detailed, incisive study of Thayer can also be found in R. Ernest Dupuy, *Where They Have Trod: The West Point Tradition in American Life* (New York: Frederick A. Stokes Co., 1940).

48. Roland, *Albert Sidney Johnston,* 13–14, 19.

49. "USMA Regulations," *American State Papers, Military Affairs,* 2:654–55.

50. Post Orders, U.S. Military Academy, 1827–30, U.S. Military Academy Archives.

"Baron" Allen, as he was known to his classmates, considered the command a personal insult, for which he demanded an apology. Failing to obtain a satisfactory response, he challenged Magruder to a duel. Dueling was prohibited by academy regulations,[51] but John viewed the matter as an "affair of honor" and readily accepted the challenge. The meeting took place, preliminaries were settled, and the final word was about to be given when Magruder's second, William N. Pendleton, interceded and insisted the matter had gone far enough. In spite of Allen's initial protestations, Pendleton brought the two would-be-duelists together and diplomatically adjusted the matter to their mutual satisfaction. All hard feelings were soon forgotten.[52]

Pendleton and Magruder were roommates and best friends. With fellow roommates, Lloyd J. Beall of Maryland and William C. Heyward of New York, they lived, studied, honed their military skills, and even devised diversionary activities that on occasion helped to alleviate the academy's Spartan lifestyle. Magruder and Pendleton both played the flute. They enjoyed their own music so much that they were frequently reported for creating a disturbance during study hours. When Beall took up playing the fiddle, he too began to receive demerits on a regular basis. The cadet trio skirted the demerit problem by confining their musical pursuits to recreation time. Then they ingeniously discovered a way to convert their music to practical value, which made the entire experience all the more rewarding. Instead of polishing the hardwood floor by hand in the usual manner, the young musicians sprinkled the floorboards with fine sand and began playing lively tunes. Reportedly, "the gay strains attracted an audience, 'put life and mettle in their heels,' and a spirited dance polished the boards in short order,"[53] all somehow within the bounds of academy regulations.

51. "USMA Regulations," *American State Papers, Military Affairs,* 2:653.

52. Lee, *Memoirs of William Nelson Pendleton,* 29. Later, on August 14, 1834, Allen was killed in a duel in Jackson, Miss., by the legendary duelist Alexander Keith McClung. One historian termed McClung "the south's most celebrated duelist," and the *London Examiner,* in a gross exaggeration, wrote that he had "killed in personal combat more than fifty persons." See Harnett C. Kane, *Gentlemen, Swords, and Pistols* (New York: William Morrow, 1951), 111; and Fred Darkis Jr., "Alexander Keith McClung (1811–1855)," *Journal of Mississippi History* 40 (November 1978): 291–92.

53. Lee, *Memoirs of William Nelson Pendleton,* 27. Author Susan P. Lee incorrectly stated that the roommate who chose not to participate in the musical endeavor was William C. Heywood of South Carolina. The cadet was William C. Heyward of New York. Heyward graduated in the class of 1830 with his roommates but later resigned from army service on February 6, 1832. He then relocated to St. Bartholomew's Parish, S.C., where he earned his living as a rice planter. Cullum, *Biographical Register,* 1:371.

Magruder was a hyperactive, mischievous lad whose deviltry went well beyond occasional flute playing. He also had a taste for liquid spirits that lasted throughout his sixty-three years. North's and Benny Havens's taverns were within a few miles of academy grounds, and although both were off-limits,[54] many cadets, including Magruder, could not resist the temptation of an occasional visit. A Board of Visitors report in the early 1820s revealed that cadets, individually, were spending an average of fifty dollars a year at the taverns.[55] Few were caught, and Magruder avoided detection until shortly before Christmas of his First Class Year, when he and Alexander J. Swift, the top-ranked cadet in the class, were reported "absent from the post without permission." For his part Magruder was deprived of his appointment as cadet captain on December 13, 1829, but on January 20, 1830, the sentence was canceled, and he was given the promotion and placed in command of the 1st Company.[56]

The free-spirited, independent-minded Magruder was often at odds with Colonel Thayer. To Magruder many of the colonel's restrictions seemed to be unreasonably harsh, while others seemed to have no purpose whatsoever. Adhering to the regulations proved to be challenging for young Magruder, who came dangerously close to being expelled from the academy when during his First Class Year he accumulated 196 demerits.[57] Thayer automatically dismissed any cadet who received more than 200 demerits in a single year.[58] It is often said that a picture is worth a thousand words, and such is the case with the only known drawing of Magruder that has survived the years. Penciled on the inside of his engineering textbook, S. F. Gay de Vernon's *Treatise on the Science of War and Fortification*,[59] is a sketch depicting a cadet being

54. "USMA Regulations," *American State Papers, Military Affairs*, 2:653.

55. Freeman, *R. E. Lee*, 1:49; Wood, *West Point Scrap Book*, 59–64.

56. Post Orders, U.S. Military Academy, 1827–30, U.S. Military Academy Archives.

57. U.S. Military Academy Register of Merit, 1817–35, U.S. Military Academy Archives. Hereafter cited as USMA Register of Merit.

58. Ambrose, *Duty, Honor, Country*, 74.

59. Magruder's copy of the Vernon textbook is in the possession of the Pennsylvania State Library, Harrisburg. Its full title is *Traite elementaire de l'art militaire et de fortification, a l'usage de l'Ecole polytechnique, et des éléves des écoles militaires*. Principal among the other textbooks in use at the time were Newton's *Principia*, Gregory's *Treatise on Mechanics*, Enfield's *Institutes of Natural Philosophy*, Henry's *Chemistry*, Lellemand's *Treatise on Artillery*, Hackett's *Traite des machines*, Szannin's *Programme d'un cours de construction*, Farrar's *Treatise on Plane and Spherical Trigonometry*, Lacroix's *Algebra and Calculus*, Legendre's *Geometry*, Bernard's *Lectur français*, Morse's *Geography*, Tytler's *Elements of General History*, Paley's *Principles of Moral Philosophy*,

strung up to the gallows by an unidentified hangman. One can surmise that Thayer is the executioner and Magruder the victim.

West Point routine was even more exacting than the discipline. At dawn reveille roused the sleeping cadets from their narrow mattresses on the floor (beds were not permitted).[60] The men dressed quickly, answered roll call, and prepared their barracks for the inspection that took place thirty minutes after reveille. Following the inspection the Corps of Cadets marched to the mess hall for breakfast. The eating utensils were of heavy iron or tin, the wooden tables and benches were old and bulky, and the food was usually unappetizing.[61] At the conclusion of the thirty-minute eating period the cadets marched hurriedly to class. Thayer fulfilled to the letter the army regulation that the cadets spend not less than nine hours per day on their studies.[62] When the three-hour morning class ended at eleven o'clock, the cadets went back to their rooms to study until dinner at one. From the time they finished the meal until two o'clock, the cadets could relax in the recreation of their choosing. Then lines were formed again, and the cadets marched to their afternoon classes for two more hours of academic instruction. Military training was given from four o'clock until sunset, after which came supper. When the evening meal was completed, the signal was given to retire to quarters, where the cadets once again wrestled with their studies. Tattoo, roll call, and a final inspection ended the day. At ten o'clock lights were extinguished.[63]

It was a long day dominated almost entirely by military and academic activities. Cadet Leonidas Polk complained that his spare time was so limited it was "impossible to devote any [time] to literary attainments privately."[64] The superintendent even discouraged cadets from reading extraneous materials by limiting students' subscriptions to a single periodical. Thayer then maintained the right to check the periodical to ensure that it was of a scholarly nature. Novels were prohibited, and the library was open only two hours

---

and Rawle's *On the Constitution*. In the case of the latter textbook it would seem that it has been given undue weight as having influenced the cadet's attitude toward the doctrine of secession. It simply reflected the prevailing legal attitude. The cadet's origin and environment probably had more influence in determining later views and attitudes than anything in Rawle's book.

60. "USMA Regulations," *American State Papers, Military Affairs*, 2:654.

61. Freeman, *R. E. Lee*, 1:50.

62. "USMA Regulations," *American State Papers, Military Affairs*, 2:650.

63. Freeman gives an excellent description of "cadet routine" in *R. E. Lee*, 1:48–85.

64. William M. Polk, *Leonidas Polk: Bishop and General*, 2 vols. (New York: Longmans, Green and Co., 1915), 1:55. Letter of November 16, 1823, Polk to his father.

per week, on Saturday afternoon from two to four o'clock, when cadets were allowed to check out but one book.[65] The superintendent believed that the cadets should devote their extra time, if any, to their course work; unrelated reading could only be distracting. In support of this philosophy Thayer instituted a regulation whereby "cadets [were] allowed to take from the library such books only as [were] calculated to assist them in their studies."[66]

Magruder had come to West Point with a solid academic background. At the Rappahannock Academy he had attained a proficiency in Latin, French, and geography, and while at the University of Virginia he had concentrated on mathematics and modern languages.[67] The military academy curricula, however, consisting of courses in French, geography, history, moral science, drawing, chemistry, mineralogy, mathematics, and natural and experimental philosophy, including astronomy, military science, and engineering,[68] was more diversified than anything he had previously experienced, and West Point academics were understandably more difficult. Nevertheless, Cadet Magruder readily profited from the instruction of such talented scholars as Charles Davies and Albert E. Church in mathematics; Jared Mansfield and William H. C. Bartlett in natural philosophy (physics); David B. Douglas in engineering; Thomas Gimbrede in drawing; and Claudius Berard in French. The faculty as a whole was highly distinguished, and the departments of physics, engineering, and mathematics were regarded as "the best in the United States."[69]

Rigorous academics and the strenuous routine proved to be too demanding a regimen for many of the cadets in spite of the excellent instruction.

65. "USMA Regulations," *American State Papers, Military Affairs,* 2:655. Douglas Southall Freeman has a listing that shows that Robert E. Lee checked out fifty-two books from the library between January 26 and May 24, 1828, and on at least two occasions he checked out six books in a single day. Freeman, *R. E. Lee,* 1:72–73. Perhaps there were special library privileges for honor students.

66. "USMA Regulations," *American State Papers, Military Affairs,* 2:655.

67. Garnett to secretary of war, February 4, 1821, Magruder's USMA File; Matriculation Register of the University of Virginia, Alderman Library, University of Virginia.

68. "USMA Regulations," *American State Papers, Military Affairs,* 2:649–50. The course in engineering, one of the most comprehensive in the academy curricula, was divided into five parts—field fortification, permanent fortification, artillery, grand tactics, and civil and military architecture. During Magruder's tenure in the academy there was no specific course on military strategy, although elementary strategic principles were studied as a part of grand tactics.

69. Ambrose, *Duty, Honor, Country,* 91–102. Brief descriptions of courses and several leading faculty members can be found in Freeman, *R. E. Lee,* 1:59–79.

Half of Magruder's eighty-three classmates who had taken the January examinations in their Fourth Class Year had departed by the time of the same examinations four years later.[70] And of the eleven Virginians who entered the academy in 1826, only Magruder and Pendleton graduated.[71] John succeeded because he was "smart and uncommonly ambitious to excel in everything he [undertook]."[72] In his first two years he ranked high in mathematics, French, and drawing, and in the last two he excelled in engineering, drawing, and artillery. Fortunately, his attraction to West Point academics prevailed over his dislike of Thayer's regulations.[73] When at last the June examinations were completed and the final class standing tabulated, Magruder ranked a respectable fifteenth of forty-two cadets in the class of 1830 headed by Alexander J. Swift, whose father, Joseph G. Swift, was the first graduate of the U.S. Military Academy in the class of 1802.[74]

The graduation and commissioning exercise was a simple affair. Following a valedictory address, each cadet received a formal diploma, signed by the superintendent and academic board.[75] The graduates next received their commissions, orders, and a two-month furlough. Then they were dismissed. Magruder had mixed emotions about the events that transpired on July 1, 1830. He was elated to receive the furlough, his first since entering the academy,[76] but he also found leaving West Point an emotionally difficult ordeal. Despite the endless drilling, poor food, and questionable regulations, the academy had been his home for four years. He had formed many close companionships there, and West Point had had a strong influence in molding his character and personality. When he departed "the Point," he left with a sense

70. USMA Register of Merit.

71. *American State Papers, Military Affairs,* 7:37–38; Cullum, *Biographical Register,* 1:362, 367–68.

72. Garnett to secretary of war, February 4, 1821, Magruder's USMA File.

73. USMA Register of Merit. In his First Class Year Magruder stood 15th of 42 class members in general order of merit, while he ranked a lowly 188th of 215 members of the Corps of Cadets in conduct. He had 196 demerits for the year, only 4 short of the maximum number allowed by the superintendent. In conduct Magruder fared best in his Third Class Year, when he received but 30 demerits. Even then he ranked only 68 of 207 members of the corps for the year. It was difficult, but not unusual, for a cadet to complete his four-year stay at the academy without receiving any demerits. As Magruder was charged with 372 total demerits, his final standing and the ranking positions of leadership he held within the Corps of Cadets were all the more remarkable.

74. Cullum, *Biographical Register,* 1:89, 360, 367.

75. "USMA Regulations," *American State Papers, Military Affairs,* 2:652.

76. Magruder to Jones, October 4, 1830, National Archives.

of pride, a feeling of accomplishment, and the finest technical instruction his country had to offer.

Second Lieutenant Magruder spent most of his furlough in the company of twenty-year-old Henrietta von Kapff of Baltimore. Her father, Bernard Johann von Kapff, was born in Bremen on July 16, 1770, and emigrated to the United States in 1794.[77] He served as German consul in Baltimore and co-founded Von Kapff and Anspach, later reorganized as Von Kapff and Brune, which became one of the most successful shipping businesses in the city.[78] On May 29, 1804, von Kapff married Hettie Henrietta Didier, who bore him seven children. Henrietta, the fourth child, was born on March 27, 1810.[79] She was a charming belle with fair skin, dark hair, large dark eyes, and a considerable inheritance.[80] Henrietta captured Magruder's eye the first time they met, and a romance began immediately thereafter. The couple was married

77. Ellinor Wilson Poultney to Thomas Robson Hay, March 7, 1962. Thomas Robson Hay Papers, Central Rappahannock Heritage Center, Fredericksburg, Va. Hereafter cited as Hay Papers. Mrs. Poultney of Garrison, Md., is the great-granddaughter of Bernard Johann von Kapff.

78. Dieter Cunz, *The Maryland Germans: A History* (Princeton, N.J.: Princeton University Press, 1948), 159; John Thomas Scharf, *Chronicles of Baltimore: Being a Complete History of "Baltimore Town" and Baltimore City from the Earliest Period to the Present Time* (Baltimore: Turnbull Bros., 1874), 209, 577; "F. W. Brune & Sons," *Biographical Sketches* from the Maryland Historical Society, Nancy G. Boles to Hay, February 22, 1971, Hay Papers. Von Kapff and Anspach was founded in Baltimore in 1795, the year after Bernard Johann von Kapff emigrated to the United States. When Henry N. Anspach, died on June 20, 1799, von Kapff brought Frederick W. Brune into the firm, which was reorganized as Von Kapff and Brune. Later, after the death of Bernard von Kapff, the firm became F. W. Brune and Sons.

79. Poultney to Hay, March 7 and 19, 1962, Hay Papers. Ellinor Poultney is in possession of the von Kapff family Bible, which lists the von Kapff children: the eldest, Eliza Margaret married Henry Rodewald; the second, Henry Christopher, returned to Bremen and married there; the third, Mary Jane, married Diedrich Mots; the fourth, Hettie Henrietta, married John Magruder; the fifth child, a son, and the sixth, a daughter, died in infancy. The seventh and last of the children, J. Frederick C. von Kapff, married Anne Donnell Smith; they are the grandparents of Ellinor Wilson Poultney.

80. One observer declared that Magruder married "an heiress rich beyond comparison." See John N. Edwards, *Shelby's Expedition to Mexico: An Unwritten Leaf of the War* (Kansas City, Mo.: Kansas City Times Steam Book and Job Printing House, 1872), 19. Henrietta von Kapff's inheritance included real estate and trust funds, and although her net worth must have been substantial, the exact value of her holdings has never been determined.

There is also some question about Mrs. Magruder's given name. It is listed in the von Kapff family Bible as Hettie Henrietta; her wedding notices recorded it as Esther Henrietta; Mrs. Magruder in her own handwritten will stated that her name was Henrietta H.; and the name given in her obituary notice in Florence, Italy, was Enrichetta Hetty.

by the Reverend Alfred Helfenstein Sr. in the Episcopal church in Baltimore on May 18, 1831.[81] Within the next ten years the Magruders had three children: Isabella in 1833,[82] Katherine Elizabeth in 1836,[83] and Henry R. in 1841.[84]

In the early years of their marriage Henrietta occasionally traveled with her husband. On October 29, 1835, the *Army and Navy Chronicle* reported, "Lt. J. B. Magruder of the Army, lady and child . . . arrived Charleston, S.C., by packet *Dolphin* from Norfolk and landed at Smithville"[85] on the way to Magruder's post at Fort Johnston near Wilmington, North Carolina. Yet because of the hardships of travel, uncomfortable living conditions, and extremes of climate found in the remote locales where Magruder was stationed during his military career, Henrietta found it more practical to live and raise her children in the comforts of Baltimore, where she could also stay closer to family business interests. She remained there with the children until 1850, when, as a consequence of Isabella's ill health, she took her children to Europe.[86] Mrs. Magruder had relatives in Germany, but she moved to Italy,

81. *Baltimore American,* May 19, 1831; *Baltimore Gazette,* May 19, 1831; *Baltimore Republican and Commercial Advertiser,* May 20, 1831; and the Fredericksburg, Va., *Political Arena,* May 27, 1831. All four entries are essentially the same. They report the name of the bride as Esther Henrietta and that she was the youngest daughter of the late Bernard Johann von Kapff. In fact, the sixth of the von Kapff children was actually the youngest daughter born, but she died in infancy.

Both of the von Kapffs had died before the Magruder wedding. Mrs. von Kapff died on August 23, 1821, and her husband expired on January 30, 1825, exactly five months before their first child, Eliza Margaret, married Henry Rodewald, on June 30, 1825. The same Reverend Helfenstein who performed the Rodewald wedding also married John Magruder and Henrietta six years later. Alfred Helfenstein Sr. was pastor of the First German Reform Church in Baltimore. Dates from the Hayward File, *Baltimore American.*

82. Marian B. Parsons to Hay, October 1, 1954, and November 15, 1956, Hay Papers. Marian Buckler Parsons (Mrs. Paul S. Parsons) of Baltimore is Isabella Magruder Buckler's granddaughter.

83. Thomas G. Magruder to Hay, December 14, 1952, Hay Papers. Thomas Garland Magruder of Arlington, Va., was an officer in the American Clan Gregor Society when Hay made his inquiry regarding the birth dates of the Magruder children. The only date that Mr. Magruder was able to pinpoint was 1836 as the year of birth for the second-born child, Kate Elizabeth.

84. Magruder to "My Dear Carlisle," January 18, 1841. Letter in possession of Brian Green of Kernersville, N.C. In this letter Magruder wrote to his lawyer, J. Mandeville Carlisle, that his wife and children had gone to spend the winter in Baltimore with Henrietta's sister, Eliza Rodewald. Magruder reported that he was gleefully awaiting the birth of "a male heir to all my fortunes." Brian Green's great-great-uncle was George Allan Magruder, John Magruder's oldest brother.

85. *Army and Navy Chronicle* 1 (October 29, 1835): 357.

86. Allan B. Magruder to Secretary of War C. M. Conrad, August 7, 1852, National Archives; Magruder to Pierce, August 14, 1852, Manuscript Division, Library of Congress.

living briefly in Rome, then in Florence. She returned to Baltimore from September 1854 to September 1855 and later visited her husband in Mexico in 1866. In both instances she returned to Florence, where she spent most of the remainder of her life. She died there on January 1, 1884, and is buried in the Allari Protestant Cemetery with her two youngest children.[87]

John Magruder saw his wife and children only infrequently even before they departed for Europe. Consequently, the family played a relatively minor role in his life story. Henrietta paid John's bills when he was in debt and served as his mistress, to whom he returned during his furloughs, but she did little else. Even when they were together, the Magruders often went their separate ways because of dissimilar interests, particularly those relating to societal affairs. Henrietta disdained society and shied away from it; John reveled in it. Of all the times that they were together, there are very few accounts of Mrs. Magruder ever being a part of the social scene. Even later, when Henrietta and the two younger children visited General Magruder and his Confederate companions in exile in Mexico following the Civil War, Kate Elizabeth and Henry made favorable impressions, but their mother was rarely seen.[88]

Mrs. Magruder's dislike of society never dampened her husband's passion for it. He seemed to be perfectly tailored to assume a leading social role and would not be denied. Professor Caleb G. Forshey, who would later serve on Magruder's staff as chief engineer both on the Peninsula in Virginia and in Texas, observed that his conversation was "fluent, persuasive and instructive. He was musical, versatile, convivial and witty. He was well-read, widely traveled and a man of the world, [equally] at ease in the cabins of the wilderness . . . [or] in the courts of State." Because of his impeccable manners and social brilliance, Magruder earned the moniker "Prince John." He was, according to Professor Forshey, "the most accomplished of American gentlemen."[89] He loved entertaining and was prone to ostentatious display whether on the parade ground or in the ballroom. He also fancied fine food, fine wine, fine

87. Last Will and Testament of Henrietta H. Magruder; Last Will and Testament of Kate Elizabeth Magruder; Last Will and Testament of Henry R. Magruder. All are on file with the Register of Wills, Baltimore, Maryland.

88. James A. Padgett, ed., "Life of Alfred Mordecai in Mexico in 1865–1866 as Told in His Letters to His Family," *North Carolina Historical Review* 23 (January 1946): 85. In a letter, Mordecai to his wife, March 15, 1866.

89. *New Orleans Times,* March 19, 1871.

horses, and fine clothing.[90] He was a man of simple tastes, easily pleased by the best of everything. Even when Magruder had no money in his pockets, he had the finest clothing that money could buy on his back.

Magruder had an eye for beautiful women and delighted in their company. He charmed them, and they found him bewitching and irresistible. Arthur Lyon Fremantle, the well-known British observer who traveled behind Confederate lines during the Civil War, declared that "few U.S. military figures have circulated through more drawing rooms, balanced more tea cups, [or] charmed more ladies with more small talk" than John Bankhead Magruder.[91] Prince John was tall, straight, well proportioned, and "had a form that the men envied and the women adored." One admirer swore that Magruder could "fight all day and dance all night."[92] Another declared that he was "full of the cavalier's dash,"[93] and others exaggerated his social prowess to legendary proportions. Because he was so devoted to social pursuits and because Mrs. Magruder was almost never by his side in society, many thought he was a bachelor, and certainly his marital status did not restrict his social life.[94] Contemporaries not intimately acquainted with John Magruder as well as a recent Magruder scholar have inferred that Prince John's penchant for wine, women, and song was the reason Mrs. Magruder took her children to Europe, and concluded that because of the separation, theirs was a "crumpled" marriage.[95]

A more careful examination of the facts reveals that the trip to Europe in 1850 was made entirely out of medical considerations, at the insistence of Mrs. Magruder's physician and with the full concurrence of her husband.[96]

90. "John Bankhead Magruder," vertical file, Center for the Study of American History, University of Texas, Austin. Undated newspaper article from the *San Antonio Light.*

91. Arthur James Lyon Fremantle, *The Fremantle Diary: Being the Journal of Lieutenant-Colonel Arthur James Lyon Fremantle, Coldstream Guards, on His Three Months in the Southern States,* ed. Walter Lord (Boston: Little, Brown, 1954), 257n.

92. "John Bankhead Magruder," vertical File, Center for the Study of American History, University of Texas, Austin. Undated newspaper article from the *San Antonio Light;* Edwards, *Shelby's Expedition to Mexico,* 19.

93. *New Orleans Times,* March 19, 1871.

94. "John Magruder," *Army and Navy Journal* 18 (September 1880): 148.

95. Paul D. Casdorph, *Prince John Magruder: His Life and Campaigns* (New York: John Wiley and Sons, 1996), 30.

96. Allan B. Magruder to Conrad, August 7, 1852, National Archives; Magruder to Pierce, August 14, 1852, Manuscript Division, Library of Congress.

When all health problems were resolved, Henrietta returned to Baltimore with her husband and remained with him until he was transferred by the War Department to escort the U.S.-Mexico boundary commissioners across the deserts of west Texas.

Magruder's alleged "womanizing" has also been misunderstood and exaggerated. He must have had countless opportunities to be unfaithful to his wife, but his relations with other women apparently were entirely social in nature, as no one closely associated with John Magruder ever charged him with moral turpitude. Young Thomas Jonathan Jackson, a man with extremely high moral values, was well acquainted with Magruder. The two fought side by side in the battles leading to final victory in the war with Mexico. Jackson would have known if his company commander had been guilty of indiscretions with the señoritas of Mexico, and he would not have tolerated it. Indeed, shortly after the war ended, Jackson reported a fellow officer who had breached the boundaries of morality by being unfaithful to his wife. But that officer was William H. French, not John Bankhead Magruder.[97]

Later, however, in early 1862, when Magruder served on the Virginia Peninsula, one of his soldiers reported that the general was involved in a "scandalous" relationship with the wife of his chief medical officer. Richard Leach, a friend of the woman's husband, wrote that "Magruder and the woman flirted and danced in public, sometimes staying together until the early morning hours."[98] As this liaison has never been reported elsewhere, it is impossible to know whether the relationship was social or sexual or if there was any such relationship at all. What is known, and documentable, is that John Magruder, throughout his military career, made every effort to spend as much time as possible with his family. In his memoirs he declared that his ties to his family were "dearer to me than anything on earth."[99] When stationed away from Baltimore, he made numerous requests for furloughs.

97. Frank Vandiver, *Mighty Stonewall* (New York: McGraw-Hill, 1957), 56–70; D. H. Hill, "The Real Stonewall Jackson," *Century* 47 (1893–94): 624–25.

98. Peter S. Carmichael, "The Great Paragon of Virtue and Sobriety: John Bankhead Magruder and the Seven Days," in *The Richmond Campaign of 1862: The Peninsula and the Seven Days*, ed. Gary W. Gallagher (Chapel Hill: University of North Carolina Press, 2000), 102.

99. John B. Magruder, "The First Battle of the War: Big Bethel," in *Battles and Leaders of the Civil War*, ed. Peter Cozzens (Urbana: University of Illinois Press, 2002), 5:35. This article first appeared in the December 28, 1878, issue of the *Philadelphia Weekly Times* and was submitted by John Magruder's brother, Colonel Allan B. Magruder, from the deceased general's unpublished memoirs. To date the memoirs have never been found.

He constantly badgered the Adjutant General's Office for reassignment to the Baltimore–Washington, D.C., area. And when recruiting along the eastern seaboard, he spent a disproportionate amount of his duty time in and around Baltimore so he could be near his family. When Henrietta left for Europe to repair Isabella's ill health but later became desperately ill herself, John rushed to her side. Then he brought the family back to Baltimore, minus Isabella, who had eloped to Leghorn, Italy, where she married Dr. Riggin Buckler.[100] Magruder remained in Baltimore with Henrietta and the children as long as possible. He delayed rejoining his company in Texas, almost to the point of insubordination. When Henrietta returned to Europe, Magruder, after a lengthy petition campaign, secured permission from the War Department to travel to the Continent as an "official military observer." He made sure that the observations took him immediately to Italy, where he rejoined his family. And after the Civil War, Henrietta and the two unmarried children left Florence intending to settle with Magruder and his companions in Mexico. But when the ill-fated Mexican venture failed, Henrietta, Kate Elizabeth, and Henry returned to Europe, and the general returned to the United States. He saw Isabella and tended to her in Baltimore during the illness that led to her death on July 20, 1869,[101] but he did not see his wife or the two youngest children again. Neither the passage of time nor the span of oceans, however, would make Kate or Henry forget their father. When Kate Elizabeth died on April 26, 1896, nearly thirty years after last seeing her father, she specified in her will that $500 (an extremely generous amount of money in the late nineteenth century) be allotted to pay "for a tombstone over the grave of my father in Galveston, Texas."[102] Eleven years later, when Henry died on January 31, 1907, his will directed that "the gold sword and silver pitcher which were presented to my father by the State of Virginia and the State of Maryland" be given to the Smithsonian Institution for proper display.[103] And according to

100. Marian B. Parsons to Hay, October 1, 1954, and November 15, 1956, Hay Papers. Although the Bucklers were married for just thirteen years before Isabella died, in 1869, the couple had six children: four daughters and two sons. The daughters were Lilly, Nelly, Isabel, and Matilda. The firstborn son, John Buckler, died in November 1863 at the age of thirteen months. The other son, Thomas Hepburn Buckler, was born on October 5, 1864, and died on December 27, 1940. Mrs. Parsons was the daughter and only child of Dr. Thomas Hepburn Buckler and Marian Stevenson Buckler. She was in possession of the consular certificate certifying the marriage of her grandparents, Dr. Riggin Buckler and Isabella Magruder, in Leghorn, Italy, on July 3, 1856.

101. *Baltimore American and Commercial Advertiser*, July 23, 1869.

102. Last Will and Testament of Kate Elizabeth Magruder.

103. Last Will and Testament of Henry R. Magruder.

close family friend John Fitzgerald Lee, Henrietta to the very end remained "in love with [her husband] to an uncommon degree."[104]

A desire to be with Henrietta led John Magruder toward a military career in the artillery. The War Department originally assigned him to serve in the 7th Infantry after his graduation from West Point,[105] but he arranged a transfer to the 1st Artillery with Albert Miller Lea, a good friend from the academy who graduated in the class of 1831. The exchange permitted Lieutenant Magruder and his new bride "to remain in more civilized society,"[106] whereas infantry service no doubt would have resulted in a frontier assignment. Such service, reported the *Army and Navy Journal,* "was in no way suited to the tastes of a man so devoted to society, good dinners, and the comforts which are to be found in the eastern cities . . . The small western garrisons did not furnish a field of sufficient magnitude for the display of John's graces and accomplishments."[107] On the other hand, Lea's duties on the Indian frontier would allow him time, free of distractions, to read law books and court reports;[108] thus, the swap was mutually beneficial. Lea would serve on topographical duty and then on the frontier in Sioux country with the 1st Dragoons, before resigning his commission on May 31, 1836, to become chief engineer of the State of Tennessee.[109] He would not see Magruder again until reporting to him on the eve of the Battle of Galveston. The following day would be one of triumph for Magruder and tragedy for Lea.

Meanwhile, young Magruder reported to the artillery school for practice at Fort Monroe, Virginia.[110] The artillery school offered an academic challenge reminiscent of West Point, and the field exercises were intriguing; certainly, they were more interesting than infantry tactics. But after concluding his artillery instruction, Magruder left Fort Monroe and spent two uneventful years in garrison duty in 1831 and 1832 at Newbern and Beaufort, North Carolina.[111] This phase of the military did not agree with Magruder because

104. J. F. Lee to unknown (1871?), Lee Family Papers, Virginia Historical Society Library, Richmond. John Fitzgerald Lee was Robert E. Lee's first cousin, once removed.

105. Cullum, *Biographical Register,* 1:367.

106. Autobiographical sketch by Albert Miller Lea in the *Iowa Historical Record* 8 (1892): 202; *Galveston Daily News,* July 30, 1922.

107. "John Magruder," *Army and Navy Journal,* 148.

108. Autobiographical sketch by Albert Miller Lea in the *Iowa Historical Record* 8 (1892): 202; *Galveston Daily News,* July 30, 1922.

109. Cullum, *Biographical Register,* 1:381.

110. Ibid., 367.

111. Ibid.

he saw in it the most burdensome features of academy life: a strenuous rou-tine, multitudinous regulations, and boring administrative work. After leav-ing the artillery school, there was no intellectual challenge, there were few field exercises, the food remained poor, and esprit de corps was nonexistent.

In 1833 Magruder was transferred to Fort McHenry, Maryland.[112] He could not have wished for better. Magruder's father had been connected to some of the best families in Maryland, and his father-in-law had been a leader in Baltimore's business, civic, and social circles. Consequently, Prince John had entrée to Baltimore's high society. He was a fascinating conversationalist—always charming, frivolous at times, but intelligent and obviously well read. Magruder could utilize points of history in intellectual conversations that others, who prided themselves on their literary attainments, had overlooked or forgotten. He was quick at repartee and, once warmed up at the dinner table, was "as good a diner out as Sam Ward ever was."[113]

Erasmus D. Keyes, who graduated behind Magruder in the West Point Class of 1832, recalled that Prince John also exhibited legendary endurance. One evening after dining with one of his lieutenants and Magruder, Keyes retired for bed, as usual, at ten o'clock. At eight the next morning, when Keyes appeared for breakfast, he found Magruder and the lieutenant al-ready at the table. When Keyes expressed surprise that Magruder had risen so early, Magruder replied, "I don't know whether we are early or late, we haven't left the dinner table yet." Keyes also speculated that his lieutenant had been asleep perhaps seven of the fourteen hours that he and Magruder had remained at the table. "But," said Keyes, "the Prince kept on talking."[114]

While stationed at Fort McHenry, Magruder occasionally stayed at Barnum's Hotel, part of which was used to house the post office. The communica-tion between Baltimore and Washington was by stage, and the stage offices were at Barnum's in Baltimore and at Gadsby's in Washington. One night

112. Ibid.

113. "John Magruder," *Army and Navy Journal*, 148. London's *Vanity Fair* reported on January 10, 1880: "Every traveller to the United States whose lot has fallen in pleasant places is sure to have met with Sam Ward . . . he is the one man who knows everybody worth knowing, who has been everywhere worth going to, and has seen everything worth stepping aside to see . . . His fund of anecdotes is inexhaustible; his very presence in a room is enough to put everybody else in good humour; his wit is ready, and his good nature so great that most Englishmen who have seen New York bring back from it as one of the most pleasant of their reminiscences, the memory of 'Uncle Sam.'"

114. E. D. Keyes, *Fifty Years' Observation of Men and Events* (New York: Charles Scribner's Sons, 1884), 128.

Magruder came home late from a "bout" and found the hotel door locked. There was a light in the stage office, so he entered, unnoticed by anyone, and collapsed unconscious on a pile of mail sacks. In the morning the stage coach came along for the mail and passengers heading to Washington. When the driver picked up his bill, noting one passenger, he concluded that Magruder must be the man. He tried to wake him but could not. So he picked him up bodily and put him into the stage and started for Washington, where he arrived early the next morning. The driver then removed the still unconscious Magruder from the stage and laid him on a bench in the bar of Gadsby's Hotel. When Magruder awoke, he had no idea where he was, but he dared not ask for fear of being judged insane. He had an eye-opener and then decided to have breakfast, hoping to get into a conversation with someone from whom he might subtly draw information about his whereabouts. But he did not succeed. After breakfast he went out into the street and saw the capital and the two rows of Lombardy poplars that lined Pennsylvania Avenue—but how could he be in Washington? As he strolled up the avenue, he met his old classmate Thomas Lee of the Topographic Bureau. Magruder rushed up to him, exclaiming: "My God, Tom, how glad I am to see you! Will you, for God's sake, tell me where I am?"[115]

Once the mystery was solved, Magruder hurried back to Baltimore pretending that nothing out of the ordinary had happened. Yet he was so inwardly shaken that he proposed to become a "total abstinence man." Magruder explained in his inimitable lisp that he would take twenty-three "eye-openerth" on the first day of his program, leaving off one each succeeding morning. Then on the twenty-third day he would take his "lasth drink."[116] Either Magruder did not follow his plan to its conclusion, or it failed to have the desired effect; whatever the case, it did not put an end to his drinking. This behavior concerned Colonel Bankhead, who took his nephew aside for a tongue lashing. The colonel took a big pinch of snuff, glared at his nephew, and then impatiently asked:

> "John, why the devil is it that you can't behave yourself? You are always in some damned scrape! Now, there's your brother George [George Magruder was a commander in the Navy], who is as quiet and well-behaved a gentleman as ever lived; why is it that you are not like him?" "Well, Uncle," said John, "George, you know, followed your precept. I suppose I followed your ex-

115. "John Magruder," *Army and Navy Journal*, 148.
116. "The Soldiers' Temperance Union," *Army and Navy Journal* 21 (October 1883): 234.

ample." The Colonel was very deaf and had to get John to repeat his remark. Drawing his red bandana across his upper lip to wipe off the snuff, he quickly turned to old Major Payne, who was sitting near him, and exclaimed: "Payne, did you hear what that God damned rascal said?"[117]

Paul D. Casdorph, Magruder's only biographer to date, asserts that his subject "surely [had] an addiction to alcohol,"[118] and historian Peter S. Carmichael, citing Casdorph as his authority on Magruder's drinking, takes the allegation one step further, writing that he was "a confirmed alcoholic."[119] Alcoholics, however, have an addiction; Magruder did not. Drinking was never a necessity in his life. In reality Magruder drank no more than his mid-nineteenth-century American contemporaries. They lived in an era in which people lived and worked hard and frequently drank hard. Sailors were customarily given regular allotments of grog or rum while at sea. Farmers and frontiersmen were as proud of their homemade ciders, brandies, and whiskeys as they were of their livestock or their tobacco crop. And many of our leading political figures were celebrated as much for the imported spirits that they stocked in their liquor cabinets as for their spirited oratory, Daniel Webster being the perfect example. Magruder was a discriminating drinker, like Webster. If the setting was social and the wine was fine, Prince John was willing. His problem, from a historical perspective, is that he was a man of extremes who never did anything in moderation. He rode the fastest horse, he wore the finest clothing, and he hosted the most lavish parties. Inevitably, at evening's end Prince John would have been in the middle of more conversations, danced more dances, and drunk more wine than anyone else in attendance. On the basis of this evidence, and nothing more, Casdorph and Carmichael conclude that Magruder had an uncontrollable drinking problem.[120]

Casdorph specifically charges that excessive drinking was a problem for Magruder, "especially in California, where he was stationed for the 1850–1853

---

117. "John Magruder," *Army and Navy Journal*, 148; Marian Gouverneur, *As I Remember: Recollections of American Society during the Nineteenth Century* (New York: D. Appleton, 1911), 211.

118. Casdorph, *Prince John Magruder*, ix.

119. Carmichael, "The Great Paragon of Virtue and Sobriety: John Bankhead Magruder and the Seven Days," *Richmond Campaign of 1862: The Peninsula and the Seven Days*, 116.

120. Dr. Catherine Hoerster, chief transplant psychologist and addictionologist of Methodist Healthcare System of San Antonio, notes that Magruder was egotistical and vain. He gloried in ostentatious display and loved to be the center of attention. She suggests that his tendency toward grandiosity and his compulsive insistence on being unsurpassed in any social activity, whether entertaining, debating, dancing, or drinking, is more indicative of narcissism than alcoholism.

period."[121] During those years, however, Magruder was reported as having been drunk only twice, and one of those times was with his men, upon their arrival in San Diego, after they had been confined aboard their transport for seven long months at sea. Many reasonable people would concede that a serious celebration might have been in order to raise the morale of the troops. Casdorph could, on occasion, find Magruder guilty of overindulgence or excessive celebration, but the charge that he was an alcoholic is without basis in fact because there was no pattern of intoxication, nor was there ever any alcoholic dependency.

There is also no credible evidence that Magruder drank while on duty, in spite of D. H. Hill's declaration that the general was "always drunk."[122] The cantankerous North Carolinian commonly criticized everyone around him, including Jeb Stuart, Braxton Bragg, Jefferson Davis, Robert E. Lee, and Magruder. He even disparaged his own brother-in-law, Stonewall Jackson. Yet of all of those close to Magruder, Hill was the only one who ever accused Prince John of being a drunkard. Others, including Joseph Lancaster Brent, Benjamin Stoddert Ewell, Jefferson C. Phillips, John Lamb, John Baytop Cary, E. J. Eldridge, L. W. Allen, and Howell and Thomas R. R. Cobb, all offered countering testimony. The Cobb brothers, for example, "denied, emphatically and repeatedly, that Magruder was guilty of drunkenness."[123] Additionally, when rumors began circulating that General Magruder was "dissipated" while in command on the Virginia Peninsula, George Wythe Randolph, who served as Magruder's chief of artillery and later Confederate secretary of war, wrote to Assistant Secretary of War Albert T. Bledsoe specifically to refute the rumors. By his own personal knowledge Randolph insisted that his commander "has not used intoxicating liquors of any sort, and has been as rigid a temperance man as Father [Theobald] Mathew himself."[124] And later, in the euphoria after Magruder's spectacular victory at Galveston, when the general

121. Casdorph. *Prince John Magruder,* 3.

122. D. H. Hill to his wife, May 30, 1861, D. H. Hill Papers, U.S. Military History Institute, Carlisle Barracks, Pa. Robert E. Lee declared that Hill had the "tongue of an adder."

123. William B. McCash, *Thomas R. R. Cobb: The Making of a Southern Nationalist* (Macon, Ga.: Mercer University Press, 1983), 267n. In a June 13, 1862, letter to his wife Cobb reported that there was "bad blood" between Hill and Magruder. Thomas R. R. Cobb, "Extracts from Letters to His Wife, February 3, 1861–December 10, 1862," *Southern Historical Society Papers* 28 (1900): 293.

124. Randolph to Bledsoe, August 26, 1861, *The War of the Rebellion: A Compilation of the Official Records of the Union and Confederate Armies*, 128 vols. (Washington, D.C.: Government Printing Office, 1880–1901), ser. 1, 51, pt. 2, 251. Father Theobald Mathew, who was known as the "apostle of temperance," was an Irish priest who gave the pledge of abstinence to 600,000 people

was offered a glass of whiskey in celebration of his triumph, he turned it down. Yet according to Sergeant Major Charles P. Bosson, one of the captured soldiers of the 42nd Massachusetts Infantry Regiment, the colonels and majors who followed Magruder "sampled a case of fine liquors . . . in such a manner that it was never seen afterwards."[125] In spite of the documentable evidence to the contrary, the perception of overimbibing continues to have a lingering, adverse effect on Magruder's historical standing. Whether Prince John performed brilliantly or badly, those seeking an explanation for his performance have conveniently and unfairly attributed everything to drinking.

Magruder left Fort McHenry in late 1833 and spent the next two years in garrison duty at forts Macon and Johnston in North Carolina.[126] The uneventful military aspect of these assignments allowed him time to study law. As Magruder was persuasive in speech, had a strong academic background, and had been raised by a father who was a practicing attorney, he was almost a natural for the legal profession. The *Raleigh Weekly Register and North Carolina Gazette* reported on August 4, 1835, that Lieutenant John B. Magruder of the United States Army had passed the bar examinations and was certified to practice in the state's county courts.[127] Shortly afterward, however, he was transferred out of North Carolina and did not begin a law practice until fifteen years later, when he was stationed in San Diego, California.

On March 31, 1836, a month before his twenty-ninth birthday, Magruder was promoted to first lieutenant. At that time he was in temporary command of little-used Fort Washington, Maryland, on the Potomac.[128] The assignment, which should have been rather uneventful, turned into a major controversy after one of the post's medical officers questioned Magruder's authority to command. The brouhaha began innocently enough when Magruder ordered a post inspection, including the hospital, for June 26, 1836. He then sent a written order to Dr. H. A. Stinnecke, the assistant surgeon, notifying him that the hospital inspection would take place at 11:00 a.m.[129] Magruder even

during his 1849–51 visit to the United States. See *New Catholic Encyclopedia,* 15 vols. (New York: McGraw-Hill, 1967), 9:461.

125. Charles P. Bosson, *History of the Forty-Second Regiment Infantry, Massachusetts Volunteers, 1862, 1863, 1864* (Boston: Mills, Knight and Co. Printers, 1886), 109.

126. Cullum, *Biographical Register,* 1:367.

127. *Raleigh Weekly Register and North Carolina Gazette,* August 4, 1835; *New York Times,* February 20, 1871.

128. Cullum, *Biographical Register,* 1:367.

129. Order of J. B. Magruder, lieutenant commanding Fort Washington, Md., June 26, 1836, National Archives.

sent his orderly, Private Farrow, to aid in "putting the hospital in good police." But Stinnecke denied Magruder's authority to order such an inspection: "I am always (cheerfully) willing to obey orders when they come from proper authorities [but] I cannot acknowledge you in the light and character of commanding officer whereby my rights and privileges can be at all interfered with . . . The document you sent me yesterday is therefore returned conceiving that your right to send me any communication of the kind is entirely assumed."[130] Stinnecke further explained that as the medical supplies of the hospital were public property, he had them locked for safekeeping in a storeroom where only trained personnel could enter. He termed Farrow "irresponsible," declared that he "could not be trusted to go into the storeroom," and promptly dismissed him.[131]

When Private Farrow returned to post headquarters with a recounting of events at the hospital, Magruder must have been overcome with rage. His character had been questioned, his orderly had been dubbed irresponsible, and his authority had been flatly rejected. Magruder immediately issued an order for the arrest and confinement of the insubordinate surgeon.[132] But Stinnecke again refused to cooperate, replying, "Until you establish your authority as being placed in command over me, your order of arrest is not acknowledged and therefore cannot be respected or in any manner regarded."[133] Magruder, now at the end of his wits, presented his case to the adjutant general of the army.[134] This time there would be no doubt about the "proper authority." The adjutant general gave Magruder permission to "relieve that officer [Stinnecke] from duty,"[135] and he readily complied.

The Stinnecke controversy was only the first frustration. During his presidency Andrew Jackson actively sponsored an Indian removal policy to obtain more farmland for a rapidly growing America. The treaties of Payne's

130. Stinnecke to Magruder, June 27, 1836, National Archives.

131. Ibid.

132. Order No. 3 of J. B. Magruder, lieutenant commanding Fort Washington, Md., June 27, 1836, National Archives.

133. Stinnecke to Magruder, June 27, 1836, National Archives. This is a different letter than that referred to in notes 130 and 131, though both bear the same date.

134. Magruder to Jones, June 27, 1836, National Archives.

135. Jones to Magruder, July 6, 1836, National Archives. Stinnecke apparently was not permanently relieved from duty because eight years later he examined Magruder for a bronchial ailment. Magruder to the adjutant-general, September 23, 1844, National Archives. The examination must have been an awkward affair for both the doctor and his patient.

Landing and Fort Gibson (1832–33) authorized relocation of the Florida Seminoles to lands beyond the Mississippi River. But these treaties were signed
by a handful of chiefs who did not accurately reflect the will of the Seminole
nation. Consequently, the treaties were repudiated, and by November 1835
the Second Seminole War had broken out.[136] Jackson immediately sent General Winfield Scott to quell the resistance. A large portion of the 1st Artillery
accompanied Scott, but Magruder had had an attack of chronic bronchitis
that temporarily rendered him "unfit for active duty in the field."[137] While
others were departing for action, Magruder received the unwelcome news
that he had been assigned as a draftsman in the Ordnance Department in
Washington. He remained there for nearly a year, but on October 19, 1837,
received orders to rejoin his company in Florida.[138]

On November 10, 1837, Magruder left Baltimore abroad the packet *South
Carolina*. After brief stops at Norfolk and Charleston, he disembarked at
New Smyrna, approximately seventy miles south of St. Augustine, and as-
sumed command of the three 1st Artillery companies there. The men packed
their equipment onto shallow-draft, flat-bottomed Mackinaw boats on the
twenty-eighth and departed at sunrise the next morning. Navy lieutenant
John T. McLaughlin led the dozen Mackinaws thirty miles south, through
Mosquito Lagoon, to a place on the western shore called the "haul-over."
This was a narrow strip of land separating the lagoon from the Indian River,
so named because the Seminoles dragged their canoes overland there from
one body of water to the other. A large number of additional troops arrived
during the following weeks, among whom were Joseph E. Johnston and Colonel Benjamin K. Pierce, commander of the 1st Artillery Regiment. Pierce
occupied his men with drills by day; at night Magruder entertained them by
playing guitar and singing in a voice that was reportedly neither disagreeable
nor always in tune.[139]

136. The most recent scholarly study of the Second Seminole War is John K. Mahon, *History
of the Second Seminole War, 1835–1842* (Gainesville: University of Florida Press, 1967).

137. Magruder to Jones, October 18, 1836; Jones to Magruder, October 24, 1836, National Archives.

138. Cullum, *Biographical Register*, 1:367; *Army and Navy Chronicle* 5 (October 26, 1837), 272.
Quoting from Special Orders No. 84, October 19, 1837.

139. Jacob Rhett Motte, *Journey into Wilderness: An Army Surgeon's Account of Life in Camp
and Field during the Creek and Seminole Wars, 1836–1838*, ed. James F. Sunderman (Gainesville:
University of Florida Press, 1953), 155–69.

The men broke camp on December 30, 1837, crossed the haul-over, and made their way ninety miles down the Indian River to its mouth. They made camp four miles farther south on the elevated western bank at a site they named Fort Pierce, in honor of their regimental commander. Two weeks later, on January 14, 1838, General Thomas Jesup, the newly appointed commander in Florida, arrived off Fort Pierce with nearly a thousand men and large quantities of materiel in preparation for a strike against the Seminoles.[140] When the heavily laden transports attempted to cross the bar into the harbor, however, several ran aground, as the water depth at the bar had been measured during the highest monthly tide. After the men were safely ashore, Jesup sent for Magruder, whom Pierce had recently appointed assistant regimental quartermaster. The army had only three days' provisions and forage. It was imperative that Magruder salvage part of the supplies from the stranded and wrecked vessels. The assault depended upon it.[141]

Magruder organized several salvage crews from Jesup's men. Working day and night without rest, they brought ashore such supplies as they could save in rowboats, which had themselves been salvaged from the grounded vessels. Twice at night Magruder's boat was upset "among swarms of sharks" in the angry surf at the bar. Nevertheless, the crews worked on relentlessly, rescuing sometimes a half-cargo, at others a third, until the army was sufficiently supplied to advance against the enemy.[142] On January 24, 1838, General Jesup dealt the Seminoles a severe defeat at the Battle of Lockahatchee. Magruder was not a participant and received no immediate credit, but his efforts were in no small part responsible for Jesup's success.

Years later, on January 4, 1853, the auditor's office wrote Magruder for a detailed account of his receipts and expenditures.[143] It seems that all of the property sent to Fort Pierce from Charleston, St. Augustine, and elsewhere had been charged to him, though only a fraction of it had been received as a consequence of the groundings at the bar. Furthermore, Magruder had had no prior experience as a quartermaster, nor did he have a clerk to assist him. He didn't even have any stationery. He had kept his accounts on the blank portions of letters that he had received from his wife and friends. And later, when Magruder was stationed in California, such records as he had were

140. Ibid., 172–78.
141. Magruder to Thompson, January 18, 1853, National Archives.
142. Ibid.
143. Thompson to Magruder, January 4, 1853, National Archives.

lost in an 1850 fire, which destroyed the office of the Pacific Mail Steamship Company in San Francisco.[144]

The entire matter was dropped after the auditor's office asked General Jesup for his recollections regarding the supplies in question. Jesup verified the wreckage of the transports and termed Magruder's actions in saving the supplies a "heroic performance." The general added, "By his [Magruder's] efforts . . . I was enabled to keep the field and bring the Indians to battle, the result of which was the surrender of more than a thousand Indians and Negroes."[145]

At the conclusion of the fighting in Florida, the 1st Artillery Regiment was transferred to Rouse's Point near Plattsburg, New York, to restore order following the burning of the steamers *Caroline* and *Sir Robert Peel* in the wake of William Lyon Mackenzie's abortive attempt to overthrow the Canadian government. President Martin Van Buren was sympathetic to the rebel cause but ordered General Winfield Scott to enforce neutrality and administer stiff punishment to those who violated it.[146] Then, with great energy and diplomacy, the American troops urged citizens along an eight hundred–mile front to act responsibly and remain calm.[147]

At the same time, Magruder, as commander of Company I, 1st Artillery, warned his men to be on their best behavior while serving in the troubled area. One night of a payday, while patrolling the streets of Plattsburg, Magruder came upon a Frenchman of his company, Bertrand by name, and cautioned him to slow his drinking. Bertrand repelled any idea of his getting drunk and behaving in a disorderly manner. He concluded by drawing himself up in true French grandeur, wrinkling his eyebrows fiercely, slapping his right hand on his heart, and exclaiming gallantly, "Parole d'honneur, Lieutenant! Je suis Français!" Magruder was impressed. He concluded that a man of such grand eloquence must be sober and continued his patrolling. An hour later, however, while returning to his quarters, Magruder turned down a side street and found a blue-clad soldier ingloriously reposing in

144. Magruder to Thompson, January 18, 1853, National Archives.

145. Endorsement of General Thomas S. Jesup, ibid.

146. Proclamations of President Martin Van Buren, January 5, November 21, 1838. James D. Richardson, *A Compilation of the Messages and Papers of the Presidents, 1789–1812*, 11 vols. (New York: Bureau of National Literature and Art, 1907), 3:481–83.

147. Winfield Scott, *Memoirs of Lieutenant-General Scott, LLD*, 2 vols. (New York: Sheldon and Co., 1864), 1:309–10.

the mud. It was Bertrand, insensibly drunk. Magruder consigned him to a patrol, and the next day "Je suis Français" was in the guardhouse on the stool of repentance.[148]

It was imperative that cordial relations be maintained between the British and American soldiers along the border, so Magruder invited several of the ranking Britishers to a dinner. The invited guests represented some of England's finest fighting units: Coldstream Guards, Grenadier Guards, 7th Hussars, Queen's Own, 1st Dragoon Guards, 1st Royals, and 73rd Highlanders.[149] No doubt they expected to find the Americans a rather ragged lot, as Mrs. Trollope had so picturesquely described. But they were mistaken— Prince John Magruder had seen to that. He had rented or borrowed elegant gold plate, cut-glass ware, and rich furniture. Then he assured his guests that the furnishings were mere remnants of the once splendid regimental mess: "Only the debris, my lord; the schooner bringing most of the mess plate from Florida was wrecked." The English gentlemen were not only astonished; they were envious. "We do not wish to be inquisitive," one of them said, "but we have been so impressed with this magnificence that we are constrained to believe the American officers must be paid enormously. What is your monthly pay?" As if he were completely indifferent to the matter, Magruder replied, "Damned if I know." He then turned to his servant, winked, and asked, "Jim, what is my monthly pay?" There was no answer, but both men were painfully aware that the salary was a meager sixty-five dollars per month.[150]

Magruder also served as master of ceremonies for a sleigh race to be held on the ice of Lake Champlain at Plattsburg, New York, near the American border encampment. After issuing a challenge to the British soldiers, Prince John solicited some of the wealthier citizens of the town for financial assistance. A series of races was arranged, purses were made up, and a course of one mile was measured off on the ice, swept clean of snow, and staked

148. William L. Haskin, *The History of the First Regiment of Artillery from Its Organization in 1821, to January 1, 1876* (Portland, Maine: B. Thurston and Co., 1879), 285.

149. Ibid., 287.

150. Daniel H. Hill, "Lee's Attacks North of the Chickahominy," in *Battles and Leaders of the Civil War*, ed. Robert U. Johnson and Clarence C. Buel, 4 vols. (New York: Century Co., 1887–88), 2:362n; Fremantle, *Freemantle Diary*, 258–59n.; Walter H. Taylor, *General Lee: His Campaigns in Virginia, 1861–1865* (Brooklyn, N.Y.: Braunworth and Co., 1906), 51–52; "John Magruder," *Army and Navy Journal*, 148. The author of the article on Magruder in the *Army and Navy Journal* stated that Prince John's salary was "about $77 per month, and it constituted the totality of his fortune."

out with green hemlock trees cut and posted in the ice. Magruder adver-
tised the event in the *Plattsburg Republican,* and when the appointed day arrived, hundreds of people were on hand to view the spectacle. The races and
supplementary festivities lasted for two days and were carried out flawlessly.
Plattsburg had never before witnessed such revelry. The shops, hotels, cafés,
and barrooms all reaped substantial profits, while the "pious of Plattsburg"
protested the violation of the state racing laws of New York. One week later
Magruder and his fellow lawbreakers were indicted by the grand jury. It took
all of the influence of Cady, Yates, Stone, McNeal, other leading citizens,
and sleigh-racing enthusiasts to suppress the indictment. Legal technicalities
notwithstanding, the races and dinner generated a spirit of friendship and
mutual trust among the troops on both sides of the border.[151]

Many of the troops were taken off alert and reassigned elsewhere when
pressures along the border began to ease. In the summer of 1840 Magruder
was assigned to recruit for the 1st Artillery in the Boston area.[152] He generally
enjoyed recruiting because it afforded him freedom from army regimentation during which time he could more actively lend his talents to social
activities. But even recruiting occasionally proved aggravating. Army regulations did not authorize the use of a physician to examine the recruits unless
the number amounted to fifteen or more per month. As there were often less
than this number and no doctor was present, Magruder was required to conduct the medical examinations personally. He was as thorough as possible,
but it was later discovered that Thomas Whitcomb, one of the recruits, had
a scrotal hernia, which had not been detected at the recruiting station. Assuming Magruder to have been negligent, the adjutant general reprimanded
him. But Magruder was bitter and did not take the reprimand lightly. He
objected to having been required to give the examination in the first place,
and then he boldly stated that he should hardly have been held accountable
for his ignorance of the medical profession.[153]

Magruder was taken off the recruiting service and assigned to garrison
duty at Hancock Barracks, in Houlton, Maine.[154] In two years there, from
1842 to 1844, he became increasingly dissatisfied with the army, and at the
same time his health began to deteriorate as a consequence of the adverse

151. Haskin, *History of the First Regiment of Artillery,* 287–88.
152. *Army and Navy Chronicle* 11 (September 3, 1840): 159, and (October 8, 1840): 239.
153. Magruder to Lewis, January 6, 1841, National Archives.
154. Cullum, *Biographical Register,* 1:367.

northern climate. On September 11, 1844, Magruder was examined by Dr. William Power, a "highly respected stethoscopist." The doctor diagnosed a bronchial infection and warned that if neglected, "it may, and in all probability [would] serve as a starting point for tubercular disease."[155] Power also stressed the importance of living in a mild climate, and on October 11, 1844, Magruder obtained a transfer to the recruiting service in Baltimore.[156]

The new assignment was a pleasant change. Magruder returned to his wife, three children, and Baltimore society. His health also improved, but overall he remained dissatisfied with his army service. Since graduating from West Point, Magruder had seen no military action and had received but one promotion, to first lieutenant, on March 31, 1836.[157] Through the years his supporters, including Congressman Robert M. T. Hunter, General Thomas S. Jesup, General William Jenkins Worth, Colonel James Bankhead, and Colonel Benjamin K. Pierce, had recommended a brevet for Magruder's services during the Florida war.[158] But no promotion came, brevet or otherwise. By this time John Magruder was "one of the eldest, if not the oldest First Lieutenant in the Army."[159] When his patience finally ran out, Magruder personally complained of his plight in a letter written on February 14, 1845, to the adjutant general: "At the last session of Congress I had the honor to lay before the commanding general, through your office my claims for promotion . . . I have been informed that I was nominated to the Senate, for the brevet rank of Captain for services rendered in Florida but that the nomination was not acted upon in consequence of its having been made only a day or two before the termination of the session. I do not wish to press my claims to the detriment of others, but . . . I have waited in silence for seven years for this promotion."[160]

155. Power to Magruder, September 11, 1844, National Archives.

156. Cullum, *Biographical Register,* 1:367; Thomas to Crane, November 14, 1844, National Archives.

157. Cullum, *Biographical Register,* 1:367.

158. Jesup to Hunter, December 8, 1841; Hunter to Spencer, January 23, 1842; Magruder to Wilkins, February 19, 1845, endorsed by Colonel B. K. Pierce, Major Justin Dimick, and others, National Archives.

159. Worth to secretary of war, January 29, 1846, National Archives.

160. Magruder to Jones, February 14, 1845, National Archives. Brief but excellent coverage of the promotion problem as one of many causes of low morale in the army can be found in Robert M. Utley, *Frontiersmen in Blue: The United States Army and the Indian, 1845–1865* (New York: Macmillan, 1967), 28–58.

———

Suddenly everything changed. War clouds were gathering between the United States and Mexico over the question of Texas's annexation. When Texas accepted the American offer, Magruder immediately volunteered for service in General Zachary Taylor's army of occupation. Such orders were issued in August 1845, and on September 1, 1845, an enthusiastic, revitalized John Bankhead Magruder boarded the U.S. storeship *Lexington* in New York.[161] War and opportunity lay ahead in Texas and Mexico.

161. Haskin, *History of the First Regiment of Artillery,* 78. Abner Doubleday reported they embarked on September 2, 1845, ibid., 304.

2

OPPORTUNITY IN MEXICO

Brevet Brigadier General Zachary Taylor moved his men from New Orleans to the small coastal settlement of Corpus Christi, Texas,[1] immediately after he had been notified that Texas, on July 4, 1845, had officially accepted the terms of annexation.[2] His orders were to hold his troops in readiness,[3] avoiding conflict with the Mexicans,[4] while Minister Plenipotentiary John Slidell negotiated with an angry government of Mexico. Taylor's Army of Occupation expanded with the arrival of continuous reinforcements, and by the time Magruder reached Corpus Christi, on October 4,[5] more than half of the regular U.S. Army was in Texas.[6] The force numbered thirty-nine hundred

1. Donelson to Taylor, June 28, 1845, House Executive Doc. 60, 30th Cong., 1st sess., 805. Taylor chose the site on the recommendation of Andrew Jackson Donelson, the American charge d'affaires in Texas.

2. The most scholarly works on Texas-Mexican relations leading up to and including the annexation process are Justin H. Smith, *The Annexation of Texas* (New York: Baker and Taylor Co., 1911); George Lockhart Rives, *The United States and Mexico, 1821–1848: A History of the Relations between the Two Countries from the Independence of Mexico to the Close of the War with the United States*, 2 vols. (New York: Charles Scribner's Sons, 1913), vol. 1; and David M. Pletcher, *The Diplomacy of Annexation: Texas, Oregon, and the Mexican War* (Columbia: University of Missouri Press, 1973).

3. Marcy to Taylor, May 28, 1845, House Executive Doc. 60, 30th Cong., 1st sess., 79–80.

4. Marcy to Taylor, July 8, 1845, ibid., 82. In his instructions Taylor was informed that the Mexicans "[had] some military establishments on the east side of the Rio Grande" but that he should "be careful to avoid any acts of aggression, unless an actual state of war should exist."

5. Haskin, *History of the First Regiment of Artillery*, 78, 305.

6. Rives, *United States and Mexico, 1821–1848*, 2:58–59.

men;[7] it was the largest American troop concentration since the close of the War of 1812.

Zachary Taylor divided his army into three brigades commanded respectively by General William Jenkins Worth, Lieutenant Colonel James S. McIntosh, and Colonel William Whistler. Magruder commanded Company B, 1st Artillery. His was one of twelve artillery companies commanded by Brevet Lieutenant Colonel Thomas Childs that served as infantry in Worth's 1st Brigade.[8] Certainly Magruder, as a trained artillerist, must have been disappointed with this assignment; nevertheless, he administered discipline and drill instruction without complaint. He was eager for battle, and when the opportunity presented itself, he was determined that his men would be ready. Magruder's diligence did not go unnoticed. Worth, who had been commandant of cadets when Magruder was at West Point, recommended him for promotion, praising him as "one of the most accomplished and soldierly men in the service."[9]

There were, however, doubts about the competency of others. Officers who had never drilled units larger than a company, or at most a battalion, were now awkwardly attempting to coordinate the movements of entire regiments.[10] Neither Taylor nor Whistler could form the brigade into a line, and Colonel David E. Twiggs of the 2nd Dragoons could do so "only after a fashion." Colonel Ethan Allen Hitchcock, commander of the 3rd Infantry,

---

7. Justin H. Smith, *The War with Mexico,* 2 vols. (New York: Macmillan, 1919), 1:143; W. S. Henry, *Campaign Sketches of the War with Mexico* (New York: Harper and Bros., 1847), 24, 39; Return of the Army of Occupation in Texas for November, 1845; Senate Executive Doc. 1, 29th Cong., 1st sess., 220; Cadmus M. Wilcox, *History of the Mexican War,* ed. Mary Rachel Wilcox (Washington, D.C.: Church News Publishing Co., 1892), 12. Wilcox estimates there were 3,860 men, but the official return for November 1845 stated that there were only 3,593 men present; these figures, however, did not include the Texas Rangers, as they were paid by the government of Texas. In mid-October 1845 Henry reported that the Army of Occupation consisted of 251 officers and 3,671 enlisted men, totaling 3,922. Justin Smith, utilizing various sources, agrees with the 3,900 figure.

8. Haskin, *History of the First Regiment of Artillery,* 78. Haskin noted that when General Taylor had "a grand review of all of the troops," the marching of Childs's artillery battalion was "pronounced by old and experienced officers to be perfect, and the state of their arms and equipment to be in keeping with the perfection of their drill."

9. Letter of recommendation from General W. J. Worth to the secretary of war, January 29, 1846, National Archives.

10. Wilcox, *History of the Mexican War,* 13.

reported that there was but one field officer in the entire camp who could "change a single position of the troops according to any but a militia mode," and that officer was himself.[11]

The morale and discipline of the troops declined noticeably after months of waiting for the governments of the United States and Mexico to resolve their diplomatic stalemate. The problem was complicated by a change of seasons that, according to Lieutenant William S. Henry of the 3rd Infantry, brought "the most shocking weather imaginable."[12] Few had ever experienced conditions when they stood ankle deep in mud with dust blowing in their faces. Moreover, it was not unusual for the weather to change from sweltering heat and humidity to bone-chilling cold within a period of twenty-four hours, so that soldiers bedded down gasping for breath, then woke up freezing. Because of the disagreeable weather, Justin Smith estimated that at one time "nearly twenty per cent of the men were on the sick list, and half of the others were more or less ill."[13] In addition, the troops suffered from inadequate shelter, menacing insects and snakes, a lack of firewood, primitive sanitary conditions, and poor drinking water, which inevitably caused dysentery. Desertion was common, and the only diversion for those who remained was found in Corpus Christi, which now numbered approximately two thousand people,[14] owing to the heavy influx of prostitutes, gamblers, liquor sellers, and other camp followers. Hitchcock reported "several disgraceful brawls and quarrels, to say nothing of drunken frolics," and he declared that the general conduct was scandalous.[15]

To divert the men from the saloons and gambling dens, the commanders persuaded Magruder to build a theater.[16] As one who was culturally refined and somewhat dramatic in his own manner, Prince John was precisely the man for the project. By November 1 Magruder had one group of volunteers building the eight hundred–seat theater and another busily painting scenery.

11. Ethan Allen Hitchcock, *Fifty Years in Camp and Field: Diary of Major-General Ethan Allen Hitchcock, U.S.A.*, ed. W. A. Croffut (New York: G. P. Putnam's Sons, 1909), 198–99, 215.

12. Henry, *Campaign Sketches*, 45.

13. Smith, *War with Mexico*, 1:143.

14. Hitchcock, *Fifty Years in Camp and Field*, 206. An officer in Worth's brigade described Corpus Christi as "the most murderous, thieving, gambling, cut-throat, God-forsaken hole" in Texas. Edward S. Wallace, *General William Jenkins Worth: Monterey's Forgotten Hero* (Dallas: Southern Methodist University Press, 1953), 66.

15. Hitchcock, *Fifty Years in Camp and Field*, 203.

16. Lloyd Lewis, *Captain Sam Grant* (Boston: Little, Brown, 1950), 129.

A dramatic company was organized from among the officers, who were required to play both male and female roles,[17] and on the evening of January 8
the Army Theater Troupe presented its first plays: *The Wife—A Tale of
Mantua*, by James Sheridan Knowles; a farce, *The Loan of a Lover*; a dance
by a Mr. Wells; and a variety of singing and dancing acts. The humorous
performances delighted the capacity crowds, who readily paid the admission
price of one dollar for the boxes and fifty cents for seats in the pit.[18] General
Worth was regularly among the spectators; Taylor and Twiggs attended occasionally. Within a short time the profits covered building and incidental
expenses, and sufficient funds remained to send to New Orleans for cos-
tumes. The actors also decided to broaden their repertoire to include tragedy,
choosing Shakespeare's *Othello*. Lieutenant Theodoric Porter, brother of Rear
Admiral David Porter, was cast as Othello and Lieutenant James Longstreet
as Desdemona. But Longstreet was six feet tall and hardly resembled a tragic
heroine, so Magruder substituted the shorter, more slender Ulysses S. Grant
in his place. Grant, however, achieved so little feminine appeal as Desdemona
that he, too, was rejected. As a last resort, the officers of the dramatic company pooled their resources and imported an actress, Mrs. Hart, and a few
other supporting professionals from New Orleans.[19] The theater murdered
tragedy and rendered farce into buffoonery, but it did so in "the most approved style."[20] More important, it succeeded in raising the general morale
and in cooling the tempers of many of the officers who were involved in a
heated dispute over rank precedence.

Twiggs was the ranking colonel in the camp, but Worth had been bre-
veted brigadier general for distinguished service in the Second Seminole
War. Worth insisted, therefore, that he outranked Twiggs, even though
Twiggs had been commissioned colonel two years ahead of him. General
Taylor ruled in favor of lineal rank but sent the question on to Washington
for a final decision. Secretary of War William L. Marcy then referred the

17. James Longstreet, *From Manassas to Appomattox: Memoirs of the Civil War in America*
(Philadelphia: J. B. Lippincott, 1896), 20; George Meade, *The Life and Letters of George Gor-
don Meade, Major General, United States Army*, ed. George Gordon Meade, 2 vols. (New York:
Charles Scribner's Sons, 1913), 1:43–44; Henry, *Campaign Sketches*, 44–45, 47.

18. *Corpus Christi Gazette*, January 8, 1846.

19. Longstreet, *From Manassas to Appomattox*, 20. Grant and Longstreet would not reclaim
their leading roles until the theater repertoire returned to comedy, an ironic reversal of their
later leading roles in the Civil War.

20. Meade, *Life and Letters of George Gordon Meade*, 1:43–44.

problem to Winfield Scott, the ranking general in the army. When Scott supported Worth,[21] reversing Taylor's earlier decision, it divided the officer corps
at Corpus Christi and reportedly brought the camp to "the verge of battle."[22]
Over 150 officers, including Twiggs, Whistler, Hitchcock, and Magruder,
signed a petition asking that Scott's ruling be reversed.[23] On the advice of
Senator Thomas Hart Benton, President Polk, on March 12, 1846, ruled in favor of lineal rank.[24] When Polk's decision reached Taylor's army, on April 2,[25]
Worth hastily tendered his resignation and went immediately to Washington
to present his case. Although he did not receive a satisfactory answer to his
grievance, he eventually withdrew his resignation and returned to his brigade at Camargo near the end of May 1846.[26] General Worth must have been
deeply disappointed with the final ruling, but to his credit he held no grudge
against those who opposed him during the controversy. Indeed, it was just
six weeks after Magruder signed the petition supporting Twiggs that Worth
recommended him for promotion.

In the meantime, after the Mexican government rejected the Slidell mission, Polk ordered General Taylor, through Marcy, to advance his camp from
Corpus Christi to the vicinity of the mouth of the Rio Grande.[27] Twiggs's cavalry and Samuel Ringgold's artillery left Corpus Christi on March 8, with the

21. James B. Fry, *The History and Legal Effect of Brevets in the Armies of Great Britain and
the United States from Their Origin in 1692 to the Present Time* (New York: D. Van Nostrand,
1877), 162–65. The legal status of brevets had been a controversial issue in the army for over
thirty years. It nearly drove Winfield Scott from the army in 1828, when the government refused to recognize his claim to command of the army by virtue of his brevet rank. Under the
circumstances it was not at all surprising that Scott supported Worth when the controversy
re-erupted.

22. Smith, *War with Mexico*, 1:144. The most concise firsthand accounts of the controversy
may be found in Meade, *Life and Letters of George Gordon Meade*, 1: 87–88; and Ulysses S.
Grant, *Personal Memoirs of U. S. Grant*, 2 vols. (New York: Charles L. Webster and Co., 1885),
1:100–101.

23. Hitchcock, *Fifty Years in Camp and Field*, 204–6; Fry, *History and Legal Effect of Brevets in
the Armies of Great Britain and the United States*, 166–79. While Hitchcock gives only a summary
of the memorial in his diary, Fry includes the document in its entirety, including the signatories.

24. Milo Milton Quaife, ed., *The Diary of James K. Polk during His Presidency, 1845 to 1849*, 4
vols. (Chicago: A. C. McClurg and Co., 1910), 1:284–85; Fry, *History and Legal Effect of Brevets
in the Armies of Great Britain and the United States*, 180–81.

25. Hitchcock, *Fifty Years in Camp and Field*, 220.

26. Fry, *History and Legal Effect of Brevets in the Armies of Great Britain and the United States*,
183–89.

27. Marcy to Taylor, January 13, 1846, House Executive Doc. 60, 30th Cong., 1st sess., 90–91.

1st, 2nd, and 3rd brigades following at one-day intervals. Magruder's company marched on the March 9 with Worth's brigade. General Taylor and his administrative entourage followed two days later in company with the 3rd Brigade. Part of the supplies were shipped by sea to Point Isabel, near the mouth of the Rio Grande, while the remainder was transported overland in 307 wagons, 80 of which were pulled by oxen. The others were drawn by mules and ill-broken horses. Only the sick and a skeletal garrison force remained behind.[28]

The march began as beautiful spring weather turned south Texas into a palette of spectacular colors. Magruder and his men found themselves enchanted by a landscape covered with bluebonnets, lantana, phlox, verbena, and new blooming prickly pear. Fleeing deer, antelope, javelina, mustangs, and wild turkey supplied natural animation to a setting that was undisturbed until the American column reached the Arroyo Colorado, approximately 130 miles south of Corpus Christi.[29] There, on the south bank, Mexican soldiers demonstrated menacingly but then fled like the wildlife, allowing Taylor's army to continue its journey to the Rio Grande without further incident.[30]

General Taylor established his headquarters directly across the river from Matamoros in a hastily constructed fieldwork named Fort Texas. While curious Mexican citizens watched the work of Taylor's men from their rooftops,[31] equally curious American soldiers, including several young officers, Magruder perhaps among them, anxiously watched from the north bank of the Rio Grande as Mexican señoritas bathed naked in the waters across from them.[32] In the evenings army bands played "Yankee Doodle," "The Star-Spangled Banner," and "Hail Columbia" for the citizens of Matamoros, who serenaded the Americans with Spanish melodies in return.[33] Occasional gun-

28. Taylor to Jones, March 8, 1846, ibid., 118; Meade, *Life and Letters of George Gordon Meade*, 1:51; Henry, *Campaign Sketches*, 52; Emma Jerome Blackwood, ed., *To Mexico with Scott: Letters of Captain E. Kirby Smith to His Wife* (Cambridge: Harvard University Press, 1917), 22.

29. Henry, *Campaign Sketches*, 53–64; Blackwood, *To Mexico with Scott*, 23–29.

30. Taylor to Jones, March 21, 1846, House Executive Doc. 60, 30th Cong., 1st sess., 123–25; Blackwood. *To Mexico With Scott*, 29–33; Grant, *Personal Memoirs*, 1: 87–88; Henry, *Campaign Sketches*, 59–63; Hitchcock, *Fifty Years in Camp and Field*, 211. Meade, *Life and Letters of George Gordon Meade*, 1:52.

31. Henry, *Campaign Sketches*, 68.

32. Blackwood, *To Mexico with Scott*, 34.

33. Samuel G. French, *Two Wars: An Autobiography of Gen. Samuel G. French* (Nashville, Tenn.: Confederate Veteran, 1901), 45; Philip Nordbourne Barbour, *Journals of the Late Brevet Major Philip Nordbourne Barbour, Captain in the 3rd Regiment, United States Infantry*, ed. Rhoda van Bibber Tanner Doubleday (New York: G. P. Putnam's Sons, 1936), 26, 29.

shots shattered the calm, yet they did not signal the beginning of hostilities. Rather, they were fired by Taylor's pickets at deserters attempting to cross to the Mexican side of the Rio Grande.[34] A widely circulated report that American soldiers were being handsomely received by the Mexicans briefly spurred the rate of desertions.[35] The flight slowed, however, when "a person from the other side" informed Magruder that the handful of Americans who had deserted to Matamoros "would soon wish themselves anywhere else, for all was misery over there."[36]

From the time the American army reached the Rio Grande, Zachary Taylor had assured the Mexicans that his mission was entirely peaceful. On March 28 he sent General Worth, Magruder, and a handful of other junior officers to negotiate an armistice with Mexican military authorities, while representatives from the two countries attempted to settle their differences through diplomacy. Worth and his assistants met with General Rómulo Díaz de la Vega, the second-in-command at Matamoros,[37] but the negotiations failed, as did subsequent exchanges with Mexican commanders Francisco Mejía and Pedro de Ampudia, both of whom insisted that a state of war existed as a consequence of Taylor's having crossed the Nueces River into "Mexican territory."[38] The volatile situation remained until April 24, when General Mariano Arista arrived to replace Ampudia. The next day the new commander ordered General Anastacio Torrejón to cross the Rio Grande above Matamoros with sixteen hundred cavalrymen. Having heard rumors of the crossing, Taylor dispatched Captain Seth B. Thornton with sixty-three dragoons to investigate. Thornton, being ignorant of both the size and location of the opposing force, walked into a trap at Carricitos Ranch. When he tried to fight his way out, eleven of his men were killed; the rest, includ-

34. Barbour, *Journals*, 28–31; Blackwood, *To Mexico with Scott*, 37; Henry, *Campaign Sketches*, 72–73; Hitchcock, *Fifty Years in Camp and Field*, 221; Meade, *Life and Letters of George Gordon Meade*, 1:53.

35. Smith, *War with Mexico*, 1:160; Henry, *Campaign Sketches*, 73; Meade, *Life and Letters of George Gordon Meade*, 1:53; Taylor to Jones, April 6, 1846, House Executive Doc. 60, 30th Cong., 1st sess., 133.

36. Barbour, *Journals*, 24–25.

37. Minutes of an interview between Worth and General Rómulo Vega, March 28, 1846, House Executive Doc. 60, 30th Cong., 1st sess., 134–38.

38. House Executive Doc. 60, 30th Cong., 1st sess., 123–41, 1202–6; Barbour, *Journals*, 17–20, 32, 34–36; Blackwood, *To Mexico with Scott*, 34, 38; Henry, *Campaign Sketches*, 65–67, 74–75; 79–81; Hitchcock, *Fifty Years in Camp and Field*, 217, 222; Meade, *Life and Letters of George Gordon Meade*, 1:52, 56–57, 70–73.

ing Thornton and his second in command, Captain William J. Hardee, were made prisoners.[39] The following day, April 26, 1846, Zachary Taylor wrote Washington, "Hostilities may now be considered as commenced."[40]

After the clash at Carricitos Ranch, events along the Rio Grande moved rapidly. Taylor reinforced Fort Texas, then hurried to obtain provisions from his supply depot at Point Isabel. Days later, on May 8, during the return trip from the coast, Taylor found that Mariano Arista had crossed the Rio Grande and was waiting for him with his 4,000-man Mexican army,[41] aligned for battle near the pond at Palo Alto, a dozen miles northeast of Matamoros. General Taylor paused briefly to allow time for his 270-wagon supply train to catch up and his men to rest and refill their canteens.[42] Then, at two in the afternoon, he ordered his 2,288-man force forward.[43] Thirty-nine-year-old John Magruder was among Taylor's advancing charges. For Magruder what to this point had been a slow-moving, uneventful military career was about to change.

Magruder's Company B and the other artillery companies that served as infantry under Childs advanced from a position near the center of Taylor's line. James Duncan's light battery was to the left of Magruder, flanked by the 8th Infantry, on the far left flank. Lieutenant Colonel William G. Belknap commanded the left wing overall. The right wing commanded by Twiggs consisted of the 4th Infantry, in the center of the American line next to Magruder's men. Then in succession to the right were Lieutenant William H. Churchill's two eighteen-pounders, the 3rd Infantry, Major Samuel Ringgold's field artillery, the 5th Infantry, and Captain Charles A. May's dragoons, which protected the extreme right flank. For security the wagon train was parked in the rear near the pond and was protected by a squadron of dragoons commanded by Captain Croghan Ker.[44]

---

39. Taylor to Jones, April 26 and May 3, 1846, with the accompanying reports of William J. Hardee, April 26, 1846, and Seth B. Thornton, April 27, 1846, House Executive Doc. 60, 30th Cong., 1st sess., 288–92 (Hardee is incorrectly identified as W. T. Hardee, and Thornton is incorrectly identified as T. B. Thornton.); Blackwood, *To Mexico with Scott*, 39–43; Henry, *Campaign Sketches*, 82–85; Barbour, *Journals*, 45–48.

40. Taylor to Jones, April 26, 1846, House Executive Doc. 60, 30th Cong., 1st sess., 288.

41. Smith, *War with Mexico*, 1:165. Smith surmised that Arista's force "seemed to number 6,000, though probably not more than two-thirds as many."

42. Charles M. Haecker and Jeffrey G. Mauck, *On the Prairie of Palo Alto* (College Station: Texas A&M University Press, 1997), 27–28.

43. Taylor to Jones, May 16, 1846, Senate Executive Doc. 388, 29th Cong., 1st sess., 2, 4, 6.

44. Ibid., 2; Henry, *Campaign Sketches*, 91; Blackwood, *To Mexico with Scott*, 47–48; Barbour, *Journals*, 54.

Zachary Taylor anticipated the battle would be fought by bayonet and lance.[45] Had his expectation been realized, Palo Alto may well have been his last battle, as Arista enjoyed a two-to-one advantage in infantry and an overwhelming advantage in cavalry. Arista commanded perhaps 1,800 cavalrymen; Taylor had approximately 200.[46] Additionally, Taylor's deficiency in cavalry was magnified because Ker's men, having been assigned to protect the vulnerable supply train, would not be available to participate in the fight. The only advantage that Taylor had was one that he did not appreciate—his artillery.[47] Ultimately, the Battle of Palo Alto would be as much of a learning experience for the veteran commander as it would be for the inexperienced John Magruder. Magruder at least understood the capabilities of the artillery. Zachary Taylor, having spent the greater part of his military service on the frontier, where artillery was rarely utilized in warfare against Indians, did not.

Taylor, despite his thirty-eight years in military service, had numerous other shortcomings.[48] He had no formal military education. He knew nothing of military maneuvers, never utilized his engineers, seldom listened to his staff, and failed utterly to appreciate the talents of the ambitious, young West Pointers in his army.[49] The old general so resented their spit-and-polish style of dress that he discarded his uniform altogether in favor of "a blue checked gingham coat, blue trousers without braid, a linen waistcoat and a broad-brimmed straw hat."[50] Historians have benevolently overlooked Taylor's shortcomings, preferring to cite his great courage, solid common sense, and keen instincts. However, the general's military contemporaries were often less generous in their assessments. Winfield Scott, for example, declared that Old Zach "was quite ignorant, for his rank."[51] And Colonel Hitchcock, likewise recognizing his commander's want of technical military skill, declared in a letter to his brother, "If Taylor succeeds, it will be by accident."[52]

45. Orders no. 58, May 7, 1846, House Executive Doc. 60, 30th Cong., 1st sess., 487; Henry, *Campaign Sketches*, 89–90.

46. Haskin, *History of the First Regiment of Artillery*, 81.

47. Smith, *War with Mexico*, 1:465n–66n.

48. Quaife, *Diary of James K. Polk*, 2:452. President Polk wrote in his diary that "Gen'l Taylor is a hard fighter, but has none other of the qualities of a great General."

49. Smith, *War with Mexico*, 1:140–41, 144–45, 161, 465n–66n; Meade, *Life and Letters of George Gordon Meade*, 1:101; Hitchcock to brother, February 10, 1846, Hitchcock Papers, Library of Congress; Hitchcock, *Fifty Years in Camp and Field*, 194, 198–99, 215.

50. Rives, *United States and Mexico, 1821–1848*, 2:147.

51. Scott, *Memoirs*, 2:382.

52. Hitchcock to brother, February 10, 1846, Hitchcock Papers.

Fortunately, Mariano Arista was Zachary Taylor's salvation. Instead of allowing the American force to advance upon the Mexican army, whereupon the battle would have evolved into a clash of infantry and cavalry in which he had the clear advantage, Arista opened fire with his artillery and immediately revealed his weakness. The Mexican guns were of light caliber; certainly, they were no match for Churchill's eighteen-pounders. Their powder was inferior, and they had only solid shot.[53] When Arista gave the order to commence firing, Taylor's men were nearly a half-mile away. Lieutenant U. S. Grant, one of many destined to play a much larger role in a later war, observed that the enemy cannonballs "would strike the ground long before they reached our line, and ricocheted through the tall grass so slowly that the men would see them and open ranks and let them pass."[54]

After the two armies drew closer, Magruder watched with pride and Taylor in amazement as the batteries of Duncan, Ringgold, and Churchill wreaked such havoc upon the Mexican infantrymen that Arista was unable to mount a coordinated offensive. Torrejón's cavalry attempted to flank the American right wing to cut off Taylor's supply train, but he was driven back by elements of the 3rd and 5th Infantries and a section of Ringgold's artillery commanded by Lieutenant Randolph Ridgley. On the left a furious artillery duel halted when a burning wad from Duncan's battery ignited dry, waist-high grass between the two armies. The resulting fire and smoke concealed the opposing forces from one another so that all firing ceased for about an hour. When the fighting resumed, Arista attacked Taylor's left wing but was driven back by Duncan's artillery and the 8th Infantry. The final, desperate Mexican thrust was against the center of the American line, where Magruder was positioned with Childs's artillery battalion, the 4th Infantry, and Churchill's eighteen-pounders. Arista's infantrymen shouted frantically as they charged, advancing to within 150 yards of the waiting Americans. In the course of the fighting Ringgold came to Churchill's aid, but he was mortally wounded by a six-pound shot, and Captain John Page of the 4th Infantry was horribly disfigured when a shot tore away his lower jaw. Magruder was also in the thick of the action. Two of the men in his company "had the bayonets of their muskets cut off by cannon balls passing just [inches] over their shoulders." Magruder also saw "a man killed on his immediate right

53. Smith, *War with Mexico*, 1:156, 461n–62n, 465n.

54. Grant, *Personal Memoirs*, 1:95; Barbour, *Journals*, 56. Barbour reported, "The enemy committed a fatal error in opening his fire upon our line at so great a distance as 700 yards."

and left,"[55] but he and his men, despite their lack of experience, "stood firm as veterans."[56] Arista's men also showed great courage under fire, but a final, devastating round of grape shot from the eighteen-pounders and a volley from Childs's men compelled them to withdraw. The time was ripe for a general attack, but darkness enveloped the battlefield, and Taylor was reluctant to leave his supply train unprotected, fearing it might fall prey to the opposing cavalry.

The first battle of the Mexican War lasted over five hours,[57] when, at dusk, Taylor stopped to collect his dead and care for his wounded. Nine Americans were killed; 44 others were wounded. But they were only a fraction of the 600 men Taylor estimated Arista to have lost in the battle.[58] Because "the chief Mexican surgeon and a number of assistants [had] made an early and rapid retreat" from the battlefield,[59] the American medics worked tirelessly through the night, caring for men irrespective of uniform. Those who escaped injury attempted to sleep amid the heartrending cries of the wounded, while General Taylor wrote his official reports and planned for the next battle.

Taylor expected the fighting to resume the following morning, but General Arista would have no part of another artillery duel against the Americans on relatively open ground. Instead, he began a predawn retreat toward Matamoros. By ten o'clock he had marched his men approximately five miles to the banks of a ravine known as the Resaca de Guerrero, through which the Rio Grande River had once flowed. Here Arista skillfully utilized the dense, rugged terrain to tactical advantage, concentrating his artillery and infantry safely behind the banks of two water-filled resacas on either side of

55. Haskin, *History of the First Regiment of Artillery*, 82.

56. Henry, *Campaign Sketches*, 92.

57. For primary accounts of the Battle of Palo Alto, see Senate Executive Doc. 388, 29th Cong., 1st sess., 2–30; House Executive Doc. 60, 30th Cong., 1st sess., 295, 1102–4; Meade, *Life and Letters of George Gordon Meade*, 1:79–80; Henry, *Campaign Sketches*, 90–95; Blackwood, *To Mexico with Scott*, 45–49; Grant, *Personal Memoirs*, 1:93–96; Haskin, *History of the First Regiment of Artillery*, 80–82; Barbour, *Journals*, 53–57; and French, *Two Wars*, 49–50.

58. Taylor to Jones, May 16, 1846, Senate Executive Doc. 388, 29th Cong., 1st sess., 2–4. Taylor wrote that the Americans ultimately lost 9 killed, 44 wounded, and 2 missing. (Major Ringgold and Captain Page were listed among the wounded but died of their injuries after Taylor submitted his report.) Arista officially reported "252 men killed, wounded and missing," but this is an obvious understatement, and in all probability Taylor's estimate of the Mexican casualties is more nearly correct than Arista's "official" count. Smith, *War with Mexico*, 1:466n; Rives, *United States and Mexico, 1821–1848*, 2:151.

59. Smith, *War with Mexico*, 1:466n.

and roughly perpendicular to the road from Palo Alto. Because the chaparral lining the road leading to the resacas seemed virtually impenetrable, Taylor could not deploy his artillery in line against Arista as he had at Palo Alto, nor would it be possible for his cavalry to flank the Mexican forces on either side. Arista calculated that Zachary Taylor would have to fight the entire battle in the open space along the road in front of the resacas. Furthermore, the Americans would have to rely principally on their infantry, and there Arista would have the advantage by virtue of his superior numbers.[60]

When General Arista vacated the field at Palo Alto, Zachary Taylor left his wagon train and Churchill's two cumbersome eighteen-pounders and began a pursuit. Most of Colonel Childs's artillery battalion was detailed to protect the wagons and supplies, but Magruder's Company B was part of the force that marched in pursuit of the Mexican army. At two o'clock in the afternoon Taylor's advance party found Arista's men entrenched and waiting at the resacas. When General Taylor arrived and surveyed the field before him, he saw to it that the battle would not unfold according to his opponent's designs. Instead of funneling his infantry down the road toward the massed Mexican artillery and infantry, where the Americans were sure to be slaughtered, Taylor brought forth Ringgold's battery, now commanded by Lieutenant Randolph Ridgely, and opened fire on the Mexican center. Then he ordered a flanking action, not with his cavalry but with his infantry. With Magruder's men temporarily held in reserve, the 3rd and 4th infantries advanced through the thorn-entangled chaparral on the right, while the 5th and 8th infantries moved through equally challenging terrain on the left.[61] Because the Mexicans could not see the advancing Americans, they could concentrate neither artillery nor infantry against them. Ridgely drew the attention of the Mexican artillery, but he was outgunned. To silence the opposing artillery, General Taylor boldly, perhaps foolishly, ordered Captain May to charge the Mexican center with his dragoons. An eyewitness reported that May was greeted with an overwhelming discharge of grape and bullets that nearly annihilated his first and second platoons, but the gallant captain was seen darting through this murderous hailstorm unhurt, and in an instant he and his men drove away or cut to pieces the enemy artillerists.[62]

---

60. Brainerd Dyer, *Zachary Taylor* (Baton Rouge: Louisiana State University Press, 1946), 175–76.

61. Taylor to Jones, May 17, 1846, Senate Executive Doc. 388, 29th Cong., 1st sess., 7.

62. Haskin, *History of the First Regiment of Artillery,* 83.

At the same time that May caused mayhem in the center of the Mexican line, the American infantrymen advanced to engage their Mexican counterparts in the chaparral, near the resacas. Dense, thorny brush rendered unit coordination impossible; thus, the battle evolved into desperate hand-to-hand combat. Reportedly, the Mexican infantrymen "fought like devils."[63] Their entire line faltered, however, shortly after General Taylor sent Magruder's company and the rest of the American reserves into the battle. On the Mexican side disorganization led to demoralization. Sensing defeat, the Mexicans broke ranks and fled toward the Rio Grande, where great numbers of them were drowned in attempting to escape.[64]

Among those who did not escape was General Rómulo de la Vega. While it is unclear who his captor was,[65] the *Fredericksburg News* reported that Magruder took charge of de la Vega and personally delivered him to General Taylor.[66] Unfortunately, Taylor's men were unable to capture General Arista, who made it safely across the Rio Grande. Arista made such a hurried escape, however, that he left behind all of his personal effects and papers, including an order from his government directing him to send Taylor to Mexico City as a prisoner.[67] Instead, Zachary Taylor was the victor in a battle that was costlier than that fought on the preceding day, with the Americans losing thirty-nine men killed and eighty-three wounded,[68] and the Mexicans losing six to seven times that number.[69] In two days Taylor had won consecu-

---

63. Blackwood, *To Mexico with Scott*, 51.

64. Haskin, *History of the First Regiment of Artillery*, 83.

65. Philip Barbour and W. S. Henry reported that Captain May captured General de la Vega. Samuel G. French, who was with General Taylor during the battle, reported that a sergeant "had captured Gen. La Vega; next an infantry officer came and reported La Vega was his prisoner; and then May returned and, riding up to Gen. Taylor drew from a scabbard a sword. He presented it to the General with these words: 'General, I have the honor to present to you the sword of Gen. La Vega. He is a prisoner.'" Justin Smith, on the other hand, gives May almost no credit for either the cavalry charge or de la Vega's capture. Smith insists that "the real captor was a bugler." While the real captor may never be known, it seems that it was the opportunistic Magruder who "delivered him to Gen. Taylor." And one can only imagine that he did it with great fanfare. Barbour, *Journals*, 58; Henry, *Campaign Sketches*, 97; French, *Two Wars*, 54; Smith, *War with Mexico*, 1:467n; and *Fredericksburg* (Va.) *News*, October 28, 1847.

66. *Fredericksburg* (Va.) *News*, October 28, 1847.

67. Otis A. Singletary, *The Mexican War* (Chicago: University of Chicago Press, 1960), 32.

68. Return of killed, wounded, and missing of the Army of Occupation at the action of "Resaca de la Palma," May 9, 1846, Senate Executive Doc. 388, 29th Cong., 1st sess., 10.

69. Rives, *United States and Mexico, 1821–1848*, 2:155. The Mexican loss was officially reported at 262 killed, 355 wounded, and 185 missing.

tive battles, one by artillery, the next by infantry. His twin victories at Palo Alto and Resaca de la Palma were the first against organized troops of a civilized nation since Andrew Jackson's defeat of the British at New Orleans on January 8, 1815,[70] and they set the tenor for things to come in the remainder of the Mexican War.

General Taylor proudly wrote Washington on May 9, 1846, that "the enemy has recrossed the river, and . . . will not again molest us on this bank."[71] He was, however, in no hurry to molest the Mexicans on the southern bank. He could have easily dispersed Arista's remaining forces, and the West Pointers within his army urged him to do so. But Taylor waited until he could transport his supplies and heavy ordnance across the river with him. By that time Arista had reorganized his army and retreated to safety. "The salvation of the Mexican army," declared one of its historians, "was owing to General Taylor not having made use of his victory."[72] Once in Matamoros he cautiously waited for additional supplies, reinforcements, and orders from Washington. In short, wrote historian Bernard de Voto, "he sat down and did nothing whatever for six weeks."[73]

On June 18, 1846, while encamped on the outskirts of Matamoros, Magruder was promoted to captain, and shortly thereafter his service under Zachary Taylor came to an end.[74] In July Company B, 1st Artillery, was temporarily dissolved in an organizational realignment. The enlisted men were transferred to other companies of the regiment, while the officers were sent back

70. For primary accounts of the Battle of Resaca de la Palma, called Resaca de Guerrero by the Mexicans, see Senate Executive Doc. 388, 29th Cong., 1st sess., 6–30; House Executive Doc. 60, 30th Cong., 1st sess., 295–96, 1104–6; Meade, *Life and Letters of George Gordon Meade,* 1:80–83; Henry, *Campaign Sketches,* 95–100; Blackwood, *To Mexico with Scott,* 49–53; Grant, *Personal Memoirs,* 1:96–99; Haskin, *History of the First Regiment of Artillery,* 82–83; Barbour, *Journals,* 57–61; and French, *Two Wars,* 51–54.

71. Taylor to Jones, May 9, 1846, House Executive Doc. 60, 30th Cong., 1st sess., 295–96.

72. Ramón Alcaraz, *The Other Side: or, Notes for the History of the War between Mexico and the United States,* trans. Albert C. Ramsey (New York: J. Wiley, 1850), 56. Taylor seldom made use of his victories. After Monterrey capitulated on September 24, 1846, he granted the Mexicans an eight-week armistice. Taylor, exclaimed President Polk, "violated his express orders" in granting the armistice; Polk termed such action "a great mistake" that would "only enable the Mexican army to reorganize and recruit so as to make another stand." Polk subsequently repudiated the armistice. Quaife, *Diary of James K. Polk,* 2:181–86; Marcy to Taylor, October 13, 1846, House Executive Doc. 60, 30th Cong., 1st sess., 355–57.

73. Bernard de Voto, *The Year of Decision: 1846* (Boston: Little, Brown, 1943), 196.

74. Cullum, *Biographical Register,* 1:367; Haskin, *History of the First Regiment of Artillery,* 83.

to the United States on recruiting assignments.[75] Magruder recruited briefly in New Orleans and New York but spent most of his time near his family in Baltimore, where he "raised a company of one hundred of our brave citizens" for service in Mexico.[76] While away from the fighting, he no doubt thought of his service under Taylor. Stifling heat, long marches, dust, and endless drilling must have crossed his mind. He must also have been dissatisfied with his temporary infantry assignment, but it would not be the last time that he would lead infantry troops into battle; hence, lessons learned at Palo Alto and Resaca de la Palma would prove valuable.

While Magruder recruited, Zachary Taylor pushed deeper into Mexico. Before 1846 came to a close, he had taken Reynosa, Camargo, Monterrey, Saltillo, and Tampico, the major cities in the states of Tamaulipas, Nuevo León, and Coahuila. But now what to do? Because of the desert and immense distance involved, it would be altogether impractical to undertake an invasion of Central Mexico from the north. Should he invade from another direction, perhaps from Vera Cruz? Or should he hold the line in northeastern Mexico, forcing the Mexicans to take the offensive? Taylor favored the latter course of action,[77] but in October President Polk decided differently.[78] The army would strike at Central Mexico via Vera Cruz, and General Winfield Scott would lead the expedition.[79]

Scott was the antithesis of Zachary Taylor. Tall in stature, possessing a commanding presence, Scott always dressed in a fine uniform and was always dignified, both in manner and speech. He received his formal education at William and Mary College and was admitted to the bar before joining the army. He became a military scholar, reading and writing extensively on war-

75. Haskin, *History of the First Regiment of Artillery,* 84–92; Cullum, *Biographical Register,* 1:367.

76. *Fredericksburg* (Va.) *News,* October 28, 1847.

77. Taylor to Marcy, October 15, 1846, House Executive Doc. 60, 30th Cong., 1st sess., 351–54.

78. Quaife, *Diary of James K. Polk,* 2:179–80, 195–200, 204–5, 221–22, 225–29, 234–35, 240–41.

79. Ibid., 241–46; Marcy to Scott, November 23, 1846, House Executive Doc. 60, 30th Cong., 1st sess., 836. The choice of Scott was not an easy one for President Polk to make. Polk had lost all confidence in Taylor's abilities, and because Scott was the ranking officer in the army, clearly he was the logical choice to lead the Vera Cruz expedition. But Scott was a Whig who had presidential ambitions. He had received sixty-two votes at the Whig National Convention in 1840, and Polk feared that success on the battlefields of Mexico might sweep him into the White House in 1848. Consequently, he seriously considered Thomas Hart Benton, William O. Butler, and Robert Patterson, but none had Scott's qualifications.

fare, and twice traveled in Europe to observe Continental armies in action. Polk complained that Scott was too scientific and visionary,[80] but there was no doubt about his effectiveness in combat. He formulated his plans carefully and executed them vigorously. Scott could manage with insufficient resources and deceive his opponent by feinting at times and striking boldly at others. "Old Fuss and Feathers," as he was affectionately called, was confident, self-reliant, and possessed of great personal courage. Perhaps equally important, he had a talent for selecting capable subordinates to assist him.[81]

Magruder was one of Scott's protégés, and the two became quite close. Years later, on the eve of the 1852 presidential election, in which Scott opposed Democrat Franklin Pierce, Magruder declared in a letter to Pierce that he was "a Whig . . . and professionally of the Scott school of military men."[82] Within four years Magruder would change his politics, but he never wavered in his respect and admiration for Winfield Scott. Scott was not perfect. He was aloof, vain, somewhat egotistical, and almost totally inept in politics, but he was also the highest-ranking and most highly regarded general officer in the United States Army.[83]

In December 1846, upon returning from recruiting duty, Magruder reached Tampico, one of the points of rendezvous for General Scott's seaborne expedition against Vera Cruz. There he briefly resumed command of the recently reconstituted Company B, but in January he was reassigned to command Company I,[84] which, together with companies B, F, and H, constituted the 1st Artillery Battalion of Major Levi Whiting.[85] Other recently arrived units included Twiggs's division of regulars and Major General Robert Patterson's volunteers. They, combined with the garrison of General James Shields, boosted the troop strength at Tampico to approximately seven thousand men.[86]

80. Quaife, *Diary of James K. Polk*, 1:401.

81. Rives, *United States and Mexico, 1821–1848,* 2:199.

82. Magruder to Pierce, August 14, 1852. Manuscript Division, Library of Congress.

83. For a more detailed study of Winfield Scott, see Charles Winslow Elliott, *Winfield Scott: The Soldier and the Man* (New York: Macmillan, 1937); Timothy D. Johnson, *Winfield Scott: The Quest for Military Glory* (Lawrence: The University Press of Kansas, 1998); and Arthur D. Howden Smith, *Old Fuss and Feathers: The Life and Exploits of Lt. General Winfield Scott* (New York: Greystone Press, 1937).

84. Official Return of the First Artillery, November 1846, January 1847, National Archives.

85. Haskin, *History of the First Regiment of Artillery,* 92.

86. Robert Anderson, *An Artillery Officer in the Mexican War, 1846–7* (New York: G. P. Putnam's Sons, 1911), 13.

When Magruder and his men were not drilling, they spent their spare time frolicking in Tampico, where an infinite variety of entertainment was available. One of four regimental bands played in the main plaza each evening, while the company of professional actors that had accompanied Twiggs and Patterson from Victoria performed their specialty at another location. There was also sightseeing, dining out at any of a number of excellent restaurants, and shopping. The variety of goods in the marketplace was as complete as in New Orleans. One could find tobacco, fruits, fish, game, vegetables, and "a poisonous description of liquor, under the denomination of brandy," which sold for a shilling per glass.[87] Because the troops had just received two months' pay, there was a good deal of money in circulation. As was the case in Corpus Christi, most of the money found its way into the hands of camp followers.[88] No doubt this was the case with Magruder's money. One of his fellow officers, William F. Barry, reported that Magruder "was distinguished for the ease with which he spent his money, and the difficulty he had in getting it." One day in June 1846, while still in Matamoros, Magruder approached the sutler and asked if he would be so kind as to cash his pay account for September. The sutler explained that he did not have the money but that he could probably raise it, as it was only three months ahead. "Oh," said Magruder casually, "it's my pay accounts for September, 1847, that I want to get cashed."[89]

On February 2 word reached Tampico that a ship carrying Colonel Lewis G. DeRussy and four companies of Louisiana volunteers had run aground approximately forty miles south of Tampico and about the same distance north of Tuxpán, which was garrisoned by a Mexican force commanded by General Martín Perfecto de Cos. Only one man had been lost in the accident, and most of the supplies and arms had been saved. But DeRussy's entire command was in danger of being captured because Cos was the first to hear of their plight. Cos immediately left Tuxpán with 980 men and two pieces of

---

87. George Ballentine, *Autobiography of an English Soldier in the United States Army, Comprising Observations and Adventures in the States and Mexico* (New York: Stringer and Townsend, 1853), 134. Ballentine wrote his autobiography from memory several years after the war. The dates that he cites are often incorrect. Nevertheless, his book is helpful on general observations, and it is important because it is the only publication by anyone closely connected to Magruder during the Mexican War. Ballentine gives an excellent description of Tampico on pp. 132–40. See also Anderson, *Artillery Officer in the Mexican War,* 13–65; and Meade, *Life and Letters of George Gordon Meade,* 1:174–86.

88. Ballentine, *Autobiography of an English Soldier,* 139.

89. *Army and Navy Journal* 17 (August 1879): 11.

artillery. Shortly thereafter, General Patterson sent Magruder and his company to DeRussy's aid. Meanwhile, Cos reached the stranded Americans first and demanded their surrender. As the message was received shortly before sunset, DeRussy replied that he would return an answer the following morning at nine. After darkness set in, however, DeRussy abandoned his encampment, leaving tents standing with candles burning in them to ensure an adequate head start. While retreating up the beach the next day, he encountered Magruder's company and determined to make a stand. He informed General Patterson of his whereabouts and intentions, but before Cos arrived, Patterson returned a messenger ordering DeRussy and Magruder to return to Tampico. The mission was Vera Cruz; any action before that was neither authorized nor deemed necessary.[90]

By the latter part of February Scott began assembling his forces near the Lobos Islands, off the Gulf Coast of Mexico, between Tampico and Vera Cruz. Magruder's men, having been drilled until "they were considered in good order for active operations," departed Tampico on February 25 aboard the barque *Caroline*.[91] When they arrived two days later they found the islands a "barren and desolate spot, on which the only signs of vegetation were a few stunted shrubs, evidently struggling hard with the difficulties of their situation for a bare subsistence."[92] Another observer speculated that the islands were "hitherto only known to pirates,"[93] and he was at least partially correct because the English had been using the location for their smuggling operations for more than a century.[94] The Lobos Islands were secluded, and they offered as good an anchorage as was available anywhere on the entire Gulf of Mexico. It was an excellent staging ground for the expedition.

While Magruder and the other company commanders practiced landings with their men in the newly designed surfboats, General Scott organized his army into three divisions. Worth commanded the first division, Twiggs the second, and the third division, consisting entirely of volunteers, was commanded by General Patterson. The 1st Artillery Regiment, including Magruder's

90. Anderson, *Artillery Officer in the Mexican War,* 26, 28, 32–34; Meade, *Life and Letters of George Gordon Meade,* 1:179–80. Meade reported the Cos expedition to consist of a thousand men, but this is probably only an estimate.

91. Haskin, *History of the First Regiment of Artillery,* 92; Ballentine, *Autobiography of an English Soldier,* 141–42. The English soldier incorrectly reported the date of departure as December 27.

92. Ballentine, *Autobiography of an English Soldier,* 142–43.

93. Blackwood, *To Mexico with Scott,* 108.

94. Jesup to Marcy, December 27, 1846, House Executive Doc. 60, 30th Cong., 1st sess., 568.

Company I, was assigned to Twiggs. Overall, Scott's army, including newly arrived reinforcements from Taylor, numbered 13,660 men.[95]

The sheer size of the force inspired confidence in the men that they would succeed at Vera Cruz against any opposition that Mexico could muster. George Ballentine, an English recruit who served in Magruder's company, exhibited an attitude of naive enthusiasm that was pervasive among Scott's men. Their only thoughts were of victory, and they seemingly had no fears. "As to the cost of life," pondered Ballentine philosophically, "that was left to the chapter of accidents; in reckoning the probable contingencies of a coming engagement, the soldier seldom includes himself in the list of the killed and wounded."[96] The Englishman indeed was destined to fight his way from Vera Cruz to Mexico City without injury. But many of his comrades, including Magruder, would not be as fortunate.

Winfield Scott's transports departed the Lobos Islands on March 2, 1847. A week later, after having effected a rendezvous with Commodore David Connor's blockading fleet, Scott positioned his army for a landing on the sandy beaches of Mocambo Bay, two and a half miles southeast of Vera Cruz, a safe distance beyond the range of the guns of the fortress San Juan de Ulúa, which protected the city. Worth's division led the surfboat invasion followed by Patterson's volunteers and then Twiggs. Magruder's company landed from the brig *Porpoise* in the third wave.[97] Everyone feared the Mexicans would give them a warm reception. And Magruder's men confessed no regret in their company's not having been selected to lead the expedition.[98] Inexplicably, Worth encountered no opposition. Patterson and Twiggs likewise came ashore unopposed, and by midnight more than ten thousand men had landed safely on Mexican soil.[99] The following day, on March 10, a triumphant and astonished Winfield Scott landed. He had expected the landing at Vera Cruz

95. Rives, *United States and Mexico, 1821–1848,* 2:378; Haskin, *History of the First Regiment of Artillery,* 92.

96. Ballentine, *Autobiography of an English Soldier,* 142.

97. Ibid., 145–46; Haskin, *History of the First Regiment of Artillery,* 92, 327; Meade, *Life and Letters of George Gordon Meade,* 1:91; Rives, *United States and Mexico, 1821–1848,* 2:382–83. The English soldier incorrectly recalled that Magruder's company landed in the second wave and that Patterson landed on the tenth with Scott.

98. Ballentine, *Autobiography of an English Soldier,* 146–48.

99. For primary accounts of the landing at Vera Cruz, see Senate Executive Doc. 1, 30th Cong., 1st sess., 216–18, 220, 222, 239–40; House Executive Doc. 1, 30th Cong., 2nd sess., 1177–79; House Executive Doc. 60, 30th Cong., 1st sess., 897, 1169; Scott, *Memoirs,* 2:413–14, 418–21; J. Jacob Oswandel, *Notes of the Mexican War* (Philadelphia: n.p., 1885), 67–70, 83; Blackwood, *To Mexico*

to be "the most formidable struggle of the war."[100] It was during the landing that the American army was most vulnerable. By not even contesting Winfield Scott's landing, Mexico lost its best chance of turning the war in its favor.

In front of Magruder and his fellow invaders was the walled city of Vera Cruz, protected by the forbidding castle of San Juan de Ulúa, located across the harbor but well within artillery range. General Juan Morales commanded forces in both the city and the fortress. According to Mexican sources, the combined troop strength was 4,390, of which approximately three-fourths were garrisoned in Vera Cruz proper.[101] The city was protected by 89 guns, generally of light caliber, while the fortress was armed with 135 pieces of heavier artillery, and both were well supplied with ammunition.[102] Many military authorities believed the fortifications to be the strongest in North America.[103]

Winfield Scott could not afford the 2,000 to 3,000 probable losses that would result from a frontal assault. Nor did he have time to reduce Vera Cruz by starvation given that early April inevitably brought wet, miserable weather and the dreaded *vómito,* or yellow fever, to the Mexican east coast. Instead, Scott formed an investment line around the city and determined upon a siege.[104] In the upcoming drama the artillery would take the honored position center stage, and Magruder would be one of the principal players. The opportunity for which he had so long waited was now before him.

Magruder's company marched with Twiggs's division to the small village of Vergara, two and a half miles up the coast from Vera Cruz. They formed the far left of the American line, with Patterson's volunteers in the center and Worth on the right at the original point of landing.[105] The American forces

with Scott, 113–14; Anderson, *Artillery Officer in the Mexican War,* 74; Grant, *Personal Memoirs,* I, 126; Ballentine, *Autobiography of an English Soldier,* 145–50; Hitchcock, *Fifty Years in Camp and Field,* 239. Accounts by naval officers include Raphael Semmes, *Service Afloat and Ashore during the Mexican War* (Cincinnati: William H. Moore, 1851), 125–28; and Philip Syng Physick Conner, *The Home Squadron under Commodore Conner in the War with Mexico* (Philadelphia: n.p., 1896), 18–20, 60–70.

100. Scott, *Memoirs,* 2:414.

101. Alcaraz, *Other Side,* 182–83.

102. Rives, *United States and Mexico, 1821–1848,* 2:385.

103. K. Jack Bauer, *The Mexican War, 1846–1848* (New York: Macmillan, 1974), 245.

104. Scott, *Memoirs,* 2:422–25.

105. Scott to Marcy, March 12, 1847, Senate Executive Doc. 1, 30th Cong., 1st sess., 216–17; Scott to Marcy, March 17, 1847, ibid., 220; Ballentine, *Autobiography of an English Soldier,* 152, 154, 157–63; Oswandel, *Notes of the Mexican War,* 74, 76–80, 84; Blackwood, *To Mexico with Scott,* 115–17; Semmes, *Service Afloat and Ashore during the Mexican War,* 129–30; Anderson, *Artillery*

had only occasional contact with the Mexicans, but on the fourteenth Company I encountered an enemy force while skirmishing in front of the brigade line. Magruder dispersed the Mexicans in short order and was subsequently commended for his actions by Twiggs.[106]

After the investment line had been completed, there began what William L. Haskin, historian of the 1st Artillery Regiment, called "the monotonous and severe labors incident to a regular siege."[107] Soldiers exchanged their weapons for shovels. Under the guidance of Scott's engineers some of them threw up breastworks and constructed gun emplacements, while others brought up the heavy artillery that Conner had landed on the beach at Mocambo Bay. Because Magruder's position on the investment line was the greatest distance from the original landing site south of Vera Cruz, he received his ordnance last. Consequently, his battery was one of the last to become fully operational. Three other batteries mounting seven ten-inch mortars were in place, however, by the afternoon of March 22. As soon as they were ready for action, Winfield Scott demanded that the town' surrender or face the consequences.[108] When General Morales defiantly refused the demand,[109] Scott opened fire. For two days the Mexicans matched the American cannonade shot for shot. Lieutenant Raphael Semmes, who would later captain the Confederate commerce raider *Alabama,* described the duel as "an awful, as well as a grand and beautiful spectacle . . . with its deafening roar of artillery, clouds of wreathing smoke, crashing of shot and shells, and flashes of lurid lightning, as the heavy pieces belched forth their destructive missiles of death."[110] The spectacular fusillade far exceeded that which Magruder had witnessed earlier at Palo Alto.

Officer in the Mexican War, 75, 78; Scott, *Memoirs,* 2:426; Hitchcock, *Fifty Years in Camp and Field,* 240; Meade, *Life and Letters of George Gordon Meade,* 1:191.

106. Twiggs to Scott, March 15, 1847, Senate Executive Doc. 1, 30th Cong., 1st sess., 246; Haskin, *History of the First Regiment of Artillery,* 93.

107. Haskin, *History of the First Regiment of Artillery,* 93.

108. Scott to Morales, March 22, 1847, Senate Executive Doc. 1, 30th Cong., 1st sess., 226–27; George C. Furber, *The Twelve Months Volunteer; or, Journal of a Private in the Tennessee Regiment of Cavalry, in the Campaign, in Mexico, 1846–1847* (Cincinnati: J. A. and U. P. James, 1849), 511.

109. Morales to Scott, March 22, 1847, Senate Executive Doc. 1, 30th Cong., 1st sess., 227; Furber, *Twelve Months Volunteer,* 517.

110. Semmes, *Service Afloat and Ashore during the Mexican War,* 131. Semmes reported that the Mexican gunners had handled their pieces skillfully throughout the battle, displaying great courage under fire. Their accuracy was also impressive, but most of their guns were too light to be effective. Ibid., 139.

The effect may have been dazzling, but the result, initially, was disappointing. The mortars wreaked havoc in the city but caused minimal damage to the fortifications. At 10:00 a.m. on March 24, however, three thirty-two-pounders and three eight-inch Paixhans borrowed from the navy began blasting massive holes in the soft coral walls of the city. The following morning Magruder's battery, consisting of three twenty-four-pounders, joined the fray and helped pound Vera Cruz into submission.[111] After Winfield Scott formally took possession of the city, on March 29, 1847,[112] Magruder granted George Ballentine leave to visit the once beautiful Mexican seaport. When the Englishman returned, he reported "a scene of desolation calculated to make the most strenuous advocates of physical force pause and reflect."[113]

The awesome power of the American artillery enabled General Scott to win an easy victory, capturing a heavily fortified city and taking some five thousand prisoners and four hundred pieces of ordnance,[114] while suffering only seventy-five casualties in the process.[115] Magruder, too, must have been proud of his service. Besides taking part in the successful skirmish on the fourteenth, he had commanded some of the larger artillery pieces that turned the tide in Scott's favor, and he had received the personal commendation of his division commander. But the time for celebrations and congratulations was over. All now worked tirelessly to sustain the invasion through its conclusion. General Worth, as temporary military governor of Vera Cruz, distributed food, cleaned up the city, and reopened the port to

111. Haskin, *History of the First Regiment of Artillery*, 93–94.

112. For primary accounts of the siege and surrender of Vera Cruz, see Senate Executive Doc. 1, 30th Cong., 1st sess., 216–55; House Executive Doc. 1, 30th Cong., 2nd sess., 1179–92; Ballentine, *Autobiography of an English Soldier*, 150–66; Oswandel, *Notes of the Mexican War*, 70–99; Semmes, *Service Afloat and Ashore during the Mexican War*, 128–47; Furber, *Twelve Months Volunteer*, 502–70; Scott, *Memoirs*, 2:421–29; Hitchcock, *Fifty Years in Camp and Field*, 240–48; Blackwood, *To Mexico with Scott*, 114–29; Anderson, *Artillery Officer in the Mexican War*, 78–101; Meade, *Life and Letters of George Gordon Meade*, 1:192–93; Grant, *Personal Memoirs*, 1:126–28.

113. Ballentine, *Autobiography of an English Soldier*, 165.

114. General Orders No. 80, March 30, 1847, Senate Executive Doc. 1, 30th Cong., 1st sess., 239.

115. No one has ever determined the exact number of American casualties suffered at Vera Cruz. Justin Smith writes that there were "about nineteen killed and sixty-three wounded." Even Scott's figures are inconsistent. Utilizing official returns of regular and volunteer units and a statement of the naval losses suffered ashore, it appears that there were sixteen killed and fifty-nine wounded, a total of seventy-five casualties. House Executive Doc. 24, 31st Cong., 1st sess., 13, 29; House Executive Doc. 1, 30th Cong., 2nd sess., 1185; Senate Executive Doc. 1, 30th Cong., 1st sess., 253–55; Smith, *War with Mexico*, 2:34.

foreign commerce.[116] Magruder drilled his men in preparation for the fighting to come, and Scott, Twiggs, and Patterson collected all available forms of transportation for the movement inland toward Mexico City by way of the National Road. They would march over virtually the same path that Hernán Cortéz had taken to conquer the Aztecs some three hundred years earlier.

Scott was woefully lacking in both animal and carriage transport. Consequently, he was forced to advance his army in piecemeal fashion, with General Twiggs leading the way on April 8, followed by Patterson.[117] Magruder and the 1st Artillery Battalion, now commanded by Colonel Thomas Childs, who had replaced Major Whiting, marched with Twiggs, who organized his division into two brigades. General Persifor F. Smith commanded the 1st Brigade, which included the 1st Artillery, and Colonel Bennett Riley commanded the 2nd.[118] By April 11 Twiggs and his men had passed through a seemingly endless expanse of sand to the village of Plan del Río, at the foot of the first range of mountains, just below the pass at Cerro Gordo. Waiting for them there was General Santa Anna. He had recovered from his devastating loss to Zachary Taylor at Buena Vista in February, recruited a new army, and had his forces well positioned for the American advance.

General Twiggs, six feet tall, powerfully built, courageous, but shy of intellect, ordered an attack on the 13th, directly into the teeth of Santa Anna's defenses.[119] On the night before the scheduled attack George Ballentine observed that "the camp wore an air of stillness unusual at other times, the men generally appearing more thoughtful, and conversing less, and in more subdued tones than usual." Magruder tried to cheer and encourage his troops but to no avail. The men had no confidence in Twiggs. They judged him "to be totally incapable of successfully directing an operation of such magnitude as the present, which any person might easily see required both military talent and skill." The enemy was strategically positioned and numerically superior, so that, according to Ballentine, "we felt that we were in danger of a defeat, or a victory purchased by a lavish and useless expenditure of life. And as we knew that General Scott with a division of the army was only two days in rear, no one could perceive the least necessity for either of these alternatives."

116. House Executive Doc. 60, 30th Cong., 1st sess., 930–34; General Orders No. 91, April 3, 1847, ibid., 914–15; General Orders No. 94, April 6, 1847, ibid., 921–22.

117. Scott to Marcy, April 11, 1847, House Executive Doc. 60, 30th Cong., 1st sess., 928–29.

118. Haskin, *History of the First Regiment of Artillery,* 94.

119. Smith, *War with Mexico,* 2:48–49.

Fortunately, General Patterson arrived and countermanded Twiggs's order to attack, instructing him to wait for Scott's arrival. "This turn of affairs gave universal satisfaction," reported Ballentine, "as General Scott deserved and possessed the confidence of both officers and men in the highest degree."[120]

The commanding general reached Plan del Río at noon on April 14 and found his opponent entrenched in a nearly impregnable position. The Mexican defensive line was approximately two miles long, stretching from the Río del Plan, on Scott's left, running roughly parallel to the highway, to the heights of Cerro Gordo and La Atalaya on the right. Santa Anna positioned thirty-five hundred of his best men and three batteries on three parallel ridges between the river and the highway and the rest of the artillery atop the two hills on the other side of the road. He held his reserves ready on the road behind the Mexican lines so that he could rush them to either side in the shortest possible time.[121]

Scott saw that it was not practical to attack the Mexican right because of the river and high, fortified ridges in that direction. He likewise recognized it would be suicidal to attempt a frontal assault along the highway. Instead, he decided to move around the Mexican left and strike at the rear of La Atalaya, with the 1st Artillery leading the way.[122] It was another splendid opportunity for Magruder.

On April 16 Worth arrived from Vera Cruz with his division, boosting Scott's troop strength to eighty-five hundred men.[123] Early the next morning Captain Robert E. Lee of the engineers led Twiggs's division around La Atalaya with the artillery companies at the head of the column.[124] The terrain was so rugged that progress was slow. Men could barely scale the deep ravines; animals could not. Ulysses Grant reported that "artillery was let down the steep slopes by hand, the men engaged attaching a strong rope to the rear axle and letting the guns down, a piece at a time, while the men at the

120. Ballentine, *Autobiography of an English Soldier*, 174–75; Scott, *Memoirs*, 2:432. Ballentine incorrectly reported that Twiggs ordered the attack on the morning of April 14.

Winfield Scott hastened his march to Plan del Rio because he too had serious doubts about Twiggs's abilities. Scott confided in a private letter that Twiggs was not qualified "to command an army—either in the presence, or in the absence of an enemy." Smith, *War with Mexico*, 2:48.

121. Alcaraz, *Other Side*, 199–202; Scott to Marcy, April 23, 1847, Senate Executive Doc. 1, 30th Cong., 1st sess., 261.

122. Scott to Marcy, April 23, 1847, Senate Executive Doc. 1, 30th Cong., 1st sess., 261.

123. Ibid., 264.

124. Ballentine, *Autobiography of an English Soldier*, 179.

ropes kept their ground on top, paying out gradually, while a few at the front directed the course of the piece. In a like manner the guns were drawn by hand up the opposite slopes."[125]

As the column neared the Mexican position, strict silence was enjoined on the men. But one of Magruder's troops stumbled over a stone and accidentally struck his musket against his canteen. The loud clattering noise enraged Magruder. He charged the terrified soldier, sword drawn, and shouted, "You infernal scoundrel, I'll run you through if you don't make less noise." In his rage, however, Magruder had made as much noise as the soldier. All "burst into a hearty and simultaneous laugh."[126] The incident eased the tension, and the advance continued.

At eleven o'clock, when it was approximately seven hundred yards from the enemy, Twiggs's vanguard was discovered. As soon as the Mexicans opened fire, General Twiggs ordered the 1st Artillery to form into a line and charge up the hill. When Magruder asked how far to carry the attack, Twiggs brusquely answered, "Charge them to hell!"[127] Colonel William S. Harney, who had temporarily taken command of the 1st Brigade during General Smith's illness, immediately led his men into action. In the course of the charge approximately sixty artillerymen led by Magruder and Lieutenant John P. Johnstone became separated from the main body and continued in pursuit of the two thousand fleeing Mexicans until they reached the base of Cerro Gordo.[128] There the Mexican artillery opened fire, stopping them. When the retreating infantrymen saw what was happening, they turned their guns on their pursuers. Suddenly Magruder, Johnstone, and their men found themselves trapped in a deadly crossfire without any support. George Ballentine reported the predicament:

> To attempt to retreat up the hill . . . would have been instant and total destruction. We were forced to remain therefore under the cover of rocks and trees, firing an occasional shot at the enemy only, who kept up an incessant, though fortunately for us a very ill-directed fire . . . At length, toward sunset, the enemy seemed preparing for a grand charge . . . we could observe their officers forming their men into the ranks, and with colours displayed, and a

125. Grant, *Personal Memoirs,* 1:132–33.

126. Ballentine, *Autobiography of an English Soldier,* 179.

127. Ibid., 180.

128. Childs to Van Dorn, April 20, 1847, Senate Executive Doc. 1, 30th Cong., 1st sess., 284–85; Haskin, *History of the First Regiment of Artillery,* 97.

band of music playing in front, they at last advanced towards our position, which at that moment seemed sufficiently perilous. We had a small [mountain] howitzer . . . prepared for their reception, being well loaded with grape, and we waited with some anxiety to see its effects. On they came till near the bottom of the ravine, and within two or three hundred yards of us, when the howitzer sent its murderous contents among them. I never saw such sudden havoc and confusion caused by a single shot.[129]

The Mexicans dashed for cover and made no further advances. When darkness finally covered the field of action, Magruder led his stranded comrades back up La Atalaya to safety.

During the night General Scott had three twenty-four-pounders brought up and positioned on the summit of La Atalaya to support the advance against Cerro Gordo the following morning. He also ordered Twiggs's 1st Brigade under Harney to lead the attack. At the same time, the 2nd Brigade was to march to the right, around and behind Cerro Gordo, seize the National Road, and block the Mexican escape route toward Jalapa. Scott ordered his left flank, under General Gideon J. Pillow, President Polk's former law partner, to engage the batteries at the eastern end of the Mexican line, drive through them, and attack the Mexican rear.[130] If successful on all three fronts and if the timing of the coordinated movements unfolded flawlessly, Winfield Scott would be able to destroy or capture Santa Anna's entire army.

On the morning of April 18, at seven o'clock, after the three twenty-four-pounders began their barrage against the Mexican artillery opposite them, Magruder led his company, in concert with the other elements of Colonel Harney's brigade, down La Atalaya and up Cerro Gordo. The men, observed Harney, "advanced intrepidly and as steadily as on a parade day" despite a heavy fusillade of grape, canister, and musketry from the Mexican defenders. In his official report the colonel wrote, "I cannot speak too ardently of their animation, zeal and courage under such trying circumstances, and without which they never could have surmounted the natural and artificial obstacles which opposed their progress."[131] Near the summit of Cerro Gordo, Magruder captured a light field battery and quickly turned its guns

129. Ballentine, *Autobiography of an English Soldier,* 181–82.
130. General Orders No. 111, April 17, 1847, Senate Executive Doc. 1, 30th Cong., 1st sess., 258–59; also in Scott, *Memoirs,* 2:433–36.
131. Harney to Brooks, April 21, 1847, Senate Executive Doc. 1, 30th Cong., 1st sess., 281.

against the enemy,[132] sending them into a panic-stricken flight along the National Road toward Jalapa. Regrettably, Twiggs's 2nd Brigade did not reach the highway to cut off the escape until the flight was well under way. Had Twiggs been able to cut the escape route, the Mexican army would have been completely destroyed. Instead, Santa Anna and 6,000 to 8,000 men escaped to fight again. Still, Scott won the contest at Cerro Gordo,[133] proving himself a brilliant strategist in the process. In his official report to Secretary of War Marcy, General Scott reported losing 63 killed and 368 wounded. He also estimated that his opponents had suffered between 1,000 and 1,200 casualties.[134] There was no official count of Mexicans killed, wounded, and missing because none of Santa Anna's officers stayed behind to make such a tabulation. Hitchcock, however, reported that 5 generals, 199 officers of other rank, and 2,837 rank-and-file soldiers had been captured.[135] Scott also captured forty-three Mexican guns, but having no means to transport them, he ordered all but a single field battery destroyed.[136] Of no military importance, yet offering tremendous personal satisfaction, was the capture of all of Santa Anna's personal effects, including a wooden leg, reportedly his.[137]

132. G. F. R. Henderson, *Stonewall Jackson and the American Civil War* (New York: David Mc-Kay, 1961), 23–24; Thomas Jackson Arnold, *Early Life and Letters of General Thomas J. Jackson* (New York: Fleming H. Revell Co., 1916), 93.

133. For primary accounts of the Battle of Cerro Gordo, see Senate Executive Doc. 1, 30th Cong., 1st sess., 255–99; Scott, *Memoirs*, 2:436–51; Hitchcock, *Fifty Years in Camp and Field*, 249–53; Ballentine, *Autobiography of an English Soldier*, 178–89; Semmes, *Service Afloat and Ashore during the Mexican War*, 175–84; Oswandel, *Notes of the Mexican War*, 116–36; Grant, *Personal Memoirs*, 1:130–33; Anderson, *Artillery Officer in the Mexican War*, 136–40.

134. Scott to Marcy, April 23, 1847, Senate Executive Doc. 1, 30th Cong., 1st sess., 264.

135. Hitchcock to Scott, April 24, 1847, House Executive Doc. 60, 30th Cong., 1st sess., 1089.

136. Scott to Marcy, April 23, 1847, Senate Executive Doc. 1, 30th Cong., 1st sess., 264; Scott to Marcy, April 19, 1847, ibid., 257–58.

137. Singletary, *Mexican War*, 81; Ballentine, *Autobiography of an English Soldier*, 197. The immense satisfaction of victory was immediately offset by the gruesome reality of its cost in humanity. Many of those who witnessed the battle's aftermath were deeply affected, including the Englishman Ballentine. Upon surveying the carnage at Cerro Gordo, he wrote: "I passed the dead bodies of a great many who had been killed the day before, both Americans and Mexicans, though principally the latter. They presented a shocking spectacle; these ghastly corpses but yesterday were as full of life and animation as I was at that moment, and now there they lay with their features distorted and blackening in the sun. I felt a sickening loathing at the idea of these human sacrifices, these offerings to Mars, which the poet and the historian dignify with the titles of glorious victories, and I cursed in my heart the infatuation which had linked me to the inhuman profession of a soldier." Ballentine, *Autobiography of an English Soldier*, 194–95.

At Cerro Gordo the 1st Artillery led the attack on both days of fighting. The men shared in the glory of battle, but they also felt its fury, losing nearly one-third of the battalion in the assault of La Atalya alone.[138] In his *Memoirs* Winfield Scott wrote that he had personally witnessed Childs's troops in action. According to Scott, the artillerymen "ascended the long and difficult slope of Cerro Gordo, without shelter, and under the tremendous fire of artillery and musketry, with the utmost steadiness, reached the breastworks . . . and after some minutes of sharp firing, finished the conquest with the bayonet." The action was, according to Scott, "most brilliant and decisive."[139] Immediately after the battle, General Scott sought out those who had led the way in the 1st Artillery companies and told them, "You have a claim on my gratitude for your conduct this day, which I will never forget."[140]

Magruder in particular was singled out in the official battle reports submitted by his superiors. Childs wrote how Magruder, in attempting to reach him, had "passed gallantly through a shower of bullets from the enemy's musketry."[141] Colonel Harney reported that he had performed his duty with "zeal and ability" and that his "gallantry was conspicuously displayed on several occasions."[142] Twiggs likewise stated that Magruder had shown "wary and good management in the face of the enemy."[143] Both Twiggs and Scott acknowledged that Magruder merited special praise,[144] and for his services at Cerro Gordo, John Magruder was breveted major.[145] Additionally, General Scott ordered Company I supplied with light artillery and horses as authorized by an Act of Congress on March 3, 1847.[146] The guns given Magruder,

138. Childs to Van Dorn, April 20, 1847, Senate Executive Doc. 1, 30th Cong., 1st sess., 284–85.

139. Scott to Marcy, April 19, 1847, ibid., 257. The same observations can be found in Scott, *Memoirs*, 2:439–40.

140. Ballentine, *Autobiography of an English Soldier*, 191.

141. Childs to Van Dorn, April 20, 1847, Senate Executive Doc. 1, 30th Cong., 1st sess., 284.

142. Harney to Brooks, April 21, 1847, ibid., 281–82.

143. Twiggs to Scott, April 19, 1847, ibid., 276.

144. Ibid.; Scott to Marcy, April 23, 1847, ibid., 263; Scott, *Memoirs*, 2:448.

145. Cullum, *Biographical Register*, 1:367.

146. *Statutes at Large and Treaties of the United States of America from December 1, 1845, to March 3, 1851* (Boston: Little, Brown, 1851), 186. Although Magruder had been given the light artillery pieces shortly after Cerro Gordo, his company was not officially mounted until it reached Puebla. See General Orders No. 218 of July 16, 1847. Smith, *War with Mexico*, 2:365n–66n; Haskin, *History of the First Regiment of Artillery*, 99; Ballentine, *Autobiography of an English Soldier*, 215–30.

two twelve-pounders and a mountain howitzer, were those he had captured in storming Cerro Gordo,[147] and the horses that would draw them were "forty of the quartermaster's best."[148]

The Mexican army was not able to mount a serious challenge to Scott for four months after its defeat at Cerro Gordo. Consequently, the Americans moved practically unopposed toward the Mexican capital. When they reached Jalapa, thirty miles from Cerro Gordo, Scott left Colonel Childs as military governor of the city, with Magruder and his men as part of its garrison. The rest of the army continued inland. On May 15, 1847, Worth ceremoniously took possession of Puebla, a town of eighty thousand inhabitants only seventy-five miles from Mexico City. Scott joined Worth in Puebla thirteen days later, but there the advance stalled and morale declined. The men were "living precariously in the midst of a hostile populace, riddled with dysentery, fatigued by too many hours on the drill field, and annoyed by too few visits from the paymaster."[149] Furthermore, the enlistments for the twelve-month volunteers had expired. Because they could not be persuaded to stay, Scott released them, leaving himself dangerously deficient in troop strength. He was forced to give up attempting to protect his entire line of supply, and on June 3 he ordered Magruder's newly mounted battery and the other units left behind in garrison to join his depleted ranks at Puebla.[150]

Magruder left Jalapa on June 18, escorting a valuable supply train that had come from Vera Cruz. The Mexicans had made several attempts to seize the train before it reached Jalapa and tried again at the mountain pass of La Hoya on June 20. They could not, however, contest Magruder's artillery. After losing four killed and six captured, they retired and did not attack again. On the following day the wagon train and its defenders reached Perote, where they rested for a week. On the twenty-eighth they began the last leg of their journey, reaching Puebla ten days later.[151]

147. Henderson, *Stonewall Jackson and the American Civil War*, 23–24; Arnold, *Early Life and Letters of General Thomas J. Jackson*, 93; Haskin, *History of the First Regiment of Artillery*, 99.

148. Ballentine, *Autobiography of an English Soldier*, 215.

149. Singletary, *Mexican War*, 82; Ballentine, *Autobiography of an English Soldier*, 213–14.

150. Scott to Childs, June 3, 1847, House Executive Doc. 60, 30th Cong., 1st sess., 997–98.

151. Haskin, *History of the First Regiment of Artillery*, 99–100; Cullum, *Biographical Register*, 1:367; Ballentine, *Autobiography of an English Soldier*, 215–30. George Ballentine incorrectly stated that Childs's battalion departed Jalapa on June 25 and reached Puebla on July 9. Official reports indicate, however, that the battalion began its march on June 18 and reached Scott's encamped army on July 8.

The arrival of the wagons, which contained specie for pay, raised the morale of the men, and the subsequent arrival of additional regular and volunteer units bolstered the strength of the army. When, in early August, Scott had nearly fourteen thousand men at his disposal, he reorganized his forces for their final push into Mexico City. Harney was placed in command of a cavalry brigade, while generals Worth, Twiggs, Pillow, and John A. Quitman each headed a division of infantry and artillery. Quitman's division was composed of volunteer troops, the other three of regulars. The 1st Artillery was still attached to the 1st Brigade of Twiggs's division, but it no longer included Magruder's company. Battery I was attached to Pillow's division,[152] yet it was a semi-independent company; hence, "the officers thereof would receive personal credit for whatever the company accomplished, as distinguished from a regiment of regulars, where what reputation was gained would be bestowed in the usual manner upon the commanding officer."[153]

Despite being in such an enviable position, Magruder found it difficult to locate capable, young lieutenants to serve under him. All shied away from the restless, hot-tempered Virginian except for a young West Point graduate named Thomas Jonathan Jackson, who observed that "if any fighting was to be done, Magruder would be on hand."[154] Indeed, the two would share many battlefield experiences in Mexico and later during the Civil War. They had little in common personally, but Magruder readily took the talented Jackson under his wing as his protégé, and they became close friends. Jackson even served as Magruder's second when Magruder reportedly challenged General Franklin Pierce, the future president, to a duel.[155] It is ironic that the usually reliable Jackson, in a rare lapse of tardiness, would contribute to the near destruction of Magruder's reputation years later during an imperfectly managed campaign on the Virginia Peninsula.

On the morning of August 7 Twiggs's division, preceded by Harney's brigade of cavalry, departed Puebla for the valley of Mexico with the divisions of Quitman, Worth, and Pillow following at day intervals.[156] The American troops, minus the sick and the garrison left at Puebla under the command of Colonel Childs, numbered 10,738 rank and file.[157] Scott was forced to leave

152. Scott, *Memoirs*, 2:460–65; Haskin, *History of the First Regiment of Artillery*, 100.

153. Arnold, *Early Life and Letters of General Thomas J. Jackson*, 95–96.

154. Ibid., 93.

155. Hill, "Real Stonewall Jackson," 624.

156. Scott to Marcy, August 19, 1847, Senate Executive Doc. 1, 30th Cong., 1st sess., 303.

157. Scott to Marcy, September 18, 1847, ibid., 384.

his base of supply behind, while ahead waited Santa Anna's reinforced army, estimated at "some thirty odd thousand, including good, bad and indifferent."[158] "A single defeat," declared a Mexican writer, "would be sufficient for the destruction of the American troops [while the defenders] might suffer several without deciding the fate of the contest."[159] Even the duke of Wellington, who observed the war from afar, stated: "Scott is lost . . . He can't take the city, and he can't fall back upon his base."[160] Nevertheless, Winfield Scott moved on toward his enemy's capital.

Mexico City was admirably suited for defense. Surrounded by vast lakes and marshlands, it could only be approached by way of a limited number of causeways, each of which was protected by heavily fortified interior and exterior lines of defense. Scott's engineers reported three entrances to the city ahead of them, but none were promising. The road on which they had traveled from Puebla was bordered by lakes Texcoco to the north and Chalco and Xochimilco to the south and was guarded by artillery strategically positioned atop El Peñón, a small hill rising about three hundred feet out of the waters of the southern edge of Lake Texcoco; a northern route would require a forty-mile march around Texcoco with no promise of an easier approach once on the other side; and the southerly route would expose Scott's flank and rear to attack from the direction of El Peñón while he attempted to take Mexicaltzingo. General Scott had decided to try the latter route when Colonel James Duncan of Worth's division reported finding a more southerly route around Lakes Chalco and Xochimilco that led to San Agustín, a lightly defended village just south of Mexicaltzingo. Scott had Twiggs demonstrate in front of El Peñón and on August 17 led the rest of his forces around the twin lakes and occupied San Agustín practically without opposition.[161] In this manner he outflanked the strongest points in the Mexican exterior line of defense and placed his army in position to strike Mexico City from the south or southwest, where the interior defensive line was weakest.

158. Scott to Marcy, July 25, 1847, House Executive Doc. 60, 30th Cong., 1st sess., 1013.

159. Alcaraz, *Other Side*, 241.

160. Scott, *Memoirs*, 2:466n.

161. Scott to Marcy, August 19, 1847, Senate Executive Doc. 1, 30th Cong., 1st sess., 303–4; letter of Captain R. E. Lee, August 22, 1847, Senate Executive Doc. 65, 30th Cong., 1st sess., 461–62; Hitchcock to *New York Sun*, October 26, 1847, ibid., 521–22; Hitchcock, *Fifty Years in Camp and Field*, 272–74; Anderson, *Artillery Officer in the Mexican War*, 289; Ballentine, *Autobiography of an English Soldier*, 238.

Scott ordered Worth north from his position at San Agustín to distract Santa Anna, who had hastily thrown together a new defensive line near San Antonio, less than two miles away. While these two forces glared menacingly at each other, Scott's engineers, led by Robert E. Lee, scouted the rugged territory to the west in the direction of Contreras. When Lee reported it possible to cut a road toward Contreras through the lava field known as the Pedregal, Scott immediately decided upon another flanking movement, hoping to seize the San Angel Road to Mexico City, thereby again bypassing the Mexican defensive strength.[162] This time, however, Santa Anna anticipated the American strategy. When the divisions of Pillow and Twiggs started across the Pedregal, they found General Gabriel Valencia waiting for them on the other side, near Padierna Ranch. At approximately 1:00 p.m., when the advancing Americans were in range and without cover, Valencia began his cannonade.[163]

General Pillow immediately ordered Magruder and Lieutenant Franklin D. Callender forward with their batteries to provide a covering fire for his exposed infantrymen.[164] Within an hour Magruder was able to advance his guns nearly a mile over almost impassible ground, to a transverse ledge that engineers Robert E. Lee and George B. McClellan selected,[165] barely nine hundred yards from the enemy. At 2:00 p.m. Magruder opened fire with his two six-pound field guns and two twelve-pound howitzers.[166] He had no cover and was far outgunned by Valencia's twenty-two pieces, most of which were eighteen-pounders. At each discharge of the Mexican guns, Magruder's men tried to protect themselves by falling flat against the lip of their protective ledge.[167] The ledge, however, provided minimal protection, and in Winfield Scott's words, Magruder "suffered much in the course of the afternoon from the enemy's superior metal."[168] Approximately an hour after the fighting commenced, Magruder's second-in-command, Lieutenant

---

162. Scott to Marcy, August 19, 1847, Senate Executive Doc. 1, 30th Cong., 1st sess., 304–05.

163. Smith, *War with Mexico,* 2:104.

164. Magruder to Hooker, August 23, 1847, Senate Executive Doc. 1, 30th Cong., 1st sess., 101, appendix.

165. Smith, *War with Mexico,* 2:104, 378n; Twiggs to Scott, August 23, 1847, Senate Executive Doc. 1, 30th Cong., 1st sess., 322.

166. Ballentine, *Autobiography of an English Soldier,* 234.

167. Smith, *War with Mexico,* 2:378n.

168. Scott to Marcy, August 19, 1847, Senate Executive Doc. 1, 30th Cong., 1st sess., 305.

John P. Johnstone, was mortally wounded, his leg having been crushed by an eighteen-pounder cannonball.[169] On Magruder's order Thomas Jackson "advanced in handsome style," took Johnstone's place, and in his commander's words, "kept up the fire with great briskness and effect."[170] However, holding Valencia's attention, while Persifor F. Smith, Bennett Riley, and George Cadwalader led their brigades in a flanking movement around the Mexican left, was costly. In addition to losing Johnstone, Magruder reported that by battle's end a sergeant and three privates of Company I had been wounded, another private was missing, ten horses were killed or wounded, one gun was dismounted by an eighteen-pounder ball that tore away the axletree, another gun was disabled, and one of the mountain howitzers was "rendered unfit for immediate use." After darkness and a heavy downpour brought a merciful end to the uneven artillery duel at Padierna Ranch, Magruder modestly reported that his battery was withdrawn "in a somewhat crippled state."[171] At the same time, George Ballentine more tersely declared that nothing but the "excessively bad firing [of the enemy artillery] had saved our battery from being totally annihilated."[172]

Valencia bedded down confident in the belief that the next day he would "destroy the miserable remains of the Anglo-Americans."[173] During the night, however, American forces seized the advantage by quietly encircling Valencia's camp. At daybreak on the August 20 Colonel Trueman B. Ransom, temporarily in command of Franklin Pierce's 9th Volunteer Infantry Regiment, opened the attack against the Mexican front. So occupied were Valencia's men that Smith, Riley, and Cadwalader were able to advance undetected from the rear until they were at their opponent's back. After their charge, the fighting lasted but seventeen minutes. Valencia's demoralized forces then broke ranks and fled via the San Angel Road toward Churubusco, leaving behind seven hundred men dead and eight hundred others captured, along

169. Magruder to Hooker, August 23, 1847, ibid., 101, appendix; Haskin, *History of the First Regiment of Artillery,* 330; Ballentine, *Autobiography of an English Soldier,* 252. John Preston Johnstone, an 1843 graduate of the U.S. Military Academy and the nephew of Joseph E. Johnston, was the first officer of the 1st Artillery Regiment to lose his life in Mexico.

170. Magruder to Hooker, August 23, 1847, Senate Executive Doc. 1, 30th Cong., 1st sess., 101, appendix.

171. Ibid., 102–3.

172. Ballentine, *Autobiography of an English Soldier,* 252.

173. Valencia to minister of war, August 19, 1847, quoted in Rives, *United States and Mexico, 1821–1848,* 2:473.

with seven hundred pack mules, a large cache of small arms and ammunition, and all twenty-two pieces of artillery. The American loss at Padierna Ranch totaled sixty killed and wounded.[174]

Santa Anna reined in Valencia's fleeing forces from Padierna Ranch and others that Worth had driven from San Antonio, at Churubusco. There, protected by stout defensive fortifications, Santa Anna stubbornly resisted repeated headlong assaults until late in the afternoon, when, low on supplies, he was forced to evacuate the town, giving Winfield Scott his second victory of the day. Scott reported taking about 3,000 prisoners, including 8 generals, two of whom were former presidents. There were also approximately 4,000 Mexicans killed and wounded, and thirty-seven pieces of artillery were captured, along with quantities of small arms, munitions, and various other military supplies. Santa Anna, however, could afford losses much more easily than Scott, who lost 139 killed, 876 wounded, and 38 missing.[175] Of those losses over 90 percent had been sustained in the assault at Churubusco.[176]

The 1st Artillery was particularly hard hit, losing captains Erastus A. Capron, Martin J. Burke, and Lieutenant Saterlee Hoffman killed and Lieutenant Joseph S. Irons mortally wounded. The loss, in proportion to its numbers, was greater than that of any other regiment of Scott's army. On the day following the battle Capron, Burke, and Hoffman were buried together with Lieutenant Johnstone in one grave; Lieutenant Irons was buried in a separate ceremony after he died on August 26.[177] These burials served as grim reminders to George Ballentine, who had once spoken so cavalierly about the list of killed and wounded, that life was fleeting. Never in his worst nightmares could he have imagined that the officer who recruited him (Burke), the com-

---

174. Scott to Marcy, August 28, 1847, Senate Executive Doc. 1, 30th Cong., 1st sess., 308.

175. Ibid., 313–14.

176. Robert Selph Henry, *The Story of the Mexican War* (Indianapolis: Bobbs-Merrill, 1950), 342. For primary accounts of the battles of Contreras (more correctly termed the Battle of Padierna Ranch by the Mexicans) and Churubusco, see Senate Executive Doc. 1, 30th Cong., 1st sess., 303–54, 35–134, appendix; Hitchcock, *Fifty Years in Camp and Field*, 276–83; Semmes, *Service Afloat and Ashore during the Mexican War*, 380–403; Ballentine, *Autobiography of an English Soldier*, 249–55; Blackwood, *To Mexico with Scott*, 197–204; Grant, *Personal Memoirs*, 1:143–45; Anderson, *Artillery Officer in the Mexican War*, 294–95. A wealth of additional information can be found in the testimony given before the court of inquiry in the case of General Pillow, whom Scott charged with writing untruthful accounts of the fighting in which he minimized Scott's role. See Senate Executive Doc. 65, 30th Cong., 1st sess.

177. Haskin, *History of the First Regiment of Artillery*, 119, 331.

mander of his company at the time that he joined the army (Capron), and his company's second-in-command (Johnstone) were destined to die within hours of one another and would be buried in the same grave.[178]

Magruder's battery did not participate in the fighting at Churubusco because several of its guns had been disabled in the action at Padierna Ranch the day before.[179] Nevertheless, Magruder and Jackson witnessed the carnage as interested spectators. They learned the value of using deception as opposed to making a frontal attack against fortified positions.[180] Magruder later proved to be a master of the former tactic, and only once did he resort to the latter. He did so against his better judgment, yet under orders, and it cost him dearly.

Winfield Scott granted Santa Anna a truce after the bloody fighting at Churubusco on August 20.[181] The Mexican army appeared demoralized and generally disorganized. Consequently, Scott believed that if they were spared the carnage and humiliation of a final, massive assault that they would be more apt to accede to his demands. While negotiations were under way, Magruder's company encamped in the small village of Mixcoac,[182] two miles west of Churubusco. Other American units were situated in various locations along the entire southwestern periphery of the city. The cease-fire at least gave Scott time to rest his weary men. Unfortunately, the lull also gave Santa Anna an opportunity to reorganize his army. When it became obvious that the Mexicans were merely stalling to strengthen their forces, an angry Winfield Scott brought the truce to an abrupt end on September 7.[183]

During the cease-fire General Scott had received reports that the Mexicans were casting church bells into cannon at Molino del Rey, near Chapultepec, on the western edge of the city. The Mexican position, consisting of several massive stone buildings, was strongly fortified and protected by in-

---

178. Ballentine, *Autobiography of an English Soldier,* 14, 33–34, 252, 255.

179. Haskin, *History of the First Regiment of Artillery,* 111. Haskin reported that Magruder rejoined Pillow's division on the night of the twentieth after replacing the broken six-pounder carriage with another that had been captured at Contreras.

180. James I. Robertson Jr., *Stonewall Jackson: The Man, the Soldier, the Legend* (New York: Macmillan, 1997), 64–65; Vandiver, *Mighty Stonewall,* 36.

181. Scott to Marcy (with enclosures), September 11, 1847, Senate Executive Doc. 1, 30th Cong., 1st sess., 354–61.

182. Ballentine, *Autobiography of an English Soldier,* 256; Haskin, *History of the First Regiment of Artillery,* 111.

183. Scott to Santa Anna, September 6, 1847, Senate Executive Doc. 1, 30th Cong., 1st sess., 359; Haskin, *History of the First Regiment of Artillery,* 111.

terlocking fields of fire. When Scott ordered Worth to take the *molino* (mill), one of the latter's officers grimly predicted that "tomorrow will be a day of slaughter."[184] When the Battle of Molino del Rey commenced early on the morning of September 8, Magruder and his men were initially held in reserve. At about the mid-point of the two-hour battle, however, they were ordered into action. Magruder attacked the enemy with such speed and abandon that one of his own men was nearly killed when he was thrown from the caisson on which he was riding. Magruder left the seriously injured soldier for dead,[185] sped to the battlefield, and joined the action just in time to drive off a large body of cavalry attempting to flank the American left.[186] When the fighting ended, Worth reported his losses as 116 killed, 653 wounded, and 18 missing—nearly a fourth of those engaged.[187] Regrettably, when his men took the *molino,* they discovered the intelligence regarding the cannon foundry to be false. "We were like Pyrrhus after the fight with Fabricius," wrote Hitchcock after the battle, "a few more such victories and this army would be destroyed."[188]

Following the fighting at Molino de Rey, Magruder was ordered to return to Pillow's division at La Piedad to occupy the road leading north into Mexico City.[189] The enemy was massed less than a mile away and occasionally fired artillery rounds toward the Americans to hold them at bay. Neither side advanced in earnest, yet each posed a serious threat to the other. During the night of September 10 Magruder built a crude road toward the Mexican position parallel to and only ten yards' distance from the La Piedad Road. He connected the two with a bridge across a wide ditch and then relocated his artillery pieces on the new road, camouflaged by rows of maguey. On

184. Blackwood, *To Mexico with Scott,* 216.

185. Ballentine, *Autobiography of an English Soldier,* 258. Ballentine wrote that the injured soldier "was left by the roadside in a seemingly dying state." He subsequently recovered, however, but was later discharged as a result of the internal injuries he had received.

186. Magruder to Hooker, September 18, 1847, Senate Executive Doc. 1, 30th Cong., 1st sess., 192, appendix.

187. Tabular statement of casualties in the command of Major General Worth, in the action of Molino del Rey, September 8, 1847, ibid., 370. For primary accounts of the Battle of Molino del Rey, see Senate Executive Doc. 1, 30th Cong., 1st sess., 354–56, 361–75, 134–66, appendix; Hitchcock, *Fifty Years of Camp and Field,* 296–99; Grant, *Personal Memoirs,* 1:152–53; Semmes, *Service Afloat and Ashore during the Mexican War,* 436–49; Ballentine, *Autobiography of an English Soldier,* 257–59; Anderson, *Artillery Officer in the Mexican War,* 311–14.

188. Hitchcock, *Fifty Years of Camp and Field,* 298.

189. Haskin, *History of the First Regiment of Artillery,* 111–12.

the following afternoon at 4:00 p.m. approximately five hundred Mexican cavalrymen advanced to investigate Magruder's disappearance. When they came within range, Battery I opened fire, causing great confusion among them. Several of the enemy cavalrymen were killed, and though most were able to retreat unharmed to the safety of their original position, Magruder termed the action "most satisfactory."[190]

The firing had hardly ceased, however, when a Mexican soldier was observed running toward the American position, shouting and waving his arms. Most of the men gathered together to receive him, when suddenly one of Magruder's officers, who had witnessed the same tactic earlier at Monterrey, warned his companions to take cover. Magruder's position happened to be at a range that the Mexican artillerists had previously measured and set their trajectory for. When the curious Americans gathered together to discuss the approaching soldier, several Mexican gunners opened fire simultaneously. The warning had been given just in time. Three or four shells burst on the location where they had been standing seconds before. Although no one was injured, Magruder indignantly termed the action "one of those miserable tricks, common only among uneducated, cruel, and cowardly nations."[191]

Winfield Scott, meanwhile, decided to attack Mexico City from the west and southwest rather than from the south. He ordered Twiggs to threaten the southern approach to the city from La Piedad, while the rest of his army moved quickly under cover of darkness on the night of September 11–12 to the west toward Chapultepec palace for a final massive strike.[192] In earlier times Chapultepec had served as a summer retreat for Spanish viceroys. More recently, since 1833, it had been the home of the Military Academy of Mexico. The palace building was situated in the eastern end of a walled, rectangular park, opposite Molino del Rey, which was approximately three-fourths of a mile away at the park's western end. Strategically, Chapultepec commanded the entrances to the Verónica and Belén causeways to the *garitas* (gates) at San Cosmé and Belén, respectively, the last defensible points before entering the Mexican capital.[193] Gaining access to the causeways was crucial for the American attackers. However, Ulysses Grant would later write in his *Personal Memoirs* that first taking Molino del Rey and Chapultepec

---

190. Magruder to Hooker, September 18, 1847, Senate Executive Doc. 1, 30th Cong., 1st sess., 192–93, appendix.

191. Ibid., 193.

192. Scott to Marcy, ibid., 376.

193. Smith, *War with Mexico*, 2:147–52.

was "wholly unnecessary," suggesting that the two positions could have been easily bypassed. "If this course had been pursued," Grant believed, "Molino del Rey and Chapultepec would both have been necessarily evacuated."[194]

Scott believed otherwise. He therefore ordered an artillery bombardment of Chapultepec palace on the twelfth. Then, early on the September 13 Quitman was to attack the palace from the south via the Tacubaya Road, while Pillow simultaneously attacked from the west from Molino de Rey. Magruder and Jackson were to support Pillow's advance with their artillery, and Worth was to follow with his infantrymen.[195]

Because Winfield Scott had so surreptitiously moved the bulk of his army from the southern approach to Mexico City to the west, Santa Anna was completely deceived about his opponent's whereabouts. He therefore cautiously held most of his force back, near the *garitas,* until he could be sure of Scott's intentions. General Nicolás Bravo, commanding the palace, called for reinforcements immediately after the American artillery bombardment commenced on the morning of the twelfth. Yet because Bravo reported no enemy infantry activity, Santa Anna still doubted that Chapultepec was going to be assaulted. Fearing that Scott was only feinting for Twiggs, he ignored Bravo's plea and remained stationary so that he could send his troops directly to the point of attack as soon as its location was certain.[196]

The American target, much to Santa Anna's chagrin, was indeed Chapultepec. And it was Magruder who fired the first shots against the palace early on the thirteenth to signal the beginning of the attack. His primary responsibility, however, was to provide a covering fire for Pillow's advancing infantrymen from a carefully chosen position among the stone buildings at Molino del Rey. In Magruder's words, "This was done at the time and in the manner prescribed, and, I believe, with full effect."[197] As soon as Pillow's troops safety reached the palace grounds, Magruder ceased firing and rejoined Jackson, who was leading the advance on the Anzures Causeway, along the northern edge of Chapultepec Park, with two regiments of infantrymen commanded by Colonel William Trousdale. Jackson and Trousdale had been assigned to seize the important three-way intersection of the Anzures, Verónica, and

194. Grant, *Personal Memoirs,* 1:154–55.

195. Scott to Marcy, September 18, 1847, Senate Executive Doc. 1, 30th Cong., 1st sess., 376–77; Magruder to Hooker, ibid., 194, appendix; Worth to Scott, September 16, 1847, ibid., 391.

196. Alcaraz, *Other Side,* 353–60.

197. Magruder to Hooker, September 18, 1847, Senate Executive Doc. 1, 30th Cong., 1st sess., 194, appendix.

Belén causeways, just to the east of Chapultepec. Possession of the cross-roads would simultaneously block the arrival of Santa Anna's reinforcements from the city and prevent the escape of Bravo's troops from the palace. Before reaching the intersection, however, Jackson and Trousdale ran into murderous fire from a Mexican gun emplacement and its supporting infantry contingent in front as well as deadly crossfire from Mexican infantrymen located on the side of the palace hill. Trousdale was severely wounded, and several of the battery horses were killed, but Jackson stood boldly by his guns.[198]

During the heat of the battle, when enemy bullets were "pouring down like hail,"[199] Magruder rode up, only to be dismounted by a blast of grapeshot. His horse was killed and he was slightly wounded. Nevertheless, he and Jackson maintained a steady fire until the Mexican force before them retreated. When the enemy began falling back, Magruder quickly retrieved his two guns, added them to the lone undamaged six-pounder from Jackson's section, and offered chase up the Verónica Causeway. The pursuit was so vigorous, however, that Magruder, Jackson, and approximately sixty men led by lieutenants D. H. Hill and Barnard E. Bee, suddenly found themselves well in advance of their fellow attackers.[200] Mexican lancers, realizing that the small American force was unsupported, turned and charged. They far outnumbered Magruder and his comrades, but as the cavalrymen had to attack in line because of the width constraints of the causeway, the advantage shifted to the Americans. Three times the Mexicans attacked. Three times Magruder drove them away. Finally, Worth's troops, commanded by Colonel John Garland arrived, streamed past Magruder's somewhat disabled guns and charged up the Verónica Causeway then to the right toward the Garita de San Cosmé.[201] Farther south, Quitman surged into the Mexican capital by way of the more direct Belén Causeway. Both roads were crowded with

198. Pillow to Scott, ibid., 401–3; Magruder to Hooker, ibid., 194, appendix; Cadwalader to Hooker, ibid., 203, appendix; Trousdale to Hooker, September 23, 1847, ibid., 219–20, appendix; Hebert to Cadwalader, September 17, 1847, ibid., 221, appendix.

199. Thomas J. Jackson to his sister, October 16, 1847, in Arnold, *Early Life and Letters of Thomas J. Jackson,* 130.

200. Robertson, *Stonewall Jackson,* 67–68. Robertson incorrectly stated that lieutenants Hill and Bee were chasing the Mexicans "down the Tacubaya causeway" (68), when, in fact, the pursuit was up the Verónica Causeway.

201. Magruder to Hooker, September 18, 1847, Senate Executive Doc. 1, 30th Cong., 1st sess., 194–95, appendix; Worth to Scott, September 16, 1847, ibid., 391; Garland to Mackall, ibid., 170, appendix.

Mexican troops and blocked by occasional barricades. The troops, however, were demoralized and without leadership. They retreated almost as fast as the Americans pursued, offering only token resistance. Even Santa Anna fled Scott's army. By nightfall both *garitas* had been taken. And on the morning of September 14, 1847, Scott formally took possession of the city.[202]

The fighting for the capital city cost the Mexicans approximately 1,800 casualties,[203] while Winfield Scott reported 130 men killed, 703 wounded, and 29 missing.[204] Magruder was officially listed among the wounded in the Battle of Chapultepec.[205] The fighting along the Anzures Causeway was the most bitter of his experience. Seven of his men were also wounded, but only one was killed. Nine of the battery horses were killed, three more were wounded, and several of the gun carriages were damaged, yet he and Jackson had opened the way for others.[206] Generals Pillow and Worth commended Magruder in their official reports.[207] Pillow, in particular, reported that Magruder and Jackson had rendered "invaluable service preparatory to the general assault."[208] Additionally, Winfield Scott, who had personally witnessed Magruder's light battery in action on more than one occasion during the fighting leading to the capture of the Mexican capital, listed Magruder among the "individuals of conspicuous merit."[209] Shortly after the fighting ended, Magruder was breveted lieutenant colonel, "for gallant and meritorious conduct in the Battle of Chapultepec."[210] Yet his most cherished honor came later, in January 1848, after returning home, when he was presented

202. For primary accounts of the Battle of Chapultepec and occupation of Mexico City, see Senate Executive Doc. 1, 30th Cong., 1st sess., 375–431, 166–231, appendix; Pillow Court of Inquiry, Senate Executive Doc. 65, 30th Cong., 1st sess.; Semmes, *Service Afloat and Ashore during the Mexican War*, 453–61; Hitchcock, *Fifty Years of Camp and Field*, 302–3; Ballentine, *Autobiography of an English Soldier*, 259–64; Grant, *Personal Memoirs*, 1:155–59.

203. Pillow to Scott, September 18, 1847, Senate Executive Doc. 1, 30th Cong., 1st sess., 408.

204. Scott to Marcy, ibid., 384.

205. Pillow to Scott, ibid., 405; Return by name of the killed, wounded, and missing, of the army, under the command of Major General Winfield Scott, incident to the capture of Chapultepec and the city of Mexico, on the thirteenth and fourteenth days of September 1847, ibid., 463.

206. Magruder to Hooker, September 18, 1847, Senate Executive Doc. 1, 30th Cong., 1st sess., 195–97, appendix.

207. Pillow to Scott, ibid., 400–405; Worth to Scott, September 16, 1847, ibid., 391.

208. Pillow to Scott, September 18, 1847, Senate Executive Doc. 1, 30th Cong., 1st sess., 404–5.

209. Scott to Marcy, ibid., 380.

210. Cullum, *Biographical Register*, 1:368.

with a splendid gold sword. The scabbard of Magruder's sword was inscribed: "To Brevet Lieutenant Colonel John B. Magruder, 1st Artillery, United States Army, for gallant conduct at Vera Cruz, Cerro Gordo, Contreras, Molino del Rey, Chapultepec and the City of Mexico from his fellow citizens of Caroline County, Virginia."[211] Prince John had made the most of his opportunity.

211. The sword, inherited by his son, Henry R. Magruder, of Baltimore, is now in the Smithsonian Institution, Washington, D.C.

3

BETWEEN THE WARS

Sporadic fighting continued in and around Mexico City even after Santa Anna had fled with the remnants of his battered army and the American flag had been ceremoniously raised over the Grand Plaza to formalize Winfield Scott's victory. However, because a civilian insurrection was anticipated, Scott kept his men on alert and ordered them to be on their best behavior so as not to antagonize local citizens further. Daily drills, inspections, and parades were the norm, as General Scott took every precaution to ensure discipline until the last Mexican resistance was quashed. He had one-third of each regiment stationed at their quarters as an in-lying picket ready for emergency duty. And all of Scott's men, whether on or off duty, carried their sidearms when away from their quarters.[1]

Because of Winfield Scott's vigilance and the firm but fair administration of Major General John A. Quitman, whom Scott had appointed military governor, calm quickly returned to the streets of Mexico City. On September 20 the English-language *American Star,* the official headquarters newspaper, reported that order had been restored, businesses had reopened, and scores of families had returned to promenade the streets without trepidation. "Whenever you see the softer sex walking the streets in confidence," declared the *Star,* "you may set it down at once that things are as they should be."[2]

---

1. Wilcox, *History of the Mexican War,* 511. Wilcox, an 1846 graduate of the U.S. Military Academy and later Confederate major general who would fight in virtually all of the major battles with Lee's Army of Northern Virginia, was a miracle survivor of the Mexican War. While storming the gate at Belén, Wilcox was struck down and thought to be killed, but his revolver, hanging to his belt, saved his life. The ball struck its barrel and was picked up as flat as a dollar, with the name of the maker and place where it was made legibly stamped upon it.

2. *American Star,* September 20, 1847.

When tranquillity returned to the Mexican capital, General Scott eased restrictions and allowed his men more freedom. The Army of Occupation became an army of tourists in a city that blended "the extremes of splendour and squalor, dirt and grandeur."[3] Scott's men frequented sites of interest, including the gates of Belén, San Cosme, Chapultepec Castle, the Grand Catholic Cathedral, Alameda Park, and the National Museum. Besides sightseeing, available entertainment ran the gamut from bullfights to American theatrical productions to the National Theatre of Mexico, which featured a troupe of Italian opera singers. Mexican restaurants made their specialties available for the dining pleasure of the Yankee soldiers, while other pleasures could be satisfied at any number of saloons, gambling halls, and whorehouses, which were later dubbed "the hells of Montezuma."[4]

Winfield Scott's officers, being somewhat more refined, organized the Aztec Club to perpetuate the memories of their military service in Mexico. This was a social and fraternal organization formed on October 13, 1847, at a meeting in the home of José María de Bocanegra, the former Mexican secretary of state and foreign relations. The original membership of 160 officers elected John A. Quitman president, with John B. Grayson and Charles F. Smith first vice presidents and Magruder second vice president. Less than two weeks after the initial election, however, General Quitman received orders to report to the War Department in Washington. When Quitman left, General Franklin Pierce succeeded him as president of the Aztec Club.[5]

The club offered excellent food, fine spirits, cards, camaraderie, and good cheer at moderate rates. It also provided Magruder with a venue in which he displayed both his social skills and a penchant for fashion. "This was the period when Prince John Magruder flourished and shaped fashionable opin-

3. Ballentine, *Autobiography of an English Soldier*, 269.

4. Alfred Hoyt Bill, *Rehearsal for Conflict: The War with Mexico, 1846–1848* (New York: Alfred A. Knopf, 1947), 308; Ballentine, *Autobiography of an English Soldier*, 269–80; Oswandel, *Notes of the Mexican War*, 445, 449, 459; Wilcox, *History of the Mexican War*, 511.

5. *Constitution of the Aztec Club of 1847 and List of Members* (London: Hanbury, Tomsett and Co., 1928), 5–6, 28–34; Wilcox, *History of the Mexican War*, 514–15, 710–11; *Army and Navy Journal* 21 (September 15, 1883): 132; reprint from the *Numistatist* 47:548–52. The *Constitution of the Aztec Club* lists only those elected annually; consequently, Franklin Pierce is not cited as having been president of the club. The book also lists 160 original members. Wilcox, on the other hand, states that Franklin Pierce was the first president of the Aztec Club, without mentioning Quitman, and that there were 149 members. Wilcox's listing was made after some of Scott's officers, including Quitman, had been returned to the United States. Membership in the Aztec Club was at first confined to officers in the Army of Occupation; thus, the officers in General Taylor's

ions," declared Edward C. Boynton, a fellow artillerist and West Point graduate who would later write one of the first histories of the academy. Boynton also disapprovingly noted that in the somewhat lax postwar period the official uniform gradually began disappearing from sight. Soldiers wore almost any garment that had at least some army blue in it,[6] and Magruder was one who led the trend away from traditional military dress. Lieutenant George H. Derby, who graduated from West Point with Boynton in the class of 1846, reported that Prince John appeared in a uniform "upon which the brilliant red facings exceeded even the generous limits of the regulations." Derby whimsically queried, "Are Magruder's pants blue with red stripes or red with blue stripes?" It was, according to the lieutenant, as evenly balanced a subject as any of which he could think.[7] Boynton, on the other hand, took exception to the fashion revolution. He condemned Magruder as "a bad example for young men to follow," suggesting that he was "ambitious, unscrupulous, treacherous and dissolute." Boynton conceded, however, that Magruder "had one good quality at least—he was a dashing, fearless soldier."[8]

Indeed, after finally having gained an opportunity to prove his mettle in combat, John Magruder won a dazzling reputation on the battlefields of Mexico. He was promoted in permanent rank to captain on June 18, 1846, and was twice cited for gallantry, receiving brevet rank of major after Cerro Gordo on April 18, 1847, and brevet lieutenant colonel on September 13, 1847, for his part in the Battle of Chapultepec.[9] His spirit was so revived and his morale so boosted that, temporarily at least, his former opinion of the army improved. His health, however, began rapidly deteriorating.

On November 24, 1847, Company I surgeon Josephus M. Steiner warned that Magruder had "a chronic affection of the liver . . . which is daily growing more serious."[10] Additionally, an accompanying surgeon's certificate signed by a Dr. Martinez of Mexico City reported that Magruder had a "very serious irritation of the brain and whole nervous system, accompanied with chronic tarpidity of the liver. The Captain has likewise a sore leg, and a fistula in

---

army in northern Mexico were not original members. Subsequently, many officers in Taylor's army were admitted to the Aztec Club, and in 1871 all officers who had served in the Mexican War were declared eligible for membership.

6. Haskin, *History of the First Regiment of Artillery*, 321.

7. George R. Stewart, *John Phoenix, Esq., the Squibob* (New York: Henry Holt, 1937), 53.

8. Haskin, *History of the First Regiment of Artillery*, 321.

9. Cullum, *Biographical Register*, 1:367–68.

10. Report of Assistant Surgeon J. M. Steiner, November 24, 1847, National Archives.

ano, which requires operation. His general health is still in a very disordered condition; and I consider that for his complete recovery, it is of the utmost importance that Captain McGruder [*sic*] should have access to a change of climate and that for four or five months he should have absolute rest from his official duties."[11] Steiner concurred and predicted that his company commander would "not be able to perform in his official duties for at least three months."[12] And time proved him right. As late as March 2, 1848, Magruder wrote the adjutant general that as a result of "the ill effects of the injury which I received in Mexico . . . I have been confined strictly to my bed . . . unable to attend to duty."[13] Shortly after surgeons Steiner and Martinez prescribed a change of climate for their patient, General Orders No. 365 released Magruder from his duties in Mexico,[14] and in late December he sailed from Vera Cruz with new orders to resume command of Battery I, 1st Artillery, at Fort McHenry in Baltimore.[15]

Prince John must have been elated. Although he had been born and raised in Virginia, he now claimed Baltimore as his home.[16] There he rejoined his wife, Henrietta, and his children, Isabella, Kate Elizabeth, and Henry, whom he had not seen for over a year. Baltimore society was also within reach, but as Magruder's health improved, he concerned himself primarily with military affairs. He proved the tactical advantages of light artillery in such stunning fashion during Scott's drive toward Mexico City that the artillery emerged as the premier branch of the army in the postwar years. And John Magruder, armed with his newly won reputation, "was anxious to hold his place in the light artillery."[17]

On July 18, 1848, Magruder submitted a detailed plan for organizing the batteries of light artillery into a battalion. In 1821 and again in 1847 Congress had authorized the consolidation of such a battalion from the light artillery

11. Surgeon's Certificate, November 24, 1847, signed by Dr. [?] Martinez, Mexico City. Dr. Martinez's certificate was attached to Steiner's report, National Archives.

12. Report of Assistant Surgeon J. M. Steiner, November 24, 1847, National Archives.

13. Magruder to adjutant general, March 2, 1848, National Archives.

14. General Orders No. 365, December 6, 1847, Adjutant General's Office, National Archives.

15. Cullum, *Biographical Register*, 1:368; *Niles National Register* 73 (January 29, 1848): 338, reported that Magruder, Major Ben McCulloch, and Colonel W. W. S. Bliss "have reached Washington."

16. Magruder to Jones, January 17, 1848, National Archives.

17. Casdorph, *Prince John Magruder*, 82; A. L. Long, "Memoir of General John Bankhead Magruder," *Southern Historical Society Papers* 12 (1884): 106–8.

companies that then existed. Separating the light artillery from the ordnance, field, and sea coast artillery would, in Magruder's opinion, result in an "enlightened division of labor," allowing each branch of the artillery to become more skilled in its specialized task. He urged the light artillery in particular to receive suggestions, examine plans, test innovations, and implement meritorious ideas that would result in improved efficiency in battle. He also challenged his fellow officers to keep abreast of foreign technological improvements and to surpass them if possible. "The science of artillery is continually advancing," observed Magruder. For the United States to be competitive with its military rivals, it was imperative that the War Department be aware of all foreign innovations and advancements. Moreover, as European armies had made significant advances in artillery, even since the commencement of the Mexican War, Magruder applied to lead a team of observers abroad to report on such improvements.[18] Unfortunately, in the postwar period governmental priorities changed in such a way that the military was deemphasized, and "farsighted planners were discouraged or ignored."[19] As evidence, the Adjutant General's Office tabled Magruder's organizational plan and rejected his European mission. Plus, the War Department, in a post–Mexican War cost-cutting move, dismounted Company I on September 30, 1848, and ordered Magruder's men to serve as "foot artillery."[20]

This triple disaster devastated Magruder. For the next several months he incessantly badgered Adjutant General Roger Jones about remounting his company.[21] Failing to get the desired response from the unyielding Jones, Magruder tried a different tack. On December 3, 1848, he attempted to get his company remounted by uniting it with Colonel James Duncan's light artillery company. Because Duncan had approximately fifty horses at Fort McHenry, Magruder reasoned that both companies could drill at minimal public expense. He further asserted that his men were "veteran light artiller-

18. "Plan for Organizing the Batteries of Light Artillery into One or More Battalions," Magruder to Jones, July 18, 1848, National Archives; "Project for Organizing into a Battalion the Batteries of Light Artillery, Now Authorized by the Acts of Congress of 1821 and 1847," Magruder to secretary of war, July 18, 1848, National Archives.

19. Fairfax Downey, *Sound of the Guns: The Story of American Artillery from the Ancient and Honorable Company to the Atom Cannon and Guided Missile* (New York: David McKay Co., 1955), 119.

20. Haskin, *History of the First Regiment of Artillery,* 122; Magruder to Jones, October 3, 1848, and April 10, 1849, National Archives.

21. Magruder to Jones, October 3 and 22, 1848, National Archives.

ists . . . and proud soldiers—without practice they will lose their efficiency and pride." Magruder closed his letter by predicting that Duncan and the officers of his company would "be fully satisfied with the plan proposed." On December 5 General Thomas Childs, the commanding officer at Fort McHenry, "approved and urgently recommended" that Magruder's recommendation be accepted. Four days later John P. Gaines, who as a member of Winfield Scott's staff had witnessed the value of light artillery during the Mexican War, added his endorsement, writing, "Every officer and soldier of every artillery regiment . . . should enjoy the benefit of such instruction . . . it is essential to the defense of the country."[22] Yet when Jones queried Colonel Duncan about the merger, Duncan pointed out that such an instructional arrangement had been tested before the Mexican War and the result was that "nothing could have been more [detrimental] to the interest, discipline and harmony of the service." "The effect," declared Duncan, "was to spoil two very good companies to make one very bad one."[23] Because of Duncan's opposition, Roger Jones once again denied Magruder's request.[24] Finally, as a last resort, Magruder turned to President-elect Zachary Taylor, and there he found a sympathetic supporter. On April 21, 1849, just six weeks after succeeding James K. Polk in office, Taylor issued Order No. 22, which remounted Company I with four artillery pieces and forty-four horses.[25]

Adjutant General Jones was miffed. For months he had put up with Magruder's backstage politicking and the fusillade of letters that were an irritating part of the remounting campaign. Magruder's action of going over Jones's head to get his company remounted caused the adjutant general to run thin on patience, and on November 13, 1849, he ordered Magruder and his men to "proceed without unnecessary delay" to California,[26] where San Diego would be their home for the next four years.

Magruder's original orders directed him to travel with his company to San Francisco by sea via Cape Horn. He asked for and received permission, however, to precede his men to California by taking the shorter route

22. Magruder to Freeman, December 3, 1848, National Archives. The endorsements of Childs and Gaines were written on the cover of Magruder's letter. William Grigsby Freeman was assistant adjutant general from 1841 to 1849.

23. Duncan to Jones, December 19, 1848, National Archives.

24. Jones to Magruder, December 30, 1848, National Archives.

25. Haskin, *History of the First Regiment of Artillery,* 122; *Niles National Register* 75 (May 9, 1849): 289.

26. Jones to Magruder, November 13, 1849, National Archives.

through Panama.[27] This course would reduce the distance of the trip by seventy-eight hundred miles and travel time by approximately three months. While awaiting the arrival of his men, Magruder could procure safe and dry storerooms, adequate stables, and comfortable quarters in advance. He also planned to meet with the commanding officer in California to ascertain the precise duty assignment of Company I so that no time would be lost. When the men arrived, they could immediately resume their ordinary duties; thus, discipline would be maintained and desertions minimized. "It is always desirable that the commanding officer should be on the spot . . . to superintend the preparations for the reception of [his] company," declared Magruder.[28] And in this instance Jones agreed. It was, however, the last time Roger Jones and John Magruder would agree on anything.

The collapse of their relationship began with a controversy involving advance pay for the men of Company I. On January 2, 1850, Magruder "urgently recommended" that the usual six months' advance pay issued to troops being sent to distant posts not be made until after the transport carrying the men was at sea; otherwise, there would be desertions, and all of the pay would be spent in Baltimore.[29] Unfortunately, nearly a week passed before Jones acted on Magruder's suggestion. Shortly before the Adjutant General's Office issued orders that the troops were "not to be paid before their embarkation,"[30] Major Andrews, the resident paymaster, paid the men, resulting in the predicted debauchery. Fifteen men of Company I deserted, taking with them all of their clothing.[31] And many of those who remained did so only because they were too drunk to leave. When informed of the turmoil, Jones placed the blame entirely on Magruder.[32]

Unbeknownst to the adjutant general, Magruder had sent an official note to Major Andrews expressing his desire that the advance pay be withheld until the troops were ready to depart. He also told Andrews that he had written the War Department on the subject and was daily expecting an an-

27. Magruder to Jones, November 22 and 26, 1849; Jones to Magruder, December 7, 1849, and January 17, 1850, National Archives.

28. Magruder to Jones, November 26, 1849, National Archives.

29. Magruder to Jones, January 2, 1850, National Archives.

30. Jones to Magruder, January 7, 1850, National Archives.

31. Magruder to Jones, January 11, 1850, National Archives. In a letter to Roger Jones dated January 22, 1850, Magruder reported that all but five of the missing soldiers had returned and that their places were immediately filled by enlistments.

32. Jones to Magruder, January 12, 1850, National Archives.

swer. The paymaster refused to wait, however, for an official order from the adjutant general. Andrews stated, "It would be defeating the object of the government to pay the troops after embarkation." Accordingly, he sent a personal message to Magruder's house announcing his intention of paying the men. Upon receiving the note, Magruder mounted his horse and galloped to Fort McHenry to prevent the payment. But he arrived too late. Andrews had already committed "the grave impropriety of paying the troops under my (Magruder's) command, without competent authority, against my expressed wishes, and without waiting [for an order from the War Department]."[33] Magruder did everything in his power to keep Major Andrews from paying the men, but he had no direct authority over Andrews; Jones did. Had Roger Jones responded immediately to Magruder's letter of January 2, requesting an order withholding pay, Andrews would have been prevented by higher authority from paying the men, and the fiasco never would have occurred.

Shortly after the pay controversy Jones blasted Magruder for his slowness to depart for his new duty station. Magruder and his men had been directed to proceed "without unnecessary delay" to California in orders dated November 13, 1849, but their transport, the *Monterey,* did not even arrive in Baltimore until December 29.[34] In the meantime Magruder had taken care of all matters relating to the procurement of supplies, ammunition, clothing, and other provisions for his men, and on January 2, 1850, he reported, "My command is now ready to embark."[35] But then the Ordnance Department ordered shipment of "a number of heavy guns" on the same transport. Several days passed before the artillery pieces arrived from the Washington arsenal. Major Samuel B. Dusenberry, the quartermaster in charge of loading the ship, ordered that the heavy guns be loaded first. The *Monterey* had to be moved to a different mooring in Baltimore harbor, however, "to procure the use of machinery powerful enough to place the guns on board." While the *Monterey* was being loaded, Magruder ascertained from several local shipping merchants who regularly loaded large vessels bound for distant ports, including California, that the normal time required to load and fit out a ship was approximately one month, depending on the weather. But in this case the weather did not cooperate. "The weather has been very unfavorable," reported Magruder, "and many articles could not go on board, without the

33. Magruder to Jones, January 11, 1850, National Archives.
34. Magruder to Jones, January 22, 1850, National Archives.
35. Magruder to Jones, January 2, 1850, National Archives.

certainty of injury and danger to the health of the troops." In the end, because Major Dusenberry overcame bad weather, inadequate loading facilities, and late arriving ordnance supplies that had to be loaded first, yet still
had the transport ready to sail in less than a month, Magruder concluded,
"The operation could not have proceeded more rapidly without injury to the
service."[36]

Adjutant General Jones, on the other hand, grew increasingly more impatient. On January 17 he noted that Magruder's men had been paid and
furnished with their supplies. He could not understand why the transport
remained in port and Magruder's men of Company I "linger[ed] on shore."[37]
Jones had no way of knowing that Company I could not board until all other
supplies had been loaded. He likewise had no concept of the difficulties that
Major Dusenberry faced. From his vantage point in Washington, D.C., he
believed the transport was waiting for Magruder, when in fact Magruder and
his men were waiting for the ship. Because of his imperfect understanding of
the situation in Baltimore, Roger Jones again blamed Magruder.

Company I finally left Baltimore on January 24, 1850,[38] and Magruder
departed shortly afterward, almost exactly two years after coming to Fort
McHenry from the battlefields of Mexico. Leaving Henrietta and the children once again must have been difficult. On the other hand, he must have
been relieved leaving Roger Jones behind. Their personalities clashed and
their styles conflicted. In John Magruder's mind Jones was so inflexible that
he seemed to lack common sense. He was also stubborn and appeared to
be overly regimented. Plus, he was traditional to the point of being ridiculous. Jones never wanted to change anything; Magruder seemingly wanted to
change everything. Prince John, however, was no match for the adjutant general of the U.S. Army. Had relations between the two men deteriorated further, Magruder was sure to be the loser. Under the circumstances Magruder's
transfer to California was perhaps a blessing in disguise. The assignment

36. Magruder to Jones, January 22, 1850, National Archives.

37. Jones to Magruder, January 17, 1850, National Archives.

38. Haskin, *History of the First Regiment of Artillery,* 124; Magruder to Jones, January 22, 1850,
National Archives. This is a different letter than that referred to in notes 34 and 36, though
both bear the same date. Several years later, on August 22, 1855, in a letter to Samuel Cooper,
Magruder recalled that Company I had left Fort McHenry for California on January 28, 1850.
Magruder to Cooper, August 22, 1855, National Archives. Major Samuel P. Heintzelman, in his
diary, reported on April 19, 1850, that Magruder's men left Baltimore on the *Monterey* on January 27, 1850. The original Heintzelman Diary is in the National Archives.

would also prove to be one of the most interesting in his entire career. In addition to commanding the post at San Diego, Magruder would find time enough to become a land speculator, lawyer, saloon owner, railroad president, and one of California's most celebrated duelists.

The West Coast adventure, however, did not begin well for Magruder. Upon arriving in San Diego on April 19, 1850, aboard the steamer *Panama*,[39] orders awaited him to report to departmental headquarters in San Francisco, where Pacific Division commander General Persifor F. Smith would brief him regarding his duties and responsibilities in southern California. While Magruder traveled overland, purchasing horses along the way for his company, his personal effects, including all of his public and private papers, were sent to San Francisco by sea. But when he arrived there he learned that the trunks containing his papers had been incinerated in a fire that destroyed the office of the Pacific Mail Steamship Company. Later, in a letter dated January 18, 1853, Magruder stated that the fire had occurred in May 1850,[40] but this appears to be in error. If the trunks were at the office of the Pacific Mail Steamship Company as reported, they would not have been destroyed in the fire of May 4, 1850. That fire, which consumed three square blocks of San Francisco's business district, came within one block of the steamship company's office but did not reach it. A subsequent fire less than six weeks later, on June 14, 1850, reduced to ashes everything between Clay and California streets from Kearney Street to the waterfront. This included the Pacific Mail Steamship Company office, which was then located at the southeast corner of Commercial and Leidesdorff streets, directly in the center of the area destroyed.[41] Because it was over two and a half years after the fire that Magruder recalled the date of the event as May 1850, his error could be attributed either to an imperfect memory, or he could have simply been given the date of the wrong fire when originally informed of his loss. At any rate the unfortunate loss of all of Magruder's pre-1850 papers and records would later cause problems for him, and it would forever handicap historians attempting to reconstruct his life.

39. Heintzelman Diary, April 19, 1850.

40. Magruder to Thompson, January 18, 1853, National Archives.

41. Hubert Howe Bancroft, *History of California*, 7 vols. (San Francisco: History Co., 1884–90), 6:172, 178n, 202–3n, 204. After the fire of June 14, 1850, the Pacific Mail Steamship Company moved its office a block south, to the northwest corner of Sacramento and Leidesdorff streets. That location was later destroyed, however, in a fire on May 3, 1851. Bancroft described San Francisco as "one of the most combustible of cities" in California.

John Magruder rejoined his men aboard the *Monterey* after the transport reached San Francisco on August 10, 1850.[42] As soon as the cargo of ordnance was unloaded and new food and fuel supplies were taken aboard, the vessel was put back out to sea with the entire compliment of officers and men of Company I, 1st Artillery, aboard. Magruder carried orders to proceed to his new duty post with his battery "without delay,"[43] and the *Monterey* obliged, completing the five-hundred-mile voyage in less than a week. By the time the ship reached San Diego on August 25, 1850,[44] Magruder's men had been sea bound aboard their transport for seven full months. Finally reaching their long-sought destination resulted in wild celebration. A fellow officer who witnessed the event reported: "Col. Magruder is having a nice time with his men. They are getting drunk."[45] Once the jubilation ceased, however, the joy of leaving the *Monterey* was no doubt tempered by the stark, sobering realities of living on the southern California frontier.

California was in a state of volatility when Magruder and his company reached San Diego. The town had just been incorporated. California was soon to become a new free state as a part of the Compromise of 1850, and thousands upon thousands of adventurers and prospectors were streaming into California as a consequence of James Marshall's discovery of gold in the American River at Sutter's Mill on January 24, 1848. Some stopped briefly at the Port of San Diego on their way, by sea, to San Francisco. Others came via the Gila Trail, the southernmost of the overland routes to the California gold fields. Those who survived cholera epidemics, starvation, attacks by Apache and Yuma Indians, and finally the trek across the southern California desert were often broken men by the time their weary eyes beheld the Pacific Ocean. A caravanist who reached San Diego in July 1849 exclaimed, "A man who has traveled the Gila route may throw himself upon his knees . . . when reaching this point and thank God for preserving him through it."[46] And a correspondent from the *New York Tribune* instructed his newspaper to warn adventurers to "avoid this way [the Gila Trail] as they would the plague."[47]

42. Heintzelman Diary, August 21, 1850; Haskin, *History of the First Regiment of Artillery*, 124. Haskin reported that the *Monterey* arrived in San Francisco on August 18.

43. Letter to Magruder, August 18, 1850, from U.S. Army Headquarters at Benicia, Calif., Records of the Tenth Military Department, 1846–51, Letters Sent, National Archives.

44. Heintzelman Diary, August 26, 1850; Haskin, *History of the First Regiment of Artillery*, 124.

45. Heintzelman Diary, August 29, 1850.

46. Richard F. Pourade, *The History of San Diego: The Silver Dons* (San Diego: Union-Tribune Publishing Co., 1963), 149.

47. Ibid., 144.

Many of the immigrants were too sick, too weak, or too poor to complete their trek to destination's end in northern California and were forced to make San Diego their temporary home. For some, including artist H. M. T. Powell, the experience was an eye-opener. He complained, "Their manners here are detestable . . . everybody gets drunk . . . the gambling and drinking . . . is very reprehensible." Bullfights, cockfights, and fistfights provided regular entertainment, and shootings were so commonplace that Powell recorded in his diary on February 13, 1850, "A Mexican soldier . . . murdered another right here in town last night. So little notice was taken of it that I did not hear of it until this evening." Other than the murder, Powell nonchalantly mentioned that it was a "beautiful day." After convalescing for three months, during which time he sold several sketches and maps of the area to replenish his exhausted financial resources, artist Powell, on March 9, 1850, left San Diego, "I hope for ever [sic]."[48]

A few months after Powell left San Diego, John Magruder and his battery arrived. When they entered San Diego Bay, they came upon one of the finest natural harbors on the Pacific coast, one that even compared favorably with San Francisco. "The harbor of San Francisco has more water," reported Lieutenant William H. Emory, an engineer serving with the U.S.-Mexico Boundary Commission, "but that of San Diego has a more uniform climate, better anchorage, and perfect security from winds in any direction,"[49] thus offering excellent protection for the *Monterey* and all other visiting ships. Additionally, Lieutenant Andrew B. Gray, chief surveyor for the Boundary Commission, judged that San Diego Bay was "large enough to hold comfortably more than a thousand vessels at a time."[50]

In 1850 the principal anchorage and longtime headquarters for whalers and ships involved in the hide trade was at La Playa, on the western part of the bay. The settlement consisted of hundreds of tents that provided shelter for an ever-changing immigrant population. There were also a few unimpressive permanent structures, including four run-down hide houses, four stores, a ramshackle customhouse, a makeshift hotel, and an assortment of

48. H. M. T. Powell, *The Santa Fe Trail to California, 1849–1852: The Journal and Drawings of H. M. T. Powell,* ed. Douglas S. Watson (San Francisco: Book Club of California, 1931), 199, 204.

49. Report of Lieutenant W. H. Emory, House Executive Doc. 41, 30th Cong., 1st sess., 113. From a commercial standpoint San Diego has an ideal climate. The area receives only ten inches of rain annually and its temperature averages seventy degrees in summer and a mild fifty-five degrees in winter.

50. William E. Smythe, *History of San Diego, 1542–1908* (San Diego: History Co., 1908), 689.

commercial buildings that were near the water's edge.[51] It was there that the *Monterey* was moored and unloaded. And it was on the nearby beach at La Playa that Magruder's men made their first West Coast encampment, had their arrival celebration, and suffered their first California hangovers.

Old San Diego, or Old Town as it was commonly called, was at the north end of San Diego Bay, slightly inland, along the Rio San Diego, which emptied into the bay. Lieutenant Thomas W. Sweeny described the town as "a collection of dilapidated adobe buildings affording but scanty shelter to a population of three or four hundred Spaniards and Indians."[52] Another even less impressed observer, Gunner Meyers, exclaimed that San Diego was "a miserable hole [with] the ugliest women I ever saw."[53] Old Town, despite its aesthetic shortcomings, was the business center and home to most of the of local citizens.

Three miles south of Old San Diego, on the eastern side of San Diego Bay, was New San Diego, or New Town. It was a new development located at Punta de los Muertos (Point of the Dead), where a Spanish expedition in 1782 had buried several of its members who had died of scurvy. Surveyor Andrew Gray selected the site for New Town. He convinced William Heath Davis and several other prominent local investors of the commercial potential of a location where a southern transcontinental railroad would have as its western terminus the Port of San Diego. Davis, in turn, convinced Major Samuel P. Heintzelman, who had preceded Magruder in command in San Diego, to build the army's new depot in New Town rather than at La Playa.[54] Magruder arrived just in time to supervise the project's completion. To celebrate the occasion, Captain Nathaniel Lyon, the army's quartermaster in San Diego, organized a "baile," or dance, for his brother officers. Lyon prevailed upon Davis and Captain Santiaguito Arguello "to invite the fair sex, from the Old Town, from the ranchos, and from the City of the Angels." According to Davis, "The assemblage of women constituted the elite of San Diego and Los Angeles . . . places [that] were noted . . . for their handsome women."[55] Gunner

51. Pourade, *History of San Diego: The Silver Dons*, 171.

52. Ibid, 142.

53. Ibid, 120.

54. Ray Brandes and James R. Moriarty III, *New Town, San Diego* (San Diego: San Diego Science Foundation, 1985), 29–30. Besides Davis and Gray, the other principal investors in New Town were Miguel de Pedrorena, José Antonio Aguirre, William C. Ferrell, and Lieutenant Thomas Denton Johns.

55. William Heath Davis, *Seventy-five Years in California*, ed. Harold A. Small (San Francisco: John Howell Books, 1967), 260.

Meyers might have missed seeing these women on his earlier visit to San Diego; chances are John Magruder did not. Contemporary sources do not specifically place Magruder at the party, but he was in San Diego at the time, and he would have never missed a social event of this nature. Davis reported that the party did not disperse until the early hours of the morning—Prince John Magruder, if true to form, was probably the last celebrant standing.

Magruder built a home in New Town near the depot, as did Captain Lyon and lieutenants Gray and Daniel M. Beltzhoover.[56] While his home was under construction, Magruder rented a house in New Town from Davis at the corner of Market and State streets. There he lived with Captain George Stoneman and lieutenants Adam Slemmer and Francis E. Patterson.[57] As there were no other available accommodations in the vicinity of the depot, the men of Company I were quartered a half-dozen miles away toward the northeast in the remains of the mission which Franciscan pioneer Junípero Serra had established on July 16, 1769.[58] Mission San Diego was the oldest Christian church in California.

The mission consisted of a church 84 feet long and 15 feet wide with a red tile roof and adobe walls 3 feet thick. Additionally, there was a granary, harness room, storerooms, guest rooms, refectory, and kitchen. These buildings and the soldiers' quarters occupied three wings of a quadrangle, each measuring 155 feet in length, while the fourth side was enclosed by an 11-foot-high adobe wall. In its heyday under the Franciscans, Mission San Diego was known as the "mother mission" and was "decidedly striking in its appearance."[59] After the missions were secularized in the early 1830s, however, many of them fell victim to neglect. By the end of the Mexican War, Mission San Diego was judged to be in a "mournful state of decay." The church was "dilapidated," and the rooms were "dirty and full of fleas."[60] Magruder complained that some of the buildings were so structurally impaired that on occasion his men had barely "escaped with their lives from the falling parts of the mission."[61]

56. Pourade, *History of San Diego: The Silver Dons,* 171–72.

57. Ed Scott, *San Diego County: Soldier-Pioneers, 1846–1866* (National City, Calif.: Crest Printing Co., 1976), 69, 129.

58. Pourade, *History of San Diego: The Silver Dons,* 177.

59. Richard F. Pourade, *The History of San Diego: Time of the Bells* (San Diego: Union-Tribune Publishing Co., 1961), 37, 58, 117, 216.

60. Pourade, *History of San Diego: The Silver Dons,* 82, 127.

61. Records of the Tenth Military Department, 1846–51, Letters Received, December 17, 1850, National Archives.

Because the accommodations were woefully inadequate and the distance between the mission and the depot made for a cumbersome command situation, Magruder urged the army to build barracks for his men in New Town.[62] But department headquarters denied the request and instructed Magruder to maintain his position at the mission.[63] He then sought money and materials to repair the mission but was told that no funds were available.[64] Magruder had to do the best that he could with whatever materials he could find locally. Improvements were made slowly but steadily. Later, in May 1852, when John Russell Bartlett of the U.S.-Mexico Boundary Commission inspected the mission, he wrote that it was "under the command of Colonel J. B. Magruder, and in consequence is kept in good repair."[65]

After his battery was settled at the mission, one of Magruder's first interests was to petition for a grant of city land. The "Index of Deeds, San Diego County" records that he made three land purchases on September 14, 1850, one on September 18, and another on October 2. The largest purchase, an eighty-acre farm in Mission Valley, made September 14, 1850, was held until September 17, 1853, when it was sold to provide funds with which to purchase a larger ranch, known as the "Rancho de Jamacha," with "all tenements, hereditaments and appurtenances thereon" for $2,500. On March 26, 1853, Magruder sold a parcel of land to J. Judson Ames, editor and owner of the *San Diego Herald,* and a month later he bought two city lots from the trustees of the city of San Diego.[66]

After departing California, Magruder apparently paid his taxes through an agent, Eugene B. Pendleton of San Diego, but he stopped the payments during the Civil War. Magruder's name consequently appeared on the delinquent tax list for 1861 as the owner of twelve blocks of property in San Diego County. He owed $5 per unit, $60 total.[67] It appears that these taxes were paid by one of Magruder's former soldiers in Battery I, Sergeant James Mc-

---

62. Robert Stephen Milota, "John Bankhead Magruder: The California Years" (master's thesis, University of San Diego, 1990), 17.

63. Records of the Tenth Military Department, 1846–51, Letters Sent, October 28, 1850, National Archives.

64. Ibid., November 28, 1850.

65. John Russell Bartlett, *Personal Narrative of Explorations and Incidents in Texas, New Mexico, California, Sonora, and Chihuahua, Connected with the United States and Mexican Boundary Commission during the Years 1850, '51, '52, and '53,* 2 vols. (New York: D. Appleton, 1854), 2:104.

66. Index of Deeds, San Diego County.

67. Delinquent Taxes, 1861, San Diego County.

Coy, who in 1861 was the San Diego County tax assessor. He may have also dropped the assessed valuation to make the payments easier. At any rate the "Estate of J. B. Magruder" in California had an assessed valuation of $3,584 in 1872, the year following his death, when the estate was settled.[68]

Magruder's private land dealings and official responsibilities, wherein he occasionally served as a land claim verifier, led him to open a law practice with "particular attention given to land claims."[69] He received his California license on February 18, 1851,[70] and joined William C. Ferrell, James W. Robinson, and Thomas W. Sutherland as the only practicing attorneys in San Diego.[71] On May 24, 1851, Magruder announced in the newspapers that he would practice in the courts of Los Angeles, San Diego, and the Supreme Court of California.[72] Also, while stationed in southern California, he would serve on several court-martial boards, where he would be able to employ his knowledge of the law in the pursuit of justice. And on the practical side the legal practice helped to keep Magruder ahead of his bills.[73]

Magruder made numerous social contacts both through his dealings in land, as a lawyer, and as post commander. His military duties were not demanding, and though he devoted much of his time and energy to social affairs, a friend wrote on January 1, 1851, that Magruder had "fallen out with old John Barleycorn, . . . and he *says* they are to be strangers for a year to come."[74] But when in Los Angeles he ran across Samuel R. Dummer, an old friend from the Mexican War, the resolution was forgotten. Joseph Lancaster Brent, a Louisiana-bred lawyer who leased office space in Los Angeles from Dummer, described his landlord as a man of "some means [who] did not do any regular business, but every now and then would take up some enterprise, which did not always succeed."[75] Business was not Magruder's forte either,

68. Assessed Land Valuations, 1872, San Diego County.

69. May 24, 1851, newspaper clipping in the newspaper collection of the Bancroft Library, University of California, Berkeley. John Barr Tompkins, then head of public services at the Bancroft Library, said the clipping "was most probably" from the *Los Angeles Star*. Tompkins to Hay, January 31, 1955, Hay Papers.

70. Casdorph, *Prince John Magruder*, 91.

71. Smythe, *History of San Diego*, 582.

72. May 24, 1851, newspaper clipping in the newspaper collection of the Bancroft Library, University of California, Berkeley.

73. Jerry MacMullen, "Selim Woodworth: A Heel or Hero?" *San Diego Union*, September 3, 1961.

74. Couts to Emory, January 1, 1851, Emory Papers, San Diego Historical Society.

75. Joseph Lancaster Brent, *Memoirs of the War between the States* (New Orleans: Fontana Printing Co., 1940), 5–7. Brent knew both Magruder and Dummer well. He occasionally rep-

but he and Dummer were a superb match on the social circuit. They were both typical hail-fellows-well-met, who knew no strangers. They were perfect boon companions, and they loved the high life.

Magruder's problem was that he was stationed in San Diego, which was "as dead as a door nail." Los Angeles was much more to his liking.[76] It was the social center of southern California and also a haven for deserters. To join Dummer there, Magruder convinced departmental headquarters of the necessity of stationing an officer and three of his men in the city to apprehend deserters.[77] Then, when Magruder's frequent "official" visits brought him up from San Diego to check on his detached men, he and Dummer began a new round of reminiscing, reveling, and carousing, which made Los Angeles howl. Major Horace Bell wrote that whenever Magruder "honored our pueblo with a visit he certainly livened things up, even here where they were already very lively." Bell also noted that his city lacked a "first class drinking place." So there, in the City of Angels, John Magruder and Samuel Dummer decided to open "a respectable saloon for the gentility . . . where two gentlemen could get on a bust in a grand manner."[78]

First they bought a lot on Main Street, adjoining the present Pico House on the south, and when the building materials arrived from Maine, they constructed an oblong frame building with an attic, which the owners used as a sleeping room. The structure was weather boarded on the outside and lined on the inside with tongue-and-groove boards. It had a shingle roof and was altogether quite an imposing curiosity in the adobe town. When the building was completed, a large sign placed over the front entrance was inscribed EL DORADO.[79]

The owners found their finances depleted before they had acquired a stock of liquor and a billiard table. Don Able Stearns, perhaps the wealthiest of Los Angeles's citizenry, loaned Magruder five hundred dollars on a note bearing 5 percent interest compounded monthly. The anxious proprietors then purchased the needed items, hired a bartender, and opened for business in grand style. The festive, elegant El Dorado never lacked customers,

---

resented Magruder in legal matters and later would serve on his staff during the Peninsula Campaign in Virginia.

76. Bell, *On the Old West Coast,* 147.

77. Records of the Tenth Military Department, 1846–51, Letters Sent, November 28, 1850, National Archives.

78. Bell, *On the Old West Coast,* 147.

79. Ibid., 147–48.

and both Magruder and Dummer kept pace with their drinking patrons to ensure that all had a good time. The management often provided drinks on the house, and one reporter wrote that "the run on [the bar] was awful." The many drunkards so filled the sleeping room that Magruder was often forced to make his bed on top of the downstairs billiard table. But the good times lasted only until the original liquor stock ran out and the proprietors discovered that they could not meet the combined overhead and new liquor costs. Their hospitality had broken the business. Magruder and Dummer "agreed to separate and divide," each selling his interests to bartender John H. Hughes, nephew of Archbishop John Joseph Hughes of New York. But Hughes also failed. Subsequently, in 1853 he sold the property to the Reverend Adam Bland, who converted the El Dorado into a Methodist church. How ironic it was that the Magruder-Dummer project, which housed the first American saloon in Los Angeles, later also became the first American church in the city.[80] The revolutionary turn of events must have been revolting to Magruder, whose social proclivities placed him in a position of conflict with the precepts of religious austerity. He once spoke of the Puritans with "intense disgust" and referred to the first immigrants to Plymouth as "that pestiferous crew of the *Mayflower*."[81]

The principals in the El Dorado went their separate ways after their venture failed. Johnnie Hughes drifted off to San Francisco, then to Tucson. In 1857 he was killed in combat by hostile Mexicans in the wake of a failed attempt to rescue filibuster Henry A. Crabb. Samuel Dummer became a pioneer sheep raiser in Tulare but later returned to New York to assist his father in business, and John Magruder fell back on the defenses of his post.[82]

Magruder's official duties, including service on several court-martial trials, the pursuit of desperadoes, and official verification of land claims, often took him away from San Diego. In his absence the men of Company I occasionally became part of the general lawlessness that pervaded the southern California frontier in the post–Mexican War period. Once, after returning from temporary duty in Los Angeles, Magruder was forced to issue Order No. 15, calling upon the members of his command to stop killing the cattle of people living in the neighborhood.[83] Unfortunately, the raucous behavior was not confined

80. Ibid., 148–51.

81. Fremantle, *Fremantle Diary,* 27.

82. Bell, *On the Old West Coast,* 150–51, 321n; Brent, *Memoirs of the War between the States,* 6–7.

83. *San Diego Herald,* June 12, 1851.

to enlisted men alone. A grand jury report written by local merchant Lewis A. Franklin "deplored the prevalence of drunkenness, even among public officials." When Franklin questioned Magruder's public deportment, the two had a fistfight in the plaza that lasted fifteen minutes. The following day Lieutenant Cave Couts reported that Magruder had whaled Franklin all over the plaza with a stick. Since that time, wrote Couts, "Franklin has been running about trying to find a civil officer to sue him [but] not one is to be found."[84]

Shortly after the fracas with Franklin, Magruder had "a big falling out" with one of his junior officers. Lieutenant Daniel M. Beltzhoover had declared that his commanding officer was a liar and a thief. Beltzhoover charged specifically that Magruder was illegally using the army horses of Battery I for private purposes.[85] Immediately afterward, on March 31, 1851, Adjutant General Roger Jones ordered Battery I dismounted.[86] This time he would not be overruled by Zachary Taylor because Taylor had died several months earlier, on July 9, 1850. Jones also wrote to General Ethan A. Hitchcock, commander of the Pacific Division, San Francisco, that he had received an anonymous letter accusing Magruder of misusing the horses. General Jones said that he normally did not entertain anonymous communications, but owing to the service of the officer implicated, the situation merited an investigation.[87] Hitchcock subsequently uncovered no irregularities, and Beltzhoover was later transferred elsewhere, so that nothing ever came of the charges. Nevertheless, Jones's letter indicates that he was still at odds with Magruder.

Beltzhoover also continued to be a nuisance. During the so-called Garra Insurrection, when rebellious Indians were raiding in southern California and then fleeing to safety across the border, he wrote anonymous letters to the *San Diego Herald* and to the commanding officer of the Southern District of the Army that Company I was without ammunition and was therefore utterly incapable of offering defense in case of further hostile attacks.[88] Two weeks later Magruder angrily replied in a letter to the *Herald* that his battery "was never more perfectly supplied with ammunition of all kinds . . . than at this moment; and being on the eve of departure to support Major Fitzgerald and his gallant volunteers, I invite the author of the above ungenerous com-

84. Pourade, *History of San Diego: The Silver Dons,* 186–87.

85. Couts to Emory, March 1, 1851, Emory Papers, San Diego Historical Society.

86. Haskin, *History of the First Regiment of Artillery,* 125.

87. Jones to Hitchcock, July 9, 1851, National Archives.

88. *San Diego Herald,* November 27 and December 11, 1851.

munication, to accompany me, in order to witness the efficiency [of the company when in action]."[89]

Beltzhoover apparently made his charge based on the situation before he had departed San Diego without checking to learn if conditions had remained unchanged since that time. In the meantime Magruder obtained ammunition from the infantry at San Diego, and the *Herald* later reported his company in pursuit of rebellious Indians.[90] Thus, Beltzhoover's allegations were disproved, and the disgruntled lieutenant never bothered Magruder again.

Daniel Beltzhoover's complaints irritated Magruder, but they did not force any changes in the way that he did things. When he returned from the Indian chase, Magruder revitalized himself with a round of drinks and then immediately moved on to the next escapade.[91] He had an enormous variety of interests. He loved adventure, and he refused to be bored. On March 6, 1852, Magruder and fourteen others, half of whom were fellow officers, signed on as charter members of the Pacific Pioneer Yacht Club. Major Justus McKinstry was president, and J. Judson Ames was first vice president. Ames was also editor of the *San Diego Herald*. He publicized well the club's first regatta to be held on April 7, followed by a catered dinner and dancing to music furnished by Señor Leandro del Sarto's quadrille band. On race day the entire town turned out to witness the twenty-two-mile contest involving fifteen vessels ranging from five to thirty tons. Magruder captained the nine-ton sloop *Contreras,* named for the battle in Mexico that contributed significantly to his military reputation. Ed Scott, who authored *San Diego County: Soldier-Pioneers, 1846–1866,* speculated that "'Prince John' would have been decked out in the latest style a gentleman wore while yachting in 1852." Style and appearance notwithstanding, Magruder placed out of the money behind lighthouse keeper Captain J. P. Keating's victorious *Platus,* Judson Ames's second-place *Livinia,* and Captain William Oliver in the *Fanny.*[92] The top finishers were all the larger, two-master schooners, which enjoyed a considerable sailing advantage over the smaller, single-masted sloops, including the

89. *San Diego Herald,* December 11, 1851.

90. Ibid., January 10, 1852.

91. Heintzelman Diary, February 8, 1852. Heintzelman reported, "Colonel Magruder is drunk in Old Town." This is one of the two instances in which Heintzelman reported Magruder as having overimbibed; the first was eighteen months earlier, on August 29, 1850, when Magruder and his men celebrated their arrival in San Diego.

92. Scott, *San Diego County: Soldier-Pioneers,* 63–68.

Contreras. Odds are that Magruder regained the advantage at the dinner and dance that climaxed the regatta festivities.

While Prince John Magruder sailed and socialized, Adjutant General Roger Jones simmered. Convinced that there was substance to the charges that Lieutenant Beltzhoover had made earlier, General Jones sent Colonel George A. McCall to inspect the military facilities at San Diego. After a thorough inspection, however, McCall found no irregularities or deficiencies. In his June 3, 1852, report the colonel stated that the weapons were in excellent condition and Magruder's men were well instructed and skilled in using them. He praised the noncommissioned officers for their personal appearance, writing that they also "perform their duties with promptitude and precision, and in all respects give evidence of a very good state of discipline." The officers, he reported, likewise performed their duties "in a very satisfactory manner." Colonel McCall concluded by declaring that "the present state of discipline and instruction of the Company show that the commanding officer has been attentive to his duties."[93]

These findings ran counter to all of the perceptions that Roger Jones held relating to John Bankhead Magruder. Jones, however, may well have never read the report, as he died on July 15, 1852. To the very end he viewed Magruder as an unconventional player in a profession that demanded strict adherence to uniformity. Although Magruder never let his off-duty escapades interfere with his military responsibilities, Jones simply could not fathom how one could be simultaneously such a maverick in private life and a professional in military service. Magruder was an anomaly that Jones and few others understood. Consequently, his talents and service, for the most part, have never been fully acknowledged.

During the time that Colonel McCall was in San Diego conducting his inspection, John R. Bartlett, American commissioner for the international survey between the United States and Mexico, was delayed in San Diego for want of a carpenter and blacksmith to repair his wagons and shoe his horses. Magruder supplied both, enabling Bartlett to depart the post on May 26, 1852, with his escort, Brevet Lieutenant Colonel Lewis S. Craig, to complete the survey.[94] On June 6, 1852, during the eastward march across the southern

93. Robert W. Frazer, "Military Posts in San Diego, 1852," *Journal of San Diego History* 20 (Summer 1974): 44–52. Frazer's article contains the full text of George McCall's report.

94. Bartlett, *Personal Narrative*, 2:107, 111. In his report Bartlett wrote the following note of appreciation: "Before leaving California, I take occasion to acknowledge the favors rendered to the Boundary Commission by the officers of the United States Army in California . . . to Colonel

California desert, Craig was murdered by deserters near Sackett's Wells, east of Carrizo Springs. Magruder immediately alerted military units and cooperative Indian tribes in the area. Within a short time the murderers, Corporal William Hayes and Private John Condon, were captured by Indians near Temecula and returned, bound hand and foot, to San Diego for court-martial.[95] Magruder personally presided over the lengthy trial, which ultimately found the defendants guilty under penalty of death by hanging. President Fillmore approved the court's actions, and the execution was scheduled to take place on January 31, 1853. When the appointed day arrived, Magruder required his troops to be present, along with several alcaldes and Indian chiefs who had helped apprehend the murderers, to witness "the efficacy of our laws." At high noon Condon and Hayes were hanged. It was the first military execution by hanging in time of peace that had occurred in the army.[96]

During one of the court recesses in the Craig murder case several of the leading citizens of Los Angeles feted Magruder with a dinner at Harry Monroe's restaurant, where, reportedly, the "wine flowed as wine had never flowed before." In the course of the evening's conversation the subject of great men came up for discussion. One of the guests declared that Henry Clay was the greatest American statesman. Another stated that Daniel Webster was, but Magruder declared that "Old Hickory Jackson was the greatest man who ever trod shoe-leather." At that moment Dr. William Osborn blurted out, "My father who was the sheriff of Cayuga County, New York, was the greatest of all Americans." Magruder indignantly declared that the doctor was "a damned fool." A challenge was issued and accepted. The matter was to be settled at once, in the ten-by-twenty-foot dining room, with derringers. Wilson Jones, Osborn's second, issued instructions, and the principals took their respective stations without shaking hands. The word was to be "Ready, fire, one, two, three." At the word *ready*, to the utter dismay of all present, the doctor blazed away. When the smoke cleared, the unscathed but furious Magruder glared directly at his opponent for a full minute, while all the spectators, including Osborn, shuddered at the thought of what was to come. He then

---

J. Bankhead Magruder, commanding at San Diego. To this gentleman in particular, both personally and on behalf of the government, I feel under the deepest obligation . . . he was of great service to me and the commission, both during our stay in the country, and while preparing for the journey before us."

95. Pourade, *History of San Diego: The Silver Dons*, 187–88.

96. Magruder to adjutant general of the Department of the Pacific at San Francisco, February 1, 1853, National Archives; *New York Illustrated News*, April 2, 1853.

leveled his derringer directly at the doctor's head and advanced toward him. The grim expression on Magruder's face reflected his extreme anger. His victim was white with fear. As Magruder drew closer, Osborn dashed underneath the main table, scurried toward Magruder, grabbed his knees, and screamed for mercy, "Colonel Magruder, for the love of God, spare me for my family." Magruder pushed him aside, kicked him in the rear, and shouted: "Damn you! I'll spare you for the hangman." He then returned his unused weapon to his second. The duel could not possibly have resulted in loss of life, for both derringers had been loaded with powder and bottle corks.[97]

In February or March 1853 Magruder may have been involved in a similar duel. His opponent this time was reportedly George P. "Two-Bits" Tebbetts, the proprietor of the Exchange Hotel in San Diego. As both duelists were Masons, all who looked on viewed the incident as an open scandal. Accordingly, one of the seconds secretly loaded the pistols with bullets molded of tallow mixed with charcoal. Magruder and Tebbetts were then given their weapons and instructions and took their positions. On the appointed command both fired. Tebbetts fell to the ground stunned and scared but uninjured, for the bullet had splattered harmlessly against his forehead. Magruder became so enraged that he threatened to shoot both seconds.[98] Because this duel was reported by Lieutenant George Derby, also known as John Phoenix, a notorious prankster, it is difficult to ascertain whether the duel is fact or fiction.

97. Horace Bell, *Reminiscences of a Ranger: or, Early Times in Southern California* (Los Angeles: Yarnell, Caystile, and Mathis, 1881), 64–66; Milota, "John Bankhead Magruder: The California Years," 68–70. William Osborn was formerly hospital steward of the New York (Stevenson's) Regiment. He took his discharge in California after the War with Mexico and became the first American pharmacist in Los Angeles.

98. George R. Stewart, *John Phoenix, Esq., the Veritable Squibob,* 101–2. John Magruder came by dueling naturally. His father, Thomas Magruder, was involved in a duel with Richard Buckner Jr. of Port Royal, Va. The Fredericksburg *Virginia Herald* reported on January 13, 1797, that the elder Magruder had sent for dueling pistols from Smith's Mount, a plantation a few miles from Port Royal. The duel, however, was fought "on the other side of the river Potomak," in Maryland. After exchanging rounds, the combatants apparently reconsidered their positions, as the *Herald* reported that their differences were "amicably settled." Years later, circa 1815, Magruder's uncle General James Bankhead fought a duel with Major Colin Buckner, Richard Buckner's cousin, in the front yard of Vauter's Church in Essex County, Va. There was "an exchange of one or two shots without physical effect," after which the men "retired satisfied." Undated article written by George Fitzhugh for *DeBow's Review* in the George H. S. King Papers, Virginia Historical Society, Richmond; Bishop William Meade, *Old Churches, Ministers and Families of Virginia,* 2 vols. (Baltimore: Genealogical Publishing Co., 1978), 1:404; Hayden, *Virginia Genealogies,* 448. Reverend Hayden's spelling reflects "Collin" Buckner and "Vawter's" Church.

Franklin Pierce, whom Magruder allegedly challenged to a duel during the Mexican War,[99] became the object of slanderous assaults while running for the presidency as the Democratic candidate in 1852. A charge of cowardice seems to have been instigated by Brevet Captain George McLane of the Mounted Rifles, who was a Scott supporter.[100] Magruder was a Scott supporter, too, but he stated that if Scott were not elected, the choice would go to "a deserving man" in Franklin Pierce. Magruder then refuted the charge of cowardice, praised Pierce for his leadership, and advised him to "pay no more attention to such slanders than to the bark of a cur."[101] He had now made amends with Pierce, who ironically won the presidency over the man Magruder had preferred to begin with.

In the spring of 1853, shortly after Pierce's election, a movement got under way to construct a rail line to be known as the Atlantic and Pacific Railroad, from San Diego eastward to Yuma along the 32nd parallel. Magruder was chosen president and prepared preliminary reports that were published in the *San Diego Herald* on May 21, 1853, and April 29, 1854.[102] The projected cost was thirty thousand dollars per mile, but an extended leave of absence in Europe forced Magruder to relinquish his position before construction began.

Not long after Magruder reached California, his wife took the three children to Europe in the hope of restoring the health of their oldest daughter, Isabella. They journeyed first to Paris, then to Bremen, Germany, to visit her father's home, and then to Florence, Italy, where Mrs. Magruder purchased a villa not far from the city. The change of climate, however, only worsened Isabella's condition.[103] Accordingly, on May 31, 1852, Magruder applied for a six-month leave of absence to visit his family.[104] When he received no response from the Adjutant-General's Office, his brother Allan B. Magruder, a practicing attorney in Washington, D.C., interceded on his behalf, writing Secretary of War Charles M. Conrad:

> It may not be known to the Department that after my brother left Baltimore, where he had been permanently stationed, for California, the health of his eldest daughter, about 17 years old, became so seriously impaired as to make

99. Hill, "Real Stonewall Jackson," 624.

100. Magruder to Sweeny, November 11, 1852, in the *New York Sun,* December 10, 1941.

101. Magruder to Pierce, August 14, 1852, Manuscript Division, Library of Congress.

102. *San Diego Herald,* May 21, 1853, and April 29, 1854; Smythe, *History of San Diego,* 352.

103. Allan B. Magruder to Conrad, August 7, 1852, National Archives; Magruder to Pierce, August 14, 1852, Manuscript Division, Library of Congress.

104. Magruder to Jones, May 31, 1852, National Archives.

an immediate sea voyage indispensable on the opinion of her physician, to her recovery . . . Mrs. Magruder, with the consent of her husband, sailed for Europe and has for some two years past, sought to repair the shattered health of her daughter having traveled on the continent with her and spent the past winter in Sicily and Italy. By the last accounts received, Mrs. Magruder and family were in Rome where her invalid daughter had been confined by violent inflammation of the lungs and unable for three months to leave her room. Mrs. Magruder's own health is suffering meanwhile, as she writes. She has no parents living or other relatives who can go to assist her. Under these circumstances, my brother whose distant station in California has hindered his receiving early and regular advises from his family, is naturally and laudably most anxious to obtain a leave of six months.[105]

Conrad replied to Allan Magruder on September 11, 1852, assuring him that "under the peculiar circumstances of the case orders will be at once given to the commanding officer, Pacific Division, to grant him [John B. Magruder] leave of absence and the Department will give him permission specially required to enable him to leave the United States and join his family in Europe."[106] General Orders No. 145 granted the leave, but because of the delay in communications and the remoteness of the post, it did not reach San Diego until early 1853. By then Magruder was involved with organizing the Atlantic and Pacific Railroad and several courts-martial so that he could not leave immediately. It was, in fact, March 28, 1853, before he officially relinquished his command to Captain Henry S. Burton.[107] Magruder then traveled by ship to New York via Panama, arriving aboard the *Georgia* on July 29, just in time to attend the Grand Military Banquet at the Astor House. Upon entering the room, Magruder was immediately called upon to address the assemblage. Prince John informed the revelers that, as he had just arrived from California, he was hardly free enough from saltwater to make a very interesting oration. He nevertheless took the stand and spoke eloquently on behalf of education, unification, and the gallantry of the volunteer soldier. At the conclusion of the address the crowd cheered wildly.[108]

After leaving New York, Magruder went to Washington to straighten out his accounts with the Auditor's Office because all of his personal and

105. Allan B. Magruder to Conrad, August 7, 1852, National Archives.

106. Conrad to Allan B. Magruder, September 11, 1852, National Archives.

107. Special Orders No. 54, March 28, 1853, noted in the returns from San Diego Barracks for May 1853, National Archives.

108. *San Diego Herald,* October 7, 1853.

public papers had been destroyed in the 1850 fire at the Pacific Mail Steamship Company office in San Francisco.[109] He finally closed out his accounts on January 4, 1854,[110] and left for Europe shortly thereafter. Upon reaching Florence, he found his wife, Henrietta, and daughter Isabella in a much improved condition, enabling the entire family to tour Europe by easy stages. In Paris Magruder met French general François-Achille Bazaine and discussed the Crimean situation with him. Magruder had not been sent abroad in any official capacity, but he had long been interested the military advancements of the European powers. The observations made and interviews conducted were effected entirely on his own.

Magruder returned from Europe in September 1854, accompanied by Henrietta and their two youngest children, Isabella having eloped to Leghorn, Italy, where she married Dr. Riggin Buckler. Shortly after arriving in Baltimore, Magruder learned that Company I had left San Diego for Texas as escort of the International Boundary Commission, which was surveying the newly established border between the United States and Mexico. Although Magruder's leave had expired on November 4, 1854,[111] he remained with his wife at her home while awaiting instructions from the War Department. Magruder had numerous conversations and exchanges of letters with Secretary of War Jefferson Davis and Samuel Cooper, who had succeeded Roger Jones as adjutant general of the army, in an effort to ascertain the location of his men. Both Davis and Cooper expressed concern that Magruder's leave had expired without his having returned to duty.[112] On the other hand, because his men had departed California before he could rejoin them, Magruder had no choice but to wait until they reached Texas before setting out to find them. Finally, in March 1855, upon learning that Company I had arrived in El Paso,[113] Magruder bade his family farewell and departed Baltimore for duty. Several months later, in September, Mrs. Magruder returned to Europe with Kate Elizabeth and Henry and would not see her husband again for five years.[114]

109. Magruder to Thompson (Auditor's Office), January 18, 1853, National Archives.

110. Magruder to Cooper, January 4, 1854, National Archives.

111. Magruder to Cooper, February 23, 1855, National Archives.

112. Ibid., Endorsements by Jefferson Davis, February 28, 1855, and by Samuel Cooper, February 26, 1855; Cooper to Magruder, December 4, 1854; Cooper to Magruder, February 21, 1855, National Archives.

113. Magruder to Cooper, March 5, 1855, National Archives.

114. Magruder to Cooper, August 20, 1855, National Archives.

Magruder's trip west through Texas took him first to San Antonio, then to Fort Clark, on Las Moras Creek just opposite the town of Brackettville. On May 9 he reported that he was 110 miles west of Fort Clark on his way to Fort Bliss, near the far western tip of Texas.[115] By the time he reached the fort, however, he learned that his men had just left, resuming their survey work under the direction of Lieutenant Nathaniel Michler. On August 8, 1855, Major William H. Emory, the U.S.-Mexican boundary commissioner, arrived with his entourage and intelligence that Company I probably would not return to Fort Bliss until the end of September.[116] This frustrating sequence of events caused Magruder to complain to Adjutant General Cooper that his men had been on severe duty almost continuously for six years. He pointed out that "the larger portion of the company has been in tents and engaged in expeditions against Indians or on escort duty across the most perfect desert on the American continent . . . while the other mounted companies of our regiment have been in garrison on the Atlantic seaboard continuously ever since the termination of the Mexican War."[117] He also declared, "I am one of the oldest captains in the regiment . . . I think after 29 years of military service . . . I might reasonably expect the command of a post."[118] Six weeks later, in another letter to Colonel Cooper, Magruder reiterated that he and his men had been assigned extended duty "in the most uninhabited regions of the continent," and he therefore requested a transfer east.[119] Instead, Magruder and his men were ordered to Fort Clark to continue escorting the boundary survey team.[120]

Magruder's primary mission was procuring mules and supplies for the commissioners and protecting them from hostile Indians. On December 8, 1855, he wrote to the Adjutant General's Office requesting that Company I be remounted and equipped with two mountain howitzers to be drawn by two mules each, upon which the necessary munitions would also be packed. The lighter mountain howitzers would be more mobile and therefore, according to Magruder, more useful against the Indians of Texas than heavier, larger-caliber field guns. By furnishing the men with cavalry equipment, they would become much better riders. Furthermore, at a moment's notice

115. Magruder to Cooper, March 5, 1855; Magruder to Cooper, May 9, 1855, National Archives.

116. Magruder to Cooper, August 8, 1855, National Archives.

117. Magruder to Cooper, August 22, 1855, National Archives.

118. Magruder to Cooper, August 20, 1855, National Archives.

119. Magruder to Cooper, December 8, 1855, National Archives.

120. Cullum, *Biographical Register*, 1:368.

one-half to two-thirds of the company could be detached on horseback in pursuit of Indians, accompanied by the mountain howitzers. If the Indians fled to mountains or broken country that was inaccessible to the horses, the men would dismount. Some of them would be detailed to guard the horses and howitzers, while the majority of the detachment would pursue the Indians on foot.[121] Magruder's request was both logical and sensible, and it was the fourth communiqué that he had sent to Samuel Cooper after Roger Jones died,[122] asking that his company be remounted. The result was no better with Cooper, however, than it had been with Jones. On February 27, 1856, Colonel Cooper rejected Magruder's request.[123]

The frustrations of dealing with the Adjutant General's Office forced Magruder to redirect his efforts toward affairs more societal in nature. Even in the remote Texas badlands Prince John found time for entertainment. On one occasion Lydia Lane, the young wife of Lieutenant William B. Lane, recalled a dinner that Magruder hosted at Fort Clark. The affair, she reported, "was of necessity as plain as it could be; but it was served in courses and in grand style. John was always magnificent."[124]

Magruder always kept one eye on society, but as the decade of the 1850s wore on and sectional tensions became increasingly more strained, he was forced to focus the other on politics. He was particularly concerned about the rise of the Know-Nothing Party and the failure of the Whigs to compromise on the important slavery and states' rights issues. On January 24, 1856, he wrote to James Lyons, a friend and prominent lawyer and politician in Richmond, declaring that the time had come for "every union man throughout the country to show his 'flag' and to be prepared to make all the sacrifices its honor and security demanded."[125] Magruder added, "I had been a Whig—a conscientious whig—but for many years past I had become satisfied that on the great issue between the whig and democratic parties the whigs were in error." Ultimately, he concluded that "no other except the democratic party

121. Magruder to Cooper, December 8, 1855, National Archives.

122. On April 24 and August 12, 1853, and March 5 and December 8, 1855, Magruder sent official communiqués to Cooper requesting that Company I be remounted. All of the letters from Magruder to Cooper cited here are in the National Archives.

123. Cooper to Magruder, February 27, 1856, National Archives.

124. Lydia Spencer Lane, *I Married a Soldier; or, Old Days in the Old Army* (Philadelphia: J. B. Lippincott, 1893), 85.

125. Magruder to James Lyons, January 24, 1856, in a pamphlet, *Presidential Contest of 1856, in Three Letters by Col. J. Bankhead Magruder of the United States Army* (San Antonio: Printed by the *San Antonio Texan*, 1856), 3.

could save the country, and [therefore] I became a Democrat in name as I had been for years in principle."[126] Magruder accordingly endorsed James Buchanan for the presidency. He mentioned his experience and skill as a diplomat and added hopefully, "God grant that the time may come when we may with truth hail him as the Savior of the Union."[127]

Republican radicalism, on the other hand, alarmed Magruder, and he was disappointed in their candidate, John C. Fremont, whom he had known in California. Magruder predicted that if elected, Fremont would "plunge his country into a civil war for the sake of that notoriety which he mistakes for glory. Vanity and self-conceit, the handmaids of ignorance, have ever waited upon his steps, and will always guide his actions."[128] In summary, wrote Magruder, "the success of the Democratic party is the safety of the Union."[129] If, however, the "agitators of the North" prevailed, Magruder grimly predicted the dissolution of the Union, "for no sane man believes the South will ever part with its slave[s] at the bidding of the North, or that there is a Southerner who will not sacrifice his life . . . in the defense of his property, guaranteed to him by the Constitution of the United States."[130]

Magruder's family had owned a small number of slaves in Caroline County while young John was growing up in Port Royal.[131] Later he occasionally employed servants when hosting special social events, but there are no records to indicate that he ever owned any slaves of his own. And while the majority of southerners likewise were non–slave owners, all were keenly aware that the Constitution guaranteed them the right of ownership. Magruder and his fellow southerners believed that abolitionist attacks upon the institution were thus tantamount to attacks on the Constitution, which in turn threatened the Union itself. He did not believe in nullification as a remedy for southern political problems. Yet "when all constitutional remedies shall have failed and the general government find[s] itself unable to protect the constitutional rights of the South," declared Magruder, "then revolution becomes the rightful remedy."[132]

126. Magruder to Lyons, August 25, 1856, ibid., 6.

127. Ibid., 9.

128. Magruder to Paschal et al., September 18, 1856, ibid., 10.

129. Magruder to Lyons, August 25, 1856, ibid., 6.

130. Magruder to Lyons, January 24, 1856, ibid., 3.

131. Report of the U.S. Census Bureau, 1810, for Caroline County, Va.; Caroline County Personal Property Tax Lists, 1794–1811, Library of Virginia, Archives Division, Richmond.

132. Magruder to Lyons, January 24, 1856, *Presidential Contest of 1856*, 3.

On February 14, 1856, Judge Lyons sent Magruder's first letter to the editor of the *Richmond Enquirer* and asked that it be published.[133] Magruder wrote again on August 25, amplifying and extending the arguments set forth in his original letter.[134] Less than a month later a group of prominent San Antonio citizens headed by I. A. Paschal and Samuel A. Maverick wrote to Magruder, asking for copies of his two letters, as well as "a full expression of your views upon the subject of the approaching Presidential election," for publication.[135] Magruder, who was then in San Antonio, immediately complied with their requests, giving them full authority to publish his correspondence.[136] Shortly thereafter, the two letters to Judge Lyons and a September 18, 1856, letter to Paschal and his group were published in a campaign pamphlet, with a one and a half page introduction by Magruder.

James Buchanan eventually won the 1856 election about the same time the boundary commission completed its work. While Buchanan began preliminarily organizing his administration, Company I moved from Texas to temporary assignment at Baton Rouge, Louisiana. It remained there for only a few months during the winter of 1856–57, when Magruder received notification of his appointment as commanding officer of Fort Adams near Newport, Rhode Island.[137] The new assignment delighted Magruder, as did Buchanan's victory. Prince John timed his travel northward to his new post so that he was in Washington on Inauguration Day, March 4, 1857. That evening he was one of over six hundred people who attended the inaugural ball. As there was no building in Washington sufficiently large to handle such a crowd, the ball was held in a temporary annex to City Hall. The interior walls of the makeshift structure were colorfully decorated with numerous national flags, and the ceiling was covered with white cloth dotted with gold stars that twinkled when reflecting light from the large gas chandeliers. President Buchanan arrived about eleven o'clock, accompanied by his niece, Miss Harriet Lane. Journalist Ben Perley Poore reported that Magruder received Buchanan at the end of what must have been an extremely long day of near nonstop activities for the sixty-five-year-old bachelor president. Perley Poore

133. Lyons to the editors of the *Richmond Enquirer,* February 14, 1856, ibid., 3.
134. Magruder to Lyons, August 25, 1856, ibid., 6–9.
135. Paschal et al. to Magruder, September 18, 1856, ibid., 2.
136. Magruder to Paschal et al., September 18, 1856, ibid., 2–3.
137. Cullum, *Biographical Register,* 1:368.

also noted that the usually verbose Magruder was discreet enough to spare Buchanan "the infliction of a speech."[138]

John Magruder had met James Buchanan in London in 1854 when Buchanan was serving as minister to Great Britain. They were among two hundred guests at a dinner given for Lord Elgin by the members of the British cabinet. Magruder observed that Buchanan was "frank, earnest and patriotic." He further declared that "nothing could exceed the delicacy with which he acknowledged the compliments bestowed upon his country and himself during the evening."[139] These remarks indicate that Buchanan favorably impressed Magruder, and apparently the sentiment was mutual. When Queen Victoria's son, Albert Edward, the prince of Wales, visited the United States in October 1860, President Buchanan personally selected Magruder, then serving on garrison duty in Washington, D.C.,[140] to be the aide for his honored guest, who would later become Edward VII.[141] Prince John seemed to be perfectly at ease with his more royally legitimate counterpart, even inviting the eighteen-year-old English prince to hunt buffalo on the Great Plains. Because of time constraints, however, the invitation was declined. In just thirty days the royal tour covered nearly three thousand miles. When completed, the duke of Newcastle, secretary of state for the colonies and Albert Edwards's mentor on the tour, said the trip "had done more to cement the good feeling between the two countries than could possibly have been effected by a quarter of a century of diplomacy."[142]

Meanwhile, following Buchanan's inauguration, Magruder made his way to Rhode Island, arriving at Fort Adams on May 29, 1857. On the same day Company I was remounted as a light artillery battery, after serving for over six years as foot artillery.[143] Magruder's morale rebounded, and his energy

138. Ben Perley Poore, *Perley's Reminiscences of Sixty Years in the National Metropolis,* 2 vols. (Philadelphia: Hubbard Bros., 1886), 1:515–16.

139. Magruder to Lyons, August 25, 1856, *Presidential Contest of 1856,* 9.

140. Cullum, *Biographical Register,* 1:368.

141. Elizabeth Lindsay Lomax, *Leaves from an Old Washington Diary, 1854–1863,* ed. Lindsay Lomax Wood (New York: E. P. Dutton, 1943), 130.

142. Fred Harrington, "A Royal Tour," *South Atlantic Quarterly* 38 (July 1939): 337–39. When the Royal Tour was at Mount Vernon, artist Thomas P. Rossiter commemorated the occasion by illustrating and then painting the group of visitors at Washington's Tomb. The painting is on display at the Museum of American Art at the Smithsonian Institution in Washington, D.C.

143. Haskin, *History of the First Regiment of Artillery,* 129.

level soared. Furthermore, at Fort Adams he found the type of social life that best suited his cultural tastes. It was reported that he fared "sumptuously every day," and he immediately surged to the head of Newport society, sparing neither pains nor expense in his pursuit of festive splendor. While entertaining guests, he employed some of the soldiers of his command as servants,[144] while others presented themselves in "dress parade, with full trappings and gold braid pomp, and this he would follow with a flawless dinner."[145] It was vintage Prince John.

In March 1858 Magruder went to Washington on a temporary assignment with Lieutenant Colonel Joseph E. Johnston and Major Nathaniel C. Macrae to a board examining knapsacks and army canteens, but he did not let his duties interfere with his social affairs. After attending early services at St. John's Church on March 28, he joined several close friends for "a delightful breakfast" at the home of recently widowed Mrs. Elizabeth Lindsay Lomax. On the following day Mrs. Lomax recorded in her diary: "I must confess I was surprised to find John Bankhead Magruder at early service. I think him a very clever man, a fine soldier, but not religious—but Who knows."[146]

On the evening of the twenty-eighth Magruder attended Lady Owsley's ball and a musical hosted by Lady Napier, the wife of the British ambassador.[147] The highlight of Washington's social season, however, was the Gwin Fancy Dress Ball hosted by California senator William Gwin and his wife on April 8. The most prominent names in Washington society—leading politicians, foreign dignitaries, and a select group of high-ranking military officers—attended the gala. The guests wore every conceivable type of costume as each tried to surpass the other in display. But it was Prince John who became the center of attention when he arrived ostentatiously dressed as the king of Prussia.[148]

The merrymaking ended when Magruder received Special Order No. 231, dated November 26, 1859, transferring him to Fort Leavenworth.[149] He found

---

144. Gouverneur, *As I Remember*, 211.

145. Freeman, *Lee's Lieutenants*, 1:15. On October 3, 1857, Magruder wrote to a friend, F. Markoe, in Washington that "we have had a charming season." Magruder to Markoe, October 3, 1857, New York Public Library.

146. Lomax, *Leaves from an Old Washington Diary*, 83.

147. *Harper's Weekly*, March 20, 1858, 82; Mrs. E. P. Ellett, *Court Circles of the Republic* (Philadelphia: Philadelphia Publishing Co., n.d.), 492 fn, 495–96.

148. *Harper's Weekly*, April 24, 1858, 262; *New York Times*, April 12 and 13 and June 14, 1858.

149. Special Orders No. 231, November 26, 1859, National Archives.

Kansas winters extremely cold and the summers oppressively hot, and on April 16, 1860, he wrote to Adjutant General Samuel Cooper directing his attention to the problem of proper dress. As a consequence of the great heat, Magruder recommended the adoption of straw hats and white pantaloons as a part of the official uniform to be worn from June through September. He also suggested the adoption of a round jacket trimmed with scarlet and decorated with Russian shoulder knots, for all duties except formal reviews and inspections, when the standard frock coat with epaulets would be worn. Magruder pointed out that his officers were mounted a great deal of the time and the epaulets were expensive and fragile and lasted for only a short time before they had to be replaced.[150] Secretary of War John B. Floyd rejected the suggestion regarding straw hats and white pantaloons but declared round jackets of dark blue cloth, trimmed with scarlet and decorated with the Russian shoulder knot, to be adopted.[151]

Magruder's joint assignment as commander of both the post and the Artillery School for Instruction at Fort Leavenworth was an important one. Since the Mexican War he had been recognized as one of the leading artillerists in the army.[152] Even Douglas Southall Freeman, who was no great admirer of Magruder, admitted that "he knew his ranges as thoroughly as his vintages."[153] Magruder's plan for organizing the batteries of light artillery into a battalion and other studies relative to light artillery maneuvers reflected his foresight and technical skill. He was pragmatic enough to recommend the use of mountain howitzers in place of heavier field guns when campaigning against Indians and six-pounders rather than twelve-pounders to maximize speed and maneuverability on the battlefield against more conventional opponents.[154] Magruder was also aware of the need to keep abreast

150. Magruder to Cooper, April 16, 1860, National Archives.

151. Floyd endorsed Magruder's letter on July 16, 1860.

152. Lyons to the editors of the *Richmond Enquirer*, February 14, 1856, *Presidential Contest of 1856*, 3; Edward A. Pollard, *Lee and His Lieutenants: Comprising the Early Life, Public Services, and Campaigns of General Robert E. Lee and His Companions in Arms, with a Record of Their Campaigns and Heroic Deeds* (New York: E. B. Treat and Co., 1867), 840. Of Magruder, Pollard wrote: "In the Mexican War his services were historical and brilliant, and he was remarkable there for the splendid performance of his light artillery—an arm the value of which he illustrated in no less than nine battles . . . It was in the rapid and effective management of field-pieces, and the combinations with which they were applied to accomplish immediate and important results, that his genius shone and his brilliant courage was most strikingly manifested."

153. Freeman, *Lee's Lieutenants*, 1:15.

154. Magruder to Cooper, December 8, 1855, and December 21, 1859, National Archives.

of technological advances made by European armies. He volunteered to lead fact-finding missions abroad on July 18, 1848, and May 31, 1852, but to no avail. In April 1853, shortly after Franklin Pierce was inaugurated, Magruder twice applied for European duty through the Adjutant General's Office,[155] but he was turned down each time. Several months later, on December 3, 1853, he sent a long letter directly to Jefferson Davis, Pierce's secretary of war.[156] Davis acknowledged that "useful results might be obtained by a board of officers properly constituted and authorized to inquire into the organization, arms, and equipment of the armies of other countries."[157] Secretary Davis, however, rejected Magruder and then promptly sent others abroad in 1854 and again in 1855. On October 21, 1859, Magruder wrote the adjutant general that he would even pay his own way.[158] He added that he had "influential friends, both in the British and French armies, whose good offices, I am sure I can command, as I have done before. I feel satisfied that I am more fortunately situated for securing the necessary facilities, to accomplish the objects in view, than most officers in the army."[159]

But even this advantage failed to evoke a favorable response. Undeterred, Magruder tried again, a year later, on October 10, 1860. He authored a plan "that would permit satisfactory tactical maneuvers of artillery, infantry, and dragoons," again stressing the need to observe similar movements in European armies.[160] This time his superiors agreed, and the following day Secretary Floyd sent Magruder orders to "proceed without delay to Europe to accomplish the objects of your letter to the Adjutant General."[161]

After turning over all government property under his charge, Magruder sailed for Europe, arriving in Paris on November 24, 1860.[162] There he visited briefly with Philip Kearny, an old friend from the Mexican War who had resigned his commission in 1851.[163] Magruder may also have talked with Bazaine, whom he had met during his first trip to Europe, but he did not remain in Paris long. On December 1 he informed Cooper that he was jour-

155. Magruder to Cooper, April 2 and 7, 1853, National Archives.

156. Magruder to Davis, December 15, 1853, National Archives.

157. Davis to Magruder, December 22, 1853, National Archives.

158. Magruder to Cooper, October 21, 1859, National Archives.

159. Magruder to Cooper, November 1859, National Archives.

160. Magruder to Cooper, October 10, 1860, National Archives.

161. Floyd to Magruder, October 11, 1860, National Archives.

162. Magruder to Cooper, December 1, 1860, National Archives.

163. Thomas Kearny, *General Philip Kearny: Battle Soldier of Five Wars* (New York: G. P. Putnam's Sons, 1937), 164, 311.

neying to Naples,[164] which had been taken by Giuseppe Garibaldi in the fight for the reunification of Italy in the name of King Victor Emmanuel II. It is not known whether Magruder was received by either Garibaldi or by Victor Emmanuel, but he no doubt met and exchanged views with his friend Roberdeau Wheat, who had volunteered his services to Garibaldi.[165] From Naples Magruder traveled to Florence to visit his wife and youngest children, whom he had not seen for five years. The family visited Genoa in January 1861, and planned to travel to Berlin, Vienna, and St. Petersburg,[166] but upon returning to Florence, Magruder received a communiqué from Winfield Scott ordering him "to return home immediately and report for duty."[167]

When John Magruder arrived in Washington about March 10, 1861,[168] he found governmental affairs in turmoil and uncertainty. During the brief period of his absence seven of the southern states had passed ordinances of secession, and everyone was talking of war. His older brother, Captain George A. Magruder, then chief of the Hydrographic Bureau, was awaiting the action of his native Virginia. If his state seceded, he planned to resign his commission, but he had no intention of serving either the Union or the Confederacy. He would leave the country and await the outcome of the likely conflict.

Younger brother Allan Magruder, a highly respected Virginia Unionist who was a partner in the Washington, D.C., law firm of Chilton and Magruder, was called upon by President Lincoln on April 3, 1861, to bring a representative from the convention then in session in Richmond that was meeting to determine Virginia's relationship to the Union. The president explained that his object was to make an arrangement that would prevent Virginia from seceding.[169] After a hasty trip to Richmond, Allan Magruder returned to Washington with John B. Baldwin, who had been endorsed by the Virginia Convention and authorized to speak their sentiments. Lincoln urged Baldwin and his Unionist colleagues to adjourn the Virginia Convention sine die. Baldwin replied that such questionable tactics would be

164. Magruder to Cooper, December 1, 1860, National Archives.

165. Charles L. Dufour, *Gentle Tiger: The Gallant Life of Roberdeau Wheat* (Baton Rouge: Louisiana State University Press, 1957), 111–15.

166. *Army and Navy Journal* 7 (June 4, 1870): 660.

167. Magruder, "First Battle of the War: Big Bethel," in *Battles and Leaders of the Civil War,* 5:34.

168. Magruder to editor, *Philadelphia Evening Telegraph,* May 8, 1870, in the *New York Times,* May 23, 1870.

169. Allan B. Magruder, "A Piece of Secret History: President Lincoln and the Virginia Convention of 1861," *Atlantic Monthly* 35 (April 1875): 438–45.

unnecessary if Lincoln would promise that the federal government had no intention of coercing the cotton states.[170] The president would make no such promise, and on April 17, 1861, Virginia seceded.

For the next four days John Magruder agonized over the inevitable. He wrote in his memoirs that "the ties which connected me with the old army were dearer to me than anything on earth except those which bound me to my own family." Yet he also had an undying loyalty to Virginia, and because he could not fight against his own people, among whom he was born and raised,[171] he sadly and reluctantly resigned his commission on April 21, 1861.[172] In Prince John's own words, it was "the most unhappy moment of my life." He left Washington immediately thereafter and offered his services to authorities in Richmond.[173]

Several years after the close of the Civil War, Senator Simon Cameron of Pennsylvania made damaging accusations against Magruder regarding his conduct after he returned to the United States from Europe in March 1861. Cameron, in a speech to the Senate on April 5, 1870, recalled having heard Magruder tell President Lincoln "that he admired him and was going to stand by him during the war." According to Cameron, who was Lincoln's secretary of war at the time, Magruder's promise of fidelity was made the evening before he left for Virginia.[174] Magruder later dismissed the charges,

170. R. L. Dabney, "Memoir of a Narrative Received of Colonel John B. Baldwin, of Staunton, Touching the Origin of the War," *Southern Historical Society Papers* 1 (1876): 449.

171. Magruder, "First Battle of the War: Big Bethel," in *Battles and Leaders of the Civil War,* 5:35.

172. Magruder to Lorenzo Thomas, April 21, 1861, National Archives. The *Papers of Jefferson Davis* noted that Magruder resigned on April 21, 1861, but that "his letter to Samuel Cooper has not been found" (7:132). It is highly unlikely that any such letter ever existed. Cooper had resigned as adjutant general of the U.S. Army six weeks earlier, on March 7. As Magruder was stationed in Washington, D.C. (after returning from Europe on March 10), he most certainly would have been aware of Cooper's resignation and would not have sent his own letter of resignation to him. Instead, Magruder's April 21, 1861, letter was addressed to Cooper's successor, Lorenzo Thomas. Magruder's resignation was accepted on April 22, 1861. See Special Orders No. 114, National Archives.

173. Magruder, "First Battle of the War: Big Bethel," in *Battles and Leaders of the Civil War,* 5:35–36; *Calendar of Virginia State Papers,* 11 vols. (New York: Kraus Reprint Corp., 1968), 11:111. Magruder's letter to Governor Letcher, offering his services to Virginia, was written from Alexandria on April 22, 1861.

174. *Congressional Globe,* 41st Cong., 2d sess., 2420. On February 10, 1868, Cameron had made similar charges against General Robert E. Lee in another Senate speech, but the allegations were immediately denied by Senator Reverdy Johnson of Maryland and nothing more was heard of them.

declaring in a May 8, 1870, letter to the editor of the *Philadelphia Evening Telegraph* that he "never was with President Lincoln in the presence of Mr. Cameron in my life."[175] Shortly after Magruder refuted Cameron's charges, however, General Samuel D. Sturgis supported them.[176] But Sturgis could not have witnessed any conversation between Magruder and Lincoln that might have taken place in mid-April 1861 given that he did not arrive in Washington, D.C., until late May 1862,[177] thirteen months after Magruder had departed for service in Virginia. Furthermore, had Sturgis or Cameron been intimately acquainted with John Magruder, they would have realized the inconceivability of his standing against Virginia during the war. Indeed, over five years earlier, in letters that had been published and widely circulated, he had stated in no uncertain terms that if degenerating politics led to Virginia's seceding, "I should at once resign my commission in the army, return to my native county of Caroline . . . [and] labor in defense of the sacred rights of our honored State."[178]

Other similar accusations were the result of misidentification rather than malice. Author Burke Davis, in his biography of "Jeb" Stuart, reported that Magruder had asked President Lincoln to make him a brigadier general in the Union army, but when Lincoln refused, Magruder came south.[179] Davis cited a December 18, 1862, letter from Stuart to General Custis Lee.[180] He failed to notice, however, that Stuart identified Magruder as W. T., rather than J. B. Magruder. W. T. Magruder indeed attempted to secure a general's commission in the federal army in exchange for remaining loyal to the Union. Captain W. T. Magruder served for over a year in the Union army but resigned in October 1862. He then joined the Confederate army and was killed at Gettysburg while serving on the staff of General Joseph R. Davis,[181] then commanding a brigade in A. P. Hill's corps of the Army of Northern Virginia. Those who heard the story of this treasonable bargaining, including Margaret Leech, author of *Reveille in Washington,* incorrectly inferred that the Magruder im-

---

175. Magruder to editor, *Philadelphia Evening Telegraph,* May 8, 1870, in the *New York Times,* May 23, 1870.

176. Sturgis to editor, *Philadelphia Evening Telegraph,* June 12, 1870, in *Army and Navy Journal* 7 (June 1870): 660.

177. Cullum, *Biographical Register,* 2:160.

178. Magruder to Lyons, January 24, 1856, *Presidential Contest of 1856,* 5.

179. Burke Davis, *Jeb Stuart: The Last Cavalier* (New York: Rinehart and Co., 1957), 258.

180. Stuart to Custis Lee, December 18, 1862, Duke University Library, Durham, N.C.

181. Cullum, *Biographical Register,* 2: 260.

plicated was the well-known Virginian John Bankhead.[182] In actuality the culprit was the younger, less-known William T. Magruder of Maryland.

John Bankhead Magruder's relations with President Lincoln and the circumstances surrounding his resignation and departure from Washington were carefully recounted in his May 8, 1870, letter answering Cameron's charges:

> The day on which President Lincoln received the telegram from the Governor of Virginia, my native state, declining to send his quota of troops under the first proclamation, or the day after that, Mr. Lincoln sent for me and informed me of that fact. My state had not yet seceded. I informed him that I regretted deeply the course events had taken; that if my state seceded, I was a soldier, obliged to fight either for or against her, and that I would fight for those among whom I was born and bred, my relations and friends, all of whom believed they were right. I stated to him that I was a graduate of West Point, but that West Point was not a charity school; that it was supported as much by the southern people, in proportion to cadets from the South, as by the North in the same proportion; that the government had always recognized the right of officers to resign, unless they were officially charged with crime, and that the obligations to which an officer subscribed were simply to obey the lawful orders of his superiors so long as he held the commission of the government, and that every officer had this right to resign when he thought proper. Mr. Lincoln acquiesced in the propriety of these views. "But," I added, "Mr. President, I will be perfectly true and faithful to the obligations of my commission as long as I hold it, and you and your family will sleep in safety whenever I am on guard." "Yes," said he, "I know it, for you are an officer of the army and a Southern gentleman, and incapable of any but honorable conduct." I thanked him warmly and said: "Mr. President, if I do resign, you shall be the first to hear of it after my resignation is placed in the hands of the Adjutant, if I can reach you, and I will remain at least twelve hours in Washington after my resignation." "Why," said he, with some surprise, "should you do that?" "Mr. President," I replied, "I wish to be gracefully off with the old love before I am on with the new." "I am sorry to lose you," he said, with great animation, "but if you must go, I'll help you to be gracefully off with the old love," meaning, I supposed, that he would accept my resignation when the time came to offer it. A day or two after this my state seceded. I handed my resignation to Col. C. F. Smith, Commanding, about 8 or 9 o'clock A.M., and repaired at once to the White House. Failing to get admission, I asked a brother officer, who said he would certainly see the President that morning, to inform him

182. Margaret Leech, *Reveille in Washington, 1860–1865* (New York: Harper and Bros., 1941), 62.

that I had resigned, which I presume he did, took leave openly of my friends, and found myself at the Long Bridge, in a hack, just three minutes after 9 P.M., too late, the orders being not to lower the draw-bridge after 9. It was a bright moon-light night, and as I got out of the coach I found my own battery guarding the bridge. The men uncovered as I passed through them to see the Lieutenant in charge. I asked him if he would be kind enough to lower the draw-bridge for me, as I was all packed and ready and was only three minutes behind the time. He touched his hat and answered courteously, "Colonel, I will lower the draw-bridge, but I would do it with far greater pleasure if you were coming from Virginia instead of going to Virginia."

I departed, taking off my hat to my old comrades, some of whom I had commanded for thirty years, and with a sad heart bade them farewell.[183]

---

183. Magruder to editor, *Philadelphia Evening Telegraph,* May 8, 1870, in the *New York Times,* May 23, 1870. Magruder also recounted his conversation with President Lincoln in his memoirs. See Magruder, "First Battle of the War: Big Bethel," in *Battles and Leaders of the Civil War,* 5:34–36.

4

PROTECTING THE APPROACH
TO RICHMOND

In Richmond, immediately following the adoption of the ordinance of secession on April 17, 1861, Governor John Letcher and a council of three advisors—Colonel Francis H. Smith of the Virginia Military Institute; Captain Matthew Fontaine Maury, the famous oceanographer who had recently resigned his commission in the United States Navy; and John J. Allen, chief justice of the Virginia Court of Appeals—began searching for dependable military leadership. They made no distinction between old Democrats and Whigs and more recent conservatives and radicals. After each man had been judged "solely on his qualifications," the committee selected Robert E. Lee on April 21 to command the state's land and sea forces with the rank of major general.[1] Four days later Letcher approved the appointments of Joseph E. Johnston as major general of volunteers, Magruder as colonel, and Richard Stoddert Ewell and Henry Heth as lieutenant colonels.[2]

Lee and his fellow appointees were given the daunting task of protecting Virginia, the most populous state of the South and the fifth in the Union. Its borders extended from the Atlantic Ocean to the Big Sandy River, within 115 miles of Cincinnati. From east to west Virginia measured 425 miles in

1. F. N. Boney, *John Letcher of Virginia: The Story of Virginia's Civil War Governor* (Tuscaloosa: University of Alabama Press, 1966), 114–22; Proceedings of the Advisory Council of the State of Virginia, April 21, 1861, *Official Records*, ser. 1, vol. 51, pt. 2, 21; Proclamation of Governor John Letcher, April 23, 1861, ibid., 2:775.

2. Proceedings of the Advisory Council, April 25, 1861, *Official Records*, ser. 1, vol. 51, pt. 2, 35–36. Governor Letcher's Advisory Council was also called the Aulic Council, reminiscent of that which had once personally served the Holy Roman emperor.

width and 300 miles in length on a north-south axis from the panhandle to the North Carolina boundary. The highways of the state were numerous but all too often of poor quality. The railroads, which totaled 1,150 miles of track, included continuous linkage from Norfolk to Bristol, from Richmond to the Allegheny Mountains, from Alexandria to Lynchburg, from the Potomac River into North Carolina, and a number of shorter lines. Strategically, Virginia occupied the line of the Potomac and of the Ohio. It had strong, defensive mountains in the west but was exceedingly vulnerable to attack from the east, where the Rappahannock, York, and James rivers reached far into the interior of the state.[3]

This vulnerability was proved on April 21, when word flashed through Richmond that the Federal warship *Pawnee* was coming up the James River to bombard the capital. The tocsin rang out an alarm from the public square that struck fear into the hearts of all those within hearing distance. Governor Letcher "rallied all the troop units in the area to something vaguely resembling combat readiness," though they were woefully short of heavy artillery. Many were armed with handguns, shotguns, and hunting rifles. Fortunately for them, the *Pawnee* never appeared, but it left a psychological scar on the minds of Richmond's citizens, who were uneasy for weeks thereafter.[4]

John Magruder knew that there was similar apprehension and disorganization north of the Potomac; thus, he recognized an early opportunity for Virginia to take the offensive against Washington, D.C. Having just been in command of an artillery unit charged with the defense of the capital, he was intimately aware of the city's defensive strengths and limitations as well as the capabilities of the soldiers who constituted its guard. To Governor Letcher's Advisory Council, Magruder made a startling proposal: "Give me 5,000 men and if I do not take Washington, you may not only take my sword, but my life." When the council members sought General Lee's opinion, Magruder confidently and zealously repeated the offer to him, but Lee shook his head and said, "We have not the men."[5]

3. Freeman, *R. E. Lee*, 1:472–73.

4. John B. Jones, *A Rebel War Clerk's Diary*, ed. Earl Schenck Miers (New York: Sagamore Press, 1958), 10–11; Boney, *John Letcher of Virginia*, 117–18. Jones incorrectly reported the date of the *Pawnee* scare as April 27. Perhaps the error is attributable to his state of panic, though he courageously declared in his diary, "The *Pawnee* is about as likely to attempt the navigation of the River Styx, as to run up this river within shelling distance of the city."

5. Dunbar Rowland, ed., *Jefferson Davis, Constitutionalist: His Letters, Papers, and Speeches*, 10 vols. (Jackson: Mississippi Department of Archives and History, 1923), 8:216. Letter, James Lyons to W. T. Walthall, July 31, 1878.

Magruder did not let the matter die. He was so convinced of the feasibil-
ity of the plan that he proposed it to President Jefferson Davis in an April 26,
1861, letter that was both insightful and self-serving. Magruder reported that
he had been commissioned in the Virginia army after his resignation had
been accepted and that he had applied to Adjutant and Inspector General
Samuel Cooper for a commission in the regular army of the Confederate
states. More important, he also informed the president that while in Washington, D.C., just prior to departing for Virginia, he had ascertained the precise plan for the occupation and defense of the capital from a conversation
that he overheard between Lieutenant Frederick E. Prime of the Corps of
Engineers and Major John G. Barnard, who had just arrived in Washington
to assume his duties as chief engineer of the city's defenses. Magruder reported:

> The Garrison of Washington is to consist of 15,000 troops—with at least
> three batteries of Lt arty, which it is proposed to strengthen, to six guns each . . .
> of this garrison, about 1000 will be regular troops . . . The Falls above George-
> town the arsenal navy yard & public buildings, are to be strongly guarded . . .
> the long bridge to be protected on the Va. Side by a Tete de Pont & the heights
> of Arlington, to be fortified— . . .
>
> Baltimore, which has been so faithful & glorious a sentinel . . . has a
> southern Communication, open only with Virginia, via Harper's Ferry—by
> means of the B. & O.R. Road—This road however is at this moment entirely
> at the mercy of the Federal troops . . . At Harpers Ferry there are I learn 5000
> Virginians—5000 more could be added, & the /continued/ possession of the
> B & O.R.R. secured . . . [By controlling the railroad between Harpers Ferry
> and Baltimore,] Balto. would be secured, the line of operations of the enemy
> cut, or at least in our power, Washington threatened, Eastern virginia, by
> diversion, secured from invasion & a line of communication, from Balto to
> Va, kept open permanently—If we do not take that line, the Federal troops
> will, as soon as they feel themselves secure in Washington . . .
>
> Everything at this moment is in confusion here—& I have thought it best
> to communicate the above for your own information—

While the military intelligence in the letter was important, it is also undeniably
obvious that Magruder was angling for a high-ranking Confederate army
commission and presidential endorsement to take command at Harper's
Ferry to implement the plan he was proposing. The closing of the letter indeed suggests more than simple courtesy, "Hoping that your life and health,
which are so important to the safety and prosperity of our new republic may

long be preserved, I remain General . . . your friend and servant in haste—J Bankhead Magruder of Virginia."[6]

Ironically, Jefferson Davis may never have seen the letter. The original correspondence had no endorsement on it from Davis, and it was catalogued as correspondence "offering military services." Because Samuel Cooper, while serving as adjutant general of the U.S. Army, had never paid the slightest bit of attention to the unending stream of communiqués that he had received from Magruder in the 1850s, there is no reason to expect that he would have attached any more importance to subsequent letters regardless of subject matter. It was something Cooper had learned from his predecessor Roger Jones. If the source was Magruder, the missive was to be ignored. In all probability Magruder's April 26, 1861, letter to President Davis was no more than screened for the purpose of filing, as it ultimately met the same fate as the numerous other proposals that he had sent to the government in the post–Mexican War period—it died for want of approval. Many would have become sufficiently discouraged and given up. But Magruder absolutely believed in the worthiness of his various plans and proposals, and he had that tenacity of purpose for which his Scottish ancestors were famous. So he tried again and again. The result, however, was always the same.

Had the proposed move against Washington, D.C., been authorized, Magruder would have been well suited to lead it. He possessed a wealth of front-line experience, having fought earlier in almost every major engagement in the War with Mexico. Lessons learned in that conflict and in his studies of Continental warfare were not lost on this now fifty-four-year-old soldier-scholar, whom historian Stephen Sears described as a man of "shrewd intelligence."[7] From his mentor, Winfield Scott, he learned to be opportunistic. He learned to use the element of surprise to his best possible advantage. Additionally, Union general and author D. H. Strother wrote that Magruder demonstrated "a genius for executing grand maneuvers."[8] Because his strategy was "deep and acute" and his planning was meticulous,[9] Magruder was

6. Magruder to Davis, April 26, 1861, in Lynda Lasswell Crist and Mary Seaton Dix, eds., *The Papers of Jefferson Davis*, 12 vols. to date (Baton Rouge: Louisiana State University Press, 1971–), 7:130–32. The original letter is in the Dearborn Collection at Harvard University.

7. Stephen W. Sears, *To the Gates of Richmond: The Peninsula Campaign* (New York: Ticknor and Fields, 1992), 26.

8. Strother, "Personal Recollections of the War," 549.

9. *New Orleans Times*, March 19, 1871. Caleb G. Forshey assessed Magruder's military capabilities in a lengthy article written for the *New Orleans Times* shortly after the general's death.

able to execute schemes that were so ambitious that they bordered on reck-lessness. One of his contemporaries wrote that he belonged to that class of men "whose genius, being unshackled, was capable of achieving the most brilliant results."[10] More important, Magruder knew as much about Washing-ton's defenses as anyone in Richmond at the beginning of the war, including Lee. He was confident that southerners in Virginia would be able to marshal their manpower and resources more rapidly than their opponents north of the Potomac. He also understood the political, military, and psychological value of the capture of the capital city and urged that it be done.[11]

Magruder's longtime friend Judge James Lyons also urged Lee to "plant his standard on the north bank of the Potomac." Lyons, who had known Lee

Forshey was educated at Kenyon College, Ohio, and the U.S. Military Academy. Although a pro-fessional engineer by trade, he taught at Jefferson College, Miss., and later, in 1855, established the Texas Military Institute. When the war began, Forshey entered the Confederate service and served on Magruder's staff, both on the Virginia Peninsula and in Texas. With respect to Magruder's plans, Professor Forshey applauded the general for his "promptness in conception, and his boldness in execution." He declared that his commander "never underrated an enemy, but habitually estimated him at his maximum." After the war ended, Caleb Forshey expressed "a profound regret . . . that General Magruder had not been assigned to the chief command of the trans-Mississippi." Had such been the case, Forshey was "strongly convinced that New Orleans would have been recaptured, and Missouri recovered and retained, to influence the fortunes of the armies further East."

10. Long, "Memoir of General John Bankhead Magruder," 110.

11. Unbeknownst to Lee, one week before Magruder vowed to the Governor's Advisory Coun-cil that he could capture Washington, D.C., Winfield Scott had confided to two Pennsylvania Republicans, Governor Andrew Gregg Curtin and Alexander K. McClure, that "the capital was not defensible." Furthermore, author Margaret Leech reported that in Washington at that time "the general opinion was that the South was prepared and the North was not." Leech, *Reveille in Washington, 1860–1865,* 56, 64.

Ben Butler, soon to be Magruder's opponent in Virginia, could not understand why Jefferson Davis did not march forces across Long Bridge, "where there were no forces to oppose him, and capture Washington." Butler wrote: "The prize to be won was gloriously magnificent. The capital of the nation, with its archives, its records and its treasure, and all of its executive organization was there . . . The capture and occupation of Washington would almost have insured the Con-federacy at once a place by recognition as a power among the nations of the earth." In summa-tion General Butler declared, "If the Confederacy had made the capture . . . it would have been a disaster to our government of almost incalculable weight and potency." Benjamin F. Butler, *Butler's Book: Autobiography and Personal Reminiscences* (Boston: A. M. Thayer and Co., 1892), 220–21. Additionally, President Lincoln believed the capture of Washington, D.C., would have resulted in "the quick collapse of the war and, with it, the Republican Party." Clifford Dowdy, *The Seven Days: The Emergence of Lee* (Boston: Little, Brown, 1964), 24.

for many years before the war and reportedly was "on the most friendly and familiar terms with him," met personally with the general and attempted to persuade him that the slaveholding states were best suited for an invasive war and weakest for a defensive war. Furthermore, Lyons declared that if the South took the offensive, Maryland would join the Confederate endeavor, bringing with it a half-million excellent horsemen and marksmen. With Maryland in the Confederate fold, Washington, D.C., would be surrounded. The judge then predicted the capture of the capital city, forcing the enemy to fall back into Pennsylvania. There, stated Judge Lyons, the fighting would be done on "[enemy] soil, and not ours." Lyons, like Magruder, realized the importance of capturing Washington City. He predicted that if Confederate forces were able to take the Federal capital, "peace would speedily follow." Lee, however, was unmoved and unpersuaded, and his reply was the same, "We have not the men."[12]

Whether Magruder could have captured Washington, D.C., at the beginning of the conflict and what impact the event might have had on the course of the war will never be known, nor will it ever cease to be debated. Almost a century afterward Clement Eaton wrote, "Although it is still a matter of controversy whether the Confederacy thus lost a golden opportunity by inactivity, it seems from the vantage point of today that the bold course of attempting to capture Washington should have been adopted."[13] In this particular instance Eaton was referring to the "golden opportunity" following the first battle of Bull Run. It was one of several opportunities the Confederates had to move against Washington. Others were after Second Bull Run, Fredericksburg, Chancellorsville, and at the very outset of the war, as Magruder and Lyons proposed.

In his book *Emancipating Slaves, Enslaving Free Men*, Jeffrey Rogers Hummel states that as time passed, it grew increasingly difficult for the Confederates to take the offensive against Washington.[14] It logically follows that the

12. Rowland, *Jefferson Davis, Constitutionalist,* 8:216. Although Robert E. Lee would not authorize Magruder to move against Washington, D.C., in 1861, he apparently later changed his mind about the worthiness of the project. Two months before the surrender at Appomattox, Lee revealed to John S. Mosby in a post-dinner conversation that he had written to Joe Johnston in the spring of 1862 urging him not to fall back from the Rapidan to Richmond but, rather, to attack Washington. John S. Mosby, *The Memoirs of Colonel John S. Mosby,* ed. Charles Wells Russell (Boston: Little, Brown, 1917), 375.

13. Clement Eaton, *A History of the Southern Confederacy* (New York: Free Press, 1954), 153.

14. Jeffrey Rogers Hummel, *Emancipating Slaves, Enslaving Free Men* (Chicago: Open Court, 1996), 199.

odds were best earlier, at the beginning of the war, when Washington was ill prepared, disorganized, and weakly defended. However, the problem for the Confederacy was always the same, regardless of timing. In each instance opportunities slipped away because of inactivity, time lost to the paralysis of analysis, or the agonizing wait for proper authorization. These were frustrations that would drive Magruder and several of his comrades in the field to the brink of lunacy in the campaigns ahead. All too often, by the time proper civilian or military authorities acted, viable military endeavors had turned from the realm of distinct possibility to that of passing fancy.

Had Governor Letcher not been so hesitant earlier, Virginia certainly would have been in a much better position militarily to have implemented the offensive against Washington that Magruder and Lyons urged. But Letcher was a moderate politician who opposed secession and insisted that the states' business be conducted in an orderly and legal manner. He refused to begin even a limited manpower mobilization because he did not wish to encourage radicalism in his state. He also resisted pressure from leading citizens, including Henry Wise, John Imboden, Oliver Funston, John and Alfred Barbour, Richard and Turner Ashby, and John Harman, to seize Federal installations in Virginia until the state formally seceded.[15] Once secession was accomplished, however, Letcher worked feverishly to put his state on a proper war footing, and John Magruder became an important part of the governor's frenetic organizational effort.

Magruder's first official responsibility was to serve on a committee with Joseph E. Johnston, Richard Stoddert Ewell, Sydney Smith Lee, Samuel Barron, and Robert Pegram to assess the qualifications of sons of Virginia who might be efficient officers in the volunteer forces of the state.[16] That committee assignment dated April 25, 1861, was followed four days later by a formal military tasking to command the artillery forces in and around Richmond.[17] Amazingly, on the very day that he was given his new assignment, Magruder sent Colonel Robert S. Garnett, the adjutant general of Virginia's state forces, a detailed inventory of all artillery in the area and suggested the precise manner in which the available batteries could be most efficiently drilled and provisioned for Richmond's defense.[18] Magruder's energy and attention to detail

15. Boney, *John Letcher of Virginia*, 109–14.

16. Proceedings of the Advisory Council, April 25, 1861, *Official Records*, ser. 1, vol. 51, pt. 2, 37.

17. Orders No. 5, April 29, 1861, ibid., 53.

18. Magruder to Garnett, April 29, 1861, ibid., 2:789–90.

did not go unnoticed. On May 8 he was elevated to command all forces in the Richmond area.[19] Then, less than two weeks later, on May 21, he was placed in command of forces, east of Richmond, on the Virginia Peninsula between the York and James rivers.[20] The assignment was an important one. In view of the *Pawnee* incident and reported troop concentrations at federally held Fort Monroe, Richmond seemed most threatened from the east.

Magruder's new command extended from Fort Monroe, on the eastern end of the Peninsula, toward Richmond, almost a hundred miles to the west. His southern departmental boundary was the James River, which ran from Hampton Roads, in the lower Chesapeake Bay, through Richmond and beyond. The James was a major waterway open to seagoing vessels inland as far as Richmond. Farther north Magruder's opposing boundary, the York River, roughly paralleled the James. Several tributaries of the York originated well to the northwest of Richmond. However, the York itself began at West Point at the confluence of the Pamunkey and Mattapony rivers. The York River had been the destination of both the French and British fleets at the end of the Revolutionary War. It was broad and deep and easily navigable to West Point. The only places at which the York might be controlled were at Yorktown, on the southern bank of the river, and Gloucester Point, opposite Yorktown on the north bank, where the river narrowed to within three-quarters of a mile in width—easily within the effective firing range of the weaponry of the day. If the Federals penetrated either river in force, not only would Richmond be imperiled, but Magruder and his men would be cut off and entrapped. The potential for disaster was enormous.

Governor Letcher and Robert E. Lee were fully aware of the importance of strongly defending the two rivers. A month before sending Magruder to the Peninsula, Letcher had dispatched the talented and highly respected engineer Andrew Talcott to select locations for batteries that would protect the York from passage by the Federals.[21] Immediately afterward, Lee sent him on a similar mission to the James.[22] Talcott had been Lee's immediate superior when both were stationed at Fort Monroe in the early 1830s. As Talcott had also earlier been assigned to construct defenses for Hampton Roads,[23] he was well acquainted with the area and completed his task quickly.

19. General Orders No. 12, May 8, 1861, ibid., 817.

20. Special Orders No. 95, May 21, 1861, ibid., 865.

21. Talcott to Lee, April 26, 1861, ibid., 781.

22. Lee to Talcott, April 29, 1861, ibid., 788–89.

23. Cullum, *Biographical Register*, 1:172–73.

Under Talcott's plan a hundred guns were to be positioned on the banks of the York and James rivers. Because these guns were large-bore artillery pieces, primarily naval in design, Virginia's naval officers were assigned to supervise construction of the batteries with orders to complete the various defensive works as quickly as possible.[24] In his original orders Magruder had been instructed to provide protection for those working at the sites selected by Talcott, including Jamestown Island and Gloucester Point. And while naval personnel worked to protect the riverine approaches to Richmond, it was also Magruder's assigned task to build defensive lines across the Peninsula to prevent overland access to Richmond.[25]

Immediately after establishing his headquarters at Yorktown, Magruder hired the local sheriff to guide him on a tour of the area, "to get some knowledge of the country."[26] What he saw led him to believe that a successful defense of the Peninsula was entirely possible. The marshy nature of the region combined with dense undergrowth, numerous watercourses that would provide serious obstacles for an advancing enemy, and the scarcity of roads all worked in Magruder's favor. On the other hand, it would take time to engineer and then build the earthworks and defensive fortifications necessary to supplement the natural obstacles already there. Once the works were completed and the defenses were sufficiently manned, Magruder firmly believed that he would be able to hold the Peninsula against "any number of men that [could] be brought against it."[27]

Magruder calculated that it would take eight to ten thousand men to defend the Peninsula,[28] yet he had only thirty-four hundred men, including

24. Talcott to Lee, April 26, 1861, *Official Records*, ser. 1, 2:781–82; April 27, 1861, ibid., 782–83; Lee to Talcott, April 29, 1861, ibid., 788–89. The mounting and use of naval ordnance had heretofore been restricted to the various systems of naval fortifications at the entry to the significant harbors of the country. The experience of the War of 1812 demonstrated the need to resist naval invasions before marines or other land soldiers could get ashore. The large naval guns had different characteristics than light artillery. Heavy guns were immobile and had to be mounted on carriages that could then be aimed by pivoting the piece in different directions. Naval officers were familiar with these guns. Whenever they were included as part of the ordnance designed to defend a point, naval officers were assigned to supervise in the areas of both gun installation and training.

25. Special Orders No. 95, May 21, 1861, *Official Records*, ser. 1, 2:865.

26. Magruder to Cooper, February 1, 1862, ibid., 4:38; Magruder, "First Battle of the War: Big Bethel," in *Battles and Leaders of the Civil War*, 5:36. The sheriff was Major George Wray.

27. Magruder to Garnett, May 29, 1861, *Official Records*, ser. 1, 2:893.

28. Magruder to Garnett, May 27, 1861, ibid., 887.

those who were sick.[29] Worse yet, many of those who were counted as available were reportedly on the verge of starvation because of inadequate food distribution.[30] Numerous others were so lacking in both experience and military essentials that they were basically ineffective.[31] The Virginia regiment of Colonel Thomas P. August could not even take the field "for want of shoes and other necessaries."[32] In these early times of turmoil Magruder reported difficulties even assembling a capable staff: "Lieutenant [George A.] Thornton, who is now sick, is my acting assistant adjutant-general. He has had no experience. I have nobody but my nephew, Mr. [George A. Jr.] Magruder, who is a citizen, and Mr. [Hugh] Stanard, who is a private. Captain [?] Lambert, assistant quartermaster, is at Williamsburg, where a quartermaster ought to be stationed. I must have an efficient one here [Yorktown]. The whole of my time nearly is occupied in doing other people's duties."[33]

Difficulties notwithstanding, Magruder and his men worked at a furious pace. Slaves borrowed from local owners labored alongside one-third of the available men constructing defensive fortifications, while the remaining two-thirds drilled under the watchful eyes of West Point graduates Daniel Harvey Hill and John Bell Hood.[34] Hood, only a first lieutenant, was assigned command of the recently arrived cavalry companies when a question of rank arose. Because the volunteer cavalry companies were commanded by captains, Magruder elevated Hood to the rank of captain by his own order without taking the time to wait for authorization from Richmond. When questions later arose regarding the dates of commission of the captains, Magruder promoted Hood to the rank of major, and the problem involving rank ended.[35]

The more immediate problem for Magruder was his newly arrived opponent

29. Magruder to Garnett, June 3, 1861, ibid., 902.

30. Magruder to Garnett, June 8, 1861, ibid., 914.

31. Magruder to Cooper, February 1, 1862, ibid., 9:38.

32. Magruder to Garnett, June 2, 1861, ibid., 2:900.

33. Magruder to Garnett, May 29, 1861, ibid., 893; June 2, 1861, ibid., 901. George A. Magruder Jr. and Hugh Stanard would serve on Magruder's staff for the duration of the war.

34. Magruder to Garnett, May 25, 1861, *Official Records,* ser. 1, 2:878; May 27, 1861, ibid., 886; June 2, 1861, ibid., 900; June 3, 1861, ibid., 902–3; Ewell to Washington, May 29, 1861, ibid., 891; Ewell to Magruder, ibid., 892.

35. John Bell Hood, *Advance and Retreat: Personal Experiences in the United States and Confederate Armies* (New Orleans: Hood Orphan Memorial Fund, 1880), 17–18. Magruder and Hill were involved in a similar controversy involving rank. See Magruder to Garnett, June 2, 1861, *Official Records,* ser. 1, 2:901.

at Fort Monroe, Major General Benjamin Franklin Butler. Butler was a well-connected war Democrat and an intimidating criminal lawyer, but tall, dark, and handsome he was not. He had puffy cheeks; droopy, squinty, crossed eyes; and very little hair. He was also overweight and on his finest day stood but five feet four inches tall. Yet for a man with such a pitiable appearance, Ben Butler had an amazing amount of self-confidence. He was also ruthlessly ambitious, which made him dangerous. Furthermore, because Butler lacked military experience and was ignorant of the standard military practices of the day, Magruder knew that his movements and tactics would be difficult to predict.

To deceive General Butler about the size and intentions of his own force, Magruder sent Major John Baytop Cary to the Hampton–Newport News area to demonstrate in the vicinity of Fort Monroe.[36] It quickly became apparent, however, that the Federals were more of a threat to Cary than he was to them. Less than a week after Magruder took command on the Peninsula, Major Cary sent him an urgent message warning that "the enemy are landing at Newport News." At the time Magruder had few men, insufficient equipment, and only fifty rounds of heavy ordnance with which to oppose them. He inferred from the alarmist tone of Cary's communiqué that an attack on his flank was imminent.[37] Yet after a few days had passed and no strike was made, Magruder personally scouted Federal lines and discovered that he and his opponents were simultaneously handicapped by a shortage of many of the same military essentials.[38]

Butler had no horses, carts, or wagons, and he had precious little ammunition.[39] His own Massachusetts regiment did not even have any cooks "because they had always taken caterers with them on the glorified picnics of their encampments."[40] The only item that General Butler had in large supply was men. The troops Butler ordered to Newport News were sent there not to attack the Confederates but because Fort Monroe had become so

36. Magruder to Cooper, February 1, 1862, *Official Records,* ser. 1, 9:38–39; Magruder to Cary, May 25, 1861, ibid., 2:877–78.

37. Magruder to Garnett, May 27, 1861, *Official Records,* ser. 1, 2:884; ibid., 886–87; George A. Magruder Jr. to Garnett, ibid., 885.

38. Magruder to Garnett, June 2, 1861, *Official Records,* ser. 1, 2:900. Magruder stated that the Federals were "in a most disorganized state" but that additional troops were arriving daily.

39. James Parton, *General Butler in New Orleans* (New York: Mason Bros., 1864), 123. Parton reported that when General Butler arrived at Fort Monroe "he had but five thousand rounds [of ammunition], less than a round and a half per man."

40. Leech, *Reveille in Washington, 1860–1865,* 77.

crowded with the new arrivals that it could no longer accommodate them,[41] even though it was the largest coastal fortress in the United States. By the beginning of June Butler commanded approximately nine thousand men at Fort Monroe and Newport News. What he did not have was patience. An informant, Dr. John M. Cuyler, reported that General Butler intended to move against Magruder as soon as fifteen thousand men were available. That number would be reached, reckoned Cuyler, "within ten days."[42]

Meanwhile, the Federal occupation of Newport News resulted in a massive exodus of pro-Confederate Virginians to safety behind Magruder's lines. From his headquarters in Yorktown Magruder observed, "The women and children have been passing here all day." Many of them were assisted by close friends and family members who were in Major Cary's Company of the Wythe Rifles. Cary's men were so preoccupied helping the refugees during the chaos of the evacuation that Magruder had to order them to retrieve their own artillery pieces, which they had inadvertently left behind.[43]

When the evacuation began, Magruder journeyed to the lower peninsula to boost the spirits of the frightened refugees and to gain whatever intelligence he could from them about the Federals.[44] Along the way he encountered Parker West and his family, who had fled from Newport News. West's twenty-two-year-old son, George Benjamin West, recalled the meeting in a postwar memoir: "After breakfast we started and met General Magruder near the picket, with some cavalry, reconnoitering. He stopped and enquired as to the number and position of the Yankees—whether they had thrown up entrenchments—and intimating that he would attack them. He seemed to feel very sorry for father and told him to go to Yorktown, and he would furnish us with quarters and would supply all our wants as long as he had anything to eat himself. We have always felt very kindly to him for his kindness and offer, and in fact, he was kind to all of the refugees and did all in his power to help them."[45]

41. Parton, *General Butler in New Orleans*, 123–26.

42. Magruder to Garnett, June 2, 1861, *Official Records*, ser. 1, 2:900.

43. Magruder to Garnett, May 27, 1861, ibid., 886. During the evacuation only sixty-five of two hundred men answered present at a company roll call; the others, presumably, were assisting the refugees.

44. Magruder to Garnett, May 29, 1861, ibid., 893; June 2, 1861, ibid., 900.

45. George Benjamin West, *When the Yankees Came, Civil War and Reconstruction on the Virginia Peninsula*, ed. Parker Rouse Jr. (Richmond: Dietz Press, 1977), 64.

At the same time that the West family and their neighbors abandoned their homes and plantations and headed for protection behind Confederate lines, several slaves, three of whom belonged to Colonel Charles K. Mallory, sought refuge behind Union lines. During a truce Major Cary asked General Butler what his intentions were regarding the slaves:

General Butler: I propose to retain them.

Major Cary: Do you mean, then, to set aside your constitutional obligations?

General Butler: I mean to abide by the decision of Virginia as expressed in her ordinance of secession . . . I am under no constitutional obligations to a foreign country, which Virginia now claims to be.

Major Cary: But you say, we can't secede, and so you can not consistently detain the negroes.

General Butler: But you say you have seceded, and so you can not consistently claim them. I shall detain the negroes as contraband of war. You are using them upon your batteries. It is merely a question whether they shall be used for or against the government.[46]

Butler's compelling argument, later endorsed by his superiors in Washington, D.C., effectively superseded the Fugitive Slave Law. It was his most significant contribution during the Civil War.

Because Ben Butler had a fertile mind and a natural talent for persuasive speaking, constructing powerful arguments and defeating lesser opponents came easily to him. He was ingenious, pompous, and unrelenting. Butler feared no one. He bullied his legal and political adversaries with an irreverent arrogance that raised many eyebrows but won him few friends. Butler was even less respectful and more condescending toward his contemporaries in the army. From the time his application for admission to the U.S. Military Academy was rejected, he was openly contemptuous of the American military establishment. Butler showed no respect for Winfield Scott, and he despised West Point graduates.[47] He believed military training and experience were

---

46. Parton, *General Butler in New Orleans*, 126–29.

47. Robert Holzman, *Stormy Ben Butler* (New York: Macmillan, 1954), 7, 9, 28, 31, 131, 188, 221; Robert Werlich, *"Beast" Butler: The Incredible Career of Major General Benjamin Franklin Butler* (Washington, D.C.: Quaker Press, 1962), 3. Both biographers are severely critical of their subject. Werlich, in particular, insists that Butler was "one of the country's most incompetent Generals and most unscrupulous politicians."

overrated.[48] After all, when he was commissioned major general on May 16, 1861, the sum total of Butler's military experience was the five days per year that he had spent in camp with his fellow Massachusetts militiamen.[49] The promotion made Butler the senior major general in the U.S. Army.[50] It also filled him with self-importance and fueled his ambition. His original orders authorized him to use his forces for "aggressive purposes,"[51] and he intended to do exactly that. The prize that he sought was Richmond,[52] newly designated as the capital of the Confederacy. Ben Butler knew if he could get past Magruder and seize Richmond, his political future would be assured.

Magruder previously decided to anchor his forward defense behind a branch of the Back River, thirteen miles below Yorktown and eight miles from Hampton, near Big Bethel Church.[53] On June 6 he ordered D. H. Hill and eight hundred North Carolinians, along with six hundred Virginians, including Major George Wythe Randolph's Richmond Howitzers, to Bethel to prepare its defense. Simultaneously, to prevent a turning movement on his right from Newport News, Magruder dispatched Lieutenant Colonel William D. Stuart and his Virginia volunteers to destroy bridges and block roads.

On the seventh Hill sent word to his commander that a superior force of Federal troops was advancing toward his position. Believing an attack was imminent, Magruder immediately proceeded to Bethel to take command in person.[54] Yet when the Federals failed to appear as anticipated, Magruder grew restless. At 3:00 a.m. on June 10 he awakened his men and led them forward in search of their opponents.[55] An irritated D. H. Hill saw no rationale for a march beginning at three o'clock in the morning. Because of previous orders of a similar nature, the disgruntled North Carolinian had earlier written to his wife that "Col. Magruder in command is always drunk and giving foolish and absurd orders. I think that in a few days the men

48. Holzman, *Stormy Ben Butler*, 28.

49. Werlich, *"Beast" Butler*, 14.

50. Parton, *General Butler in New Orleans*, 120.

51. Scott to Butler, May 18, 1861, *Official Records*, ser. 1, 2:641.

52. Holzman, *Stormy Ben Butler*, 45. The ambitious Butler had obtained plans of Richmond through private sources, and not through Washington, so that the War Department would not know what his intentions were.

53. Hill to Magruder, n.d., *Official Records*, ser. 1, 2:93.

54. Magruder to Garnett, June 8, 1861, ibid., 912–13.

55. J. W. Ratchford, *Some Reminiscences of Persons and Incidents of the Civil War* (Richmond, Va.: Whittet and Shepperson, 1909), 13.

will refuse to obey any order issued by him."[56] Marching orders that Hill judged to be foolish instead proved to be fortuitous. In the dark of night the Confederates encountered a local resident, Hannah Tunnell, who warned Magruder that the Yankees were approaching in large number. Based on that intelligence, Magruder hurried his troops back to the protection of their earthen fortifications at Big Bethel to await the enemy.[57]

In the meantime the oncoming Federal force, commanded by Brigadier General Ebenezer Pierce, sustained losses before it ever reached Magruder's line. Pierce's two columns of troops, one marching from Hampton and the other from Newport News, were supposed to have rendezvoused before completing their predawn journey to Big Bethel. When they met in the darkness, however, one of the Federal columns, thinking the other was the enemy, fired upon it, killing two and wounding nineteen.[58] The noise of the gunfire also alerted Hannah Tunnell, who then courageously sought out Magruder to warn him of the approaching danger. By the time the Federals realized their mistake, tended to the dead and wounded, and resumed their march, Magruder had returned his men to Big Bethel and skillfully positioned them for battle. Prince John thus gained a decided advantage over General Pierce, who knew neither where the Confederates were nor what their strength was. Furthermore, after the unanticipated delay and loss of the advantage of surprise, Pierce was forced to fight on unfamiliar ground, in broad daylight, and at a place of Magruder's choosing.

Shortly after the Federals reached Big Bethel at 9:00 a.m. on June 10, they were met with a well-directed fusillade from Major Randolph's artillery. The

56. Hill to his wife, May 30, 1861, D. H. Hill Papers, U.S. Military History Institute.

57. Ratchford, *Some Reminiscences of Persons and Incidents of the Civil War*, 13–14; Edward J. Hale, "The Bethel Regiment, the First North Carolina Volunteers," in *Histories of Several Regiments and Battalions from North Carolina in the Great War, 1861–65*, ed. Walter Clark, 5 vols. (Raleigh: State of North Carolina, 1901), 1:86; Magruder, "First Battle of the War: Big Bethel," in *Battles and Leaders of the Civil War*, 5:38. After the battle the officers and men of the "Bethel Regiment," as it was subsequently called, collected a $225 reward and presented it to Hannah Tunnell for her gallantry.

58. Frederick Townsend to R. A. Pierce, June 12, 1861, *Official Records*, ser. 1, 2:86; Ebenezer W. Pierce to Butler, ibid., 84; Butler to Scott, June 10, 1861, ibid., 79. Townsend, of the 3rd New York Infantry, led the column that was accidentally fired upon by members of the 7th New York Infantry, commanded by Colonel John E. Bendix. Both Colonel Townsend and General Pierce, in their official reports, stated that there were two killed and nineteen wounded. Butler attempted to minimize the losses in his report to Scott, which said there were two killed and eight wounded in the mishap, which he called an "almost criminal blunder."

deadly greeting seemed to stun the Federals, whose return fire was brisk but inaccurate. D. H. Hill observed in his official report that the enemy's "organization was completely broken up,"[59] and they never recovered. In a battle that lasted two and a half hours, all subsequent Federal thrusts against the Confederate lines were executed in piecemeal fashion, allowing Magruder, in each instance, to send reinforcements to assist at the point of attack. A battlefield correspondent from the *Richmond Whig* observed that "during the entire engagement, Colonel Magruder was in every part of the field, and, displaying consummate generalship and courage, directing every movement in person and exposing himself with a recklessness of danger which was seen and admired by all in camp,"[60] even D. H. Hill. In the end Magruder orchestrated the fighting in such a way that the Confederate manpower disadvantage was of no consequence to the outcome.[61]

Only seven Confederates were wounded, and Private Henry Lawson Wyatt of the North Carolina regiment was killed—"First at Bethel."[62] The less fortunate Federals suffered seventy-six casualties, including Lieutenant John T. Greble, the first graduate of West Point to lose his life in the Civil War, and Major Theodore Winthrop, who was General Butler's chief military assistant.[63] Afterward Confederate authorities returned Winthrop's posses-

59. Hill to Magruder, n.d., *Official Records*, ser. 1, 2:94.

60. *Richmond Whig*, June 14, 1861. The *Whig* had earlier reported that "during the entire conflict, [Magruder's] voice was heard above the roar of cannon and musketry, and had the effect of magic on the men." Ibid., June 12, 1861. Similarly, Richmond diarist Sallie Putnam wrote that Prince John "calmly smoked his cigar and gave orders with coolness and deliberation." Sallie Putnam, *Richmond during the War: Four Years of Personal Observation* (New York: G. W. Carleton and Co., 1867), 53.

61. For battle reports and important correspondence relating to the battle at Big Bethel, consult the *Official Records*, ser. 1, 2:77–104. For additional information, see Magruder to "My Dear Colonel," June 12, 1861, Chicago Historical Society; Magruder, "First Battle of the War: Big Bethel," in *Battles and Leaders of the Civil War*, 5:34–41; Joseph B. Carr, "Operations of 1861 about Fort Monroe," ibid., 2:144–52; J. M. Drake to "Dear Father," June 25, 1861, Southern Historical Collection, University of North Carolina, Chapel Hill; Ratchford, *Some Reminiscences of Persons and Incidents of the Civil War*, 14–18; Hale, "Bethel Regiment, The First North Carolina Volunteers," 1:86–98; and Benjamin Huske, "More Terrible than Victory," ed. Walter Brown Jr., *Civil War Times Illustrated* (October 1981): 28–30.

62. Magruder to Garnett, June 10, 1861, *Official Records*, ser. 1, 2:92; Magruder to "Sir," June 12, 1861, ibid., 92.

63. Butler to Scott, June 16, 1861, *Official Records*, ser. 1, 2:82. On the day following the battle, Lieutenant Greble's father arrived at Fort Monroe to visit his son. Instead, the elder Greble returned to his family in Pennsylvania with his son's remains. John T. Greble died at age twenty-

sions with a note stating that he had been given a military funeral,[64] adding that in their opinion he was the only Union officer "who exhibited even an approximation [of] courage."[65]

On the day following the battle General Butler sent a detachment of troops, under a flag of truce, to collect the dead and remove the wounded. Much to their surprise, the Federals found that their dead and wounded had already been taken care of by Magruder's men.[66] Furthermore, the members of Butler's burial detail were received with such civility that it made a considerable impression upon them, as evidenced in a letter that one of the Federal soldiers wrote to his father: "Our wounded that were left in that murderous and disgraceful affair at Bethel were by the enemy sent to Yorktown and well cared for. Our dead they decently buried not even so much as taking from their persons the least thing, I know this to be true because . . . we dug them up. One man had in his pocket quite a sum of gold . . . Colonel Magruder the secession commander of Bethel Forces gave us a good dinner, the best I have seen since I left Boston and sent by us word to our commander that he was ready for us if we desired to attack him and that he should send as many of us to bloody graves as he was able to do."[67]

There was, however, no immediate resumption of hostilities. Instead, officers and men of both forces set aside their firearms, sheathed their swords, and seized their pens. Because Big Bethel was the first battle of the Civil War and the first time that the vast majority of the men had ever been involved in combat, many of them wrote of the experience in journals, diaries, or letters sent home to their loved ones. It was also the first time that most of the officers, Ben Butler included, had ever written official battle reports. Butler, who just days earlier, had envisioned military and political grandeur, now found himself scrambling to survive. Not surprisingly, he blamed the entire debacle on General Pierce.[68] Then, on two occasions he attempted in vain to

seven. The other Federal officer killed, thirty-three-year-old Theodore Winthrop, was directly descended from Massachusetts Bay Colony's first governor, John Winthrop, and Jonathan Edwards. Additionally, seven of his ancestors were presidents of Yale College, from which Winthrop himself was a distinguished graduate. Parton, *General Butler in New Orleans,* 149.

64. Parton, *General Butler in New Orleans,* 146.

65. Hill to Magruder, n.d., *Official Records,* ser. 1, 2:95.

66. Magruder to Butler, June 12, 1861, ibid., ser. 2, 3:3.

67. Drake to "Dear Father," June 25, 1861, Southern Historical Collection, University of North Carolina, Chapel Hill.

68. Werlich, *"Beast" Butler,* 25; Butler, *Autobiography and Personal Reminiscences,* 268–70.

convince Winfield Scott that he and his men had "gained much more than we have lost."[69] Such logic failed to impress either Scott or President Lincoln, both of whom favored results over rhetoric. Almost any other general would have been removed from command, but Lincoln was too politically savvy to be drawn into battle with Butler's Democratic Party supporters. For the time being General Butler remained on the Peninsula. However, Lincoln had lost confidence in his military capabilities.

The mood was significantly more positive on the Confederate side. Magruder, in his official reports and in private correspondence written shortly after Big Bethel, was generous in giving credit to all of his subordinates, particularly to the distinguished grandson of Thomas Jefferson, George Wythe Randolph—who would soon become Confederate secretary of war—and D. H. Hill.[70] Likewise, each of Magruder's unit commanders confirmed that their outnumbered men had performed gallantly in the face of enemy fire, even though most of them lacked previous battle experience. All had remained steadfastly at the posts assigned them, including those who did not get to see action but were eager to participate. "The men are influenced by high moral and religious sentiments," declared D. H. Hill, "and their conduct has furnished another example of the great truth that he who fears God will ever do his duty to his country."[71]

The praise and celebration that followed Big Bethel far exceeded the military importance of the battle. Not more than three hundred of Magruder's fourteen hundred men were engaged simultaneously, and the combined contesting forces totaled slightly less than six thousand men.[72] Later in the war

69. Butler to Scott, June 10, 1861, *Official Records,* ser. 1, 2:80; June 16, 1861, ibid., 82.

70. Magruder to Garnett, June 10, 1861, *Official Records,* ser. 1, 2:91; Magruder to "Sir," June 12, 1861, ibid., 92; Magruder to "My Dear Colonel," June 12, 1861, Chicago Historical Society. While Magruder praised D. H. Hill, Hill's biographer, Hal Bridges, was not at all generous in assigning any credit to Magruder. Bridges's statement that "Magruder who as over-all commander had given few battle orders, while allowing Hill to control most of the fighting" is incorrect. Hal Bridges, *Lee's Maverick General: Daniel Harvey Hill* (New York: McGraw-Hill, 1961), 29. Two of D. H. Hill's officers, North Carolinians Edward Hale and Benjamin Huske, neither of whom is mentioned in Bridges's book, both gave proper credit to Magruder. Hale, "Bethel Regiment, the First North Carolina Volunteers," 1:93–94, 96, 98; and Huske, "More Terrible than Victory," 28, 30. Additionally, in his official report of the battle D. H. Hill cited four instances in which Magruder rushed troops to assist at critical points when the Confederate line began to falter. Hill to Magruder, n.d., *Official Records,* ser. 1, 2:94–96.

71. Hill to Magruder, n.d., *Official Records,* ser. 1, 2:97.

72. Ibid.

such a clash would be the subject of a brief dispatch, but it was altogether different in June 1861. The war's first battle had a profound psychological impact. It shocked the North. "Occurring just when it did," wrote pro-Unionist author James Parton, "it was a calamity." Conversely, it reconfirmed the belief of many southerners that their soldiers were superior and their cause was righteous.[73]

Word of the victory traveled quickly and raised morale in the far corners of the Confederacy. From New Orleans Mrs. Braxton Bragg wrote to her husband about the cheerful news.[74] In South Carolina Mary Boykin Chesnut, whose husband, James, would serve as an aide to Jefferson Davis for most of the war, gleefully recorded in her diary that "Colonel Magruder has done something splendid on the Peninsula."[75] And in the Confederate capital a writer for the *Richmond Examiner* exhibited a keen understanding of the ramifications of the battle when he stated that Magruder "turned the hateful current of retreat, and sent the first gleam of sunlight through that somber shadow which has for some time past hung over public opinion in the South."[76]

The battle's end, however, did not conclude the fighting between Magruder and Butler. Immediately afterward, the two commanders became involved in an exchange of caustic letters regarding the status of prisoners that served as quick reminder to Prince John that his opponent had not gone away. It was galling to Magruder that the one Confederate soldier who had been captured was not taken in battle and the other three prisoners were civilians. In a June 12 letter to General Butler, Magruder declared, "The citizens in your possession are men who doubtless defended their homes against a foe who to their certain knowledge had with or without the authority of the Federal government destroyed the private property of their neighbors, breaking up even the pianos of the ladies and committing depredations numberless and of every description."[77] Magruder was willing to exchange a Federal prisoner for his captured vedette, Private Carter, but he demanded that the civilians be released immediately.

The following day Butler defended his decision to detain the civilians. Two of them, he wrote, had been captured with weapons in their hands,

73. Parton, *General Butler in New Orleans*, 148; Long, "Memoirs of General John Bankhead Magruder," 108; *Richmond Examiner*, June 18, 1861.

74. Don C. Seitz, *Braxton Bragg: General of the Confederacy* (Columbia, S.C.: State Co., 1924), 43.

75. Mary Boykin Chesnut, *A Diary from Dixie*, ed. Ben Ames Williams (Boston: Houghton Mifflin, 1949), 58.

76. *Richmond Examiner*, June 18, 1861.

77. Magruder to Butler, June 12, 1861, *Official Records*, ser. 2, 3:3.

and the other, Mr. Whiting, had fired on Federal troops. As far as Butler was concerned, armed citizens with hostile intentions were either soldiers or assassins. About the charge that Federal soldiers had indiscriminately destroyed the property of area residents, General Butler admitted to Magruder "that there have been too many sporadic acts of wrong to private property committed by bad men under my command,"[78] but, he stated, he had issued orders wherein he pledged to punish severely any of his men who failed to respect the property rights of loyal citizens.[79] Toward the end of his June 13 communiqué Ben Butler shifted from defense to offense by charging that Confederate cavalrymen fired into a Union ambulance that was carrying the wounded back from the battle. According to Butler: "My men complain that the ambulance having the wounded was fired into by your cavalry and I am informed that if you have any prisoners they were taken while in the pious duty to their wounded comrades and not in battle. It has never occurred to my mind that either firing into the ambulance or capturing persons in charge of the wounded was an act authorized, recognized, or sanctioned by any gentleman." Finally, he chided Magruder by admitting that the latter was technically correct in stating that his vedette had not been taken in battle; he had been captured while asleep at his post.[80]

John Magruder, whose blood must have been near the boiling point, was not to be denied in this poison pen exchange, which the *Wilmington Daily Journal* described as "rich if not racy."[81] He replied on June 15, 1861, that the allegation of firing shots into the ambulance was "entirely untrue" because the Confederate cavalry was unable to get in front of Butler's fleeing troops, who had departed the field of action so rapidly that they left behind many of the Federal wounded whom they should have evacuated. Magruder also denied General Butler's assertion that the captured civilians were either soldiers or assassins. They were "brave men, defending their firesides against piratical invasion, and are entitled to the respect of all good men." He stated that they had taken up arms because they knew what had happened to their neighbors—a charge that Magruder claimed was verified by Butler himself. Prince John also judged that Butler's order pledging to respect the property rights of "citizens at peace with the United States" was a farce because it applied "only to persons who think as you think," leaving every other citizen

78. Butler to Magruder, June 13, 1861, ibid., ser. 1, 2:682.
79. General Orders No. 2, May 28, 1861, ibid., 664.
80. Butler to Magruder, June 13, 1861, ibid., 682.
81. *Wilmington Daily Journal,* July 3, 1861.

at risk and without protection. Magruder ended his letter by pointing out to his Federal counterpart that when a picket of four is sent on a twenty-four-hour reconnoitering assignment toward enemy lines, at least one is permitted to sleep. The vedettes had orders to retreat in the face of a large force of the enemy. Four men against five thousand constituted such great odds as to have justified the retreat of three of the vedettes, who, regrettably, left the other behind. "Had Private Carter been awake," wrote Magruder with biting sarcasm, "perhaps a retreat would not have been necessary."[82] Magruder's June 15 letter ended the rhetorical battle; Butler offered no reply.

The *Wilmington Daily Journal* judged that Magruder "got the better of the Lowell general" in the letter exchange,[83] just as he had prevailed earlier when his force exchanged shots with Butler's at Big Bethel. Several newspapers also reported that Magruder challenged General Butler to a duel after their rhetorical tussle,[84] but one never occurred. If the prince was as handy with a dueling pistol as he was with his sword and his pen, Butler was sure to lose again. The Lincoln administration realized that the Massachusetts politician turned general was overmatched and had become an embarrassing liability. Less than three months after taking command at Fort Monroe, Benjamin Franklin Butler was replaced by seventy-eight-year-old Mexican War hero General John E. Wool.[85] Worse yet for Butler, he was not given another command but, rather, was kept on the Virginia Peninsula and placed in charge of whatever troops were outside of the fortress.[86] After being stripped of his command, Butler seemed to disappear like a passing storm.

Richmond could, at least for awhile, breathe easily again. The topic of conversation as well as the focus of local newspapers became not the Federal threat but Prince John Magruder. He was "a brave and daring officer," according to one correspondent.[87] And when in full uniform directing his troops in battle, the prince reportedly looked "every inch a King."[88] Several newspapers declared that Magruder was the "hero of the Peninsula."[89] Yet the most gen-

---

82. Magruder to Butler, June 15, 1861, *Official Records*, ser. 1, 2:686.

83. *Wilmington Daily Journal*, July 3, 1861.

84. *Baltimore Sun*, June 27, 1861; *Richmond Dispatch*, June 29 and July 4, 1861.

85. Scott to Wool, August 8, 1861, *Official Records*, ser. 1, 4:600. General Wool assumed command at Fort Monroe on August 17, 1861. See General Orders No. 1, August 17, 1861, ibid., 601.

86. Special Orders No. 9, August 21, 1861, *Official Records*, ser. 1, 4:602.

87. "The First Regiment (N.C.) Volunteers," *Southern Historical Society Papers* 19 (1891): 228.

88. *Richmond Dispatch*, July 10, 1861.

89. *Richmond Whig*, July 4, 1861; *Richmond Dispatch*, June 17, 1861, note from the *Fredericksburg News*.

erous praise—and the most ridiculous—came from the *Richmond Dispatch,* which on June 13, 1861, proclaimed the triumph at Big Bethel to be "the greatest victory in the annals of modern warfare."[90] When Magruder followed his military victory with what was proclaimed as his intellectual defeat of Ben Butler in their widely circulated and eagerly read exchange of letters following the battle, his stature was further enhanced in the public mind. Suddenly, in the opinion of Douglas Southall Freeman, John Magruder had become "a hero second only to Beauregard in the esteem of the Confederacy."[91]

So far, however, Magruder had proved very little to Jefferson Davis. Davis and Magruder had a long history that started when they were cadets at the U.S. Military Academy. Davis graduated in the class of 1828 in the bottom third of his class; Magruder graduated in the class of 1830, one slot away from the top third of his class. Davis left the army in 1835 as a first lieutenant but later returned to lead Mississippi volunteers in the War with Mexico. He served under Zachary Taylor, fought at Buena Vista, where he was wounded, and again left military service. Conversely, Magruder's army career was uninterrupted after West Point. In the Mexican War he had fought under both Taylor and Scott and participated in every major engagement of the war except Buena Vista. By the time the war ended, Magruder had spent eighteen years in military service; Davis had served eight.[92] Yet in spite of Davis's lim-

90. *Richmond Dispatch,* June 13, 1861. Accurate, objective reporting was a rare commodity in mid-nineteenth-century American journalism. Reporters and editors in both sections had fanned the flames of hatred in the 1850s to the point of "hyperemotionalism." In an already emotionally charged political environment it was the press that radicalized the American people, thus rendering productive communications impossible. Indeed, the war between the North and South was fought in the newspapers long before it reached the fields of battle of the American Civil War. Then, when it started, the press continued to report events with a shameless disregard for either accuracy or objectivity. Throughout the war it was the northern press that, without a shred of evidence, promoted the notion that Magruder was continually under the influence of alcohol while in command. The southern press, on the other hand, lionized Magruder and other successful Confederate leaders and exaggerated their accomplishments. The statement in the *Dispatch* calling Big Bethel "the greatest victory in the annals of modern warfare" should serve as warning to any scholar in search of an honest, unbiased historical perspective that Civil War–era newspapers must be read with considerable skepticism.

91. Freeman, *Lee's Lieutenants,* 1:19. George Shackleford, George Wythe Randolph's biographer, agreed with Freeman, writing that Magruder was "probably Virginia's greatest war hero" until the Seven Days' battles. George Shackleford, *George Wythe Randolph and the Confederate Elite* (Athens: University of Georgia Press, 1988), 62.

92. Cullum, *Biographical Register,* 1:333–34, 367–68. Davis graduated number twenty-three in a class of thirty-three; Magruder graduated number fifteen in a class of forty-two.

ited time in uniform and scant battle experience, he had an extremely high opinion of his military capabilities.[93] Magruder had a high opinion of his abilities too, but he believed that his reputation had been earned, not arrogated.

Magruder became a thorn in Davis's side when Davis served as Franklin Pierce's secretary of war from 1853 to 1857. During those years Magruder made innumerable requests to have his artillery company remounted. At one point he had even charged that Davis failed to make good on his promise to remount his company following its service as escort for the U.S.-Mexico Boundary Survey.[94] However, Adjutant General Samuel Cooper returned a short, direct note to Magruder on Jefferson Davis's behalf, stating that the secretary of war had no recollection of having made any such promise.[95] Magruder also bombarded both Davis and Cooper with requests to lead an entourage of American military officers abroad to observe the advancements of Continental armies. Although Davis acknowledged the merits of the suggested fact-finding missions,[96] and twice sent delegations to Europe, he never selected Magruder. John Magruder became such an irritant to the War Department that Davis's chief clerk, Archibald Campbell, suggested facetiously that it might be more fruitful to send him to China.[97] In his excellent study on the Confederate command system Frank Vandiver observed that once a person had fallen out of favor with Jefferson Davis, it was "impossible for Davis to forgive an enemy or to see much good in him."[98] It was only after Davis had departed as secretary of war that Magruder's company was remounted and he was given choice assignments, including command of the prestigious Artillery School for Instruction at Fort Leavenworth and the long-sought mission to observe European armies in action on the Continent.

Jefferson Davis's skepticism was undoubtedly fueled by his adjutant and inspector general, Samuel Cooper, who had an extremely low opinion of

---

93. Frank E. Vandiver, *Rebel Brass: The Confederate Command System* (Baton Rouge: Louisiana State University Press, 1956), 24. Vandiver wrote that Davis's "experience as a field officer in Mexico had a lasting effect on his self-estimate. Mexican service seems to have convinced him that he was something of a military expert, not to say genius."

94. Magruder to Cooper, December 8, 1855, National Archives.

95. Cooper to Magruder, February 27, 1856, National Archives.

96. Davis to Magruder, December 22, 1853, National Archives.

97. Archibald Campbell to "My Dear Sir" (Davis), August 20, 1853, Crist and Dix, eds., *The Papers of Jefferson Davis*, 5:39. Original in Jefferson Davis Papers, Transylvania University, Lexington, Ky.

98. Vandiver, *Rebel Brass,* 28.

Magruder. Cooper had been Roger Jones's protégé in the War Department. He had served under Jones for ten years until the Jones died on June 15, 1852. He had also witnessed the bickering between Jones and Magruder. Then, after succeeding Jones, Cooper and Magruder developed their own adversarial relationship. Not surprisingly, Jefferson Davis invariably supported Samuel Cooper, with whom he had worked closely for many years. That Davis held Cooper's opinions in high regard was unfortunate for John Magruder because Samuel Cooper was Magruder's principal detractor in the Confederate governmental hierarchy. It was Cooper who later warned Davis never to rely on Magruder, stating that he was "addicted to the vice of intemperance."[99]

When Jefferson Davis arrived in Richmond on May 29, 1861, to relocate and reorganize his government's operations, he immediately met with Governor Letcher to discuss transferring Virginia's forces to Confederate control. Letcher was particularly concerned about preserving the rank of officers in the state's forces who were about to be transferred into Confederate service.[100] President Davis promised that virtually every officer switching from Federal to Virginia to Confederate service would retain his original rank. Davis added that probably not a single man would lose rank by transfer, but he could not absolutely guarantee this in every case.[101] Given the turbulent working relationship between Davis and Magruder, combined with the enmity of Samuel Cooper, one can only speculate that Davis would not guarantee the preservation of rank in all cases because of Magruder. However, the matter became a moot point shortly afterward, when Prince John won his victory at Big Bethel. As a result of the instant popularity he won with both southern people and the press corps, it would have been impossible for the president to have reduced his rank. On the contrary, a promotion appeared to be in order, but Davis was reluctant. So concerned was he about past rumors of alcoholic impropriety that he had Robert E. Lee ask Magruder for a verification or denial of the rumors before he would even consider granting a promotion.[102]

99. Cooper to Davis, July 12, 1862, Dearborn Collection, Harvard University.

100. Boney, *John Letcher of Virginia*, 132; Proceedings of the Advisory Council of the State of Virginia, June 1, 1861, *Official Records*, ser. 1, vol. 51, pt. 2, 124.

101. Boney, *John Letcher of Virginia*, 132; Davis to Letcher, June 2, 1861, *Official Records*, ser. 1, vol. 51, pt. 2, 133.

102. The letter from Robert E. Lee to Magruder regarding Magruder's alleged alcoholic impropriety has never been located. Its substance can be clearly ascertained, however, from Magruder's June 18, 1861, response to General Lee's communication.

Magruder answered on June 18, 1861, in a letter written from Bethel Church that was marked "Private." He acknowledged Lee's communication as being "kind" and "generous." He also told Lee that he appreciated "the delicacy of your letter and the truth of your friendship for me," even though "the reports of the nature alluded to by you do me great injustice." Magruder closed in a straightforward manner when he told Lee, "I do not hesitate to authorize you to state I will never during this war give the slightest cause for these reports."[103]

Three days later, on June 21, General Lee sent Magruder a reply:

> Upon reception of your letter on the 18th I stated to the President what you authorized me to say, quoting your written words. He replied that the only construction he could give to your resolve [that] never during [the war would you] give the slightest cause for reports referred to, was your intention to abstain altogether from the use of intoxicating drink . . . Accordingly, I have great pleasure of enclosing your commission of Brigadier General and of offering you my sincere congratulations. I believe you will so act as to bring honor on yourself and the service. I requested your commission to be dated the 17th; the date of appointment of others, that your relative position might not be disturbed.[104]

Six weeks later, on August 7, 1861, John Magruder was promoted to major general.[105] On the following day, to assure Jefferson Davis that his new confidence in him was justified, Magruder promised the president, through Lee, that he was strictly adhering to his pledge of sobriety: "I think I shall never use any stimulant so long as I live, as my health is perfect without it and as I consider myself as bound in honor to abstain from it during this war."[106]

Still the rumors persisted. Shortly after Magruder was promoted to major general, George Wythe Randolph left his station on the Peninsula for a visit to Richmond. He stated that he was shocked to find that "reports very injurious to General Magruder were rife in the community, and that he is currently represented as being very dissipated." Randolph immediately wrote to Assistant Secretary of War Albert T. Bledsoe to diffuse the gossip. "As these

103. Magruder to Lee, June 18, 1861. Original in the New York Public Library.

104. Lee to Magruder, June 21, 1861. Original in the New York Public Library.

105. Marcus J. Wright, *General Officers of the Confederate Army* (New York: Neale Publishing Co., 1911), 23; Ezra J. Warner, *Generals in Gray* (Baton Rouge: Louisiana State University Press, 1959), 207.

106. Magruder to Lee, August 8, 1861. Original in the New York Public Library.

statements do him great injury, not only with the public, but must impair his standing at the Department, I deem it but justice to contradict them," wrote Randolph. He declared "most positively and upon my own personal knowledge [that] General Magruder, since his appointment as a brigadier-general, has not used intoxicating liquors of any sort." The letter, said Randolph, was addressed to Bledsoe because "you have it in your power to remove any injurious impression about the general, should any exist in high quarters."[107]

Contemporary diaries, journals, letters, and newspaper accounts do not indicate, as Randolph reported, that rumors connecting John Magruder to alcoholic abuse were "rife in the community." In fact, after Big Bethel such gossip was uncommon, even in northern newspapers, until the turmoil following the Seven Days' campaign. Yet Magruder knew from the two letters he received from Lee that President Davis had lingering concerns. Whether he also knew that General Cooper thought him to have a problem with alcohol is conjectural. Clearly, however, if rumors were rife anywhere prior to the Seven Days' battles, it was in the "high quarters" that Randolph alluded to and not with either the public or the southern press. In all probability both Magruder and Randolph were aware of this, and Randolph wrote the August 26 letter to Albert Bledsoe in an effort to win support for his commander with his superiors in Richmond. Without it Magruder's calls for soldiers, laborers, and supplies would go unheeded, which, in turn, would render a successful defense of the Peninsula impossible.

Even if Magruder had been on the best of terms with his superiors, he was destined to face supply shortages because the Confederacy was woefully lacking in resources. It also lacked manufacturing capabilities and would find it increasingly difficult to obtain military supplies from abroad. Furthermore, as Magruder discovered, those supplies that the government was able to send were often of such inferior quality that they were useless. On August 14, 1861, he complained through Colonel Robert Johnston, commander of the 2nd Virginia Cavalry, to Josiah Gorgas, the chief of Confederate ordnance, that the gun carriages at Yorktown were "carelessly constructed, of very inferior pine timber, and are already much damaged from slight exposure to the weather and from their use."[108] Reports from the field indicated that after

107. Randolph to Bledsoe, August 26, 1861, *Official Records,* ser. 1, vol. 51, pt. 2, 251. Bledsoe, from Kentucky, graduated immediately behind Magruder in the West Point Class of 1830.

108. Johnston to Gorgas, August 14, 1861, ibid., 4:633; Magruder to Deas, August 2, 1861, ibid., vol. 51, pt. 2, 209.

firing only a few rounds, the guns often dismounted themselves. Further-more, the manner of construction prevented their being elevated sufficiently to explode a fifteen-second fuse; thus, their greatest range could not be at-tained.[109]

The ammunition was also defective. Magruder reported that about half of his artillery shells exploded near the muzzle of the gun that fired them rather than at the intended target. He had earlier experienced the same problem in battle at Bethel and warned Gorgas, "We shall be ruined unless you can send me good shell and spherical case shot and good friction primers."[110] Later, after receiving a new shipment of ordnance supplies, Magruder wrote in disgust that the new friction primers that were sent in place of "others which were worthless, turned out to be worthless themselves."[111]

The Confederates on the Peninsula were further handicapped by poor-quality working stock. On October 25 General Magruder informed Samuel Cooper that "the artillery horses which have been furnished this department are, almost without exception, worthless." Consequently, his artillery pieces were reportedly "drawn by miserable horses [and] the caissons by miser-able mules." In anger Magruder charged that the neglect in supplying the Peninsula with military essentials was "criminal." He thus implored General Cooper to order "from the Quartermaster Department one hundred good horses for artillery" in order to keep his forces in a condition in which they could at least take the field in battle against an enemy.[112]

Magruder needed guns, ammunition, tents, halters, riding saddles and bridles, picket rope, girths, horse blankets, horseshoes, running gear, har-nesses, ambulances, caissons, and wagons.[113] His need for wagons was espe-cially pressing. There existed an ample supply of forage on the Peninsula, but without sufficient wagons to transport the feed where it was needed, it was of no value. As it was, artillery and cavalry horses in Magruder's department were dying from want of long forage. "I am endeavoring to remedy this," he wrote, "but cannot do it without at least fifty wagons more." He complained

---

109. Magruder to Benjamin, September 23, 1861, *Official Records*, ser. 1, 4:656. Also found ibid., vol. 51, pt. 2, 307.

110. Magruder to Gorgas, October 8, 1861, *Official Records*, ser. 1, 4:674–75.

111. Magruder to Cooper, October 25, 1861, ibid., 691.

112. Ibid.

113. Magruder to Garnett, April 29, 1861, ibid., 2:789; June 3, 1861, ibid., 903; Magruder to Northrup, August 24, 1861, ibid., 4:635; Alston to Myers, October 3, 1861, ibid., 667; Magruder to Cooper, October 23, 1861, ibid., 687; October 25, 1861, ibid., 691.

that "requisitions have been made and repeated, messengers have been sent again and again, and standing agents kept in Richmond to procure these supplies but with very inadequate results, both as to quantity as well as quality." Although obviously frustrated, Magruder assured Samuel Cooper that his purpose in writing the letter of complaint was not to criticize but, rather, to focus the government's attention on the inadequacy of supplies.[114] In actuality Cooper was already well aware of the problem. Unfortunately, he had no solution.

Another vexing problem was a shortage of manpower. From the time that John Magruder and D. H. Hill arrived on the Peninsula, they made impassioned pleas to Richmond for additional troops. When Magruder first announced his victory at Big Bethel in a June 10, 1861, letter to Secretary of War Leroy Pope Walker, he ended the communiqué with an urgent solicitation, "Please send re-enforcements immediately."[115] Less than a week later Hill wrote Lee from his command post at Yorktown, warning that the enemy was "burning for revenge." He insisted that unless substantial reinforcements were sent, "the York line may be lost at any moment."[116] General Lee replied the following day, urging Hill to adopt every means possible to hold his position. However, as for the request for reinforcements, Lee could only promise that he would send troops as they became available.[117]

Because Richmond could not supply the Peninsula with enough defenders, Magruder had to look elsewhere for troops. His situation was facilitated somewhat after June 6, 1861, when Governor Letcher officially turned all state forces over to Confederate control. The transfer included Magruder and the Virginia volunteer units that he commanded plus all state militiamen, who were to be used "as . . . their services may be required." Letcher enjoined his

114. Magruder to Cooper, October 23, 1861, *Official Records,* ser. 1, 4:687; October 25, 1861, ibid., 691.

115. Magruder to Walker, June 10, 1861, *Official Records,* ser. 1, 2:91.

116. Hill to Lee, June 15, 1861, ibid., 927. Benjamin Stoddert Ewell, in command of Magruder's forces at Williamsburg, also pointed out the need for reinforcements. In a May 29, 1861, letter to Lee's headquarters Ewell stated: "I beg you to call the attention of the Commanding General to the fact that the force now here is not sufficient to repel a serious attack. If Yorktown, Jamestown, or the defenses below Williamsburg fall, the way will be open to Richmond. To defend them more troops are necessary, well supplied with artillery." Ewell to Washington, May 29, 1861, ibid., 891.

117. Lee to "the Commanding Officer Yorktown, Va.," June 16, 1861, *Official Records,* ser. 1, 2:930.

fellow Virginians "to respect and obey all lawful orders emanating from the President, or those commanding under his authority."[118] Because Magruder had been released from state control and now commanded under President Davis's authority, he opportunistically called the 68th and 115th regiments into active service on June 15 with orders to rendezvous at Yorktown on the twenty-fourth.[119] These militiamen were from James City, York, Warwick, and Elizabeth City counties. They were assigned to duty near their homes so that they could play a productive role in defending their own property. Magruder only required them to meet three times a week "to organize, drill, and be ready in case of an emergency."[120]

There was never any doubt in John Magruder's mind that he was acting well within his authority when he called up Virginia militiamen. He stated in a March 4, 1862, letter to Samuel Cooper that he had "authority from the Governor of this State to call out all militia from any counties in the State."[121] Furthermore, President Davis, through George W. Randolph, had earlier authorized Magruder to call out all of the militia that he could arm.[122] Magruder requested the call-ups through the War Department, which usually acquiesced, although the department limited his calls to the counties within his military jurisdiction. He did not deem it necessary to seek permission from Governor Letcher or any other state official before calling militiamen into active service.[123] As evidence, when he informed the governor that the first call-up had been made, it was five weeks after the fact. F. N. Boney, who authored John Letcher's biography, wrote that "Letcher was far from pleased with Magruder's conduct but allowed him to keep the militia."[124] In reality, because Governor Letcher had officially turned control of the state militia over to Confederate authorities, he had no power to countermand Magruder. Letcher could endorse or criticize Magruder's call-ups, but he could not overrule them; that power now rested with Confederate authorities alone.

118. General Orders No. 25, June 8, 1861, ibid., 911–12. General Orders No. 25, dated June 8, 1861, circulated the proclamation that Governor Letcher had signed on June 6, 1861. June 6, then, is the date that Letcher officially turned all state forces over to the Confederacy.

119. Proclamation of J. Bankhead Magruder, June 15, 1861, ibid., vol. 51, pt. 2, 140.

120. Magruder to "His Excellency the Governor," July 21, 1861, ibid., 2:988.

121. Magruder to Cooper, March 4, 1862, ibid., vol. 51, pt. 2, 484.

122. Magruder to "His Excellency the President of the Confederate States," January 10, 1862, ibid., 4:721. This letter is also published ibid., 9:32–33. See also Magruder to Cooper, December 20, 1861, ibid., 4:713.

123. Magruder to Cooper, December 11, 1861, *Official Records*, ser. 1, 4:709–10.

124. Boney, *John Letcher of Virginia*, 151.

In December 1861, when Magruder feared that he was about to be attacked by forty thousand Federals,[125] he called up local militiamen again. Yet this time it was not Governor Letcher but, rather, Secretary of War Judah P. Benjamin who overruled the emergency call-up.[126] It was the one and only time that Confederate authorities objected to Magruder's militia requests, and they did so on this occasion primarily because they feared he would be unable to provide the militiamen with adequate arms.[127] Authorities in Richmond were also unable to assist with arms, nor could they provide any government troops. An exasperated Samuel Cooper declared on December 18, 1861, "There are no troops in Richmond that can be sent anywhere."[128] Under the circumstances Confederate officials were hardly in a position to object too strenuously when Magruder and his fellow commanders in the field were trying to help the southern cause by utilizing the only military manpower resource available to them—the militia.

The South was also as badly in need of labor throughout the war years as it was in need of troops and munitions.[129] Robert E. Lee made Governor Letcher aware of this problem when he wrote on June 14, 1861, that the defensive works around Richmond were progressing very slowly "from the want of laborers."[130] Yet the problems involved in protecting Richmond were miniscule compared with those that Magruder faced in his department. Defending a peninsula seven miles wide at its narrowest point and nearly a hundred miles long, in order to protect the approaches to Richmond, was a daunting task.[131] It was, however, the primary task that Magruder had been assigned when originally ordered to the Peninsula in May 1861.

Magruder realized that "there was but one way that furnished the remotest hope that the Peninsula could be defended at all with the means then

125. Magruder to Benjamin, December 7, 1861, *Official Records*, ser. 1, 4:707; December 8, 1861, ibid.

126. Benjamin to Magruder, December 9, 1861, *Official Records*, ser. 1, 4:708; Richardson to Benjamin, January 3, 1862, ibid., vol. 51, pt. 2, 431. William H. Richardson, then the adjutant general of the State of Virginia, makes reference to a telegram that Benjamin sent to Magruder on December 9, 1861. In the telegram Benjamin said, "The President . . . does not deem it expedient to call out the militia."

127. Benjamin to Magruder, December 9, 1861, *Official Records*, ser. 1, 4:708; Cooper to Magruder, ibid.

128. Cooper to secretary of war, December 18, 1861, *Official Records*, ser. 1, 4:710.

129. Bernard Nelson, "Confederate Slave Impressment Legislation, 1861–1865," *Journal of Negro History* 31 (October 1946): 392.

130. Lee to Letcher, June 14, 1861, *Official Records*, ser. 1, 2:926.

131. *Richmond Dispatch*, June 15, 1861.

at the disposal of the Republic, and that was by active and threatening operations, in front, to make the enemy fear for himself, while the positions
were being most vigorously fortified in rear."[132] The victory at Bethel Church
stunned the Federals and made them overly cautious. It also gave Magruder
the time he needed to assemble manpower sufficient for the construction of
his trans-peninsular defenses with minimal opposition from his opponents.

Early on, slave owners on the Peninsula willingly provided Magruder
with Negro laborers whenever he requested them.[133] After all, the planters
could not in good conscience deny the use of their slaves to the government, which was, in part, fighting to maintain the planters' ownership of the
slaves.[134] The degree of cooperation was such that owners in many instances
even provided tools and rations for their slaves. When Magruder returned
borrowed slaves to their owners as promised and his labor supply ran short,
he ceased drilling his own men, put them to work building fortifications,[135]
then immediately appealed to area planters for more help.

In June 1861 Magruder called upon the slave owners of York, Warwick,
and Elizabeth City counties to send half of their slaves to work on the entrenchments at Yorktown.[136] After those slaves were returned, Magruder in
July issued a similar call, asking the slave owners in Charles City and New
Kent counties to send half of their slaves to work on the defenses at Williamsburg.[137] Then he sought slaves from the citizens of Gloucester, Middle-
sex, and Mathews counties to finish the defensive works around Gloucester
Point. Pay was fifty cents per day, plus rations. Magruder reckoned that six
hundred laborers could make Gloucester Point impregnable in ten days by
deepening ditches, thickening parapets, and constructing traverses.[138]

132. Magruder to Cooper, February 1, 1862, *Official Records,* ser. 1, 9:39.

133. Tinsley Lee Spraggins, "Mobilization of Negro Labor for the Department of Virginia
and North Carolina, 1861–1865," *North Carolina Historical Review* 24 (April 1947): 169; Nelson,
"Confederate Slave Impressment Legislation, 1861–1865," 393.

134. Harrison A. Trexler, "The Opposition of Planters to the Employment of Slaves as Laborers by the Confederacy," *Mississippi Valley Historical Review: A Journal of American History* 27
(1940): 211.

135. Magruder to Garnett, May 25, 1861, *Official Records,* ser. 1, 2:878; May 27, 1861, ibid., 886;
June 3, 1861, ibid., 903; Ewell to Washington, May 29, 1861, ibid., 891; Ewell to Magruder, ibid.,
892.

136. *Harper's Weekly,* June 15, 1861.

137. Tyler and Carter to the secretary of war, August 26, 1861, *Official Records,* ser. 1, 4:636.

138. Cosby to Crump, July 28, 1861, ibid., 2:1007.

Maintaining this large workforce was no easy task for Magruder. Slave laborers found out very early that the Union offered them more than the Confederacy.[139] Consequently, when opportunities presented themselves, the slaves melted into the swamps and later reappeared in Hampton to petition General Butler for protection. Butler also regularly sent out raiding parties to seize food, supplies, and slaves from the nearby countryside. Magruder countered by dispatching cavalry units under Robert Johnston and John Bell Hood to round up runaways and to "destroy or capture all parties of the enemy which may venture far from their posts."[140] Both Johnston and Hood engaged the Federals to good effect, plus they captured and returned approximately 150 slaves, who, according to Colonel Johnston, "evidenced the strongest dislike of being taken."[141]

In spite of Magruder's best efforts to confine his laborers to the defensive works where they were assigned, several were among the hundreds of runaway slaves that had fled to the protection of the Federals at Fort Monroe by July 1861.[142] Because so many slaves had defected to the fort and others were streaming in regularly, overcrowding quickly became a problem. Butler's solution was to colonize the new arrivals in Hampton. This Magruder learned from a captured issue of the *New York Tribune* that contained a copy of General Butler's report to Secretary of War Simon Cameron. He also knew for some time that Hampton "was the harbor of runaway slaves and traitors." And because it was of increasing importance to Butler, Magruder ordered his forces to destroy the town by fire.[143] Eliminating this shelter for the run-

139. Spraggins, "Mobilization of Negro Labor for the Department of Virginia and North Carolina, 1861–1865," 161.

140. Magruder to Johnston, July 22, 1861, *Official Records,* ser. 1, 2:991.

141. Johnston to Cosby, July 27, 1861, ibid., 1004; Magruder to Deas, August 2, 1861, ibid., 4:570; August 9, 1861, ibid.

142. Spraggins, "Mobilization of Negro Labor for the Department of Virginia and North Carolina, 1861–1865," 178.

143. Magruder to Deas, August 9, 1861, *Official Records,* ser. 1, 4:570–72. When Magruder was criticized for razing Hampton, a correspondent from the *Richmond Whig* explained the action in a letter to his newspaper:

I deem it nothing more than an act of justice to write the facts in the case . . . Since the homes of these loyal and good citizens had been occupied by runaway negroes, Lincoln soldiers and traitors, these latter had slaves there and were engaged giving aid and comfort to the enemy and the place was being strongly fortified by General Butler . . . He [Magruder] had seen in Butler's report to Secretary Cameron that he intended to make Hampton the

aways made the Federals scale back their efforts to round them up and bring them in. The slaves, however, came on their own and in ever-increasing numbers.[144] Thus, the challenge for Butler and Wool was to provide for the runaways. Simultaneously, the challenge for Magruder was to complete his defensive works without them.

As time passed and the need for manpower became more acute, Magruder kept borrowed laborers at work on his defenses for longer periods of time. Such actions tested both the patience and the patriotism of local planters, among them former President John Tyler and Robert E. Lee's cousin, Hill Carter. On August 26, 1861, Tyler and Carter met with Secretary of War Walker and asked for an opinion on the legal authority of General Magruder's actions. They explained that Magruder's retention of their slaves delayed the thrashing of the wheat crop and generated discontent among local slave owners. Tyler and Carter suggested that an official opinion might "quiet all further uneasiness."[145]

The opinion that Walker rendered, however, was not at all what the planters had hoped for. The secretary wrote that General Magruder and his fellow commanders in the field were expected to exercise power "with caution and discretion." But he also insisted that in times of war the generals in command had to be the sole judges of that which constituted military necessity in their respective departments.[146] A month later, on September 24, 1861, Albert Bledsoe made it clear that the War Department stood solidly behind Magruder when he stated, "I am directed by the Secretary of War to say that your course in impressing labor for work upon fortifications in cases of absolute necessity and for a fair price is fully approved."[147]

---

base of his operations up the Peninsula . . . He [Butler] stated moreover that the negroes were coming in to him rapidly and that deprived of the possession of Hampton, he was much embarrassed to know what to do with them. He had in fact determined to form a colony of blacks in the houses of their masters and the general at once decided to prevent it by burning the place to the ground . . . We occupied the town about 11 o'clock p.m., until near daylight . . . Special care was taken by the General to have the few remaining citizens notified in turn . . . Our General has succeeded in out-generaling old Furioso in every instance and now has him confined in a small space surrounded by friendly marshes, whose malaria will do them more harm this month and next than our shells could possibly do. *Richmond Whig,* August 9, 1861.

144. Edward L. Pierce, "The Contrabands at Fortress Monroe," *Atlantic Monthly* 8 (1861): 628.
145. Tyler and Carter to the secretary of war, August 26, 1861, *Official Records,* ser. 1, 4:636.
146. Walker to Tyler, August 26, 1861, ibid., vol. 51, pt. 2, 252.
147. Bledsoe to Magruder, September 24, 1861, ibid., 9:35. Also found ibid., vol. 51, pt. 2, 310.

Whether laborers were hired or impressed, slave or free, they were supposed to be paid a fair wage by the Confederate government. Slave owners were to be paid the wages that their slaves earned; free blacks were to be paid directly.[148] Magruder urged the government to send the funds necessary for the payment of his workers without delay, as he had promised "prompt payment" to all of those working on his fortifications. He pointed out that "a great many of them are free negroes who have families, who must starve if they are not paid."[149] Without timely payment the labor force would vanish, peninsular defenses would never be completed, and Richmond would be imperiled.

Robert E. Lee and Secretary of War Walker understood the importance of the Virginia Peninsula as it related to Richmond's vulnerability. However, after encouraging and supporting Magruder's early efforts to build stout defensive lines, Lee was reassigned first to western Virginia, then to coastal South Carolina. He would not return to Richmond until March 1862. John Magruder thus lost a valuable and influential ally at a critical time. After Lee left, only Leroy Walker remained to back Magruder within the Confederate hierarchy. He consistently supported Magruder by providing him with men and arms when such resources were available. But when Walker turned the War Department over to Judah P. Benjamin in September 1861, the situation abruptly changed for the worse.

Difficulties with the new secretary of war became immediately apparent when in November 1861 Magruder sought permission from Benjamin to hire five hundred men to work on his defensive lines. Secretary Benjamin, in what was to become standard practice in his dealings with Magruder, turned down the request. He did not believe that the Federals would undertake a winter campaign against the Peninsula. He also reasoned that it would be too expensive to hire the laborers requested by Magruder; plus, he claimed that it would be detrimental to keep the slaves away from their agricultural labors.[150]

Benjamin's rejection, and the reasoning behind it, made very little sense. Regardless of whether an attack was launched against the Peninsula during the winter, it was imperative that the defenses be completed. Postponing construction would only cost Magruder valuable time that he did not have and would never be able to recover. Furthermore, the assertion that Benjamin did not want to keep the slaves away from their agricultural labors was

148. Magruder to Cooper, September 20, 1867, *Official Records,* ser. 1, 4:654. See the enclosed Impressment Proclamation dated September 7, 1861.

149. Magruder to Deas, August 9, 1861, ibid., 573.

150. Leadbetter to Magruder, November 9, 1861, ibid., 697.

without merit. By November all crops had been harvested, and the growing season had ended. Because no more agricultural work loomed until the following spring, winter was, in actuality, the most opportune time to hire the slaves. And finally, to remove objections to the cost, Magruder's agents located blacks who would work for one hundred dollars per year,[151] which would result in a savings of 45 percent to the government. When informed of Magruder's proposal, Samuel Cooper immediately authorized him to hire the laborers that he needed, at the stated rate.[152]

General Magruder sent his quartermaster, Benjamin Bloomfield, to Richmond to recruit laborers for the Peninsula. Bloomfield ran advertisements in all of the local newspapers soliciting Negro laborers, mechanics, and teamsters. Hired workers were promised comfortable quarters, free medical care, and a clothing allowance. Furthermore, slave owners were assured by the advertisement that the government would be responsible for the value of any slaves who were captured, escaped, or killed in action.[153] When this clause was brought to the attention of Confederate authorities, Colonel Abraham C. Myers, the quartermaster general, instructed Bloomfield to withdraw from the ads the portion holding the Confederacy responsible for the value of the slaves. Myers stated, "No law existed authorizing you to bind the government to these terms." The retraction of this guarantee made it so difficult to recruit laborers that Bloomfield gave up the effort altogether.[154]

Because the government refused to shoulder responsibility for losses involving paid laborers but agreed to accept liability when the loss involved impressed slaves, Magruder logically concluded that most planters in Virginia "would rather have their slaves impressed than hired."[155] The principal problem with impressments on the Peninsula at least was that Magruder was forced to call upon the same planters time and time again to use their slaves. In three letters written to Adjutant General Cooper between January 23 and

151. Magruder to Cooper, December 28, 1861, ibid., 715.

152. Cooper to Magruder, December 29, 1861, ibid., 716.

153. Bloomfield to Magruder, January 30, 1862, ibid., vol. 51, pt. 2, 458. In the letter to Magruder, Bloomfield enclosed a copy of the advertisement that he ran in the newspapers.

154. Ibid. Upon receiving Bloomfield's communiqué indicating that Myers had, in effect, sabotaged the effort to hire slaves, General Magruder immediately sent a letter to Samuel Cooper insisting that the quartermaster general's decision was incorrect. "No law of Congress was required to enable the Government to pay for slaves if lost, any more than to pay for the labor of slaves if impressed," he wrote. Magruder to Cooper, January 30, 1862, ibid., 457. Magruder's point of view, however, was not shared by authorities in Richmond.

155. Magruder to Cooper, January 30, 1862, *Official Records*, ser. 1, vol. 51, pt. 2, 457.

February 1, 1862, Magruder lamented that he had prevailed upon the planters in the counties comprising his department so many times that he feared any additional slave impressments would result in widespread dissatisfaction.[156] To solve the problem, General Magruder impressed slaves from Mecklenburg, Lunenburg, Brunswick, Chesterfield, and Dinwiddie counties,[157] all of which were outside of his military jurisdiction. Secretary Benjamin again reversed Magruder's action, declaring that "it is impossible to concede that any general can proceed to the department commanded by another and there exercise authority to impress."[158]

An obviously frustrated John Magruder wrote that it was now impossible to hire slaves given the constraints placed upon him by the government.[159] Furthermore, he stated, unless he received orders to the contrary, he would not ask the planters of the Peninsula to provide more laborers because to call upon them again would be "oppressive and unjust in the extreme."[160] It seemed to be both fair and logical to call upon counties that had never furnished any labor. Magruder reminded Richmond authorities that "the quantity of labor necessary in this department is greater, perhaps, than that required in all the [other] departments in Virginia put together."[161] If Confederate authorities could mobilize Virginia's militiamen and send them wherever they were required to face the enemy, why could not the War Department authorize the impressment of slaves in places where they were not needed and send them to places where they desperately were needed?

Magruder reported that as many as nine-tenths of the citizens in the recently called upon counties were more than willing to send their slaves to work on the defenses of the Peninsula. Yet Benjamin countermanded Magruder's impressment order when a handful of dissidents employed a lawyer who raised objections at the War Department.[162] Later, after realizing that his actions had left the peninsular defensive works incomplete, Secretary Benjamin relented somewhat, allowing Magruder to impress half of the

156. Magruder to Cooper, January 23, 1862, ibid., 9:34; January 30, 1862, ibid., vol. 51, pt. 2, 456; February 1, 1862, ibid., 9:42.

157. Magruder to Cooper, January 23, 1862, *Official Records,* ser. 1, 9:33–34; January 30, 1862, ibid., vol. 51, pt. 2, 456–57.

158. Magruder to Cooper, January 30, 1862 (second endorsement), *Official Records,* ser. 1, vol. 51, pt. 2, 457; Benjamin to Magruder, January 27, 1862, ibid., 9:36; March 4, 1862, ibid., 52.

159. Magruder to Cooper, January 30, 1862, *Official Records,* ser. 1, vol. 51, pt. 2, 456.

160. Ibid., 457; Ewell to Joynes, February 7, 1862, ibid., 9:43.

161. Magruder to Cooper, February 1, 1862, *Official Records,* ser. 1, 9:42.

162. Magruder to Cooper, January 23, 1862, ibid., 33; February 1, 1862, ibid., 42.

slaves in Dinwiddie County.[163] No authorization was given, however, to utilize the labor resources of Chesterfield, Mecklenburg, Lunenburg, or Brunswick counties. Magruder thus continued to be handicapped and frustrated by the labor shortage.

John Magruder finally reached the point of no return in his dealings with Judah Benjamin. On March 1, 1862, he sent a passionately written letter to Jefferson Davis, through Samuel Cooper, protesting that "two months fully have already been lost in consequence of the War Department disapproving of my arrangements and countermanding my orders." He also complained that Benjamin had discharged 135 slaves from Greensville County who were actively working on the defenses of the Peninsula. And the secretary had done so without even informing Magruder of the fact. "The people have got an idea that the influence of the Government will be cast against my efforts," wrote an exasperated Magruder. It was a situation that he described as demoralizing and psychologically "evil."[164]

Benjamin's penchant for interference and making decisions without the knowledge or counsel of his commanders in the field had caused Stonewall Jackson to resign from the Confederate army a month earlier.[165] Jackson declared: "My duty to Virginia requires that I shall utter my protest against it [Benjamin's interference] in the most energetic form in my power, and that is to resign. The authorities at Richmond must be taught a lesson."[166] Fortunately for the South, Jackson was persuaded to withdraw his letter of resignation. Unfortunately for Magruder, Judah P. Benjamin did not end his regrettable habit of attempting "to control military operations in detail from the Secretary's desk at a distance."[167]

Magruder's March 1 letter charging Secretary Benjamin with interference and a lack of support was of such a caustic nature that, under normal circumstances, it could have jeopardized his position in command. Yet in the wake of the Jackson controversy and the losses of Forts Henry and Donelson and of Nashville in the west and of Roanoke Island in the east, the heat was on Benjamin. In spite of having President Davis's support, he was severely criti-

---

163. Chilton to Magruder, February 15, 1862, *Official Records*, ser. 1, vol. 51, pt. 2, 472–73.

164. Magruder to Cooper, March 1, 1862, ibid., 9:49–50.

165. Jackson to Benjamin, January 31, 1862, ibid., 5:1053.

166. Henderson, *Stonewall Jackson*, 155. Henderson does not give a citation for Jackson's quoted words.

167. Jackson to "Governor," January 31, 1862. This important letter, which was lost for many years and is not in the *Official Records*, was published in the *Richmond Whig*, April 26, 1873.

cized by the southern press and by powerful politicians, including Stonewall Jackson's former neighbor Governor Letcher, for the recent military setbacks and for failing to cooperate with his commanders in the field. Mounting criticism reached a climax on March 4, 1862, when the Confederate Congress offered a resolution asserting that neither the army nor the people had any confidence in the controversial secretary of war. The resolution insisted that Benjamin's retirement was "a high military necessity,"[168] and in less than two weeks he was gone.

Nevertheless, Judah Benjamin tormented Magruder to the end. On the same day that members of Congress called for Mr. Benjamin's "retirement," the beleaguered secretary ordered General Magruder to send five thousand of his men to Benjamin Huger south of the James River in defense of Suffolk.[169] The call amounted to over half of Magruder's disposable force.[170] Worse yet, it came at a critical time when Magruder was emphatically warning Richmond that the Federals were substantially bolstering their strength against him.[171]

Such dire warnings were not new. Magruder had sounded the alarm months earlier, in early December 1861, warning that attacks by the enemy were imminent.[172] When none came, however, critics concluded that Prince John was overreactive, that he "imagined a Yankee behind every ripple in

168. *Journal of the Congress of the Confederate States of America, 1861–1865*, 7 vols. (Washington, D.C.: Government Printing Office, 1904–5), 5:57. The resolution was offered by Representative James W. Moore of Kentucky.

169. Benjamin to Magruder, March 4, 1862, *Official Records*, ser. 1 , 9:51; ibid., 52–53. These are different letters, though both bear the same date.

170. Magruder to Cooper, March 6, 1862, *Official Records*, ser. 1, 9:57.

171. Magruder to Cooper, February 1, 1862, ibid., 42; February 24, 1862, ibid., 44; March 6, 1862, ibid., 57. In late February and early March 1862, Magruder's signal officer, William Norris, reported that large numbers of enemy troops had landed at Newport News. Magruder estimated their strength at "six regiments, in addition to six companies of light artillery, with their horses." Less than three weeks later he would report to Benjamin's successor, George Wythe Randolph, "The enemy are in great force at Fort Monroe, Newport News, and between those places; not less, I think, than 35,000 men." Magruder to Randolph, March 24, 1862, ibid., vol. 11, pt. 3, 392–93.

172. The alarms had come on December 7 and 8, 1861, when Magruder had sent urgent communiqués to the War Department warning that he would soon be attacked by forty thousand Federals. Secretary of War Benjamin scoffed at the report. In an extremely sarcastic letter dated December 9, 1861, Benjamin declared: "It is not believed that any such forces . . . can possibly be within the enemy's line . . . We have no news whatever of any fleet at Fort Monroe threatening your department, but are glad to find that you are vigilant and hopeful." Magruder to Benjamin, December 7, 1861, *Official Records*, ser. 1, 4:707; December 8, 1861, ibid., 708; Benjamin to Magruder, December 9, 1861, ibid., 708.

the water."[173] Because he was thought to be an alarmist, nobody in Richmond took him seriously.[174] Furthermore, Benjamin thought Magruder erred in reporting that the Peninsula was the target of the Federals. "Suffolk is the aim of the enemy," the secretary insisted. Then, with absolute confidence, he declared, "We do not believe that you are in the slightest danger of an attack at present, either in front or by being outflanked by naval forces."[175]

A month earlier Benjamin had been just as confident that Roanoke Island was in no danger of attack, in spite of numerous warnings from North Carolina governor Henry T. Clark and impassioned pleas for assistance from former Virginia governor Henry A. Wise, who commanded Confederate forces along the North Carolina coast. When Wise appealed directly to Benjamin for munitions, the secretary of war replied, "At the first indication . . . of an attack on Roanoke Island a supply will be sent to you."[176] General Wise stated that if Richmond waited until he was attacked to send him the supplies that he needed, they would arrive too late to help.[177] Sure enough, three weeks later, when Federals under Ambrose E. Burnside arrived in force, Wise was left to oppose them in a battle that he had no chance of winning. Subsequently, when a committee of the Confederate Congress investigated the debacle at Roanoke Island, it directed the blame toward Wise's commander, Benjamin Huger, and "the late Secretary of War, J. P. Benjamin."[178] The committee's finding was supported by the attorney general of the Confederacy, Thomas Bragg, who wrote in his diary that "[Benjamin] will say he left all to Huger and he will say he had no troops to spare. The truth is Mr. Benjamin could not be brought to believe that Burnside was going to North Carolina."[179]

173. Boney, *John Letcher of Virginia*, 151.

174. *Memphis Daily Appeal*, January 10, 1862; Brent, *Memoirs of the War between the States*, 100, 102; Freeman, *Lee's Lieutenants*, 1:16. Freeman wrote that Magruder's early dispatches were eagerly read, but after constantly bombarding the War Department with dire warnings, his later exhortations evoked groans.

175. Benjamin to Magruder, March 4, 1862, *Official Records*, ser. 1, 9:53.

176. Benjamin to Wise, January 12, 1862, ibid., 132.

177. Wise to Benjamin, January 15, 1862, ibid., 135–36.

178. Report of the Investigating Committee Confederate House of Representatives, n.d. ibid., 183–91. Approximately twenty-five hundred Confederates were captured at Roanoke Island, and although the loss in killed and wounded was small, among the Confederate dead was Captain Obadiah Jennings Wise, General Wise's twenty-eight-year-old son. Until the day that he died, Henry Wise held Judah Benjamin responsible for the death of his son. Robert Douthat Meade, *Judah P. Benjamin: Confederate Statesman* (New York: Oxford University Press, 1943), 227.

179. Diary of Thomas Bragg, Southern Historical Collection, University of North Carolina, Chapel Hill.

Judah Benjamin was a brilliant man and an extremely talented lawyer. Unfortunately, it seemed that his brilliance did not extend beyond the courtroom to the military field.[180] He consistently misread the intentions of the Federals. Additionally, Benjamin was so self-righteous that he could not admit error and therefore failed to profit from his mistakes. The disastrous consequences of ignoring the warnings of Governor Clark and General Wise prior to the Confederate loss at Roanoke Island did not make the secretary of war any more inclined to believe General Magruder when, in March, he warned Richmond that large numbers of Federals were arriving at Fort Monroe. After all, Magruder had been wrong before. But this time, to Benjamin's complete dismay, the troops that Magruder reported to be arriving were real and not imagined. They were the vanguard of General George B. McClellan's Union Army of the Potomac, soon to be the largest army ever assembled in the Western Hemisphere. Within a month 389 vessels would deliver to the fortress 121,500 men, 14,592 animals, 1,150 wagons, 74 ambulances, 44 artillery batteries, and an enormous amount of equipment.[181] The very Peninsula that Secretary of War Benjamin had perceived to be in no danger of attack was soon to become the epicenter of the war. And because Benjamin had failed to provide Magruder with even minimal military assistance, Prince John, with only 11,000 Confederates,[182] stood alone to block McClellan's march to Richmond.

180. Clifton Rodes Breckenridge, the second son of John C. Breckenridge, wrote many years after the war that Virginians generally believed that "Benjamin's great talents did not extend to the military field." Meade, *Judah P. Benjamin*, 239–40.

181. Report of John Tucker, April 5, 1862, *Official Records*, ser. 1, 5:46.

182. Magruder to Cooper, May 3, 1862, ibid., vol. 11, pt. 1, 405.

5

MAGRUDER DEFENDS, JOHNSTON
RETREATS

The arrival on the Virginia Peninsula of Major General George Brinton Mc-
Clellan and his Army of the Potomac was a long time in coming. Months
earlier, on July 25, 1861, President Lincoln had selected the thirty-five-year-
old McClellan to reorganize the dispirited Union army, which staggered back
toward Washington, D.C., following its humiliating loss at Bull Run.[1] After
"Little Mac" did a superb job of restoring order in Washington and refortify-
ing the capital's defenses, he turned his attention to his primary task of building an army and formulating a scheme that would quell the rebellion and
force the seceded states to return to their former positions in the Union.

General McClellan planned to turn the war decisively in the North's favor
by attacking the Confederate capital with an army so large, so powerful, and
so well trained that it would be invincible in the face of any force the enemy
could bring in opposition to it. Rather than marching due south through
open country, however, he ultimately planned to bypass Joseph E. Johnston's
rebel army in northern Virginia altogether by way of an amphibious expedition into the Chesapeake and then to Urbanna on the Rappahannock River.

1. General Orders No. 47, July 25, 1861, *Official Records,* ser. 1, 2:763. On July 27, 1861, George B.
McClellan took command of what was then officially called the Division of the Potomac, com-
prising the Military Departments of Washington and Northeastern Virginia. General Orders
No. 1, July 27, 1861, ibid., 766. Later, on August 17, 1861, the Departments of Washington and
Northeastern Virginia were united to form the Department of the Potomac. General Orders
No. 15, August 17, 1861, ibid., 5:567. When McClellan formally took command of the newly cre-
ated Department on August 20, he termed it the "Army of the Potomac." It is by that name that
McClellan's army is still known today. General Orders No. 1, August 20, 1861, ibid., 575.

Once ashore, McClellan would move swiftly overland to West Point on the York, isolating Magruder and his men on the Peninsula and leaving the Federal navy in position to seize both the York and James rivers. Finally, from West Point McClellan would utilize the Richmond and York River Railroad, race the remaining thirty-four miles to the west, and capture Richmond before Johnston could arrive to defend it.[2] In both scale and concept the plan reflected the genius of one who was admiringly referred to by his supporters as the "Young Napoleon."

From the beginning, however, nothing about this expedition seemed to work as planned. Before McClellan could move, Joe Johnston retreated with his army to a position behind the Rappahannock River, placing him closer to Richmond than the Army of the Potomac would have been at Urbanna.[3] When Johnston's unanticipated move rendered the Urbanna plan impractical, McClellan decided instead to land at Fort Monroe and march to Richmond via the Peninsula. Simultaneously, Irvin McDowell's 1st Corps was to operate on the right and turn Magruder's position in the event that he proved to be a serious obstacle in McClellan's path. It appeared to be a good alternative plan. The fortress was secure. It was relatively close to the rebel capital. And McClellan could still utilize the York and James rivers for supply and artillery support from the navy.[4]

The new plan assumed that the Union navy would be able to control the two important river passages. Coincidentally, however, on March 8, 1862, the same day that Johnston had begun his retreat, the curious-looking CSS *Virginia*, built on the hull of the salvaged USS *Merrimack*, lumbered out of its moorings at Norfolk and laid waste to the Federal blockading squadron in Hampton Roads. On the following day the disaster was allayed somewhat when the USS *Monitor* arrived and fought the *Virginia* to a draw. Still, the threat that the powerful Confederate ironclad ram continued to pose against

2. McClellan to Stanton, February 3, 1862, *Official Records,* ser. 1, 5:44–45. This lengthy and very important letter may also be found in George B. McClellan, *McClellan's Own Story* (New York: Charles L. Webster and Co., 1887), 229–36.

3. Joseph E. Johnston, *Narrative of Military Operations* (Bloomington: Indiana University Press, 1959), 96–102. Johnston had anticipated that as the weather improved and travel became more practical, McClellan would move against Richmond. To protect the capital and to place his army in "a less exposed position," he retreated with his men to the south bank of the Rappahannock River. It was purely coincidental that Johnston moved his army out of northern Virginia just before McClellan implemented the Urbanna plan.

4. McClellan to Stanton, February 3, 1862, *Official Records,* ser. 1, 5:45; also in *McClellan's Own Story,* 235.

the wooden ships of the U.S. Navy left the rebels in control of the James. It was only after McClellan received assurances from his naval advisors that the *Monitor* could continue to neutralize the *Virginia*[5] that he decided to proceed with the peninsular plan of attack, even though he conceded its prospects were now somewhat "less promising . . . than when the James River was in our control."[6]

By this time northerners cared little which plan was adopted; they wanted action.[7] McClellan had been given the best equipment, "the most distinguished of the old officers, the most promising of the young," and the largest number of troops that had ever been assembled by the U.S. Army.[8] The longer McClellan delayed, the more he was criticized. In October, 1861, senators Zachariah Chandler, Lyman Trumbull, and Ben Wade had demanded an advance against the enemy, declaring that a defeat was no worse than a delay.[9] Even President Lincoln, who had been so supportive of his young commander, seemed to have run out of patience, as was evidenced by his famous quip that if General McClellan did not want to use his army, he would like to borrow it so that it could be made to do something.[10]

5. Telegram, Wool to McClellan, March 13, 1862; telegram, Fox to McClellan, March 13, 1862, *Official Records of the Union and Confederate Navies in the War of the Rebellion,* 30 vols. (Washington, D.C.: Government Printing Office, 1894–1922), ser. 1, 7:100. The telegram from Fox to McClellan may also be found in *Official Records,* ser. 1, 5:753. Gustavus V. Fox, the assistant secretary of the navy speculated to McClellan that the *Monitor* would destroy the *Virginia* in their next fight. He added, however, that "this is hope, not certainty."

6. McClellan's Report on the Operations of the Army of the Potomac from July 27, 1861, to November 9, 1862. Report submitted on August 4, 1863, *Official Records,* ser. 1, 5:51.

7. John G. Nicolay and John Hay, *Abraham Lincoln: A History,* 10 vols. (New York: Century Co., 1890), 5:151. In this prodigious work, written by Lincoln's talented secretaries, the authors wrote that Lincoln had in private earnestly urged McClellan to act. The president tried to impress upon him that "a free people, accustomed to considering public affairs as their own, can stand reverses and disappointments; they are capable of making great exertions and great sacrifices. The one thing that they cannot endure is inaction." Likewise, Alexander Webb, assistant to General William F. Barry, who commanded McClellan's artillery during the Peninsula Campaign, stated that "the delay was protracted too long, even for a patient people." Alexander S. Webb, *The Peninsula: McClellan's Campaign of 1862* (New York: Charles Scribner's Sons, 1881), 11. And John G. Barnard, who headed McClellan's Engineering Corps, judged that of all his commander's mistakes, the greatest was when he failed to "do something to confirm, continue and justify the nation's confidence [in him]." John G. Barnard, *The Peninsular Campaign* (New York: D. Van Nostrand, 1864), 8.

8. Nicolay and Hay, *Abraham Lincoln,* 4:441–43; 5:152, 155.

9. Leech, *Reveille in Washington, 1860–1865,* 117.

10. Henry J. Raymond, *The Life and Public Serves of Abraham Lincoln* (New York: Derby and Miller, 1865), 773.

Finally, eight months after having been placed in command of the Army of the Potomac, McClellan began moving his men to the Virginia Peninsula to commence what he believed would be the decisive campaign of the Civil War. He intended to silence his critics—"wretched politicians," he called them—by "drubbing Magruder" at Yorktown, then moving quickly on toward Richmond.[11] General McClellan had expected support from the navy, but Flag Officer Louis M. Goldsborough, commander of the North Atlantic Blockading Squadron, was forced to concentrate his largest and most powerful warships against the *Virginia* at Norfolk. The remaining smaller vessels that were available to be sent to the York lacked sufficient firepower to contest Magruder's artillery batteries at Yorktown and Gloucester Point. The Confederates thus maintained control of both riverways, forcing McClellan to rely entirely on his land forces against Magruder.[12]

General McClellan was still optimistic, however, reporting after his meeting with Goldsborough that all was well and he was in "good spirits." Indeed, private letters written from the Peninsula revealed he had so much confidence in his army that he seemed not to have been overly concerned by the lack of support from the Union navy. If the navy could not gain control of the York River by besting the Confederate batteries at Yorktown, McClellan would simply move overland and seize the enemy artillery positions with his army. Then he would proceed toward Richmond, using the York as his main line of supply. To his wife he wrote, "I see my way very clearly, and . . . will move rapidly." He confidently predicted that within two days he would be in possession of Yorktown.[13]

McClellan's plan for a rapid advance against Magruder was based on the expectation that his army would be able to utilize good natural roads that were reportedly sandy and well drained.[14] Yet as Federal commanders in the

11. *McClellan's Own Story,* 83, 167, 307.

12. Webb, *Peninsula,* 30. Webb noted that in December 1861 Goldsborough, Gustavus Fox, and John G. Barnard had pointed out to General McClellan "the necessity of his taking Norfolk." Had Norfolk and the Gosport Naval Yard been taken, as advised, the *Virginia* would never have been completed, and the U.S. Navy would have had command of both the James and York rivers during the Peninsula Campaign. In short, wrote Webb, "The capture of Norfolk would have changed everything." Ibid., 31.

13. *McClellan's Own Story,* 307. Letter to his wife, April 3, 1861.

14. Van Vliet to McClellan, January 3, 1862, Virginia topographical study, McClellan Papers, Library of Congress; McClellan to Stanton, February 3, 1862, *Official Records,* ser. 1, 5:44. From the information that he had received, McClellan had been led to believe that the roads on the Peninsula were "passable at all seasons of the year" and that the country was level with more cleared land, less dense woods, and more sandy soil.

field would soon discover, nothing was well drained on the low-lying land between the York and James rivers, and passage overland was often challenging, even under the best of conditions. Joseph E. Johnston's early biographer Robert M. Hughes described the topographical nature of the Peninsula:

> A prominent feature is its abundance of swamps, which make up from the rivers on either side, or from the creeks or estuaries emptying into them. These swamps are practically impassable, except at occasional points, where corduroyed roads or embankments of earth for mill ponds form a crossing. The region is so level that such an embankment will make a mill pond miles in length, while every cave or hollow that drains into it will become a swamp more difficult of passage than the pond itself, as it is at once too soft for the pedestrian and too solid for the boatman. Streams of small volume, but with marshes of great extent on either side, take their rise and flow into one or the other of these rivers. The ebb and flow of the tide make these tributaries for long distances above their mouth quite deep and extensive while the swamps and ponds nearer their heads are equally difficult of passage.[15]

It was there, an area that George Wythe Randolph described as "the pestilent marshes of the Peninsula,"[16] that John Bankhead Magruder and George B. McClellan squared off against one another to open what would become the largest campaign of the Civil War.[17]

McClellan had a huge advantage in both manpower and resources. But because he had targeted the Peninsula only after the Urbanna plan had been shelved, his secret service, headed by the well-known Chicago-based detective Allan Pinkerton, had time to collect very little information on the new theater of operations. McClellan, for example, knew the approximate size of the rebel force opposing him, but he did not know how it was deployed, nor did he know anything about the strength or location of Magruder's defensive

---

15. Robert M. Hughes, *General Johnston* (New York: D. Appleton and Co., 1897), 112.

16. Randolph to Bledsoe, August 26, 1861, *Official Records,* ser. 1, vol. 51, pt. 2, 251.

17. By the strangest of ironies, Magruder and McClellan first met on a battlefield in an earlier war. In August 1847 young George McClellan, as a member of Winfield Scott's engineering staff, assisted with the placement of Magruder's guns at Contreras. In the heat of the ensuing battle McClellan took charge of a section of Magruder's artillery when its commander, Lieutenant John P. Johnstone, was mortally wounded. Shortly after Magruder sent McClellan's West Point classmate Thomas J. Jackson to take the place of the fallen Johnstone, Lieutenant Franklin D. Callender was wounded at the head of his section of mountain howitzers. Again, McClellan filled in admirably. After the battle Magruder, McClellan, and Jackson were all cited for gallantry by their superiors.

works.[18] The maps that McClellan had of the Peninsula were inaccurate,[19] plus other information that the Federals possessed about the terrain was later discovered to have been "all erroneous." In hindsight Brigadier General John G. Barnard, McClellan's chief engineer, lamented that his commander had "carried his army into a region of which he was totally ignorant."[20]

Magruder, on the other hand, had been on the Peninsula for over ten months prior to the Federal invasion, and he had used the time well. Immediately after arriving at Yorktown, he had made it a priority to familiarize himself with the geographical characteristics of his new command. He personally scouted the Peninsula,[21] with the help of knowledgable guides, until he was "as familiar with the field in which he had been ordered to operate as if he had spent his boyhood there."[22] Then he organized his command, made arrangements for supplies of rations and ammunition, designed a plan of fortification, and set his engineers to work.[23] He restricted civilian access to military zones,[24] dispatched lookouts to peninsular coastal areas to watch

18. Webb, *Peninsula,* 50, 52; Barnard, *Peninsular Campaign,* 18. General Barnard later wrote that he was astounded when he learned that "within twelve miles of the outposts of troops under [McClellan's] command a powerful defensive line had been thrown up during the winter and spring, of which he knew nothing whatever, though it lay across his meditated line of march, and altered the whole character of the problem."

19. *Report of the Joint Committee on the Conduct of War,* 8 vols. (Washington, D.C.: Government Printing Office, 1863–66), 1:429. Testimony of Major General George B. McClellan before the committee on February 28, 1863. (In 1:419 the date of the commencement of General McClellan's testimony is incorrectly given as February 28, 1862. *McClellan's Own Story,* 253; McClellan's Report, August 4, 1863, *Official Records,* ser. 1, vol. 11, pt. 1, 7–8). Neither side possessed accurate maps; the Confederates, however, were advantageously operating on their own ground; plus, Magruder always had an abundance of reliable guides who lived in the area. McClellan, on the other hand, complained that he could not even count on local slaves because they knew little about the country except for the very plantations on which they had passed their entire lives. He further stated that the slaves were "ridiculously inaccurate" when it came to providing the Federals with accurate estimates of enemy troop strengths. "If a Negro were asked how many Confederates he had seen at a certain point," wrote McClellan in frustration, "his answer was very likely to be: 'I dunno, massa, but I guess about a million.'" *McClellan's Own Story,* 253–54.

20. Barnard, *Peninsular Campaign,* 18.

21. Magruder, "First Battle of the War: Big Bethel," in *Battles and Leaders of the Civil War,* 5:36; Magruder to Cooper, February 1, 1862, *Official Records,* ser. 1, 9:38.

22. Baker P. Lee, "Magruder's Peninsula Campaign in 1862," *Southern Historical Society Papers* 19 (1891): 61.

23. Magruder, "First Battle of the War: Big Bethel," in *Battles and Leaders of the Civil War,* 5:36.

24. General Orders No. 5, May 31, 1861, U.S. War Department, Rebel Records, "Correspondence of the Department of the Peninsula," National Archives.

for unusual enemy naval activity,[25] organized foraging parties to locate and gather feed for his horses and mules,[26] and constructed telegraph lines in an effort to establish efficient communications with Richmond.[27] Magruder also established several field hospitals, recruited volunteer nurses, and requisitioned medicines and supplies from the War Department to minimize the number of soldiers he anticipated losing to malarial illnesses in the notoriously unhealthy marshlands of the Peninsula.[28] And to keep his men sober, alert, and in good discipline, he ordered that all hard liquor be destroyed.[29]

Magruder superintended every detail in preparing his army for the upcoming battles. To ensure that he could get the most out of his men, he restricted leaves of absence and furloughs and put his troops through a rigorous training and work regimen.[30] Soldiers who were not occupied building fortifications drilled four times per day;[31] plus, on Sundays there were reviews and parades, one of which lasted for six hours. Thomas R. R. Cobb, the well-known Georgia politician who was just beginning his military service, grumbled that the lengthy parade "nearly killed some of [the men]."[32] His

25. Magruder to Cary, May 25, 1861, *Official Records,* ser. 1, 2:877; Magruder to Johnston, July 22, 1861, ibid., 991; General Orders No. 89, October 3, 1861, ibid., 4:669.

26. Magruder to Garnett, May 29, 1861, *Official Records,* ser. 1, 2:893; June 3, 1861, ibid., 903; Magruder to Cooper, October 25, 1861, ibid., 4:691; Magruder to McLaws, November 25, 1861, ibid., 703.

27. Magruder to Cooper, November 17, 1861, *Official Records,* ser. 1, 4:701.

28. Magruder to Ewell, February 15, 1862, ibid., 9:43; Richardson to Crowell, August 8, 1861, ibid., 4:632–33; Magruder to Cooper, August 21, 1861, ibid., vol. 51, pt. 2, 246.

29. General Orders No. 5, May 31, 1861, U.S. War Department, Rebel Records, "Correspondence of the Department of the Peninsula," National Archives. Later, in a March 10, 1862, letter to Jefferson Davis, through Samuel Cooper, Magruder asked Davis to declare martial law on the Peninsula, in part to suppress "the clandestine sale of poisonous liquors to our soldiers." Magruder to Cooper, March 10, 1862, *Official Records,* ser. 1, vol. 51, pt. 2, 498. After President Davis declared martial law, Magruder, on March 19, 1862, issued General Orders No. 163, which warned, "The distillation and sale, or either, of spirituous liquors of any kind is positively prohibited and will be promptly punished, and all establishments for the making or sale of the same are hereby suppressed." The order was to be rigidly enforced. Magruder appointed provost-marshals in every camp to "institute strict search in order to the prompt detection, arrest, and punishment of all offenders." General Orders No. 163, March 19, 1862, ibid., vol. 11, pt. 3, 386.

30. General Orders No. 25, June 20, 1861, *Official Records,* ser. 1, vol. 51, pt. 2, 144–45.

31. General Orders No. 9, May 31, 1861, U.S. War Department, Rebel Records, "Correspondence of the Department of the Peninsula," National Archives.

32. Thomas R. R. Cobb to Marion Cobb, September 29, 1861, Thomas R. R. Cobb Collection, University of Georgia, Athens. Thomas Cobb reported to his wife that the six-hour Sunday parade made him "angry to sinfulness." He called the exercise a "Heaven-daring, God-defying

older brother Howell understood the importance of the exercises, however, "for without them our soldiers would forget that it was war—and that would unfit them for their work."[33]

The reviews and parades occurred regularly, according to a schedule. On the other hand, Magruder's emergency simulation exercises came without warning and with no regard for weather or time of day. In a July 18, 1861, letter to his wife, Colonel Lafayette McLaws, commander of the 10th Georgia Infantry, wrote that he had been "awakened at three o'clock by a dispatch from Magruder." It was but a routine drill, yet before breakfast McLaws had hurried his men, along with two six-pounders, to a new position seven miles away from their encampment. McLaws, like the elder Cobb, viewed the exercises as a necessity; he registered no complaint, only commenting to his wife that he was impressed "by the alertness of the commanding general."[34]

Ultimately, Magruder convinced his men that if they were better disciplined, better prepared, and were willing to serve the Confederate cause with zealous determination, they could triumph over their Federal opponents regardless of manpower and resource disadvantages, just as their forefathers had defeated the British in "our first war of Independence . . . on these very plains of Yorktown."[35] Prince John believed that those who served a righteous cause could prevail against unfavorable odds. He had seen it happen before—with Zachary Taylor in south Texas and with Winfield Scott in Mexico. Magruder's men were also keenly aware of the brilliant reputation that their commander had won earlier in those well-chronicled campaigns. Consequently, they placed their full trust in him. A reporter from the *New Orleans Delta* observed: "The soldiers have unbounded confidence in General Magruder. It is true that they growl at his long marches and continual movement, in which he keeps them employed; but, then his bonhomie of manner, his firm, decisive style of command, and his inflexible resolution inspire them all with confidence, and they cheerfully execute duties which under other commanders would be deemed impossible. No portion of the

---

sin." Just ten weeks later, however, Cobb admitted that he was getting used to the "infractions of God's day . . . I am gradually becoming habituated to the idea that a military necessity overrides all our accustomed ideas." Ibid., November 10, 1861.

33. Howell Cobb to Meyon [Mary Ann, his daughter], January 13, 1862, Howell Cobb Collection, University of Georgia, Athens.

34. Lafayette McLaws to his wife, July 18, 1861, McLaws Papers, Southern Historical Collection, University of North Carolina, Chapel Hill.

35. Magruder to the Army of the Peninsula, March 4, 1862, *Official Records*, ser. 1, 9:53–54.

Confederate army has performed anything like such severe marches or encountered such fatigues and hardships as the army under Magruder."[36]

On November 10, 1861, Magruder divided his Army of the Peninsula into
two divisions; Gabriel James Rains commanded the 1st Division at Yorktown,[37] and Lafayette McLaws led the 2nd Division at Young's Mill.[38] The two
newly minted brigadier generals had received their formal military training
at West Point, Rains having graduated in the class of 1827, McLaws in the
class of 1842. Coincidentally, Rains and McLaws had fought together when
Fort Texas was under siege during the early days of the War against Mexico.[39]
At the same time, Magruder had been just a few miles away, participating in
his first actions at Palo Alto and Resaca de la Palma. The three men would
have to call upon everything they had learned in class at West Point and in
battle in Mexico in their search for an advantage, any advantage, that would
enable them to defend the Virginia Peninsula successfully in the face of a
larger, more powerful foe.

Defense, of course, had been John Magruder's priority from the time that
he arrived from Richmond to take command. Immediately after surveying
the area between Yorktown and Fort Monroe with his engineers, he had put
his men to work building fortifications. Before McClellan arrived on the
Peninsula, Magruder had completed his first line of defense several miles
below Yorktown. The line ran from the mouth of the Poquosin River, on
the York, to the mouth of Deep Creek, on the James, with Harwood's and
Young's mills in between. The Poquosin River and Deep Creek protected

36. *Richmond Whig,* September 17, 1861. In his article, published in the *Richmond Whig,* the
correspondent from the *New Orleans Delta* reported that the Louisiana troops in Magruder's
army "have been marched some four or five times over the whole length of the peninsula. They
say they know it as familiarly as they do the streets and localities of New Orleans."

37. Rains was an expert with explosives. One of the innovations that he originated during the
campaign on the Peninsula was the "land torpedo," or anti-personnel mine, which he sowed in
the roads in large quantities, causing numerous Union casualties. Ezra J. Warner noted in his
reference work, *Generals in Gray:* "This hitherto unknown mode of warfare excited much com-
ment and criticism from Federals and Confederates alike. General Longstreet forbade its further
employment as 'not proper.' By the end of the war, however, even its most violent opponents
were converted to its use." Warner, *Generals in Gray,* 250.

38. General Orders No. 105, November 10, 1861, *Official Records,* ser. 1, 4:697–98. Prior to organizing his army into two divisions, Magruder had experimented with an eight-brigade arrangement. He abandoned the scheme after just five weeks, however, as it resulted in unsatisfactory
overall coordination. See General Orders No. 89, October 3, 1861, ibid., 668–70.

39. Cullum, *Biographical Register,* 1:313; 2:67.

Confederate defenders from any opposing land force that attacked from the direction of Fort Monroe. In addition, the left flank was defended by elaborate fortifications at Ship Point, which commanded the entrance to the Poquosin, while the right flank was protected by the heavy artillery batteries at Mulberry Point, opposite the mouth of Deep Creek. Plus, artillery at Yorktown and Gloucester Point sealed the entrance to the York River on the extreme left, and on the far right the powerful *Virginia* still controlled access to the James. Of the three defensive lines that Magruder built across the Peninsula, he considered the forward line, which he termed "my real line of defense," to be the strongest. As long as Confederate forces controlled access to the York and James rivers, Magruder believed that holding this line was a viable possibility. And if manned by twenty-five thousand troops, he was confident that the line could have been held in the face of "any force the enemy could have brought against it."[40]

Thomas R. R. Cobb, who was stationed with his Georgia Legion at Cockletown, near Harwood's Mill, described Magruder's defensive initiatives as "Capital." He also observed that his commander "works day and night, and does not receive half the credit for which he is entitled," nor did Magruder receive much support from his superiors in Richmond. "I know of no officer in the service," wrote Colonel Cobb to his wife, Marion, on October 26, 1861, "who with the same means has done so much and I know of none for whom the government has done so little."[41]

General Magruder had been specifically assigned to protect the approach to Richmond from the Peninsula, yet Confederate authorities gave him nowhere near the number of troops needed to hold the defensive lines that he had constructed. And when Judah Benjamin transferred five thousand troops from the Army of the Peninsula to Benjamin Huger near Suffolk on March 4, 1862, Magruder was forced to withdraw all but a token force from his forward line and fall back to a second defensive line, which ran from Yorktown on his left, along the Warwick River to Mulberry Point, and the James River on his right.[42] The second line was "incomplete in its preparations," wrote Magruder, because the War Department in December had

40. Magruder to Cooper, May 3, 1862, *Official Records*, ser. 1, vol. 11, pt. 1, 405; February 1, 1862, ibid., 9:39. Harwood's Mill was also known as Harrod's Mill and Howard's Mill.

41. Thomas R. R. Cobb to Marion Cobb, October 26, 1861, Thomas R. R. Cobb Collection, University of Georgia.

42. Magruder to Cooper, March 4, 1862, *Official Records*, ser. 1, 9:52; March 6, 1862, ibid., 57; Magruder to Lee, March 14, 1862, ibid., 67.

discharged a thousand Negro laborers who were working on its defenses. Nevertheless, the manner in which the Warwick meandered perpendicularly across the Peninsula over flat land afforded exceptional defensive potential, a detail that did not escape Magruder's notice. He skillfully dammed the river at numerous strategic points to flood the lands intervening between the higher ground at Wynn's Mill and Lee's Mill several miles down the river. This flooding created marshlands through which the movement of troops was exceedingly difficult and that of artillery or wagon transport virtually impossible. Simultaneously, the higher ground at each of the dams was defended by continuous earthworks, strong artillery batteries, and rifle pits.[43] And behind the defensive line, but parallel to it, a military road was constructed that afforded rapid communication between all parts of the line, so that troops could be moved to counterbalance any point attacked or threatened by the enemy.[44]

Joseph Lancaster Brent, who had only recently arrived from California to join Magruder's staff, wrote in his postwar memoirs that his commander was meticulous in preparing his defenses:

> He exhibited then the greatest care in providing for all emergencies, and devoted himself constantly to a careful study how he could strengthen his position. It was almost impossible for any man to have more vividly [comprehended] the duties and responsibilities of his position. He fully realized that he was defending one of the passes to Richmond with very inadequate forces for the purpose, and he kept constantly busy the engineer officers and the negroes and other labourers under them. He himself had a very excellent eye for defensive positions and rode up and down his extended line, eight or ten miles in extent, almost daily, changing or strengthening the line of fortifications here and there.[45]

After Prince John had made every preparation possible, given the resources that he had, all he could do was await the arrival of his opponent.

In the meantime Magruder's superiors in Richmond also found themselves playing a waiting game. Robert E. Lee, who had just returned from the Georgia–South Carolina coast to become Jefferson Davis's military coordina-

43. Magruder to Cooper, May 3, 1862, *Official Records*, ser. 1, vol. 11, pt. 1, 405–6.

44. Hugh Thomas Douglas, "A Famous Army and Its Commander: Sketch of the Army of the Peninsula and General Magruder," *Southern Historical Society Papers* 42 (1917): 192; McLaws to his wife, March 31, 1862, McLaws Papers.

45. Brent, *Memoirs of the War between the States,* 100–101.

tor, and new secretary of war, George Wythe Randolph, who had succeeded
Judah Benjamin, anticipated a Federal attack against either Richmond, via
the Virginia Peninsula, or Norfolk, south of the James.[46] Yet because the Confederacy had limited resources and could not concentrate significant forces at
both locations simultaneously, authorities in Richmond could only wait until
the Federals made their intentions known. The danger was that if enemy
forces moved quickly and forcefully, they might be able to seize their target
before a sufficient force could be dispatched to oppose them.[47] Magruder on
the Peninsula, Huger at Norfolk, and Joe Johnston below the Rapidan were
all made aware of the situation. Their orders were to stand by until receiving
the command from General Lee to "move at once."[48] Magruder, however,
was forced to stand by without any prospect of receiving significant military
support from Richmond because Lee, by April 1, had concluded that the Federal activity on the Peninsula was entirely diversionary and that their "real
object is to attack Norfolk."[49] An anxious John Magruder believed with equal
certainty that he was the target. It was a very nervous time for everyone in
and around the Confederate capital. As Douglas Southall Freeman succinctly
wrote, "Disaster was in the air."[50]

George McClellan had no intentions of aiding his Confederate opponents
by allowing them adequate time to concentrate their forces against him.[51] On
April 4, 1862, less than two days after arriving at Fort Monroe, he began his
advance toward Richmond without even waiting for his entire force to join
him on the Peninsula. McClellan's move was three pronged. Samuel Heintzelman advanced on the right toward Yorktown with his 3rd Corps. On the
left Erasmus D. Keyes led the 4th Corps toward Warwick Courthouse, en
route to the Halfway House between Yorktown and Williamsburg, where
he expected to flank Magruder and cut the escape route of the Confederates
fleeing Heintzelman. And in the center Edwin V. "Bull" Sumner moved his
2nd Corps to Big Bethel, where he was to stand in reserve to assist either of
his fellow corps commanders in the event that they encountered any signifi-

46. Lee to Huger, March 25, 1862, *Official Records*, ser. 1, vol. 11, pt. 3, 396–97; Lee to Johnston,
March 25, 1862, ibid., 397; Lee to Magruder, March 26, 1862, ibid., 398–99.

47. Freeman, *R. E. Lee*, 2:19.

48. Lee to Johnston, March 25, 1862, *Official Records*, ser. 1, vol. 11, pt. 3, 397; Lee to Huger,
March 25, 1862, ibid., 396–97; Lee to Magruder, March 26, 1862, ibid., 398–99.

49. Lee to Holmes, April 1, 1862, *Official Records*, ser. 1, 9:455.

50. Freeman, *R. E. Lee*, 2:1.

51. Webb, *Peninsula*, 36.

cant opposition. All went well the first day. Sumner reached his objective. Heintzelman and Keyes moved their men and supplies twelve miles without encountering much resistance, and the weather was perfect.

On the second day nothing went right for McClellan. A torrential rain that lasted through the morning hours turned the Peninsula into a quagmire and slowed the Federal advance to a snail's pace. Roads that McClellan had been told would be passable under any conditions, Keyes described as "execrable." He could not advance his artillery through the knee-deep mud, nor could he even move empty ambulances.[52] Worse yet, when the Federals finally slogged forward with their infantry late in the day, Heintzelman encountered heavy resistance near Yorktown, as expected, but Keyes ran into Magruder's heavily fortified Warwick River defenses at Lee's Mill, which had not been anticipated. From spies and Confederate deserters McClellan knew of Magruder's first line of defense near Fort Monroe, but he had no intelligence whatsoever regarding the second line behind the Warwick.[53] Additionally, Federal maps indicating that the river ran harmlessly along the Warwick Road, parallel to the Peninsula, were wrong. Instead, the Warwick River ran perpendicular to the road and across the Peninsula in such a way that it served as a formidable barrier in the path of General Keyes's advance.[54]

Keyes's attempt to turn Magruder's flank quickly went awry. At 3:00 p.m. on April 5 he reported to Randolph B. Marcy, McClellan's chief of staff, "I am stopped by the enemy's works at Lee's Mill, which offer a severe resistance." He also relayed the intelligence that the Warwick ran across and obstructed his path. The river had no bridges and was "nowhere fordable, having been dammed up in several places all the way to the head of it, which is only a few miles from Yorktown."[55] Keyes was astounded by the magnitude of the watery barrier that lay before him. Later, in May 1884, after revisiting the Peninsula, he would write in his memoirs, "I was unable to imagine how human ingenuity could have collected so much water as I saw there in 1862."[56]

52. Keyes to Marcy, April 5, 1862, *Official Records*, ser. 1, vol. 11, pt. 3, 69–70.

53. *Report of the Joint Committee on the Conduct of War*, 1:428–29. Testimony of Major General George B. McClellan before the committee on February 28, 1863; Webb, *Peninsula*, 50, 52; Barnard, *Peninsular Campaign*, 18.

54. McClellan's Report, August 4, 1863, *Official Records*, ser. 1, vol. 11, pt. 1, 7; *McClellan's Own Story*, 263.

55. Keyes to Marcy, April 5, 1862, *Official Records*, ser. 1, vol. 11, pt. 3, 70. This Keyes to Marcy letter is different from the Keyes to Marcy letter cited in note 52, although both bear the same date.

56. Keyes, *Fifty Years' Observation of Men and Events*, 442.

Shortly after reaching the Warwick River near Lee's Mill, General Keyes wrote to his good friend, Senator Ira Harris of New York, describing in detail what he and his men faced:

> We were stopped by a line of defense nine or ten miles long, strongly fortified by breastworks erected nearly the whole distance behind a stream or succession of ponds, nowhere fordable, one terminus being Yorktown and the other ending in the James River which is commanded by the enemy's gunboats. Yorktown is fortified all around by bastioned works, and on the water side it and Gloucester are so strong that the navy is afraid to attack them . . . The enemy is in great force, and is constantly receiving reinforcements from the two rivers. The line in front of us is, therefore one of the strongest ever opposed to an invading force in any country.[57]

When Erasmus Keyes stated that he would not be able to reach the Halfway House, still six miles away, and would require reinforcements from Sumner's reserve corps,[58] McClellan and General Barnard conducted their own inspection of Magruder's defensive line, only to find that Keyes had not been exaggerating when describing its strength. The enemy defenses were "far more extensive" than had been anticipated, conceded Barnard in his official report. He acknowledged that Magruder had skillfully used every type of obstruction that the country afforded to construct a barrier he described as "formidable." Indeed, in General Barnard's judgment Magruder's defensive line was "certainly one of the most extensive known to modern times."[59] McClellan deduced from the length of the line that the Confederates must have been present in much larger numbers than had been thought possible. Under the circumstances neither he nor Barnard could disagree with Keyes, who stated, "No part of [Magruder's] line . . . can be taken by assault without an enormous waste of life."[60]

Just as it seemed that nothing could go worse for McClellan, it did. On the evening of April 5, while contemplating his options at his field headquarters, General McClellan received notification from Lorenzo Thomas, adjutant general of the Union army, that President Lincoln had, at least for the time being, canceled the movement of McDowell's 1st Corps to the

57. Ibid., 442–45. General Keyes's letter to Senator Harris was also included in McClellan's official report. *Official Records*, ser. 1, vol. 11, pt. 1, 13–14.

58. Keyes to McClellan, April 5, 1862, *Official Records*, ser. 1, vol. 11, pt. 3, 69.

59. Report of John G. Barnard, May 6, 1862, ibid., vol. 11, pt. 1, 318.

60. Report of Erasmus D. Keyes, April 16, 1862, ibid., 359.

Peninsula in order to ensure more protection for Washington.[61] The move deprived McClellan of thirty-seven thousand men; it left the Confederates firmly in control of the area between West Point and Gloucester Point, north of the York River, making it impossible for the Federals to trap Magruder at Yorktown; and it filled Little Mac with anger. He called the order "the most infamous thing that history has recorded."[62] McClellan, who just two days earlier had been brimming with confidence, now helplessly watched as his master plan began to unravel. He blamed everything on Lincoln, writing that the president's actions left him "incapable of continuing operations which had begun": "It compelled the adoption of another, a different, and a less effective plan of campaign."[63] Thus, McClellan halted his advance and began the month-long process of preparing for the siege of Yorktown—probably the most crucial mistake of his military career.[64]

On the Confederate side the plan remained the same: hold firm until help arrived. Magruder and a council of his officers unanimously resolved that if the government promised to send desperately needed reinforcements, they would defend the Yorktown–Mulberry Point line "to the last extremity," regardless of the enemy's designs against them. They realized that if the Peninsula was lost, Norfolk would fall, the *Virginia* would be captured, Richmond would be endangered, and the confidence of citizens and soldiers alike would be shattered.[65] They earnestly believed that the fate of the Confederacy was in their hands, yet they were so vastly outnumbered and lacking in supplies that they had no reason to be optimistic.[66] Lesser men might well have abandoned the Peninsula, rather than run the risk of being overwhelmed or cut off from Richmond, but Magruder's troops stood their ground. They drew strength from Prince John's words, "The enemy is before us—our works are strong—our cause is good—we fight for our homes and must be careful.

61. Thomas to McClellan, April 4, 1862, ibid., 10; ibid., vol. 11, pt. 3, 66; *McClellan's Own Story,* 261.

62. *McClellan's Own Story,* 308.

63. McClellan's Report, August 4, 1863, *Official Records,* ser. 1, vol. 11, pt. 1, p. 10.

64. Emma-Jo Davis, "Mulberry Island and the Civil War, April, 1861–May, 1862," MS, Fort Eustis Historical and Archaeological Association, Fort Eustis, Va., 31.

65. Magruder to Randolph, March 25, 1862, *Official Records,* ser. 1, vol. 11, pt. 3, 395; Douglas, "Famous Army and Its Commander: Sketch of the Army of the Peninsula and General Magruder," 193–94.

66. Brent, *Memoirs of the War between the States,* 110; Magruder to Lee, April 5, 1862, *Official Records,* ser. 1, vol. 11, pt. 3, 422. Magruder wrote to Lee, "I have made my arrangements to fight with my small force, but without the slightest hope of success."

Every hour that we hold out brings us reinforcements."[67] By night the men slept in the trenches with their weapons;[68] by day they worked to strengthen their defenses.[69] Their commander, proud of the army he had crafted, reported to General Lee, "Everybody behaving beautifully."[70]

Magruder's work as a military commander was also commendable. As he could not match his opponents with either manpower or firepower, he ingeniously utilized a variety of deceptive ploys to give Federal observers the impression that the Confederate Army of the Peninsula was infinitely larger and more powerful than it really was.[71] He boldly displayed "Quaker guns," painted logs mounted on wagon carriages, beside what little artillery he possessed. At night extra campfires gave the impression of a larger force, and during the day Magruder had his buglers sounding assembly and his men rushing to and fro as if preparing for battle. Mary Chesnut wrote that Confederate soldiers appeared and disappeared like fireflies in the night, utterly deceiving McClellan.[72] On one occasion Magruder sent a column into a wooded area through which there ran a road in plain view of the enemy. Hour after hour anxious Union soldiers watched rebel troops emerge from a thicket, cross the road, and vanish again in the pines on the other side.[73] They thought they had seen a Confederate army of thousands, but Magruder had marched the same few men in a circle "like an army of supernumeraries on a stage."[74] In observation of Magruder, admirer Baker P. Lee wrote, "Here, there, everywhere, by night and by day, he showed himself to the enemy in a magnifying glass, not only exaggerating the numerical proportions of his army, but in making illusive and confusing dispositions of his troops, in carefully concealed changes, and in transformations as deceptive

67. Pollard, *Lee and His Lieutenants*, 843.

68. Magruder to Cooper, May 3, 1862, *Official Records*, ser. 1, vol. 11, pt. 1, 406–9; A. B. Magruder to Taliaferro, April 4, 1862, ibid., vol. 11, pt. 3, 421; Magruder to Rhett, April 30, 1862, ibid., 479.

69. Magruder to Lee, April 6, 1862, *Official Records*, ser. 1, vol. 11, pt. 3, 425; Jubal Anderson Early, *War Memoirs: Autobiographical Sketch and Narrative of the War between the States* (Philadelphia: J. B. Lippincott, 1912), 59.

70. Magruder to Lee, April 6, 1862, *Official Records*, ser. 1, vol. 11, pt. 3, 425.

71. Early, *War Memoirs*, 59.

72. Chesnut, *Diary from Dixie*, 261.

73. Sears, *To the Gates of Richmond: The Peninsula Campaign*, 37–38; Pollard, *Lee and His Lieutenants*, 843.

74. Freeman, *R. E. Lee*, 2:18.

as a juggler's tricks."[75] Such tactics, along with inclement weather, delayed Federal operations until April 16, when McClellan moved against what he believed to be the weakest point of Magruder's line at Dam No. 1, between Lee's and Wynn's mills. After several hours of bitter fighting, with alternating successes, Federal infantrymen made a final desperate attack on the dam but were driven back by massed Confederate sharpshooters.[76] One hundred and sixty-five Federal troops were lost at Lee's Mill, while Confederate casualties numbered but seventy-five.[77] The Federal loss confirmed in the mind of their commanding general "the inexpediency of a direct assault upon Magruder's lines." Thereafter, McClellan devoted all his efforts to his regular siege operations at Yorktown.[78]

On the day following the engagement at Lee's Mill, Joseph E. Johnston reached Magruder and superseded him in command after Magruder, with just 13,600 men, had valiantly held his position on the Peninsula for nearly a month against 105,000 Federals. This successful stand, at such a critical time, was Prince John's greatest contribution to the Confederacy. It was an accomplishment that Lee's adjutant general, Walter Taylor, described as "one of the most heroic of the war."[79] General Magruder, however, gave the entire credit to his men, as he had earlier after his victory at Big Bethel. In his official report he wrote that his men held their ground under the worst of circumstances, yet they neither faltered nor complained. In Magruder's words:

> From April 4 to May 3 this army served almost without relief in the trenches. Many companies of artillery were never relieved during the long period. It rained almost incessantly; the trenches were filled with water; the weather was exceedingly cold; no fires could be allowed; the artillery and infantry of the enemy played upon our men almost continuously day and night . . . and yet no murmurs were heard . . . The best drilled regulars the world has ever seen would have mutinied under a continuous service in the trenches for twenty-nine days, exposed every moment to musketry and shells, in water to their knees, without fire, sugar, or coffee, without stimulants, and with an

75. Lee, "Magruder's Peninsula Campaign in 1862," 64.

76. For battle reports and important correspondence relating to the engagement at Dam No. 1 (Lee's Mill), see *Official Records*, ser. 1, vol. 11, pt. 1, 363–422.

77. Smith to Marcy, April 24, 1862 (Inclosure), ibid., 367; Magruder to Cooper, May 3, 1862; ibid., 408.

78. William Allan, *The Army of Northern Virginia in 1862* (Boston: Houghton Mifflin, 1892), 13.

79. Taylor, *General Lee: His Campaigns in Virginia, 1861–1865*, 50.

inadequate supply of uncooked flour and salt meat. I speak of this in honor of these brave men, whose patriotism made them indifferent to suffering, disease, danger, and death.[80]

Typical of the additional praise was that of Jubal Early, who wrote in his *War Memoirs,* "The assuming and maintaining of the line by Magruder with his small force in the face of such overwhelming odds was one of the boldest exploits ever performed by a military commander."[81] Most Virginians believed, as did journalist E. A. Pollard, that it was "a service which saved Richmond."[82] Years later, in his *Narrative of Military Operations,* Joe Johnston would acknowledge that Magruder's defensive effort was "of incalculable value," even concurring with Pollard that it had saved the capital from capture.[83] Johnston's sentiments, however, were altogether different in mid-April 1862, when his opinion mattered most.

At this early point in the war, when Jefferson Davis thought highly of Joe Johnston,[84] Johnston did not think very highly of John Magruder. He intimated to President Davis that the Virginia Peninsula had been held not because of Magruder's defensive proficiency but, rather, because of his opponent's offensive incompetency. Johnston expressed the same opinion to General Lee, when on April 22, 1862, he made his well-known declaration that "no one but McClellan could have hesitated to attack."[85] After the war Johnston would write that it had not been his purpose to denigrate Magruder, conceding that the general had done the best he could do with the resources that he had.[86] Nevertheless, Johnston's complaints about the indefensibility of the Peninsula cast Magruder in an entirely negative light in Richmond, regardless of the intent. Davis, who had always been skeptical of Magruder,

80. Magruder to Cooper, May 3, 1862, *Official Records,* ser. 1, vol. 11, pt. 1, 408–9.

81. Early, *War Memoirs,* 59.

82. Pollard, *Lee and His Lieutenants,* 842.

83. Johnston, *Narrative of Military Operations,* 111.

84. Steven E. Woodworth, *Davis and Lee at War* (Lawrence: University Press of Kansas, 1995), 81, 97, 147. Jefferson Davis and Joe Johnston had clashed on at least two occasions earlier in the war, and it was a well-known fact that Davis did not care for Johnston personally. Nevertheless, according to Woodworth, President Davis "retained an amazing degree of faith in Johnston, partly because of Johnston's genuine theoretical skill and partly because his cautious, low-risk approach to the war mirrored Davis' own." Woodworth also noted that "Davis had had a high estimate of Johnston's military skill before the war and was not quick to change his opinions."

85. Johnston to Lee, April 22, 1862, *Official Records,* ser. 1, vol. 11, pt. 3, 455–56.

86. Johnston, *Narrative of Military Operations,* 112–13.

interpreted Johnston's criticisms as evidence of negligence. Consequently, he offered no official expression of gratitude for Magruder's service on the Peninsula,[87] just as he had previously sent no congratulatory letter to Magruder after his victory at Big Bethel. Davis's animosity notwithstanding, it was Joe Johnston who had the most significant adverse effect on Magruder's reputation. Had Johnston condemned Little Mac less and credited Prince John more, Magruder's standing, both in the eyes of his superiors and in the judgment of historians, would have been significantly different.

The hypercritical Johnston, however, rarely complimented anyone. He was by nature "a fault-finder," observed Stephen Sears.[88] The only performances that consistently pleased him were his own. Otherwise, Johnston was perpetually dissatisfied with everything—his superiors, his subordinates, his circumstances.[89] He stood in such marked contrast to the optimistic and fun-loving Magruder that it is difficult to imagine how either could have worked harmoniously with the other. Shortly after Johnston arrived on the Peninsula, Lafayette McLaws noted the differences between the two commanders in an April 25, 1862, letter to his wife:

> General Magruder is fond of dress and parade and of company, conceals nothing and delights to have a crowd about him to whom he converses freely upon any and all subjects. He never moves from his headquarters without having five or six aides and a dozen or more orderlies . . . can talk twenty-four hours incessantly . . . Our (new) commander in chief, General Johnston who is a very quiet, stern man, letting his plans to no one . . . will never speak on official matters but to the person interested, dislikes to have a crowd about him, never mentions military matters when away from the office—often rides off alone . . . Dresses neat, but, not pompous—interviews are yes/no with no detailed discussion of the matter.[90]

Johnston and Magruder were close in age and provenance, born in Virginia just eighty-seven days apart and eighty-seven miles apart.[91] Both were

---

87. Gary W. Gallagher, "The Undoing of an Early Confederate Hero: John Bankhead Magruder at the Seven Days," in *Lee and His Generals in War and Memory,* ed. Gary W. Gallagher (Baton Rouge: Louisiana State University Press, 1998), 123; H. J. Eckenrode and Bryan Conrad, *George B. McClellan: The Man Who Saved the Union* (Chapel Hill: University of North Carolina Press, 1941), 49.

88. Sears, *To the Gates of Richmond: The Peninsula Campaign,* 46.

89. Woodworth, *Davis and Lee at War,* 124.

90. McLaws to his wife, April 25, 1862, McLaws Papers.

91. Johnston was born on February 3, 1807, at Cherry Grove in Prince Edward County, Virginia.

of Scottish ancestry, the sons of lawyers, West Point educated, and yet, as McLaws observed, they were totally different by nature. Unlike the extroverted, eternally optimistic Magruder, Johnston was a solemn, dour individual, consumed by pessimism and negativism; nothing ever suited him. Mary Chesnut reported an occasion when her uncle Hamilton Boykin and Wade Hampton invited Joe Johnston, an excellent wing shot, to hunt quail with them in South Carolina. During the outing Boykin and Hampton shot frequently, but Johnston was never quite satisfied with the conditions, whether it was the flight of the birds, the position of the dogs, or the location of his hunting companions. Johnston preferred to wait until everything was just right for the perfect shot. At day's end, after Boykin and Hampton had had a successful hunt, Joe Johnston was still waiting—with an empty gamebag. He was "too fussy . . . too cautious . . . too hard to please."[92] Not surprisingly, when Johnston made a hasty inspection of Magruder's defenses on April 13, four days before assuming command on the Peninsula, he found nothing to his liking. The very defensive lines that generals McClellan and Barnard, two of the most highly respected engineers in the U.S. Army, had described as "formidable," Johnston suddenly perceived to be "indefensible."[93] Immediately upon returning to Richmond, General Johnston complained mightily before a war council including Davis, Lee, and Secretary of War Randolph that there were a multitude of problems on the Peninsula. He charged that the engineering had been done by young, inexperienced officers. The Yorktown–Mulberry Point line was too long and insufficiently fortified to defend. Offensive operations were rendered impossible as a consequence of the artificial flooding of the Warwick. And it was inevitable, insisted Johnston, that the Federals, with their naval superiority, would soon gain control of the York or James River. Defending Yorktown against a force that he believed to number 133,000 men, armed with an enormous superiority in artillery, seemed far too risky to Johnston. Under the circumstances he concluded that "a different plan of operations should be adopted without delay."[94]

Johnston advocated withdrawing Magruder's entire force from the Peninsula, as well as Huger's from Norfolk, and adding them all to his army. The

92. Chesnut, *Diary from Dixie,* 175.

93. Jefferson Davis, *The Rise and Fall of the Confederate Government,* 2 vols. (New York: D. Appleton and Co., 1881), 2:87.

94. Johnston, *Narrative of Military Operations,* 112–13; Johnston to Lee, April 22, 1862, *Official Records,* ser. 1, vol. 11, pt. 3, 455–56.

combined force would begin a controlled retreat toward the capital, buying
time until reinforcements could arrive from South Carolina and Georgia.
Johnston ultimately planned to fight McClellan in a grand battle near Richmond after the Federals had been drawn away from their base of supplies
at Fort Monroe. Conversely, Secretary Randolph pointed out that a retreat
from the Peninsula would result in the losses of Norfolk, the important Gosport naval facility, as well as the *Virginia*. Additionally, Lee warned that the
removal of Confederate troops from South Carolina and Georgia would en-
danger Charleston and Savannah. He also argued that Magruder's Yorktown–
Mulberry Point line offered the best opportunity for a smaller force against a
larger one.[95] In contrast to Johnston's criticisms, Lee contended, as Magruder
had all along, that this line could be held as long as its flanks were not turned
by the passage of the enemy up either the York or the James.[96] After listening
to over thirteen hours of debate, Davis finally sided with Randolph and Lee.[97]

Johnston did not protest the decision, but he assumed command on the
Peninsula convinced that it was a mistake and that he would not be able to
obey it.[98] He knew that artillery would determine Yorktown's fate. He also believed it was a fight that he could not win. Clearly, his smoothbore field guns
were no match for McClellan's heavy siege guns, which included thirteen-
inch mortars and two hundred–pounder Parrott rifles, weapons far more
powerful than anything in the Confederate artillery arsenal. Johnston grimly
predicted that once the enemy siege batteries were operational, he would be
able to hold his position for no more "than a few hours."[99]

However, that which Johnston saw as a calamity, Magruder saw as an opportunity. He proposed launching a "vigorous, large-scale surprise attack at

95. Davis, *Rise and Fall of the Confederate Government,* 2:87; Johnston, *Narrative of Military Operations,* 113–16.

96. Lee to Magruder, March 15, 1862, *Official Records,* ser. 1, 9:68; March 26, 1862, ibid., vol. 11, pt. 3, 399; Douglas, "Famous Army and Its Commander: Sketch of the Army of the Peninsula and General Magruder," 192, 194.

97. Davis, *Rise and Fall of the Confederate Government,* 2:87; Johnston, *Narrative of Military Operations,* 115–16.

98. Johnston, *Narrative of Military Operations,* 116; Freeman, *R. E. Lee,* 2:22–23.

99. Johnston to Lee, April 29, 1862, *Official Records,* ser. 1, vol. 11, pt. 3, 473. Hal Bridges writes that when Johnston first inspected Magruder's transpeninsular defenses, he asked D. H. Hill, who commanded the Confederate left at Yorktown and Gloucester Point, how long he could hold Yorktown after McClellan opened fire with his heavy siege guns. "About two days," Hill replied. "I had supposed," said Johnston, "about two hours." Bridges, *Lee's Maverick General: Daniel Harvey Hill,* 7.

daylight" in order to capture McClellan's nearly completed siege batteries. Although Magruder only specified that "we might cautiously, but energetically, press our success to the extent of our ability,"[100] it is likely that he envisioned driving the Federals all the way back to Fort Monroe. There he hoped to utilize the captured heavy artillery pieces against the fort in such a way that McClellan could neither receive supplies nor be evacuated to safety. If successful, Magruder's surprise attack would turn the tables on the Peninsula in dramatic fashion, placing McClellan in exactly the same position occupied by Lord Cornwallis prior to his surrender to George Washington at Yorktown in October 1781. Given that Cornwallis's capitulation ended the Revolutionary War and won independence for the United States, could not the capture of McClellan's huge army at Fort Monroe win independence for the Confederacy? The war-ending scenario was improbable, yet to the audacious Magruder it was not impossible. To Prince John nothing was impossible. The fact that he had urged the capture of Washington, D.C., at the beginning of the war showed his willingness to attempt the improbable. That he would later plan and execute the successful recapture of Galveston despite enormous odds against him would prove that the improbable was not impossible. In Magruder's mind, if the reward was great enough, he was willing to take the risk.

Joe Johnston was of an entirely different school of thought. As one "who always calculated risks before profits,"[101] he had no interest in Magruder's daring offensive scheme. Nor would he even listen when Magruder urged him to hold his position on the Peninsula. Colonel Hugh T. Douglas, Magruder's chief engineer, wrote that his commander "urged his views on General Johnston with all the force he could bring to bear."[102] Magruder's plea, however, fell on deaf ears. Johnston had already convinced himself that he had no choice except to abandon the Peninsula in spite of urgings from Magruder, as well as orders from President Davis, to defend it. It was Johnston's belief that "events on the Peninsula would soon compel the Confederate Government to adopt my method of opposing the Federal army."[103] Unfortunately, his method was not to fight the Federals but, rather, to retreat from them.

Johnston began his withdrawal from the Yorktown–Mulberry Point line under cover of darkness on the night of May 3. By daybreak on the fourth

---

100. Magruder to Rhett, April 24, 1862, *Official Records*, ser. 1, vol. 11, pt. 3, 462–63.

101. Sears, *To the Gates of Richmond: The Peninsula Campaign*, 46.

102. Douglas, "Famous Army and Its Commander: Sketch of the Army of the Peninsula and General Magruder," 193.

103. Johnston, *Narrative of Military Operations*, 116.

he and his men were gone. The evacuation was executed flawlessly and with perfect timing, as McClellan was no more than forty-eight hours away from having his full compliment of siege guns ready for action.[104] The sudden move also caught McClellan by surprise and deprived him of the satisfaction of winning by bombardment that which he had been preparing for a full month. Yet the withdrawal came at a cost—Johnston was forced to leave behind at Yorktown fifty-six heavy artillery pieces,[105] ammunition, and other supplies that the Confederacy could ill afford to lose.

On the opposite side of the Peninsula, across Hampton Roads, the loss was even more consequential. Benjamin Huger's ordered withdrawal toward Richmond left to the Federals Norfolk and the Gosport Naval Yard at Portsmouth as well as irreplaceable machinery and material, which effectively eliminated the Confederacy's ability to develop a naval capability during the war. The evacuation also doomed the *Virginia*. As the bulky ironclad drew too much water to retreat up the James River toward Richmond, it was blown up by its commander, Josiah Tatnall, on May 11, 1862, to prevent its falling into the hands of the enemy. "No one event of the war," wrote Confederate ordnance department chief Josiah Gorgas, "created such a profound sensation as the destruction of this noble ship."[106] Similarly, J. Thomas Scharf, who wrote *The History of the Confederate States Navy,* judged that the vessel's loss was equivalent "to the loss of an army of many thousand men."[107] The demise of the *Virginia* also opened the James as far as Drewry's Bluff, just seven miles south of Richmond. These losses dealt a severe blow to southern morale, an important factor that Joe Johnston appears never to have contemplated. Indeed, according to author Clifford Dowdey, it seemed that "Johnston was conducting a private campaign with no objective beyond the immediate purpose of avoiding combat until he retired to Richmond."[108]

Magruder was unavailable for duty during much of Johnston's retreat, having fallen victim to the ravages of malaria. He had first contracted the mosquito-borne disease in early April, forcing him to seek several days

104. McClellan's Report, August 4, 1863, *Official Records,* ser. 1, vol. 11, pt. 1, 18.

105. Barnard's Report, May 6, 1862, ibid., 337. General Barnard reported that fifty-three of the fifty-six captured Confederate artillery pieces were "in good order."

106. Josiah Gorgas, *The Journals of Josiah Gorgas, 1857–1878,* ed. Sarah Woolfolk Wiggins (Tuscaloosa: University of Alabama Press, 1995), 45.

107. J. Thomas Scharf, *History of the Confederate States Navy from Its Organization to the Surrender of Its Last Vessel* (New York: Rogers and Sherwood, 1887), 238.

108. Dowdey, *Seven Days: The Emergence of Lee,* 56.

of rest away from his duties to restore his health.[109] The respite, however, brought little relief. A month later, when Johnston's withdrawal order arrived, Magruder was again bedridden. The cumulative, debilitating effect of anxiety, exhaustion, and disease took its toll on the now fifty-five-year-old general. Furthermore, the decision to abandon the Peninsula was an enormous disappointment that left him deeply depressed. After calling Colonel Douglas to his side to assist with the details of the evacuation, a teary-eyed Magruder became so distraught that he could not even discuss the matter. In the words of historian Mark Grimsley: "Prince John received Douglas from his sickbed. As the colonel looked on, Magruder slowly got up and stumbled to a window. Staring out across the position he had defended for nearly a year—the last month in the face of daunting odds—Magruder became emotional. His voice broke. He said in hushed tones: '*Sic transit gloria Peninsula.*'"[110] Magruder had hoped and expected to battle McClellan on the Peninsula, but as Douglas noted, "General Johnston . . . was the commander of the army and he had determined otherwise." As a soldier, it was Magruder's duty to obey orders, and Johnston's order was to retreat.[111]

When the withdrawal began, General Magruder gamely left his sickbed and led his 17,302-man division in retreat from Lee's Mill, toward Williamsburg, Virginia's old colonial capital and the site of William and Mary College, the oldest institution of higher learning in the South. James Longstreet marched along the same route with his division, numbering 13,816 men, while D. H. Hill and Gustavus W. Smith led their divisions toward Williamsburg from Yorktown. Hill commanded 12,634 men and Smith 10,592. Jeb Stuart's 1,289 Confederate cavalrymen formed the rear guard. By noon on May 4, Johnston's 55,633-man army, minus Stuart's rear guard, had reached its destination several hours ahead of its Federal pursuers.[112]

During the retreat Magruder's health worsened to such a degree that he could no longer continue in command. Upon reaching Williamsburg, he

109. Magruder to Randolph, April 5, 1862, *Official Records,* ser. 1, vol. 51, pt. 2, 532.

110. Mark Grimsley, "Inside a Beleaguered City: A Commander and Actor, Prince John Magruder," *Civil War Times Illustrated* 21 (September 1982): 17; Douglas, "Famous Army and Its Commander: Sketch of the Army of the Peninsula and General Magruder," 193.

111. Douglas, "Famous Army and Its Commander: Sketch of the Army of the Peninsula and General Magruder," 193–94.

112. Johnston, *Narrative of Military Operations,* 119; Organization of the Army of Northern Virginia, commanded by General Joseph E. Johnston, on the Peninsula, about April 30, 1862, *Official Records,* ser. 1, vol. 11, pt. 3, 479–84.

applied for and immediately received from General Johnston a leave of absence,[113] "to turn myself over to the care of a doctor, to re-establish my health, which sadly needed repair."[114] He left General David R. Jones temporarily in charge of his division and then rode in the company of his staff to the James River, where the group embarked on a steamer for Westover, the magnificent colonial mansion that once belonged to William Byrd. There, in what aide Joseph Lancaster Brent described as "the comfort and luxuries of Westover . . . beautiful with flowers and spacious lawns facing the broad James River," the general began his convalescence. Brent reported that Magruder had originally intended to seek medical attention in Richmond. Whether because of time constraints, the delicacy of his health, or the irresistible luxury and hospitality he found at Westover, he never made it to the capital city.[115]

Meanwhile, Johnston decided to make a stand against his Federal pursuers in order to buy precious time for his retreating columns. He posted a portion of Longstreet's division along Magruder's third and final defensive line, approximately two miles east of Williamsburg, near the convergence of the Lee's Mill and Yorktown roads. Commanding this important road junction was Fort Magruder, the anchor of the Williamsburg line. The fort was an earthen redoubt several hundred yards long, with ramparts six feet high and nine feet thick, protected by a ditch nine feet wide and nine feet deep, filled with water. A line of twelve smaller redoubts and numerous rifle pits protected each flank, and impenetrable marshes and woods rendered passage around the redoubts impossible.[116] In order to strike Johnston's retreating army and its vulnerable supply train, the Federals would have to take Fort Magruder.

Shortly after daybreak on May 5, Joe Hooker launched the Federal attack against the fort. He received little support, sustained significant casualties, and failed to dislodge the rebel defenders from their works. Later in the day the battle unfolded more favorably for the Federals, at the opposite end of the defensive line on the Confederate left. Winfield Scott Hancock opportu-

113. Brent, *Memoirs of the War between the States,* 114.

114. Magruder to Randolph, May 5, 1862, *Official Records,* ser. 1, vol. 11, pt. 3, 494.

115. Brent, *Memoirs of the War between the States,* 114–15.

116. McClellan's Report, August 4, 1863, *Official Records,* ser. 1, vol. 11, pt. 1, 19; Hughes, *General Johnston,* 124–25. Having been a student at William and Mary College, and having frequently hunted in the area, Hughes was personally acquainted with the battlefield at Williamsburg. In commenting on the woods and marshes that protected Magruder's flanks, he wrote, "The former are almost impenetrable, and even a dog cannot cross the latter, much less a man." Ibid., 133n.

nistically occupied two of Magruder's redoubts that Johnston had failed to locate.[117] From these captured redoubts Federal artillerymen initiated an enfilading fire that posed a serious threat to Fort Magruder and its occupants. When the Confederates attempted to reclaim the enemy-held redoubts, they suffered their heaviest losses of the day. Jubal Early was severely wounded in the shoulder while advancing with the 24th Virginia Infantry. He was but one of 190 casualties the Virginians sustained in their futile charge against Hancock's protected positions. When Colonel Duncan K. McRae and his 5th North Carolina Infantry Regiment attacked in support of their Virginia comrades, they met an even worse fate, losing 290 of their 410 men, a casualty rate in excess of 70 percent.[118] Years later, in a letter to James Longstreet, D. H. Hill wrote: "I cannot think of it, till this day, without horror. The slaughter of the Fifth North Carolina Regiment was one of the most awful things I ever saw."[119] By the time darkness ended the Battle of Williamsburg the Federals had lost 2,239 men,[120] the Confederates 1,611.[121] Through it all and into the night Johnston continued his retreat.

Days later, when General Magruder was informed of the particulars of the battle, he must have derived at least some satisfaction from the fact that

117. Johnston, *Narrative of Military Operations*, 124. In his war memoirs Johnston wrote that he had no knowledge of the redoubts; later he would declare otherwise. See note 122.

118. D. K. McRae, "The Battle of Williamsburg—Reply to Colonel Bratton," *Southern Historical Society Papers* 7 (1879): 360.

119. Hill to Longstreet, August 31, 1885, Longstreet Papers, Perkins Library, Duke University.

120. Return of Casualties in the Union Forces at the Battle of Williamsburg, *Official Records*, ser. 1, vol. 11, pt. 1, 450.

121. Historians agree that the Federals lost 2,239 men at the Battle of Williamsburg because Union regimental casualty returns were complete; Confederate returns, however, were not. No totals were listed for the 10th Alabama of Cadmus Wilcox's brigade or the 5th North Carolina of Early's brigade. Fortunately, the losses for the 10th Alabama, 70 total, were noted in Wilcox's battle reports, but no such accurate reports were recorded for the 5th North Carolina. As Jubal Early was seriously wounded at Williamsburg, he did not submit his report until June 9, 1862. Even then he deferred to his regimental commanders, stating that his own numbers were "so inaccurate that I forbear to send them." Colonel Duncan McRae, commander of the 5th North Carolina, reported sending in his losses with his May 10, 1862, battle report. Inexplicably, his losses were not included with the other regiments of Early's brigade. Years later, however, in 1879, in a report submitted to the *Southern Historical Society Papers*, McRae reported having lost 290 men at Williamsburg. That number and the 70 casualties that the 10th Alabama had sustained, plus the 1,251 losses suffered by the other regiments of Johnston's army, makes the Confederate losses at Williamsburg 1,611 men. For battle reports and important correspondence relating to the Battle of Williamsburg, see *Official Records*, ser. 1, vol. 11, pt. 1, 447–613.

Johnston had utilized one of his purportedly "indefensible" lines to thwart his Federal pursuers. Yet Magruder must have been appalled to learn that the Confederates had sustained 36 percent of their casualties attacking the very defensive works that he and his men had earlier constructed. In the battle's aftermath it was clear to everyone, including President Davis, that had Johnston been more thorough earlier when inspecting Magruder's defenses, the redoubts that Hancock occupied without opposition would have been in Confederate hands and the unfortunate massacre of the 24th Virginia and 5th North Carolina Infantry regiments would have never occurred.[122]

The fighting around Williamsburg necessarily brought Magruder's medical leave of absence to an abrupt end. On the morning of May 9 the general and his staff departed Westover. That evening, after a hard day's ride, the traveling entourage arrived at Bottom's Bridge,[123] twelve miles east of Richmond, where Magruder rejoined his men and reassumed command from D. R. Jones. From Jones, Magruder received the disquieting news that during the brief time he had been away, his division had been placed, for administrative purposes, under the command of Joe Johnston's deputy, Gustavus W. Smith,[124] whom he did not like. It galled Magruder that Smith and his colleague, Mansfield Lovell, had not resigned their positions as street commissioner and deputy street commissioner of New York City until September 1861,[125] and then both were hastily appointed major generals with Smith's September 19, 1861, commission predating Magruder's, and Lovell's commission bearing

---

122. Davis, *Rise and Fall of the Confederate Government*, 2:94. In his Civil War memoirs Jefferson Davis wrote that Magruder's illness and medical leave of absence were regrettable, "as it appears that the positions of the redoubts he had constructed were not all known to the commanding General, and some of them being unoccupied were seized by the enemy, and held subsequently to our disadvantage" (2:94). Joe Johnston, on the other hand, emphatically insisted that "the positions of the redoubts were 'all known.'" Joseph E. Johnston, "Manassas to Seven Pines," in *Battles and Leaders of the Civil War*, 2:205. This he wrote in spite of having earlier stated in his *Narrative of Military Operations* that the "existence [of the redoubts] was unknown to us" (124). Either way, Johnston is to be censured. Whether his error was an observational shortcoming or a failure to properly man the unoccupied redoubts, it was a mistake that, in part, cost him 480 casualties.

123. Norris to Randolph, May 9, 1862, *Official Records*, ser. 1, vol. 51, pt. 2, 554.

124. Gustavus W. Smith, *The Battle of Seven Pines* (New York: C. G. Crawford, 1891), 7.

125. Cullum, *Biographical Register*, 2:45–46. Smith and Lovell had been friends since their days together at West Point. Both graduated in the class of 1842. Smith graduated eighth in the class, Lovell ninth.

the same date—October 7, 1861.[126] Smith, in fact, had been commissioned a major general in the Confederate army a day before his resignation as New York City's street commissioner was even official.[127] Smith and Lovell had been close friends of Mississippi's powerful soldier-politician, John A. Quitman, who in turn had been a friend, Democratic Party comrade, and political supporter of Jefferson Davis. Such ties, however, failed to impress John Magruder. And after his successful defense of the Peninsula, Magruder was distinctly displeased by this subordination to the younger, less-experienced, and late-arriving Gustavus Smith, in whose ability he had little confidence.

Friction between the two men developed at once. Smith became irritated at Magruder's incessant communications, which arrived at all hours of the day and night but which he deemed generally unimportant. On Smith's direction Assistant Adjutant General Major Samuel W. Melton replied that the general would be glad to entertain Magruder's correspondence, if important militarily, but he requested "that information, unless of that nature, will be sent at such time as not to deprive him [Smith] of his necessarily limited hours of rest."[128]

Immediately after receiving Major Melton's letter, Magruder sarcastically replied that he regretted "to have disturbed the rest of the major-general commanding the reserve and my wing."[129] That would not happen again. Magruder terminated all correspondence with his superior, then refused to obey orders,[130] and finally asked Johnston that his command "no longer be attached to that of General Smith."[131] Before Johnston could reconcile or separate the disputing generals, Special Orders No. 118 arrived from Richmond, assigning Magruder command of the Trans-Mississippi District, Department No. 2.[132] Reassignment would have ended his troubles with Smith, but

126. *Journal of the Congress of the Confederate States of America, 1861–1865,* 1:473; Wright, *General Officers of the Confederate Army,* 22–23. James Longstreet was likewise outraged by the commissioning of Smith and Lovell. In protest he wrote, "The placing of persons above me whom I have always ranked and who have just joined this service, I regard as a great injustice." Longstreet to Jordan, September 24, 1861, *Official Records,* ser. 1, vol. 51, pt. 2, 310.

127. *Journal of the Congress of the Confederate States of America, 1861–1865,* 1:473; Wright, *General Officers of the Confederate Army,* 22; Cullum, *Biographical Register,* 2:45.

128. Magruder to Melton, May 21, 1862, *Official Records,* ser. 1, vol. 11, pt. 3, 528.

129. Ibid., 529.

130. Smith to Magruder, May 25, 1862, Henry E. Huntington Library, San Marino, Calif.

131. Magruder to Rhett, May 23, 1862, *Official Records,* ser. 1, vol. 11, pt. 3, 537.

132. Special Orders No. 118, ibid., 540.

Magruder requested that Secretary Randolph delay the implementation of his transfer until the conclusion of the anticipated battles with McClellan.[133] Randolph agreed, and Magruder was reassigned to Johnston.[134]

McClellan, in the meantime, advanced with a portion of his army up the York to West Point and then up the Pamunkey River to White House, where he established his headquarters and supply base. Simultaneously, the larger part of his army cautiously followed Johnston's retreating Confederates overland toward Richmond. McClellan pursued slowly, in part because he was awaiting the late arrival of Irvin McDowell's corps, now 41,000 strong, which President Lincoln had finally promised to send to him from Fredericksburg. Instead, on May 24 Lincoln ordered approximately half of McDowell's force to assist in the Shenandoah Valley,[135] where Stonewall Jackson was wreaking havoc against Nathaniel Banks, James Shields, and John C. Fremont. Having McDowell's men available would have been reassuring to McClellan. Nevertheless, he was confident, even with the number of his reinforcements reduced, that he could take Richmond by siege just as he had earlier taken Yorktown.

In preparation for his final push toward Richmond, McClellan organized his army into five two-division corps, designated the 2nd through 6th corps. The alignment did not include McDowell's 1st Corps because McDowell, at least for the time being, was unavailable. Of those with McClellan and under his charge, Sumner commanded the 2nd corps with Israel Richardson and John Sedgwick as division commanders; Heintzelman the 3rd, with Joe Hooker and Phil Kearny; Keyes the 4th, with Darius Couch and Silas Casey; Fitz John Porter the 5th, with George Morell and George Sykes; and William B. Franklin the 6th Corps, with Henry Slocum and William F. Smith as his division commanders.[136] According to official Union returns, 102,236 men

133. Randolph to Davis, June 23, 1862, ibid., 13:837.

134. Special Orders No. 120, May 26, 1862, ibid., vol. 11, pt. 3, 551. In the brief time that had elapsed between the issuance of these orders, Johnston had given Magruder's old command to Lafayette McLaws. Special Orders No. 117, ibid. The assignment was rescinded, however, when Magruder returned to command in Johnston's army.

135. Lincoln to McDowell, May 24, 1862, *Official Records*, ser. 1, vol. 12, pt. 3, 219.

136. William Starr Myers, *General George Brinton McClellan* (New York: D. Appleton-Century, 1934), 280; the 5th and 6th corps of Porter and Franklin were newly constituted on May 18, 1862, in General Orders No. 125, *Official Records*, ser. 1, vol. 11, pt. 3, 181. Porter and Franklin were two of McClellan's favorite generals.

were present and equipped for duty as of May 20, 1862.[137] With these troops George B. McClellan prepared to fight what he described as "one of the great historic battles of the world—one of those crises in a nation's life that occur but seldom."[138]

By May 24 the Federal army had advanced to the north bank of the Chickahominy River and was deployed along a thirteen-mile front that extended angularly from Bottom's Bridge, due east of Richmond, to Meadow Bridge, five miles north of the capital city, near Mechanicsville.[139] As Magruder's forces south of the river controlled access to Meadow, Mechanicsville, and New Bridge,[140] the westernmost of the bridges opposite the Federal line, McClellan on the twenty-fifth ordered Keyes and Heintzelman to cross the river via newly rebuilt Bottom's Bridge, at the east end of his line, where there was no enemy resistance. By the thirtieth Keyes had moved his 4th Corps west to Seven Pines, near Fair Oaks Station, just six miles east of Richmond. Heintzelman's 3rd Corps had also crossed the Chickahominy but remained four miles behind Keyes.[141] Yet before McClellan could send Sumner, Porter, and Franklin across the river to join Keyes and Heintzelman, the skies opened, and huge rains fell.

The storm of May 30–31, 1862, was so intense that soldiers in both armies were killed by lightning. Few men had ever witnessed such a violent downpour. From Magruder's headquarters Major Brent succinctly termed the rain "excessive." He also noted that during the storm a local resident visiting Magruder informed the general that "a heavy rain like the one then falling would flood the Chickahominy bottom, and that by next day the river would be so high that probably every bridge across the river would be swept away." When Magruder asked whether this statement was supposition or fact, Brent recorded that the visitor "gave an instance of when every bridge over the Chickahominy except a stone bridge had been swept away as a result of a rain storm like this."[142] Magruder immediately urged Johnston to act, emphasizing to his commander in a hand-delivered letter that the flooding would

137. Abstract from Return of the Army of the Potomac, May 20, 1862, *Official Records*, ser. 1, vol. 11, pt. 3, 184.

138. *McClellan's Own Story*, 395–96. In a letter to his wife, May 22–23, 1862.

139. McClellan's Report, August 4, 1863, *Official Records*, ser. 1, vol. 11, pt. 1, 25.

140. Magruder to Rhett, May 30, 1862, ibid., pt. 3, 560.

141. McClellan's Report, August 4, 1863, ibid., pt. 1, 38.

142. Brent, *Memoirs of the War between the States*, 132.

isolate over 30,000 Federal troops under Keyes and Heintzelman south of the Chickahominy,[143] in the presence of 73,928 Confederates.[144] The god-sent opportunity was of enormous potential.

Johnston realized it too. Before the rains came he had been uncertain where or when to battle his opponent. His first inclination was to strike north of the river, but on May 30 he changed his mind. During the deluge Johnston issued instructions for his division commanders to attack Keyes's isolated corps south of the Chickahominy. The attack was scheduled to begin shortly after daylight on the thirty-first with Longstreet in overall command. The plan called for Longstreet's division and those of D. H. Hill and Benjamin Huger to converge simultaneously on Keyes via three nearly parallel roads that led from the eastern outskirts of Richmond toward Seven Pines. At the same time on the Confederate left, A. P. Hill and Magruder, from their positions on the south bank, were to occupy Porter and Franklin north of the river. William H. C. Whiting, commanding Gustavus Smith's division, was posted to Magruder's immediate right at Old Tavern, approximately equidistant from the Chickahominy to the north and Seven Pines to the southeast. Thus positioned, Whiting was to assist Longstreet, if necessary, or to stand firm to prevent Sumner's corps from crossing the river to reinforce Keyes. If the three-pronged Confederate attack was well timed and properly coordinated, Keyes and then Heintzelman would be overwhelmed by superior numbers and trapped against a flooded river that would seal off any possibility of their escape.[145] After the war, when Keyes reflected upon the position in which he had found himself, he wrote, "The Union cause was in greater danger on the 31st of May, 1862, than at the date of any other battle except Gettysburg."[146]

Fortunately for Erasmus Keyes and the Union, the brilliance of Johnston's plan and the magnificence of the opportunity were offset by disastrous execution on the part of the Confederates, much of which was Johnston's

143. Ibid. From Magruder's headquarters Major Brent correctly surmised that McClellan had "not less than 30,000 men on the Richmond or south side of the Chickahominy." Official Union returns indicated that on May 31, 1862, Keyes had 17,132 men present for duty; Heintzelman 16,999, for a total of 34,131. *Official Records*, ser. 1, vol. 11, pt. 3, 204.

144. Johnston, "Manassas to Seven Pines," in *Battles and Leaders of the Civil War*, 2:208–9. Included in Johnston's totals were seven thousand men under Benjamin Huger, who had just arrived.

145. Johnston, *Narrative of Military Operations*, 132–33; Smith, *Battle of Seven Pines*, 144–48.

146. Keyes, *Fifty Years' Observation of Men and Events*, 450.

fault. In his haste to take advantage of the flooded Chickahominy, Johnston gave only unclear oral instructions to Longstreet and brief, imprecise written orders to Magruder and his other division commanders. Benjamin Huger's instructions, for example, simply advised him to be ready for action without specifying when the battle was to be fought or even who was to command.[147] Longstreet must also have been confused because when he attacked, he did so by the wrong road, which destroyed the timing of the entire operation. The battle, which was supposed to be over by 8:00 a.m., did not commence until 1:00 p.m. Even then, D. H. Hill attacked without support from either Longstreet or Huger. Never did the Confederates utilize their numerical advantage by concentrating their full force against Keyes, as was Johnston's intention.[148] Keyes was therefore able to fight his opponent on relatively even terms. Furthermore, the late, disjointed nature of the Confederate attack bought time enough for Keyes to be reinforced by Heintzelman and even by Sumner, who was able to send Sedgwick's division across flood-battered Grapevine Bridge in time to inflict severe losses on Whiting.

For the Confederates, Magruder and A. P. Hill performed their assigned tasks successfully on the left wing. Everywhere else there was mayhem. When Johnston realized how badly the fighting was progressing, he was reported to have remarked that he wished his men were back in their camps and the battle had never occurred.[149] Had the execution of the plan matched its conception, the wish would not have been necessary. Instead, faulty instructions, inadequate staff work, a lack of accurate maps, and woeful unit coordination contributed to a Confederate failure that Douglas Southall Freeman described as "a battle of strange errors."[150]

Joe Johnston was among the 6,134 casualties sustained by the Confederates in the two-day Battle of Seven Pines,[151] having been wounded in the right shoulder by rifle fire and in the chest by artillery fragments late in the

147. Johnston to Huger, May 30, 1862, *Official Records*, ser. 1, vol. 11, pt. 1, 938; May 31, 1862, ibid.

148. Edward Porter Alexander, *Military Memoirs of a Confederate* (New York: Scribners, 1907), 75–93. Porter Alexander stated that twenty-three of the twenty-seven brigades of Johnston's army were to have been deployed simultaneously against McClellan's left wing. Yet nowhere were over four brigades ever in action at one time. It was Alexander's judgment that Johnston's effort to handle his army in battle was "an utter failure" (93).

149. Freeman, *Lee's Lieutenants*, 1:236. Johnston made the remark to S. B. French.

150. Ibid., 225.

151. "Opposing Forces at Seven Pines, May 31–June 1, 1862," in *Battles and Leaders of the Civil War*, 2:219.

afternoon on the May 31.[152] With Johnston's wounding, command devolved to a seemingly disoriented Gustavus Smith. When queried by President Davis about his plan of action, Smith hesitated, then rambled on by referring to Johnston's intentions. Having no interest in Johnston's intentions, Davis again asked Smith what his plans were. The repeated question unnerved Smith, who again answered unsatisfactorily. He judged that "Mr. Davis did not seem pleased with what I said."[153] Indeed, Jefferson Davis was not at all pleased. He sensed that his new commander was simultaneously ill prepared, uninformed, and lacking in self-confidence. Clearly, he was not the type of commander Davis once thought him to be.[154] Accordingly, on June 1, after Smith led a feeble attack to conclude the fighting at Seven Pines,[155] the president formally removed him from command in favor of Robert E. Lee.[156]

Magruder very rarely wished ill of anyone,[157] yet he shed no tears over Smith's removal and Johnston's incapacitation. He clearly disliked Smith and believed him to be unfit for command. On the other hand, while Prince John never questioned Johnston's capabilities, the two men were altogether different by nature, as Lafayette McLaws had earlier pointed out; plus, they rarely

152. Drury L. Armistead, "The Battle in Which General Johnston Was Wounded," *Southern Historical Society Papers* 18 (1890): 187. Drury Armistead was General Johnston's personal courier; Johnston, *Narrative of Military Operations*, 138–39.

153. Smith, *Battle of Seven Pines*, 103–4.

154. Sears, *To the Gates of Richmond: The Peninsula Campaign*, 140–41; Freeman, *Lee's Lieutenants*, 1:262–63.

155. For battle reports and important correspondence relating to the Battle of Seven Pines—or Fair Oaks, as it was called by the Federals—see *Official Records*, ser. 1, vol. 11, pt. 1, 746–994.

156. Davis to Lee, June 1, 1862, ibid., pt. 3, 568–69; Special Orders No. 22, ibid., 569. On the day after he was relieved by Lee, Smith was incapacitated by what, in all probability, was a psychoneurotic disorder known today as conversion hysteria. Typically, anxiety is converted into debilitating symptoms, including episodes of paralysis involving voluntary muscles or special sense organs. Occasionally, the disorder is exacerbated by an accompanying dissociative reaction whereby an overwhelming sense of anxiety results in a gross personality disorganization. Evidence of the disorder was provided by Major Jasper S. Whiting, Smith's assistant adjutant general, who reported to Lee that "General Smith finds himself utterly unable to endure the mental excitement incident to his actual presence with the army . . . there is danger of his entire prostration. He goes to town today to gain a few days respite. All business and all exciting questions must be kept from him for awhile . . . partial paralysis has already commenced. The case is critical and the danger imminent." Whiting to Lee, June 2, 1862, ibid., 685–86.

157. Cobb, "Extracts from Letters to His Wife, February 3, 1861–December 10, 1862," 293. In a letter to his wife, June 13, 1862. During the entire time that Cobb served with Magruder, he reported that he had never heard his commander "abuse but one man and that was [D. H.] Hill."

agreed on anything. After their rift over the defensive viability of the Peninsula, their relationship turned irreconcilably sour. Subsequently, Johnston avoided personal contact with Magruder, ignored his recommendations, routinely turned down his requests, and seldom responded to his written communiqués. Ultimately, the six weeks that Magruder served under Joe Johnston was the most frustrating period of his entire military career. Never had he encountered a commander so unapproachable, so closed-minded, so negative. For Magruder service under Johnston was unhappily reminiscent of his earlier travails with Roger Jones. But suddenly, after the Battle of Seven Pines, both Smith and Johnston were gone, and Magruder's former chief, Robert E. Lee, commanded in their stead. Because Prince John had earlier worked harmoniously with Lee, he welcomed the change. He knew that at the very least Lee would give him a fair chance, whereas Johnston had given him nothing.

Most of Magruder's colleagues, many of whom had served under Joe Johnston from the beginning of the war, were less enthusiastic about their new commander. By and large they viewed Lee with reactions that ranged from skeptical to hostile.[158] James Longstreet, in particular, was unconvinced. "The assignment of General Lee to command the army of Northern Virginia," he wrote, "was far from reconciling the troops to the loss of our beloved chief, Joseph E. Johnston."[159] The rank and file had become accustomed to General Johnston. They knew what to expect from him, but they knew little about General Lee. They knew that he had come from one of Virginia's most distinguished families. His service record indicated that he was an honor graduate of West Point with impeccable credentials as an engineer. He also enjoyed the full support of President Davis. Yet Lee had served essentially as a staff officer, and he had never before led an army into battle. Longstreet reported that there were "some misgivings as to the power and skill for field service of the new commander." Nevertheless, he conceded that Lee's policies, whatever they might be, would in all likelihood afford "a happy relief from the existing, halting policy of the late temporary commander," Gustavus W. Smith.[160]

---

158. Robertson, *Stonewall Jackson*, 462; Porter Alexander, Lee's chief ordnance officer, conceded that Lee's accession to command "did not at once inspire popular enthusiasm." Alexander, *Military Memoirs of a Confederate*, 109.

159. Longstreet, *From Manassas to Appomattox*, 112.

160. Ibid.

Lee quickly extinguished Longstreet's concerns about a slow, indecisive superior by moving at a pace uncharacteristic of either of his dawdling predecessors. In his first order, dated June 1, 1862, he asked for the support of every officer and man and directed his generals to "take every precaution and use every means in their power to have their commands in readiness for immediate action."[161] Shortly afterward Lee instructed his chief engineer, Major Walter Stevens, to lay out plans for the construction of fortifications, placement of field guns, and digging of entrenchments at commanding points from the New Bridge Road toward the James River. "My object," stated Lee, "is to make use of every means in our power to strengthen ourselves and enable us to fight the enemy to the best advantage."[162] Those digging the trenches would facetiously refer to their commander as the "King of Spades."[163] Nevertheless, it was noted, "after the Battle of Seven Pines, our soldiers seemed to have learned to appreciate the advantages of entrenched positions, and their approval of Genl Lee's policy was very cordial."[164]

On June 3, the same day that Lee sent engineering instructions to Stevens, he met with his division commanders at the Chimneys, a prominent country home located on Nine Mile Road near Magruder's new headquarters.[165] Magruder, Longstreet, D. H. Hill, Whiting, and Robert Toombs were present when the meeting commenced.[166] Others, including President Davis, joined the gathering in due course.[167] Lee listened carefully as his generals enumerated their problems and advanced their proposals. After the lengthy conference concluded and the generals returned to their camps, he and Davis continued the discussion in private. Ever the diplomat, Lee carefully cultivated a friendship with the president, frequently sought his advice, and

161. Special Orders No. 22, June 1, 1862, *Official Records,* ser. 1, vol. 11, pt. 3, 569.

162. Lee to Stevens, June 3, 1862, ibid., 571–72.

163. Freeman, *R. E. Lee,* 2:86.

164. Brent, *Memoirs of the War between the States,* 151.

165. Charles Marshall, *An Aide-de-Camp of Lee,* ed. Sir Frederick Maurice (Boston: Little, Brown, 1927), 77; Longstreet, *From Manassas to Appomattox,* 112–13; Brent, *Memoirs of the War between the States,* 150. Brent reported that on the morning of May 31, Magruder left his headquarters at Fairfield Race Course and established a new headquarters at a house on New Bridge Road, approximately a half-mile from Nine Mile Road.

166. Jeffrey D. Wert, *General James Longstreet: The Confederacy's Most Controversial Soldier—A Biography* (New York: Simon and Schuster, 1993), 130.

167. Davis, *Rise and Fall of the Confederate Government,* 2:130–31.

always endeavored to keep him informed. In return, Davis placed far more trust in Lee than he ever had in the noncommunicative Joe Johnston.[168] He also allowed his new commander more discretionary authority in making appointments,[169] and he gave him a free hand in reorganizing the Army of Northern Virginia in preparation for the battles upcoming.[170]

With Davis's concurrence, General Lee displaced Johnston's organizational scheme of two wings and a reserve in favor of a divisional alignment.[171] Magruder was among the division commanders whom Lee retained. His 13,000-man force was expanded into three divisions of two brigades each.[172] Robert Toombs and George T. Anderson commanded brigades in David R. Jones's division; Paul J. Semmes and Joseph B. Kershaw headed brigades under McLaws; and Howell Cobb and Richard Griffith led brigades under Magruder.[173] Additionally, Lee retained James Longstreet, D. H. Hill, A. P. Hill, and Benjamin Huger to command divisions near Richmond, while Stonewall Jackson and Richard Stoddert Ewell commanded divisions in the Shenandoah Valley, with Jackson in overall command there.[174] Not surprisingly, the ineffective Gustavus W. Smith was dismissed and his wing dissolved altogether. Two of Smith's former brigades under Whiting and Hood were sent to Jackson,[175] while the brigades of Wade Hampton, Dorsey Pender, and James Archer were added to A. P. Hill's "Light Division."[176] Of the newly arrived brigades Lee sent Alexander Lawton's Georgians to Stonewall Jackson,[177]

168. William C. Davis, *Jefferson Davis: The Man and His Hour* (New York: HarperCollins, 1991), 426–27, 429, 431.

169. Davis to Lee, June 2, 1862, *Official Records,* ser. 1, vol. 11, pt. 3, 569–70.

170. Davis, *Jefferson Davis: The Man and His Hour,* 431.

171. Chilton to Magruder, June 10, 1862, *Official Records,* ser. 1, vol. 11, pt. 3, 586. Chilton explained to Magruder that by utilizing "the system of divisional commanders greater harmony may be preserved throughout the army, as all questions involving differences of opinion may be referred to a common superior and promptly settled."

172. Magruder's Report on the Seven Days' battles, August 12, 1862, ibid., pt. 2, 661.

173. General Orders No. 71, June 22, 1862, ibid., pt. 3, 612; Organization of the Confederate forces during the engagements around Richmond, Va., ibid., pt. 2, 485–86.

174. Taylor, *Four Years with General Lee,* 53–54.

175. Lee to Magruder, June 11, 1862, *Official Records,* ser. 1, vol. 11, pt. 3, 589; Lee to Jackson, ibid.; Special Orders No. 130, ibid., 594.

176. Lee to Hill, June 11, 1862, *Official Records,* ser. 1, vol. 11, pt. 3, 589.

177. Cooper to G. W. Lee, June 10, 1862, ibid., 585; Cooper to Ransom, ibid.; Lee to Jackson, June 11, 1862, ibid., 589.

Roswell Ripley's South Carolinians to D. H. Hill,[178] and Robert Ransom's North Carolinians to Benjamin Huger,[179] and he posted Theophilus Holmes's North Carolinians at Petersburg and Drewry's Bluff to protect Richmond from the south.[180] With the addition of the reinforcements the 56,612-man army that Lee inherited from Joseph E. Johnston grew to approximately 90,000 men prior to the commencement of the Seven Days' battles around Richmond.[181] It would be the largest force that Robert E. Lee would have at his disposal during the Civil War.[182]

General Lee had still not decided on a strategy to employ against Mc-Clellan, but his objective, to defend his capital, was clear. With emotions that he rarely displayed, Lee had earlier insisted, "Richmond must not be given up—it shall not be given up."[183] Thus resigned, he began making preparations for the upcoming battles, knowing full well that the fate of Richmond, as well as the Confederacy, was in his hands.

178. Sears, *To the Gates of Richmond: The Peninsula Campaign*, 156; Organization of the Confederate forces during the engagements around Richmond, Va., *Official Records*, ser. 1, vol. 11, pt. 2, 484–85.

179. Report of Robert Ransom, July 19, 1862, *Official Records*, ser. 1, vol. 11, pt. 2, 791–93; Report of Benjamin Huger, July 21, 1862, ibid., 787. Ransom was temporarily detached from Holmes's command and assigned to Huger. See Organization of the Confederate forces during the engagements around Richmond, Va., ibid., 488.

180. Lee to Holmes, June 18, 1862, *Official Records*, ser. 1, vol. 11, pt. 3, 607; June 21, 1862, ibid., 610; Special Orders No. 140, ibid., 611.

181. Taylor, *Four Years with General Lee*, 51–52.

182. Sears, *To the Gates of Richmond: The Peninsula Campaign*, 156. Steven Sears states that Lee commanded 92,400 men, and Brian Burton, in his 2001 study of the Seven Days' battles, places the effective strength of the Army of Northern Virginia on June 25, 1862, at 89,772 men. On the other hand, Jubal Early, who in 1876 wrote a lengthy article on the subject, concluded that "the whole of General Lee's strength" was no more than 80,000 men. See Brian K. Burton, *Extraordinary Circumstances: The Seven Days Battles* (Bloomington: Indiana University Press, 2001), 401–3; and "Strength of General Lee's Army in the Seven Days Battles around Richmond," *Southern Historical Society Papers* 1 (1876): 421. Because official Confederate returns were tallied on May 21, nearly five weeks before the Seven Days' battles began, and not again until July 20, nearly three weeks after the fighting ended, any accounting of Confederate troop strength during the critical time in between will always be subject to question.

183. John H. Reagan, *Memoirs* (Austin: Pemberton Press, 1968), 139.

Miniature of Thomas Magruder, painted ca. 1795
Courtesy of Amelia Fisher, Hanover, Pennsylvania, in the Thomas Robson Hay Papers,
Central Rappahannock Heritage Center, Fredericksburg, Virginia

Young John Magruder from the 1913 yearbook of the American Clan Gregor Society
Courtesy of the American Clan Gregor Society

Miniature of Henrietta Magruder, painted in Italy, ca. 1850
Courtesy of Marion B. Parsons, Baltimore, Maryland, in the Thomas Robson Hay
Papers, Central Rappahannock Heritage Center, Fredericksburg, Virginia

Miniature of the Magruder children—(*left to right*) Katherine Elizabeth,
Isabella, and Henry—painted in Italy ca. 1850
Courtesy of Marion B. Parsons, Baltimore, Maryland, in the Thomas Robson Hay
Papers, Central Rappahannock Heritage Center, Fredericksburg, Virginia

Magruder shortly after the Civil War
Thomas Robson Hay Papers, Courtesy Central Rappahannock Heritage
Center, Fredericksburg, Virginia

6

"IN OBEDIENCE TO YOUR ORDERS, TWICE REPEATED"

Robert E. Lee was extremely fortunate that McClellan allowed him the time to reorganize and strengthen his new command after the Battle of Seven Pines because there was little to prevent the Federals from moving immediately on toward Richmond. Their only obstacle was a smaller, badly wounded, and disorganized Confederate force that had lost its leader. Yet because McClellan had lost over five thousand of his own men in battle,[1] and numerous others had been rendered ineffective after contracting "Chickahominy Fever" in the swampy environs east of the rebel capital, he deemed it prudent to move cautiously.[2] He gradually shifted Sumner and Franklin south of the Chickahominy to join Keyes and Heintzelman, while Porter alone remained north of the river to protect the Federal supply line to White House. McClellan, meanwhile, remained at his headquarters awaiting the arrival of reinforcements. However, unremitting rains in early June 1862 turned the ground into "a sea of mud" and caused additional delays over which he had no control.[3] McClellan wrote to Secretary of War Stanton that "the whole face of the country is a perfect bog, entirely impassable for artillery, or even cavalry, except directly in the narrow roads, which renders any gen-

---

1. Official Federal losses totaled 5,031 men. Return of Casualties in the Army of the Potomac at the Battle of Fair Oaks, or Seven Pines, Va., May 31–June 1, 1862, *Official Records,* ser. 1, vol. 11, pt. 1, 757–62; "Opposing Forces at Seven Pines, May 31–June 1, 1862," in *Battles and Leaders of the Civil War,* 2:218–19.

2. *McClellan's Own Story,* 386, 407.

3. Ibid., 399. A frustrated McClellan described the weather as "horrid in the extreme."

eral movement, either of this or the rebel army, entirely out of the question until we have more favorable weather." Nevertheless, the confident young commander assured his superiors that as soon as more reinforcements arrived and the weather improved, he would be "in perfect readiness to move forward and take Richmond."[4]

Lee, on the other hand, did not have the luxury of waiting on the weather, nor was he disposed to tarry until the Federal army was fully reinforced and in position to lay siege to his capital. Instead, he intended to strike the first blow. He planned to concentrate swiftly and secretly the combined forces of Longstreet, A. P. Hill, and D. H. Hill, plus Stonewall Jackson's army from the Shenandoah Valley on the north bank of the Chickahominy River against Fitz John Porter's 5th Corps at Mechanicsville. Simultaneously, Magruder and Huger, with 21,930 men combined,[5] were tasked to hold back the entire 69,500-man Federal army south of the Chickahominy,[6] on a front that extended to White Oak Swamp.[7] If Magruder and Huger could mask Lee's intentions by holding in place the large body of Federals opposing them, Lee would be free to concentrate 61,500 Confederates against Porter's isolated 30,000-man corps without having to worry about his opponent receiving reinforcements from south of the river.[8] It was then Lee's intent to overwhelm Porter, cut McClellan off from his base of supplies at White House, and force him to withdraw his remaining forces from the outskirts of Richmond.

Magruder's task south of the Chickahominy was clearly critical, and consequently, there was "great excitement" at his headquarters. Major Brent

4. Ibid., 387. Telegram, McClellan to Stanton, June 7, 1862.

5. Magruder's Report, August 12, 1862, *Official Records*, ser. 1, vol. 11, pt. 2, 661; "Strength of General Lee's Army in the Seven Days Battles Around Richmond," 420–21. Magruder reported his strength at "about 13,000 men," while Jubal Early, utilizing reports from Benjamin Huger's subordinates, states that Huger had 8,930 men, for a combined total of 21,930. Theophilus Holmes commanded an additional 6,573 men; thus, the total Confederate strength south of the Chickahominy was 28,503. However, as Holmes was assigned to protect Richmond from the south from Petersburg and Drewry's Bluff, he was in no position to immediately assist either Magruder or Huger.

6. Abstract from Return of the Army of the Potomac, June 20, 1862, *Official Records*, ser. 1, vol. 11, pt. 3, 238. Sumner, Heintzelman, Keyes, and Franklin commanded a total of 69,582 troops south of the Chickahominy who were "present for duty, equipped."

7. General Orders No. 75, June 24, 1862, ibid., pt. 2, 498–99.

8. Abstract from Return of the Army of the Potomac, June 20, 1862. ibid., pt. 3, 238. To Porter's 20,535 men were added 9,501 reinforcements commanded by Brigadier General George A. McCall. McCall's division arrived on June 12 and 13.

reported that when he and his fellow officers considered and discussed the plan, "all thought that the position of holding our front lines against Mc-Clellan and thereby protecting Richmond, was the post of honor as well as danger." They knew that if Sumner, Heintzelman, Keyes, and Franklin overpowered them and captured their capital, all would be lost, regardless of the outcome of the attack against Porter north of the river. Despite the dangers of the assignment, the young major had full confidence in Magruder, judging that he was "well fitted for the task confided to him." Because just seven weeks earlier Magruder had held the defensive line between Yorktown and Mulberry Point for a month against a Federal force nearly eight times the size of his own, Brent reckoned that his commander would have no difficulty briefly holding the defensive line east of Richmond against less than four times as many of the enemy.[9] Not surprisingly, President Davis was less assured, fearing that if Lee's real objective was discovered by the Federals, Richmond would, in all probability, fall victim to an enemy counterstroke. But Lee, who had a full appreciation of Magruder's deceptive artistry, as well as McClellan's timidity, persuaded the president that Prince John would be able to hold his position.[10]

Lee's plan called for Stonewall Jackson to signal the beginning of the battle early on June 26 by assaulting Porter's right flank behind Beaver Dam Creek, just to the east of Mechanicsville. A. P. Hill, D. H. Hill, and Longstreet were then to cross the Chickahominy via the Meadow and Mechanicsville bridges and join the fight, with A. P. Hill leading the way.[11] Lee did not intend to attack directly against Porter's powerful defensive line. Instead, he hoped to attack the Federals after Jackson forced them to abandon their defenses.[12] Jackson's flanking movement was therefore critically important to the plan's success. Yet in the first of four uncharacteristic lapses over the next several days, Jackson failed to appear. As the hours passed on the morning of June 26, anticipation among the Confederates poised to cross the Chickahominy turned to apprehension. Where was Jackson? "He had promised to be there," stated Longstreet's aide, G. Moxley Sorrell. Had Jackson attacked in accordance with Lee's plan, Sorrell judged that "the enemy would have melted

9. Brent, *Memoirs of the War between the States,* 158–59.

10. Davis, *Rise and Fall of the Confederate Government,* 2:232.

11. General Orders No. 75, June 24, 1862, *Official Records,* ser. 1, vol. 11, pt. 2, 498–99; Lee's Report, March 6, 1863, ibid., 490.

12. Freeman, *R. E. Lee,* 2:110–11.

before us."[13] Without Jackson nobody knew what to do. "It was evident," reported Brent from Lee's headquarters, "that the military situation was grave, and that with each hour it became more perilous."[14] Finally, at three o'clock in the afternoon of the twenty-sixth, the battle on the north bank began when the impetuous A. P. Hill, fearful of losing everything, attacked without Jackson and without orders.[15] Thus committed to battle, Lee ordered D. H. Hill and Longstreet to join the attack against Porter.[16]

South of the river the fighting had begun well in advance of A. P. Hill's midafternoon attack on the north bank. In the morning Stephen D. Lee, Magruder's artillery commander, shelled Federal positions at James Garnett's farm near New Bridge. After an hour's long lull Lee repeated the shelling in the evening.[17] Between Lee's attacks Magruder superintended an elaborate deception wherein officers shouted orders to nonexisting units; buglers sounded meaningless calls; troops, wagons, and artillery moved menacingly in plain sight of the enemy.[18] It was a show of strength so convincing that D. H. Hill wrote: "Each of McClellan's corps commanders was expecting a special visit from the much-plumed cap and the once-gaudy attire of the master of ruses and strategy. He put on naturally all those grand and imposing devices which deceive the military opponent."[19] Because of Magruder's trickery, McClellan

13. G. Moxley Sorrel, *Recollections of a Confederate Staff Officer,* ed. Bell Irvin Wiley (Jackson, Tenn.: McCowat-Mercer Press, 1958), 74.

14. Brent, *Memoirs of the War between the States,* 161.

15. A. P. Hill's Report, February 28, 1863, *Official Records,* ser. 1, vol. 11, pt. 2, 835. Hill stated that he took the initiative to begin the battle without Jackson, "rather than hazard the failure of the whole plan by longer deferring it." Interestingly, at 3:00 p.m., the time of Hill's attack, Joseph Lancaster Brent was with Lee, having been sent by Magruder "to find out the state of affairs." Brent quoted Lee as saying, "We have been waiting for Genl. Jackson, from whom I have not heard, but I cannot wait longer, and have just sent orders to Genl. Hill (A. P. Hill) to cross at Meadow Bridge." Brent, *Memoirs of the War between the States,* 160–61. If both accounts are correct, it appears that Lee and Hill decided at the same time that the attack had to be made, with or without Jackson. Such would explain why Lee never reprimanded Hill for launching the attack without proper authorization. See Burton, *Extraordinary Circumstances: The Seven Days Battles,* 65.

16. Brent, *Memoirs of the War between the States,* 162.

17. Report of Stephen D. Lee, July 22, 1862, *Official Records,* ser. 1, vol. 11, pt. 2, 746.

18. Jeffrey L. Rhoades, *Scapegoat General: The Story of Major General Benjamin Huger, C.S.A.* (Hamden, Conn.: Anchor Books, 1985), 69.

19. Hill, "Lee's Attacks North of the Chickahominy," in *Battles and Leaders of the Civil War,* 2:362.

sent Porter no reinforcements from below the Chickahominy.[20] But because Jackson had failed to attack and dislodge Porter from his defenses behind Beaver Dam Creek, the entrenched Federals, backed by their superior artillery, were able to hold their position and inflict approximately 1,350 casualties on the attacking Confederates,[21] while losing but 361 of their own.[22] After darkness stopped the fighting, Porter retired to another strong position southeast of Gaines's Mill, behind a small, sluggish stream known as Boatswain's Swamp.[23]

As Jackson had taken no part in the fighting at Mechanicsville, he at least had not revealed his whereabouts to Porter. Lee therefore elected to utilize basically the same plan on the twenty-seventh as before. While A. P. Hill and Longstreet attacked the Federal front, Jackson and D. H. Hill were to sweep down against Porter's right flank and force him to withdraw along the north bank of the Chickahominy. Lee likewise instructed Magruder and Huger to follow their original orders: threaten and deceive the enemy wherever possible south of the river; pursue them if they retreat; hold firm if they attack.[24]

Shortly after daybreak on June 27, Magruder had his men organized and ready for action. At 8:45 a.m. he boldly paraded six to eight infantry regiments in front of Sumner, then massed another large force near Old Tavern, opposite Franklin, while Stephen D. Lee's artillerymen shelled the Federals in both locations. According to one Federal officer, "Furious outbursts of artillery fire, and a resort to every device known [led] to the belief that an attack in force was imminent."[25] Throughout the day McClellan's commanders believed that they were about to be assailed at numerous points south of the river.[26] Even Professor Thaddeus S. C. Lowe, the chief aeronaut of the

20. McClellan was so confused about his opponent's intentions that at 2:30 p.m. on June 26 he telegraphed Stanton, confessing that he did not know where to send newly arriving Federal reinforcements. McClellan to Stanton, June 26, 1862, *Official Records*, ser. 1, vol. 11, pt. 1, 52.

21. Alexander, *Military Memoirs of a Confederate*, 121; Return of Casualties in the Confederate Forces during the Seven Days' Battles, June 26–July 1, 1862, *Official Records*, ser. 1, vol. 11, pt. 2, 973–84.

22. Return of Casualties in the Union Forces Engaged at the Battle of Mechanicsville, Va., June 26, 1862, *Official Records*, ser. 1, vol. 11, pt. 2, 38–39.

23. Porter to Williams, July 8, 1862, ibid., 222–23; July 7, 1862, ibid., 223–24.

24. General Orders No. 75, June 24, 1862, *Official Records*, ser. 1, vol. 11, pt. 2, 498–99; Lee's Report, March 6, 1863, ibid., 490–93; Magruder's Report, August 12, 1862, ibid., 660.

25. Webb, *Peninsula*, 135.

26. McClellan's Report, August 4, 1863, *Official Records*, ser. 1, vol. 11, pt. 1, 58–59.

Army of the Potomac, was so deceived from the vantage point of his reconnaissance balloon that he warned, "By appearances I should judge that the
enemy might make an attack on our left at any moment."[27] Later in the day
McClellan agreed to send Brigadier General Henry W. Slocum's division of
Franklin's corps north of the river in response to Porter's repeated pleas for
reinforcements.[28] Afterward, however, when McClellan requested additional
reinforcements, Franklin replied that it would not be prudent to send any
more of his troops elsewhere. Likewise, when Sumner was asked if he could
spare any of his men for Porter, he replied, "Everything is so uncertain that I
think it would be hazardous to do it."[29] Keyes and Heintzelman, across from
Huger, were similarly bewildered. Overall, the threatening maneuvers executed by Magruder and Huger so duped McClellan that he stated in his official report, "It was impossible to decide until the afternoon [of the twenty-
seventh] where the real attack would be made."[30] Not until 5:00 p.m. did he
direct Sumner to send brigades commanded by brigadier generals Thomas F.
Meagher and William H. French north of the Chickahominy.[31] However,
Meagher and French did not reach Porter until dusk, too late to be of any help.

Luckily for McClellan, the Confederate attack against Porter at Gaines's
Mill occurred without coordination and, for the most part, without Jackson,
who had taken the wrong road and then showed no sense of urgency in
correcting his mistake. Such dalliance, according to Porter Alexander, was

27. Lowe to Humphreys or Marcy, June 27, 1862, ibid., ser. 3, 3:290.

28. In *Lee's Lieutenants*, 1:555, Douglas Southall Freeman stated that while the battle was being
fought at Gaines's Mill, "one of the two Divisions opposite Magruder was taken out of line . . .
and then was hurried across the Chickahominy to reinforce the troops behind Boatswain's
Swamp." Freeman then censured Magruder for failing to discover the enemy's movements. In
reality, had Prince John faced only two of the enemy's divisions, he no doubt would have known
if one of them had moved to a new position. But he faced four divisions—the entire corps of
William B. Franklin and Edwin V. Sumner. Furthermore, Magruder's primary task on June 27
was not to observe the Federals but to threaten and deceive them. The Federal line was of such
length and strength that, in order to accomplish his assigned task, Magruder moved his men
rapidly from one location to another, striking the enemy in force, then retreating to attack again
in a different place. Because Magruder was constantly on the move, it is not realistic to expect
that he would be able to keep track of the enemy's forces at any particular point in their line after
he had become disengaged and moved on to attack them elsewhere.

29. McClellan's Report, August 4, 1863, *Official Records*, ser. 1, vol. 11, pt. 1, 59.

30. Ibid., 57.

31. Ibid., 56.

"unlike anything ever seen in Jackson before or after these Seven Days."[32] Jackson did not join the battle until about 4:30 p.m., two hours after A. P. Hill initially attacked, and it was nearly two and a half hours later before Lee was able to launch the large-scale, coordinated attack along Porter's entire line that had been his original intention. Each side then bloodied the other in a fierce battle, often fought hand to hand, until the numerically superior Confederate army broke through and forced a massive Federal retreat toward the Chickahominy. The victory at Gaines's Mill, Lee's first, helped make up for the debacle at Mechanicsville. Unfortunately, it was trifling compared with what it would have been had Jackson been poised to attack in coordination with A. P. Hill. Had the timing been in accordance with Lee's design, the Federal retreat would have commenced two hours earlier, which would have given Lee sufficient time and daylight to have crushed Porter's reeling army against the banks of the Chickahominy.[33] But darkness intervened and brought the fighting to an end before the Confederates could achieve total victory. That night, while Porter retreated to safety, an unfulfilled Robert E. Lee struggled with the realization that because of inadequate staff work, inaccurate maps, and unit coordination that paralleled that of Joe Johnston's army at its worst, his victory was altogether incomplete. And certainly the casualty count—over 8,000 of his men lost,[34] versus 6,837 for the Federals,[35] made Lee appreciate the high cost of missed opportunities.

Lee anticipated a resumption of fighting north of the Chickahominy on the following day, believing that the Federals surely would battle to protect their supply line to White House. Instead, Porter retreated with such supplies as he was able to transport south of the river, burned the rest, and destroyed

32. Alexander, *Military Memoirs of a Confederate,* 125. Alexander wrote: "Lee's official report of this battle was not written until eight months afterward, during which period Jackson's great military genius had manifested itself undimmed by any spell; and with increasing brilliancy on the fields of Cedar Mountain, Second Manassas, Harper's Ferry, Sharpsburg, and Fredericksburg. There was, most wisely and properly, every disposition to ignore and forget the disappointments felt during the Seven Days and the facts are glossed over with but brief and, as it were, casual mention, but they are plainly apparent." (128).

33. Ibid., 124–32.

34. Return of Casualties in the Confederate Forces during the Seven Days' Battles, June 25–July 1, 1862, *Official Records,* ser. 1, vol. 11, pt. 2, 973–84; Alexander, *Military Memoirs of a Confederate,* 131. Alexander fixed the Confederate loss at 8,358 men.

35. Return of Casualties in the Union Forces at the Battle of Gaines's Mill, June 27, 1862, *Official Records,* ser. 1, vol. 11, pt. 2, 41.

the bridges behind him. This unexpected move left Lee in a dangerous position. His army was now awkwardly divided, with the larger part of it isolated on the far side of the Chickahominy, out of position to protect the capital. Furthermore, as the Federal artillery commanded the river crossings, Lee could neither pursue Porter, nor could he immediately reinforce Magruder and Huger,[36] who stood alone between Richmond and the reunited Army of the Potomac, which with Porter's arrival numbered ninety-two thousand men. A nervous Robert E. Lee sent repeated warnings to Magruder during the night of June 28, urging "utmost vigilance, directing the men to sleep on their arms, and to prepare for whatever might occur." Magruder was equally apprehensive, later writing, "I considered the situation of our army as extremely critical and perilous."[37] He did not sleep that night, preparing instead for the anticipated Federal onslaught. He realized, "Had McClellan massed his whole force in column and advanced it against any point of our line of battle, as was done at Austerlitz under similar circumstances by the greatest captain of any age [Napoleon], though the head of his column would have suffered greatly, its momentum would have insured him success, and the occupation of our works about Richmond, and consequently of the city, might have been his reward."[38]

General McClellan, however, lacked the nerve of a great commander. He was too slow, too cautious, and too timorous to be effective. After Lee's attacks against Porter north of the Chickahominy, Magruder's threatening movements south of the river, and a bold yet ill-advised assault by Robert Toombs at dusk on June 27 against Winfield Scott Hancock's brigade at James Garnett's farm, near McClellan's headquarters, the once confident Union commander suddenly began to fear for the safety of his troops.[39] At a time when Richmond was within his grasp, McClellan hesitated. He was, according to biographers Bryan Conrad and H. J. Eckenrode, too upset and too

---

36. Freeman, *R. E. Lee*, 2:159–63; Taylor, *General Lee: His Campaigns in Virginia, 1861–1865*, 72.

37. Magruder's Report, August 12, 1862, *Official Records*, ser. 1, vol. 11, pt. 2, 662. Prince John's Caroline County neighbor and West Point roommate, William Nelson Pendleton, who commanded the Confederate artillery reserve opposite McClellan, agreed that at this time Richmond was in grave danger of being captured. See Lee, *Memoirs of William Nelson Pendleton*, 195.

38. Magruder's Report, August 12, 1862, *Official Records*, ser. 1, vol. 11, pt. 2, 662.

39. Marcy to Stanton, June 27, 1862, *Report of the Joint Committee on the Conduct of the War*, 1:339. General McClellan's communiqué was sent to Stanton via Chief of Staff Randolph B. Marcy; McClellan's Report, August 4, 1863, *Official Records*, ser. 1, vol. 11, pt. 1, 59; *McClellan's Own Story*, 422, 442.

unstrung on the evening of the twenty-seventh to reason clearly.[40] He instead became irrational and accepted as fact Allan Pinkerton's grossly overstated estimate that the rebel force opposing him numbered 180,000 men and perhaps more.[41] Given odds that he now perceived to be insurmountable, McClellan eschewed an attack against his enemy's capital in favor of a hasty retreat toward the James River. Thus, by failing to move against Richmond between June 27 and 29, 1862, he let pass his best chance of seizing the Confederate capital during the brief time when it was most vulnerable. Clearly, the "Young Napoleon" bore little resemblance to the real Napoleon. For that Lee and Magruder could count their blessings.

McClellan ordered Keyes and Porter to lead the withdrawal, while Franklin, Sumner, and Heintzelman were to hold their positions south of the Chickahominy, across from Magruder and Huger, and form a barrier behind which a 3,000-wagon supply train and a 2,500-head herd of cattle could safely move from White House across the Virginia Peninsula toward Harrison's Landing.[42] Magruder's scouts reported that the Federals were still in place behind their defensive works as late as 3:30 a.m. on the twenty-ninth.[43] By daybreak, however, they had abandoned their entrenchments and were several hours deep into a retreat toward the James.

The massive Federal withdrawal presented General Lee with one final chance to force McClellan into a major battle, away from the protection of his defenses and with his supplies out of reach. But first Lee would have to overcome his enemy's head start. He immediately ordered Magruder to advance cross-country along the Williamsburg Road and the Richmond and York River Railroad to engage the Federal rear guard and slow its retreat. Huger was to parallel Magruder to the south along the Charles City Road, while Jackson and D. H. Hill were to cross Grapevine Bridge, over which Porter had retreated, march south, and support Magruder against the Federals near Savage Station, north of White Oak Swamp. Meanwhile, Longstreet and A. P. Hill were to cross New Bridge, circle around just beyond the outskirts

40. Eckenrode and Conrad, *George B. McClellan: The Man Who Saved the Union,* 97.

41. E. J. Allen (Allan Pinkerton) to McClellan, June 26, 1862, *Official Records,* ser. 1, vol. 11, pt. 1, 269. Pinkerton warned McClellan that his estimate could well be "considerably short of the real strength of their army"; McClellan's Report, August 4, 1863, ibid., 51.

42. McClellan's Report, August 4, 1863, *Official Records,* ser. 1, vol. 11, pt. 1, 60; *McClellan's Own Story,* 423.

43. Magruder's Report, August 12, 1862, *Official Records,* ser. 1, vol. 11, pt. 2, 662; Brent, *Memoirs of the War between the States,* 178.

of Richmond, and then, joined by Huger and Theophilus Holmes, block the Federals on the south side of the swamp before they reached the safety of Malvern Hill and the protection of the Union gunboats on the James.[44]

Magruder began his pursuit of McClellan's rear guard early on June 29, advancing east along the railroad, with D. R. Jones on his left and Lafayette McLaws to his right. With Prince John, mounted on two railroad cars pushed by a locomotive, was a thirty-two-pounder Brooke naval rifle commanded by Lieutenant James E. Barry. The armor-plated mobile gun was in concept the predecessor of the tank. The Confederates called their new weapon the "Land Merrimack."[45]

At approximately 9:00 a.m. "Tige" Anderson's brigade of Jones's division became engaged in a spirited artillery duel with E. V. Sumner's rear guard at Allen's farm, two miles west of Savage Station. The Confederate artillery, aided by Magruder's rail-mounted thirty-two-pounder, forced the Federals to retreat. However, because Stonewall Jackson had not yet arrived to assist on the left, Jones made no attempt to pursue.[46] Meanwhile, as Magruder and McLaws advanced with their divisions along a front that extended between the railroad and the Williamsburg Road, the Federals increased their artillery fire against them. The fusillade was generally ill directed, yet a single shell exploded in the midst of Magruder's men, mortally wounding one of his brigade commanders, Brigadier General Richard Griffith of Mississippi. Griffith, who had seen his first military action during the Mexican War while serving under Jefferson Davis, was succeeded in command by Colonel William Barksdale.[47]

44. Brent, *Memoirs of the War between the States,* 179; Lee's Report, March 6, 1863, *Official Records,* ser. 1, vol. 11, pt. 2, 494.

45. Report of Lafayette McLaws, July 20, 1862, *Official Records,* ser. 1, vol. 11, pt. 2, 717–18; Brent, *Memoirs of the War between the States,* 182–83.

46. Report of D. R. Jones, July 28, 1862, *Official Records,* ser. 1, vol. 11, pt. 2, 691; Report of George T. Anderson, July 14, 1862, ibid., 707.

47. Brent, *Memoirs of the War between the States,* 180. Richard Griffith and Jefferson Davis were longtime acquaintances and close personal friends, the former having served as regimental adjutant when the latter commanded the 1st Mississippi Rifles during the Mexican War. Davis happened to be nearby when the badly wounded Griffith was being removed from the battlefield. Trying to provide comfort, the president leaned over his friend and said, "My dear boy, I hope you are not seriously hurt." Griffith grasped Davis's hand and replied, "Yes, I think fatally; farewell, Colonel." He died shortly afterward in Richmond. See Warner, *Generals in Gray,* 120; and Varina Howell Davis, *Jefferson Davis: Ex-President of the Confederate States of America, a Memoir by His Wife,* 2 vols. (New York: Belford Publishers, 1890), 2:316n.

While Jones was engaged on the left flank, Magruder received intelligence from McLaws that Kershaw's brigade had encountered Federal troops "in works well manned" on the right.[48] Additional reports from scouts and pickets convinced Magruder that he faced a foe in numbers far exceeding his own. He therefore dispatched Major Brent to Lee, begging assistance from Huger. When Brent tendered the request, he reported that Lee "seemed surprised and a little incredulous." Given the information that he had received, Lee saw no basis for Magruder's alarm. He nevertheless agreed to send two of Huger's brigades to Savage Station on the proviso that if they were not engaged by 2:00 p.m., they were to return. Later, in his postwar memoirs, Brent wrote that General Lee appeared to be amused by Magruder's anxiety.[49] He no doubt recalled earlier times when repeated warnings from the Peninsula had convinced authorities in Richmond that Prince John was delusional. Because Brent could not confirm having seen the enemy in force, Lee surmised that Magruder's imagination had once again taken charge of his senses.

Magruder's situation late in the morning on June 29 was in reality far more perilous than Lee assumed. He was opposed by Sumner's corps, W. F. Smith's division of Franklin's corps, and Heintzelman's corps.[50] Although Heintzelman's force would later withdraw through White Oak Swamp, the Federal rear guard at Savage Station numbered approximately 45,000 troops,[51] while Magruder reported having "about 13,000 men."[52] His orders, personally delivered by General Lee earlier in the day, were to attack. Yet Lee had also promised that Stonewall Jackson, after crossing Grapevine Bridge, would be available to assist. If Jackson advanced in concert with Huger and Magruder, the Confederates would be able to concentrate 46,600 men

48. Magruder's Report, August 12, 1862, *Official Records,* ser. 1, vol. 11, pt. 2, 663.

49. Brent, *Memoirs of the War between the States,* 180–81. Much has been made of the fact that Magruder misunderstood Lee's instructions to General Huger. Magruder had thought that Huger was to advance with his men along the Williamsburg Road when, in fact, he had been ordered to march further south, parallel to the Williamsburg Road, along the Charles City Road. Because Huger was still close enough to send reinforcements to Magruder on short order, Prince John's misunderstanding had no effect on the fighting at Savage Station, nor did it hinder Huger in moving his men on June 29. See Magruder to Davis, August 16, 1862, *Official Records,* ser. 1, vol. 11, pt. 2, 687–88.

50. Allan, *Army of Northern Virginia in 1862,* 102.

51. Abstract from Return of the Army of the Potomac, June 20, 1962, *Official Records,* ser. 1, vol. 11, pt. 3, 238.

52. Magruder's Report, August 12, 1862, ibid., pt. 2, 661; Brent reported that Magruder had approximately twelve thousand men. See Brent, *Memoirs of the War between the States,* 179.

against the retreating Federals at Savage Station,[53] striking them simultaneously in flank and rear. With Jackson's 25,000 men, Magruder believed that he had a chance to capture a large portion of the enemy's forces.[54]

Shortly before noon, Stonewall Jackson's chief engineer, Lieutenant James K. Boswell, informed Magruder that Jackson was within a couple of hours from crossing the Chickahominy.[55] Because Grapevine Bridge was only three miles from Savage Station and Jackson seemed to be close at hand, Magruder delayed his advance, hoping that his former lieutenant would arrive before 2:00 p.m., when Huger was scheduled to depart. At 2:00 p.m., however, with Jackson still nowhere to be found, Huger left as he had been ordered. Soon afterward, Magruder received a note from D. R. Jones indicating that Jackson would be unavailable to cooperate at Savage Station, "as he had been ordered on other important duty."[56] With all prospects of receiving the support that Lee had promised now having vanished, Magruder reluctantly readied his men for battle. He positioned D. R. Jones's division on the left wing, with Howell Cobb's brigade in the center, left of the Richmond and York River Railroad. Lafayette McLaws's division was on the right, between the railroad and the Williamsburg Road. William Barksdale's brigade was held in reserve behind Cobb and McLaws.

At approximately 5:00 p.m. Magruder ordered his generals "to attack the enemy in whatever force or works he might be found." He later recalled that the attack "was executed promptly and in beautiful order,"[57] but such was not the case. After the initial advance there was very little coordination along the Confederate line, particularly on the left and in the center. On the far left, just as D. R. Jones had maneuvered into a favorable position to attack the Federal right flank, he was recalled by Magruder's order and repositioned between Orchard and Savage stations. This move accomplished little and ultimately removed Jones's division from the fighting altogether. In the center Howell Cobb and his men watched in awe as the rail-mounted Brooke rifle pounded the enemy lines, but like Jones's men, they too did not participate in the battle. Overall, nineteen of Magruder's twenty-eight regiments, including his entire

53. Sears, *To the Gates of Richmond: The Peninsula Campaign*, 262–63, 267.

54. Magruder's Report, August 12, 1862, *Official Records*, ser. 1, vol. 11, pt. 2, 664.

55. Ibid., 663; Brent, *Memoirs of the War between the States*, 182.

56. Magruder's Report, August 12, 1862, *Official Records*, ser. 1, vol. 11, pt. 2, 664; Jones to Magruder, June 28, 1862, ibid., 675. General Jones's communiqué is incorrectly dated June 28. The Federal retreat and Confederate pursuit did not begin until the next day.

57. Magruder's Report, August 12, 1862, *Official Records*, ser. 1, vol. 11, pt. 2, 664.

force on the north side of the Richmond and York River Railroad, stood idly by while McLaws's brigades under Semmes and Kershaw, with the support of a portion of Barksdale's brigade, fought a vigorous battle south of the railroad against Sumner's corps and Smith's division of Franklin's corps. Because Sumner, like Magruder, failed to deploy a large portion of his men for battle, the opposing forces at Savage Station were approximately the same size. Brisk fighting lasted until 9:00 p.m., when darkness and a heavy rainfall brought the battle to an end.[58]

During the night the Federals retreated through White Oak Swamp, leaving behind the charred remains of tons of food, stores, and military supplies that they could not transport to safety. They also left to the Confederates approximately 3,000 non-ambulatory sick and wounded in their field hospital.[59] Those losses, in addition to the 1,038 battlefield casualties sustained at Allen's Farm and Savage Station, loomed large when compared with Magruder's total of 473 men killed and wounded.[60] Still, the battle would have ended even more favorably for the Confederates had Jackson arrived to assist or if Magruder had fought the Federal rear guard with his entire force. Because neither happened, General Lee was displeased; he lamented that "the result was not decisive."[61] And in a tersely worded message to Magruder, written on the afternoon of June 29, he stated: "I regret very much that you have made so little progress today in the pursuit of the enemy. In order to reap the benefits of our victory the pursuit should be most vigorous. I must urge you then to press on his rear rapidly and steadily. We must lose no more time or he will escape us entirely."[62]

For Lee the reprimand was uncharacteristically harsh. He initially blamed Magruder and Magruder alone for the slow developing attack and disappointing outcome at Savage Station. But by the time he wrote his official report

58. Brent, *Memoirs of the War between the States,* 180–89; Magruder's Report, August 12, 1862, *Official Records,* ser. 1, vol. 11, pt. 2, 663–65; McLaws's Report, July 20, 1862, ibid., 716–17; Report of Joseph B. Kershaw, July 14, 1862, ibid., 726–27; Report of Paul J. Semmes, July 4, 1862, ibid., 720–21; Jones's Report, July 28, 1862, ibid., 691; and Report of William Barksdale, July 24, 1862, ibid., 750.

59. Guild to Cole, July 3, 1862, *Official Records,* ser. 2, 4:798.

60. Sears, *To the Gates of Richmond: The Peninsula Campaign,* 274; Return of Casualties in the Army of the Potomac during the Operations before Richmond, June 25–July 2, 1862, *Official Records,* ser. 1, vol. 11, pt. 2, 24–37; Return of Casualties in the Confederate Forces during the Seven Days' Battles, June 25–July 1, 1862; ibid., 977–79.

61. Lee's Report, March 6, 1863, *Official Records,* ser. 1, vol. 11, pt. 2, 494.

62. Lee to Magruder, June 29, 1862, Enclosure No. 26 in Magruder's Report, August 12, 1862, ibid., 687.

over eight months later, on March 6, 1863, he had changed his tone. His original understanding of the battle, gleaned from his headquarters at the J. B. Williams farmhouse on the Williamsburg Road, several miles from Savage Station, was based on the assumption that the action had taken place as he had anticipated, exactly according to plan. Yet poor communications, imprecise orders, and unexpected delays at Grapevine Bridge, problems of which Lee was unaware at the time, resulted in a battle that, on the field, bore little resemblance to the one that had unfolded in his mind. Lee's principal biographer stated that his subject was lost in "the same 'fog of war' that somehow had prevailed on the Peninsula from the beginning of the campaign."[63] At the time Lee scolded Magruder, he had heard nothing from Jackson, and his own couriers had brought little information from the battlefield. Lee was more unaware of the happenings at Savage Station than of any of the other battles during the Seven Days'. Only later did he realize that several of the leading participants had made mistakes that not only cast Magruder in an erroneous and misleading light but also rendered impossible the implementation of the original plan of action.

At Savage Station, Stonewall Jackson once again performed in subpar fashion. Because Jackson failed to keep anyone apprised of his progress or intentions (a regrettable practice throughout the Seven Days'), Lee was left to anticipate his moves. The assumptions that he made regarding where Jackson should have been or what he should have done, though logical, proved to be entirely unfounded. Lee, for example, was wrong when he informed Magruder early on the morning of June 29 that General Jackson "had crossed or was crossing the Grapevine Bridge."[64] This erroneous statement was rooted in hope rather than fact. Subsequent assumptions were based on the belief that Jackson had crossed the Chickahominy by midmorning and was available to help thereafter,[65] but he never helped at all.

Lee also incorrectly assumed that the Federals had detailed but a token force as their rear guard. Based on that assumption, he doubted that they would attack Magruder, believing that their sole purpose was to protect their supplies while they retreated. What Lee had no way of knowing was that E. V. Sumner was opposed to the retreat altogether and had determined to stand

63. Freeman, *R. E. Lee*, 2:171.

64. Magruder's Report, August 12, 1862, *Official Records*, ser. 1, vol. 11, pt. 2, 662.

65. Clifford Dowdey, *Lee* (Boston: Little, Brown, 1965), 255. Dowdey states that "Brent was not instructed to inform Lee that Jackson had not come up on the left. Lee, assuming he was there, did not ask."

and fight.[66] After Sumner stood firm, Magruder needed all the help that he could get; thus, he asked Lee to send Huger. Reluctantly, Lee acquiesced. When Huger returned without having been utilized, however, Lee concluded that Magruder had overreacted in asking for assistance in the first place. Unbeknownst to Lee, Magruder was still waiting for Jackson at the time that Huger was obligated to return. Without Jackson's twenty-five thousand men, Magruder could not have attacked the numerically superior Federals successfully, even with Huger's help. Magruder had earlier witnessed the folly of D. H. Hill's attack at Seven Pines without the support of Longstreet or Huger. And he had been nearby less than a month later when A. P. Hill marched into battle at Mechanicsville and Gaines's Mill before Stonewall Jackson and his men had arrived. Since as in all three instances the unsupported advances had regrettable consequences for the Confederates, Magruder was not about to make the same witless mistake.[67] So he waited, and waited, but Jackson never came. Ultimately, Jackson's nonappearance, for the third time during the Seven Days' battles, proved to be the most important factor in preventing the Confederates from fully capitalizing on the opportunity at Savage Station.[68]

What had become of Jackson? According to Porter Alexander, he had lapsed into a peculiar "spell." His orders from Lee to pursue the retreating Federals via the Grapevine Bridge Road implied immediate performance and were given at an early hour on June 29. However, as that was a Sunday, Alexander stated that Jackson's priorities were of a religious nature.[69] Bridge building seemed to be his last concern. As evidence, Jackson sent his chief engineer to deliver a message to Magruder, which left Major Robert L. Dabney, who had no bridge building expertise whatsoever, in charge of the construction effort. Had Jackson deemed it important to move south of the Chickahominy, a suitable ford was available nearby. Yet he made no attempt to cross. His mind appeared to be elsewhere. Throughout the Seven Days'

66. William B. Franklin, "Rear-Guard Fighting during the Change of Base," in *Battles and Leaders of the Civil War,* 2:375. After the fighting on June 29, the stubborn Sumner initially refused to continue the retreat toward the James, declaring to General Franklin: "I never leave a victorious field. Why! if I had 20,000 more men, I would crush this rebellion." McClellan finally had to order Sumner to retreat or face arrest.

67. Brent, *Memoirs of the War between the States,* 183.

68. James Longstreet, "'The Seven Days,' Including Frayser's Farm," in *Battles and Leaders of the Civil War,* 2:405. Longstreet placed the blame squarely on Jackson. He judged that conditions were right for a substantial Confederate victory "had Jackson come up and taken part in Magruder's affair on the 29th near Savages' Station."

69. Alexander, *Military Memoirs of a Confederate,* 116–17, 135–36, 145.

Jackson seemed to have had his own priorities and timetable, regardless of orders or exigencies. He prayed when he should have slept; he stayed when he should have moved. He was never in the right place at the right time. Stonewall Jackson, judged Alexander, "was really not Jackson": "He was a different individual . . . Nothing that he had to do was done with the vigor which marked all the rest of his career."[70]

Jackson's situation became further muddled on the afternoon of the twenty-ninth after he received notice from Lee's chief of staff, Colonel Robert H. Chilton, via Jeb Stuart, to be on guard in the event that McClellan attempted to recross the Chickahominy.[71] Jackson interpreted the letter as a directive from Lee to maintain his position north of the river to prevent the Federals from escaping down the Peninsula to the safety of Fort Monroe.[72] He thus informed D. R. Jones that he had another important duty to perform and would not be available to help at Savage Station. The letter, which originated from Chilton on the Charles City Road rather than from Lee's headquarters at the Williams's farmhouse, was intended to be an order for Stuart but no more than an advisory for Jackson. Later in the day, when Walter Taylor, Lee's adjutant general, told his commander that D. R. Jones had informed Magruder of Jackson's unavailability, Lee quickly attempted to eliminate the confusion that Chilton had caused. He wrote to Magruder: "I learned from Major Taylor that you are under the impression that General Jackson has been ordered not to support you. On the contrary, he has been directed to do so, and to push the pursuit vigorously."[73] Unfortunately, the clarification came too late. Lee later conceded that Jackson's notice of non-availability to Jones had "originated in some mistake,"[74] a mistake that he obviously attributed to Chilton. At some point in time, though, he must have realized that had Jackson more expeditiously rebuilt Grapevine Bridge or utilized the nearby available ford, he would have crossed the Chickahominy and fought with Magruder at Savage Station before ever having received Chilton's communiqué. Immediately after the battle, however, Lee assigned the blame to Magruder, not Jackson.

70. Ibid., 116–17.

71. Chilton to Stuart, June 29, 1862, Stuart Collection, Henry E. Huntington Library, San Marino, Calif.

72. Vandiver, *Mighty Stonewall*, 312; Lenoir Chambers, *Stonewall Jackson*, 2 vols. (New York: William Morrow, 1959), 2:59–61; Robertson, *Stonewall Jackson*, 488–89.

73. Lee to Magruder, June 29, 1862, *Official Records*, ser. 1, vol. 11, pt. 2, 687.

74. Lee to Randolph, August 14, 1862, ibid., 680.

At sunrise on June 30 General Lee appeared at Magruder's headquarters and announced that Stonewall Jackson would take charge of the pursuit of McClellan's rear guard. Lee directed Magruder to march west from Savage Station on the Williamsburg Road, across to the Darbytown Road, thence east to the Long Bridge Road, and northeast toward Glendale, a small but strategically important crossroads community through which McClellan's retreating army would have to pass en route to Malvern Hill. There Magruder would reinforce Longstreet and A. P. Hill. Longstreet was to occupy a position in the Confederate center, with A. P. Hill to his right and Theophilus Holmes to Hill's right at New Market, three and a half miles west of Malvern Hill. Benjamin Huger was to move via the Charles City Road to a position on Longstreet's left and open fire with his artillery as soon as he was within range of the enemy. Simultaneously, Jackson was to advance through White Oak Swamp and attack the enemy's rear while driving its front toward the guns of Huger, Longstreet, and A. P. Hill.[75] If all occurred according to Lee's carefully designed plan, 71,000 Confederates would be in position to cut McClellan's army in two and envelop 61,500 retreating Federals, who were encumbered with a great wagon train.[76] The opportunity was enormous, one of the best the South would have during the entire war.[77] In order to be successful, however, Lee's commanders would have to accomplish their assigned tasks on time and without fail.

Magruder was not long into his circuitous march toward Glendale when he began acting peculiarly. Those closest to him knew that he had been unwell for a couple of days. But on the morning of June 30 he took a turn for the worse. Illness, combined with physical and mental exhaustion exacerbated by want of food and sleep, produced in Magruder "a loss of equilibrium." In Brent's words: "Genl. Magruder was on horseback, galloping here and there with great rapidity. He seemed to me to be under a nervous excitement that strangely affected him. He frequently interposed in minor matters, reversing previous arrangements and delaying the movement he was so anxious to hasten." This uncharacteristic behavior so concerned Magruder's subalterns

75. Lee's Report, March 6, 1863, ibid., 495.

76. Freeman, R. E. Lee, 2:176; Sears, To the Gates of Richmond: The Peninsula Campaign, 279.

77. Edward Porter Alexander, Fighting for the Confederacy: The Personal Recollections of General Edward Porter Alexander, ed. Gary W. Gallagher (Chapel Hill: University of North Carolina Press, 1989), 110. After the war Alexander stated that of the opportunities the South had had to win a victory of such magnitude "that we might have hoped to end the war with our independence . . . This chance of June 30th '62 impresses me as the best of all."

that Major Henry Bryan, the general's chief of staff, prevailed upon Brent to "speak to the General and endeavor to calm him." As Brent had been Magruder's legal counsel in California and was more closely acquainted with him than any of the other staff members, he reluctantly accepted the onerous assignment. Soon afterward, while stopped to water the horses, the major engaged his commander:

> "General," I said, "I am sorry to see that you are not feeling well this morning."
> "Why do you think so?"
> "Well, General, I hope you will pardon me, but I have never seen your usual calmness so much lost by an extreme irritability, sometimes exhibited without any apparent cause, and hence I inferred that you must be feeling badly."
> "Well, Major, you are right. I am feeling horribly. For two days I have been disturbed about my digestion, and the doctor has given me medicine, and I fear he has given me some morphine in his mixture, and the smallest quantity of it acts upon me as an irritant. And besides that, I have lost so much sleep that it affects me strangely; but I fully appreciate your kindness in speaking to me, and I will endeavor to regain my self control."[78]

Within a remarkably short time following the candid conversation, Magruder was able to regain his composure, overcome the ill effects of his combined maladies, and resume his march, much to the relief of his entire staff. By 2:00 p.m. he had moved his 12,500-man force approximately twelve miles from Savage Station to Timberlake's store, on the Darbytown Road, a half-dozen miles due west of Glendale. By Lee's order Magruder halted his men for rest behind A. P. Hill and Longstreet, who were in their assigned positions waiting for Huger and Jackson to signal the beginning of the battle. At 4:30 p.m., however, before the fighting began, Magruder received orders from Longstreet to reinforce Theophilus Holmes on the New Market Road to prevent a possible drive on the Confederate right flank against Hill. Immediately upon receipt of Longstreet's order, Magruder prepared to march. He obtained information from a local farmer about the shortest route to Holmes's position.[79] Then he sent Major Brent ahead to give Holmes an estimated time of arrival and to ascertain from him the most advantageous positioning for his troops.[80]

78. Brent, *Memoirs of the War between the States,* 190–92.
79. Magruder's Report, August 12, 1862, *Official Records,* ser. 1, vol. 11, pt. 2, 666.
80. Brent, *Memoirs of the War between the States,* 193.

Holmes, meanwhile, had become involved in a furious artillery duel against the enemy gunboats *Aroostook* and *Galena* to his right, on the James, as well as several of Fitz John Porter's field batteries on his front at Malvern Cliffs, on the western face of Malvern Hill. During the bombardment a number of Holmes's unseasoned men fled in terror directly past a visiting President Jefferson Davis. Davis, who was approximately a half-mile behind Holmes, later reported that he had nearly succeeded in stopping the flight of Holmes's men, but "another shell fell and exploded near us in the top of a wide-spreading tree, giving a shower of metal and limbs, which soon after caused them to resume their flight in a manner that plainly showed no moral power could stop them within the range of those shells."[81] Such a cowardly performance in the presence of the president humiliated General Holmes,[82] who had retired to consider his misfortune in the solitude of his tent when Major Brent arrived. Brent unknowingly happened upon a commander who was angry, embarrassed, and in no mood to receive visitors. When Brent asked if the general had any suggestions regarding what position Magruder should take to contest the enemy most effectively, Holmes brusquely answered that he had none. The major then asked if the general could give him any current information relative to the enemy's strength and location. An emphatic no was the reply. And finally, when Major Brent stated that he was returning to Magruder and would convey any message the general desired to send, Holmes coldly replied that he had no message. "His bearing was the most singular that I have ever seen and was marked by the absence of even a simulation of ordinary courtesy," declared Brent. "I road [*sic*] away from him almost paralyzed by amazement to find such a man in command of troops."[83]

Luckily, instructions that Brent had failed to obtain from Theophilus Holmes, Magruder received from Robert Chilton, whom he met at the junction of the Darbytown and Long Bridge roads at approximately 5:00 p.m. Chilton accompanied Magruder to New Market and directed him to occupy the woods on Holmes's right. The colonel then immediately left to find Lee, while Magruder sought out Holmes. Later, at dark, while positioning his men in accordance with Chilton's instructions, Magruder received new orders to relieve Longstreet, who during the afternoon of the thirtieth had

81. Davis, *Rise and Fall of the Confederate Government*, 2:144.

82. Report of Theophilus Holmes, July 15, 1862, *Official Records*, ser. 1, vol. 11, pt. 2, 907. General Holmes described the conduct of his men as "shameful in the extreme."

83. Brent, *Memoirs of the War between the States*, 193–94.

fought the desperate battle of Glendale or Frayser's Farm without the assistance of either Jackson or Huger. As the new orders were of an urgent nature,
Magruder immediately redirected his men to the east along the Long Bridge
Road toward Glendale, not even pausing for food or rest. At 3:00 a.m. on
July 1 the travel-weary troop reached its destination, relieved Longstreet, and
finally went into bivouac at the end of what had been an extremely long and
frustrating day.[84] After their early departure from Savage Station, Magruder
and his men had marched eighteen hours and covered twenty miles. By the
time they reached Longstreet's encampment, they were more exhausted than
the troops they replaced.[85] Magruder himself had had only one hour of sleep
during the preceding forty-eight hours and no food for nearly twenty-four
hours. He was tired, frustrated, and distressed by acute stomach pain that
medicine only made worse.[86]

General Lee was also exhausted and frustrated following the fighting at
Glendale. Moreover, Longstreet and D. H. Hill observed that he was noticeably disappointed after once again witnessing the unraveling of a carefully
designed plan because of poor execution by his division commanders.[87] In
this case Benjamin Huger and Stonewall Jackson were the culprits. Huger
was unable to reach the battlefield because felled trees and other purpose-
fully placed obstructions prevented him from advancing by the Charles City
Road to his assigned position on Longstreet's left.[88] He was handicapped by
a shortage of axes, and he moved far too cautiously. Nevertheless, Huger at
least attempted to reach his objective, which is more than can be said for
Jackson. Once Jackson perceived that he faced a large Federal rear guard,
he halted his men north of partially destroyed White Oak Swamp Bridge
and did nothing. "For the first time in his martial career," wrote Douglas
Southall Freeman of Jackson, "he quit." On the afternoon of June 30, 1862,

84. Magruder's Report, August 12, 1862, *Official Records,* ser. 1, vol. 11, pt. 2, 666–67; McLaws's
Report, July 20, 1862, ibid., 718; Lee's Report, March 6, 1863, ibid., 495.

85. Alexander, *Military Memoirs of a Confederate,* 154; Anderson's Report, July 14, 1862, *Official
Records,* ser. 1, vol. 11, pt. 2, 707; Jones's Report, July 28, 1862, ibid., 691; McLaws's Report, July 20,
1862, ibid., 719. General McLaws reported that his battle weary troops "had been on the march
for about twenty hours."

86. Magruder's Report, August 12, 1862, *Official Records,* ser. 1, vol. 11, pt. 2, 662, 665; Brent,
Memoirs of the War between the States, 191–92, 196.

87. Longstreet, *From Manassas to Appomattox,* 142; D. H. Hill, "McClellan's Change of Base
and Malvern Hill," in *Battles and Leaders of the Civil War,* 2:391.

88. Report of Benjamin Huger, July 21, 1862, *Official Records,* ser. 1, vol. 11, pt. 2, 789–90; Lee's
Report, March 6, 1863, ibid., 495.

with the sound of gunfire clearly audible, when Jackson was needed most, he lay down and went to sleep under a tree.[89] It was his fourth and most costly failure during the Seven Days' battles. A bitterly disappointed James Longstreet insisted until the day he died that "Jackson should have done more for me than he did."[90] Lee was more charitable, only lamenting, "Could the other commands have cooperated in the action the result would have proved most disastrous to the enemy."[91] But there was no Jackson, no Huger, and no victory. Later, in his Pulitzer Prize–winning biography of Lee, Freeman judged:

> Frayser's Farm was one of the great lost opportunities in Confederate military history. It was the bitterest disappointment Lee had ever sustained, and one that he could not conceal. Many times thereafter, he was able to discover a weak point in his adversary's line or a mistake in his antagonist's plan, but never again was he able to find the enemy in full retreat across his front. Victories in the field were to be registered, but two years of open campaign were not to produce another situation where envelopment seemed possible.[92]

After the war Longstreet complained that there were 50,000 Confederate troops within a radius of three miles from the battlefield at Frayser's Farm, yet none came to help.[93] Magruder, with his 12,500 men, could have made a difference, perhaps a dramatic difference, but he had been ordered away, ultimately to no purpose. Longstreet implied that Lee had ordered Magruder to General Holmes's assistance,[94] which is entirely possible because Lee had personally scouted Holmes's situation before Magruder received his orders. This is consistent with the fact that Lee's chief of staff, Robert Chilton, specified where Magruder was to position his men defensively. Magruder and D. H. Hill, on the other hand, contended that the order to assist Holmes had come from Longstreet.[95] Regardless of the source, the order was a mistake. Sending Magruder away from the Glendale front grievously weakened the Confederacy's chances of victory there, particularly because Jackson and

89. Freeman, *Lee's Lieutenants*, 1:576.

90. Longstreet, "'The Seven Days,' Including Frayser's Farm," in *Battles and Leaders of the Civil War*, 2:402.

91. Lee's Report, March 6, 1863, *Official Records*, ser. 1, vol. 11, pt. 2, 495.

92. Freeman, *R. E. Lee*, 2:199.

93. Longstreet, "'The Seven Days,' Including Frayser's Farm," in *Battles and Leaders of the Civil War*, 2:402.

94. Longstreet, *From Manassas to Appomattox*, 139.

95. Magruder's Report, August 12, 1862, *Official Records*, ser. 1, vol. 11, pt. 2, 666; Hill, "McClellan's Change of Base and Malvern Hill," in *Battles and Leaders of the Civil War*, 2:391.

Huger never arrived and never fired a shot.[96] Those attempting to assign culpability for the battle's disappointing outcome have been nearly unanimous in criticizing Benjamin Huger but surprisingly lenient in overlooking the failings of Stonewall Jackson. Freeman was one of few scholars who properly faulted Jackson, yet he simultaneously chided Prince John, derisively referring to him as "Magruder, the ever galloping,"[97] as if the unproductive marching on June 30 was of his own accord. Author Brian Burton was more factually correct in pointing out that "he [Magruder] was ordered everywhere he went, so if he could have been used elsewhere, the fault was not his."[98]

Magruder slept about an hour on Sunday morning, July 1, his second hour's sleep in three days.[99] Then he rose to organize his men in anticipation of renewed early-morning fighting near Glendale. During the night, however, Franklin, Heintzelman, and Sumner had quietly withdrawn their forces, two miles to the south, to a more secure position atop Malvern Hill, where they rejoined Porter and Keyes, who had arrived on the previous day. There Fitz John Porter; John G. Barnard, McClellan's chief engineer; and Henry J. Hunt, in command of the Union artillery reserve, worked tirelessly through the night, adding the newly arrived Federal commands to a skillfully designed defense, which was configured in a convex arc facing north, anticipating that the Confederates would move directly against them from Glendale. George Sykes's division of Porter's 5th Corps guarded the western approach to Malvern Hill, where Theophilus Holmes had been driven away a day earlier. Porter's other division, commanded by George Morell, was posted to Sykes's right, on the western portion of the northern defensive line. Darius Couch's division of Keyes's 4th Corps was to the right of Morell, completing the heavily fortified northern front. Heintzelman's 3rd Corps, Sumner's 2nd Corps, and Franklin's 6th Corps were stacked behind Couch, in position to protect the eastern approach to the hill or assist elsewhere, if needed.[100] By the time the last of the Federal units reached Malvern Hill, shortly after daybreak on July 1, 1862, the Army of the Potomac, with over eighty thousand men and 268 guns, not including siege artillery, was united on the same field for the first time during the Seven Days'.[101] Additionally, the Federals

96. Sears, *To the Gates of Richmond: The Peninsula Campaign*, 291.

97. Freeman, *Lee's Lieutenants*, 1:586.

98. Burton, *Extraordinary Circumstances: The Seven Days Battles*, 393.

99. Magruder's Report, August 12, 1862, *Official Records*, ser. 1, vol. 11, pt. 2, 667.

100. McClellan's Report, August 4, 1863, ibid., pt. 1, 68.

101. Burton, *Extraordinary Circumstances: The Seven Days Battles*, 307.

held ground, superbly suited for defense, which gave them a considerable advantage over their rebel pursuers. "Had the Union engineers searched the whole countryside below Richmond," stated Freeman, "they could not have found ground more ideally set for the slaughter of an attacking army."[102]

Malvern Hill was a broad, moderately elevated plateau, more than a mile and a quarter across north to south and less than a mile wide from east to west. Water encircled three sides of the hill, presenting significant obstacles for attackers. Western Run, which originated near Glendale, meandered in a southerly direction along the eastern base of the plateau, then turned back to the northwest, and flowed at the foot of the bluff on the southern edge of Malvern Hill. Similarly, Turkey Run rimmed the west side of the plateau below Malvern Cliffs and then flowed to the east along the southern base of the hill until it joined Western Run. At the confluence of the two streams the watercourse flowed less than a half-mile to the south until it emptied into the James River at Turkey Bend.[103] The firepower of the Union gunboats on the James precluded any rebel advance against Malvern Hill from the south, while swampy ground, thick underbrush, and forests made difficult the approaches from the east, across Western Run, or from the west, across Turkey Run. Malvern Hill was therefore most easily accessible from the north, where the Willis Church Road from Glendale, after crossing Western Run and its accompanying marshes, ran gradually uphill over firm, unobstructed ground to the plateau's summit. But while the approach from the north provided the Confederates with the fewest obstacles, it simultaneously offered the Federals advantages of excellent observation, fine artillery positions, and wide fields of fire.[104] After a local citizen, the Reverend L. W. Allen, described the topographical features of the enemy-held position to D. H. Hill, Hill reportedly "became satisfied that an attack upon the concentrated Federal army so splendidly posted, and with such vast superiority in artillery, could only be fatal to us."[105] Upon meeting Lee and Longstreet at Willis's Church, Hill

---

102. Freeman, *R. E. Lee*, 2:204.

103. Jennings Cropper Wise, *The Long Arm of Lee or the History of the Artillery of the Army of Northern Virginia*, 2 vols. (Lynchburg, Va.: J. P. Bell Co., 1915), 1:221–22; Allan, *Army of Northern Virginia in 1862*, 123; Fitz John Porter, "Battle of Malvern Hill," in *Battles and Leaders of the Civil War*, 2:409. General Porter judged that Malvern Hill "was better adapted for a defensive battle than any with which we had been favored [during the Seven Days']."

104. McClellan's Report, August 4, 1863, *Official Records*, ser. 1, vol. 11, pt. 1, 68.

105. Hill, "McClellan's Change of Base and Malvern Hill," in *Battles and Leaders of the Civil War*, 2:390.

repeated Allen's description of Malvern Hill and warned, "If General Mc-Clellan is there in force, we had better let him alone." Longstreet laughingly replied, "Don't get scared, now that we have got him whipped."[106]

General Lee shared Longstreet's optimism. His army, like the opposing army, was now fully united, and enthusiasm among his men ran high. Conversely, the Yankees, because of the heavy losses they had sustained in men and supplies during their hurried retreat from the outskirts of Richmond, appeared to be somewhat demoralized. Stragglers and Union deserters at least conveyed that impression to the Confederates, and Lee and his generals had no reason to believe otherwise. D. H. Hill reported, "It was this belief in the demoralization of the Federal army that made our leader risk the attack."[107] Lee hoped he could force the Federals to withdraw from their defenses at Malvern Hill just as he had earlier done at Gaines's Mill. Then he would have them trapped against the banks of the James River, where finally, he would be in position to win the decisive victory that he had sought since assuming command from Joe Johnston. Lee believed that such a victory would surely turn the war in the South's favor. On the other hand, he also realized that if he failed, McClellan would likely make good his escape.

Shortly after daylight on July 1, General Lee announced in a meeting with his principal commanders that Jackson, Magruder, and Huger would lead the attack. Stonewall Jackson was ordered to move his divisions directly down the Willis Church Road toward Malvern Hill.[108] Magruder, after advancing via the Quaker Road, was to form on Jackson's right,[109] in front of the hill, with Benjamin Huger to his right. Theophilus Holmes was to remain in position west of Malvern Hill near New Market, while Longstreet and A. P. Hill, who had borne all of the fighting at Glendale on the previous day, held their battle-weary troops in reserve southwest of the Long Bridge–Charles City crossroads.[110]

Jackson's four divisions and two of Huger's brigades, those commanded by Lewis Armistead and Ambrose Ransom Wright, reached their assigned positions by noon. Huger was not far behind with his other two brigades, Robert Ransom's and Billy Mahone's, but Magruder was nowhere to be

106. Ibid., 391.

107. Ibid.

108. Lee's Report, March 6, 1863, *Official Records*, ser. 1, vol. 11, pt. 2, 495.

109. Magruder's Report, August 12, 1862, ibid., 667; Brent, *Memoirs of the War between the States*, 203.

110. Lee's Report, March 6, 1863, *Official Records*, ser. 1, vol. 11, pt. 2, 495.

found. According to Major Brent, after Lee had sent his generals back to their camps to bring up their troops, Magruder and his staff promptly prepared for the march toward the Quaker Road.[111] Leading the way were guides S. B. Sweeney, L. T. Gatewood, and Charles Watkins, lifelong residents of Henrico County who were intimately acquainted with all of the local roads and byways. Sweeney and his companions led Magruder's divisions down the Long Bridge Road onto another, which turned left near Mr. Nathan Enroughty's gate and continued two miles to the south-southwest until it intersected with the River Road, a half-mile below Sweeney's Tavern. That road, insisted the guides, "was the only road regarded as the Quaker Road by persons living in the neighborhood."[112] Unfortunately, the path of travel to the Quaker Road led Magruder angularly away from Malvern Hill. Clearly, it was not the Quaker Road that Lee intended for him to take.

Several writers have claimed that the Willis Church Road was also known locally as the Quaker Road, which runs counter to the unanimous testimony of Magruder's guides. Nevertheless, based on the assumption that the two roads were one and the same, these writers have concluded that General Lee intended for Magruder to follow Stonewall Jackson down the Willis Church Road toward Malvern Hill. They have not explained why, if Prince John was to do nothing more than follow Jackson down the same road, he would have needed three guides. Moreover, if Lee had intended for Jackson and Magruder to have used the same road, he no doubt would have used the same name when referring to it. He would not have termed the road the "Willis Church Road" when giving verbal instructions to Jackson and then in his next sentence called it the "Quaker Road" when issuing orders to Magruder.[113] And finally, from logistical and time management standpoints,

111. Brent, *Memoirs of the War between the States,* 203.

112. Testimony of Charles Watkins, Enclosure No. 4 in Magruder's Report, August 12, 1862, *Official Records,* ser. 1, vol. 11, pt. 2, 677. See also Testimony of S. B. Sweeney, L. T. Gatewood, and J. W. Binford, ibid., 675–77; John Lamb, "Malvern Hill—July 1, 1862," *Southern Historical Society Papers* 25 (1897): 212–13, 216–17. John Lamb, one of Magruder's couriers, stated that the road to which Magruder had been conducted by his guides had been known for sixty years as the "Quaker Road." Furthermore, a third of the century after the Civil War ended, Lamb wrote, "You may go there and the same road will be pointed out as the Quaker Road."

113. Lee's Report, March 6, 1863, *Official Records,* ser. 1, vol. 11, pt. 2, 495; Brent, *Memoirs of the War between the States,* 203. Lee specified in his official report that he had directed Jackson to march down the Willis Church Road. Then, immediately after he had given marching orders to Jackson, Major Brent quoted Lee as saying, "And you, Genl. Magruder advancing down the Quaker Road, will form on our right, attacking from the most favorable position."

it would have been impracticable for Lee to have sent Jackson's four divisions, two brigades of Huger's, and Magruder's three divisions, in tandem, down the Willis Church Road. The concentration of over forty thousand troops with their equipment on the same narrow roadway would have caused massive confusion and unacceptable delay and would have rendered the efficient deployment of Confederate forces near Malvern Hill an impossibility. Robert E. Lee would have never been so shortsighted.

It is not known what map Lee used on July 1, 1862.[114] If, however, the Quaker Road on his map was neither the Willis Church Road nor the road that Magruder's guides identified as the Quaker Road, it is highly probable that a byroad known locally as the Carter's Mill Road, which ran between the two aforementioned roads, was the Quaker Road that Lee intended for Magruder to take. This infrequently used artery left the Long Bridge Road a little more than a mile west of Glendale and ran south through the Carter Farm until it joined the Willis Church Road, a short distance north of Malvern Hill. Had Magruder initially taken the Carter's Mill Road, he would have ended his march in front of Malvern Hill on time and on Jackson's right exactly in accordance with Lee's intentions. Instead, after several hours of useless marching and counter-marching, he arrived late and moved into position on the extreme right of the Confederate line, next to Huger rather than Jackson, as Lee had originally ordered.[115]

Freeman blamed the delay on "poor guides and poorer maps."[116] He failed to mention that the guides were not employed by Magruder. They were provided for him,[117] almost certainly by Lee's staff, specifically to lead him to his assigned position via the Quaker Road. The guides were also the best that could be found.[118] They knew every square foot of the country; hence, Magruder had no reason to doubt them. Had Lee's staff simply provided Magruder and his fellow commanders in the field with copies of General Lee's

114. Sears, *To the Gates of Richmond: The Peninsula Campaign*, 432n; Burton, *Extraordinary Circumstances: The Seven Days Battles*, 315, 459n. Burton's statement, "Lee's map showed the Willis Church road as the Quaker road," is without basis in fact given that he also conceded, "The exact map Lee used is not known."

115. Magruder's Report, August 12, 1862, *Official Records*, ser. 1, vol. 11, pt. 2, 668; Lee's Report, March 6, 1863, ibid., 496. Because Magruder was late arriving, Lee changed his original deployment plan, placing Huger next to Jackson, then ordering Magruder to position his troops to the right of Huger.

116. Freeman, *R. E. Lee*, 2:205.

117. Magruder's Report, August 12, 1862, *Official Records*, ser. 1, vol. 11, pt. 2, 668.

118. Testimony of J. W. Binford, Enclosure No. 4 in Magruder's Report, ibid., 677.

map, the advance toward Malvern Hill would have been effected without any missteps, regardless of road nomenclature. Overall, the work of Lee's staff was abominable during the Seven Days'. James Robertson cleverly stated in his superb biographical study of Stonewall Jackson: "Some previous writers are wrong in asserting that Lee's staff work was poor. It was nonexistent."[119] With proper staff preparation the Quaker Road mix-up would have never occurred.

Poor staff work was also evidenced in General Lee's July 1 battle plan, which was signed by Robert Chilton. The plan read: "Batteries have been established to act upon the enemy's line. If it is broken as is probable, Armistead, who can witness the effect of the fire, has been ordered to charge with a yell. Do the same."[120] The order was imprecise, poorly constructed, and untimed. Major Brent, for one, was stupefied. "Who ever heard of such an order to bring on a battle?" he asked rhetorically.[121] It is highly unlikely that the order was drawn by Lee—that he would have left to the discretion of one of his brigade commanders, who was commanding in his first battle, the responsibility for determining the precise moment when to begin one of the most important Confederate assaults of the war. Furthermore, stated Stephen Sears, "the only signal for a simultaneous charge by fifteen brigades— the Rebel yell of a single charging brigade—was likely to generate as much confusion as cooperation."[122] In all probability the directive was an expression of Lee's desires in Colonel Chilton's poorly chosen words. Because Chilton had authored the order to Jeb Stuart on June 29 that so confused Stonewall Jackson that it prevented him from assisting Magruder at Savage Station, Lee should have at least checked the order for clarity. Apparently, he did not. Given the ambiguous nature of the unfortunate order, Confederate coordination on July 1, 1862, was destined to fall considerably short of Lee's intentions.

Ultimately, nothing went right for the Confederacy on this crucially important day. Lee himself was reportedly "feeling unwell and much fatigued" on the morning of the first.[123] He asked Longstreet to accompany him and to assume command if the need arose.[124] Because of what Major Brent described

119. Robertson, *Stonewall Jackson,* 474. See also Dowdey, *Seven Days: The Emergence of Lee,* 189–90.

120. Chilton to Magruder, July 1, 1862, Enclosure No. 5 in Magruder's Report, August 12, 1862, *Official Records,* ser. 1, vol. 11, pt. 2, 677; Brent, *Memoirs of the War between the States,* 220.

121. Brent, *Memoirs of the War between the States,* 221.

122. Sears, *To the Gates of Richmond: The Peninsula Campaign,* 317.

123. Longstreet, *From Manassas to Appomattox,* 142.

124. Freeman, *R. E. Lee,* 2:201.

as "the stress of long continued strain, anxieties, fatigue and loss of sleep beyond the capacity of any man to endure,"[125] General Lee seemed to have lost his edge. Suddenly his temper soured.[126] He failed to supervise his staff properly, while simultaneously he appeared to have no control of the movements of his forces in the field. Clearly, like Stonewall Jackson, Robert E. Lee was not himself. Furthermore, in all previous actions during the Seven Days' battles, Lee's plans had been carefully considered and skillfully formulated. But at Malvern Hill his battle plan simply evolved. William Swinton, who studied the campaigns of the Army of the Potomac, wrote: "Lee never before or since that action delivered a battle so ill judged in conception, or so faulty in its details of execution. It was as bad as the worst blunders ever committed on the Union side."[127]

Lee had scouted Malvern Hill on the afternoon of the thirtieth.[128] He should have realized the importance that his artillery would have to play against an enemy that awaited his attack from a superior position. Yet the use of artillery was not even mentioned until late in the morning of the first, when Lee endorsed a plan, suggested by Longstreet, to establish "grand batteries," one on either side of the Willis Church Road, from which a deadly crossfire would be directed against the massed Federal artillery on Malvern Hill. Sixty guns were to be positioned on the Confederate right and up to a hundred on the left. If successful, the artillery attack would batter an opening in the enemy line and pave the way for Armistead's infantry assault.[129]

Had the potential of the Confederate artillery barrage been recognized by Lee on the afternoon of the thirtieth, rather than by Longstreet in late morning of the following day, McClellan's army might have been crushed. Yet because Lee had made no call for his artillery when he had issued the early-morning marching instructions to his division commanders on the first, most Confederate artillery units had remained behind after the infantry had moved toward the front. D. H. Hill had even sent his artillery back to Seven Pines to be refitted.[130] When the order came to advance the artillery, those

---

125. Brent, *Memoirs of the War between the States*, 204.

126. Wert, *General James Longstreet*, 146.

127. William Swinton, *Campaigns of the Army of the Potomac: A Critical History of Operations in Virginia, Maryland, and Pennsylvania from the Commencement to the Close of the War, 1861–5* (New York: Charles B. Richardson, 1866), 163.

128. Holmes's Report, July 15, 1862, *Official Records*, ser. 1, vol. 11, pt. 2, 907.

129. Longstreet, *From Manassas to Appomattox*, 143.

130. Report of H. P. Jones, July 15, 1862, *Official Records*, ser. 1, vol. 11, pt. 2, 653; Report of A. Burnet Rhett, July 12, 1862, ibid., 655.

units that could be located were forced to move a considerable distance over narrow roads, then through the infantry toward the two positions that Lee and Longstreet had belatedly selected. Not surprisingly, the few batteries that reached the front arrived too late. Furthermore, on the right the ground was so rough and obstructed that only one or two batteries could move forward for positioning at a time. "The result," wrote Longstreet, "was the enemy concentrated the fire of fifty or sixty guns upon our isolated batteries, and tore them into fragments in a few minutes after they opened piling horses upon each other and guns upon horses."[131] Likewise on the left, Jackson's artillery units were so badly scattered that when brought into position piecemeal, the Federals were able to overwhelm them almost before they were unlimbered and placed in position to return fire. Only eight batteries participated in the bombardment against Malvern Hill from the Confederate left. Six more saw action on the right, while forty-nine additional batteries lagged behind and did not fire a single round. In disgust D. H. Hill made his well-known declaration to Jackson, "The firing from our batteries was of the most farcical character."[132]

The Confederates might have more effectively contested the Federals had Magruder's old West Point roommate General William Nelson Pendleton assisted with the Army of Northern Virginia's artillery reserve. Incredibly, however, Lee issued no orders to Pendleton.[133] And Pendleton spent the better part of the first searching for his commander in an attempt to ascertain how and where his seventeen batteries might be most productively utilized. After failing to locate Lee, Pendleton stated that he could do nothing more than "await events and orders, in readiness for whatever service may be called for."[134] He later pointed out the obvious—that "too little was thrown into action at once; too much was left in the rear unused."[135] Similarly, J. Thompson Brown of the 1st Virginia Artillery wrote in regret of "the great superabundance of artillery and the scanty use that was made of it."[136] Never was there any concentration of fire against the enemy's artillery. And never was there even minimal coordination among the sixty-three Confederate

131. Longstreet, "'The Seven Days,' Including Frayser's Farm," in *Battles and Leaders of the Civil War*, 2:402. See also Lamb, "Malvern Hill—July 1, 1862," 214.

132. Report of D. H. Hill, July 3, 1863, *Official Records*, ser. 1, vol. 11, pt. 2, 628.

133. Gallagher, "Undoing of an Early Confederate Hero," 132.

134. Report of William Nelson Pendleton, July 21, 1862, *Official Records*, ser. 1, vol. 11, pt. 2, 536.

135. Ibid., 537.

136. Report of J. Thompson Brown, July 14, 1862, ibid., 550.

batteries that could have been engaged at Malvern Hill. Lee's artillery, which had been less than impressive throughout the Seven Days' battles, had its worst day on July 1, when it was needed most.

At approximately 4:00 p.m., near the end of the one-sided artillery duel, Magruder reached the front ahead of his men.[137] By the time he arrived, Armistead was in the process of advancing three of his regiments up Malvern Hill. Magruder dutifully reported this movement to Lee via one of his staff officers, Captain A. G. Dickinson. Lee received Magruder's report at about the same time that Whiting, from the left flank, reported that the enemy across from Jackson was retreating across Malvern Hill.[138] The retreat, however, was simply E. V. Sumner's men falling back to a more protected position away from Confederate artillery fire.[139] And Armistead's advance was intended only to drive away a forward line of Union skirmishers that had moved up to harass the Confederate right-wing artillery batteries.[140] As the hour was late, General Lee did not undertake a personal reconnaissance. He simply accepted as fact that McClellan was beginning another retreat and that Armistead had finally begun his advance as ordered. Thus, on the basis of two misunderstood sightings, Lee ordered his commanders to attack Malvern Hill. Magruder's order, carried by Captain Dickinson, was urgent and unequivocal: "Advance rapidly . . . the enemy is getting off. Press forward your whole line and follow up Armistead's successes."[141]

Magruder had just received the untimed, hours-old order from Chilton directing him to follow Armistead into battle when Dickinson arrived with the newly issued command from Lee. All questions raised by the imprecision of the first order to arrive were quickly eliminated by the clarity of the second. It began with the explicit statement, "General Lee expects you to advance rapidly."[142] Fresh on Magruder's mind were the words of Lee's stinging reprimand on the twenty-ninth: "I regret very much that you have made so little progress today in the pursuit of the enemy . . . the pursuit should be most vigorous . . . press on his rear rapidly . . . we must lose no more time

137. Report of A. R. Wright, July 12, 1862, ibid., 814.

138. Report of William H. C. Whiting, July 1862, ibid., 566.

139. Report of Alfred Sully, July 6, 1862, ibid., 88; Alexander, *Military Memoirs of a Confederate,* 160–61.

140. Report of Lewis Armistead, July 14, 1862, *Official Records,* ser. 1, vol. 11, pt. 2, 819.

141. Dickinson to Magruder, n.d., Enclosure No. 6 in Magruder's Report, August 12, 1862, ibid., 677–78.

142. Ibid., 677.

or he will escape us entirely."[143] This time, if Lee expected a rapid advance, Prince John would not let his commander down.

Based on the assumption that all of his forces would be available for service, Magruder hoped to send fifteen thousand men into battle against the Union left.[144] Because of the Quaker Road mix-up, however, his divisions and artillery were still en route to the front when Lee's order to advance arrived. At that time the only troops available to Magruder on the Confederate right were Huger's. Armistead was to the right of the Carter's Mill Road–Willis Church Road mergence; Rans Wright was to the right of Armistead; and behind Wright were Huger's other two brigades commanded by Robert Ransom and Billy Mahone. As time was short and General Huger was approximately two miles behind his most advanced brigades, Lee instructed Magruder to lead Huger's troops into battle.[145]

Lee's order infuriated Benjamin Huger. The sensitive South Carolinian was still simmering after his authority had been usurped earlier at Seven Pines, when he had been placed in a subordinate position to James Longstreet, despite being Longstreet's senior in rank. Huger also outranked Magruder.[146] Not surprisingly, Lee's order assigning Huger's troops to command under Magruder on the Confederate right was not well received. When Major Brent sought information from General Huger for Magruder about the exact positioning of his trailing brigades, he found Huger to be altogether uncooperative.[147] Huger lied and told Brent that he did not know where his brigades were.[148] He also made it clear that he resented Armistead and Wright having been moved to the front without his knowledge and by another officer's orders.[149] After Brent left to report his encounter with Huger to Magruder, General Huger ordered Ransom and Mahone not to obey any

143. Lee to Magruder, June 29, 1862, Enclosure No. 26 in Magruder's Report, August 12, 1862, ibid., 687.

144. Magruder's Report, August 12, 1862, ibid., 669.

145. Lee's Report, March 6, 1863, ibid., 496.

146. Benjamin Huger had outranked both Longstreet and Magruder in the "old army." Furthermore, in the Confederate army, although all three had been promoted to major general with commissions dated October 7, 1861, Huger's name preceded those of Longstreet and Magruder on the official list that was confirmed by the Confederate Congress; hence, Huger was the senior officer of the three. *Journal of the Congress of the Confederate States of America, 1861–1865,* 1:473.

147. Brent, *Memoirs of the War between the States,* 212.

148. Rhoades, *Scapegoat General: The Story of Major General Benjamin Huger, C.S.A.,* 102–3.

149. Brent, *Memoirs of the War between the States,* 212.

order unless it came directly from him.[150] Consequently, when Magruder first appealed to Ransom and Mahone for their assistance, he was turned down. Later, after a second appeal, Mahone volunteered his brigade for service, but Ransom continued to deny Magruder's urgent requests for help, as per Huger's instructions. Four times, in fact, he refused to assist.[151] Finally, at 7:00 p.m. Huger issued a discretionary order allowing Ransom to go or not to go but not to place himself under General Magruder's control.[152] Thus, on one of the most important days of the war for the Confederacy, while John Magruder was trying to fight the battle that Lee had instructed him to fight, Benjamin Huger was stubbornly fighting to protect his seniority. He steadfastly refused to yield his authority to an officer of inferior standing, regardless of the consequences.

Because Magruder was not "at liberty to hesitate under the stringency of [his] instructions [from Lee]," he had to move on, with or without Huger's cooperation.[153] Accordingly, at 4:45 p.m. he issued an order to Wright through Henry Bryan to advance in line and attack the enemy in front.[154] Magruder's personal appeal also brought forth Billy Mahone's brigade; plus, he sent in his own recently arrived division consisting of brigades commanded by William Barksdale and Howell Cobb. These brave men advanced against "a murderous fire of shot, shell, canister, and musketry."[155] In his official report Magruder vividly described the action:

> The fire of musketry and artillery now raged with terrific fury. The battle-field was enveloped in smoke, relieved only by flashes from the lines of the contending troops. Round shot and grape crashed through the woods, and shells of enormous size, which reached far beyond the headquarters of our gallant commander-in-chief, burst amid the artillery parked in the rear. Belgian missiles and Minie balls lent their aid to this scene of surpassing grandeur and sublimity. Amid all our gallant troops in front pressed on to victory, now cheered by the rapid fire of friends on their left, as they had been encour-

150. Ransom to Magruder, July 1, 1862, Enclosure No. 7 in Magruder's Report, August 12, 1862, *Official Records*, ser. 1, vol. 11, pt. 2, 678; Magruder's Report, ibid., 670.

151. Brent, *Memoirs of the War between the States*, 212–13, 216–17.

152. Report of Robert Ransom, July 11, 1862, *Official Records*, ser. 1, vol. 11, pt. 2, 794.

153. Magruder's Report, August 12, 1862, ibid., 669.

154. Wright's Report, July 12, 1862, ibid., 814; Magruder's Report, August 12, 1862, ibid., 670. Magruder incorrectly recalled that the time was "about 5:30 p.m."

155. Wright's Report, July 12, 1862, *Official Records*, ser. 1, vol. 11, pt. 2, 814.

aged in their advance by the gallant brigades on the right, commanded by Generals Wright and Mahone. Nevertheless the enemy, from his strong position and great numbers, resisted stoutly the onset of our heroic bands, and bringing into action his heavy reserves, some or our men were compelled to fall back.[156]

The "rapid fire of friends on the left" that Magruder referenced came from D. H. Hill, who, in compliance with Chilton's original instructions, attacked when he heard the rebel yell from his right. Unbeknownst to Hill, the yell was not from Armistead but, rather, from Wright and Mahone when they charged in support of Armistead. By the time Hill began his advance from the Confederate center, the Federals had already repelled the initial move against their left (the Confederate right). Therefore, the Federals, after concentrating all of their firepower against Magruder's attackers, were then able to redirect their guns against Hill. In each instance the Federals inflicted severe losses upon the Confederates, more than half of which, according to Hill, were caused by their superior artillery.[157] Hill's statement "is probably an exaggeration," judged Keith Bohannon, in his study on the Union and Confederate artillery at Malvern Hill.[158] Even so, Bohannon declared that July 1, 1862, "was undoubtedly the finest day of the Civil War for the Army of the Potomac's Artillery Reserve."[159]

At approximately the same time that Hill commenced his attack in the center, Magruder ordered Tige Anderson and Robert Toombs of D. R. Jones's Division to the front on the right. Anderson moved up quickly and supported Howell Cobb's men as instructed, but in the course of advancing through thick woods and ravines, Toombs lost contact with Anderson as well as some of his own regiments in a move that was later charitably described as having been "imperfectly accomplished." Ultimately, Toombs's Georgians strayed so far to the left, near the Confederate center, that they were in no position to assist on the right wing, where Magruder needed

156. Magruder's Report, August 12, 1862, ibid., 670.

157. Hill, "McClellan's Change of Base and Malvern Hill," in *Battles and Leaders of the Civil War,* 2:394; Hill's Report, July 3, 1863, *Official Records,* ser. 1, vol. 11, pt. 2, 628–29. Hill stated that the Federals had the advantage of "position, range, caliber, and number of guns."

158. Keith S. Bohannon, "One Solid Unbroken Roar of Thunder: Union and Confederate Artillery at the Battle of Malvern Hill," in *The Richmond Campaign of 1862: The Peninsula and the Seven Days,* ed. Gary W. Gallagher (Chapel Hill: University of North Carolina Press, 2000), 234.

159. Ibid., 240.

them. Furthermore, Toombs's advancing troops became entangled with D. H. Hill's retreating forces, causing such "great confusion" that unit integrity in the center was destroyed.[160] The two commanders became so angry with each other that in the battle's aftermath Toombs challenged Hill to a duel.[161]

At about 6:00 p.m., in response to a late order from Lee via Chilton to press the enemy on the right,[162] Magruder's last available troops, commanded by Lafayette McLaws, began moving to the front. The march began with Joseph Kershaw's brigade on the left and Paul Semmes's on the right, one hundred yards apart. The distance between the two brigades increased, however, as they advanced toward the battlefield until they, like Toombs and Anderson, lost contact with one another. Kershaw eventually wound up behind Toombs in the confusion at the center, while Semmes and Robert Ransom, who had finally been released by Huger, made their way to the front on the right to aid Magruder. With Toombs and Kershaw out of position and unavailable, Magruder had to initiate the final attempt to break the Union line on Malvern Hill with Semmes and Ransom alone.

Near dusk Ransom began the advance with his fellow North Carolinians from their position on the extreme right flank. At about the same time, Semmes's force, which was joined by the remnants of Armistead and Wright's brigades, moved forward on Ransom's left. The oncoming Confederates immediately faced the full fury of the Federal artillery. Each volley cut wide gaps in their ranks, yet they kept moving forward. Ransom's men were able to advance within twenty yards of the Federal batteries until "a fire the intensity of which [was] beyond description" forced their withdrawal.[163] Likewise, Semmes described the enemy fire on his front as being "unsurpassed for severity in any conflict during the war."[164] The Federal fusillade halted some of Semmes's men in their tracks, but others moved inexorably forward in quick time with the 10th Louisiana Volunteers in the lead. The Louisianians, commanded by Lieutenant Colonel Eugene Waggaman, battled newly arrived Federal reinforcements under Thomas Meagher of Sumner's Corps in desperate hand-to-hand combat that lasted until Waggaman and 37 of his

160. Report of Robert Toombs, July 7, 1862, *Official Records,* ser. 1, vol. 11, pt. 2, 697–98.

161. Cobb, "Extracts from Letters to His Wife, February 3, 1861–December 10, 1862," 294. In a letter to his wife, July 16, 1862; Freeman, *Lee's Lieutenants,* 1:627.

162. Magruder's Report, August 12, 1862, *Official Records,* ser. 1, vol. 11, pt. 2, 671; Chilton to Magruder, July 1, 1862, Enclosure No. 8 ibid., 678; McLaws's Report, July 20, 1862, ibid., 719.

163. Ransom's Report, July 11, 1862, *Official Records,* ser. 1, vol. 11, pt. 2, 795.

164. Semmes's Report, July 4, 1862, ibid., 723.

men were cut off and forced to surrender. The bloody assault was extremely costly for both Semmes and Ransom, the latter losing 499 of his men, the highest loss sustained by any Confederate brigade at Malvern Hill. "It was a bitter disappointment to be compelled to yield when their guns seemed almost in our hands," wrote Ransom. His only consolation was that his "officers and men behaved in every way as becomes the soldier of the Southern Confederacy."[165] Praising Ransom and his fellow brigade commanders, D. H. Hill wrote:

> I never saw anything more grandly heroic than the advance after sunset of the nine brigades under Magruder's orders. Unfortunately, they did not move together, and were beaten in detail. As each brigade emerged from the woods, from fifty to one hundred guns opened upon it, tearing great gaps in its ranks; but the heroes reeled on and were shot down by the reserves at the guns, which a few squads reached. Most of them had an open field half a mile wide to cross, under the fire of field—artillery in front, and the fire of the heavy ordnance of the gun-boats in their rear. It was not war—it was murder.[166]

At Malvern Hill, Lee lost 5,965 of his men, approximately 3,000 more than were lost by McClellan in the bloody assault that, according to Porter Alexander, should not have been made in the first place.[167] Years later historian Robert Selph Henry agreed, judging that "Malvern Hill was Lee's great tactical mistake."[168] General Lee, on the other hand, believed that the attack had failed because his subordinates had not advanced in concert.[169] The losses were particularly severe on Magruder's front, on the Confederate right, where the fighting had been heaviest. Magruder lost 2,014 of his own men, plus 1,609 more of Huger's, for an aggregate of 3,623, or 61 per cent of the total Confederate losses for the day.[170] Following the battle an angry Robert E. Lee sought out and found Magruder, who was preparing to retire for his first full night of sleep in the last four days. "General Magruder," demanded Lee,

165. Ransom's Report, July 11, 1862, ibid., 795.

166. Hill, "McClellan's Change of Base and Malvern Hill," in *Battles and Leaders of the Civil War,* 2:394.

167. Alexander, *Military Memoirs of a Confederate,* 167; Return of Casualties in the Confederate Forces during the Seven Days' Battles, June 25–July 1, 1862, *Official Records,* ser. 1, vol. 1, pt. 2, 973–84; Organization of Troops and Return of Casualties in the Army of the Potomac during the Operations before Richmond, Va., June 25–July 2, 1862, inclusive, ibid., 24–37.

168. Robert Selph Henry, *The Story of the Confederacy* (Indianapolis: Bobbs-Merrill, 1931), 162.

169. Lee's Report, March 6, 1863, *Official Records,* ser. 1, vol. 11, pt. 2, 496.

170. Alexander, *Military Memoirs of a Confederate,* 167.

"Why did you attack?" Magruder glared back at his superior and immediately replied, "In obedience to your orders, twice repeated!" The orders had indeed been given. And as Lee could not rightfully criticize Magruder for being too rash at Malvern Hill after chastising him just two days before for not being aggressive enough at Savage Station, he offered no reply, for there was nothing to say.[171]

During the night McClellan's army withdrew from its positions on Malvern Hill to Harrison's Landing, seven miles away on the James River, where powerful Union gunboats offered ample protection. Lee elected not to pursue, thus ending the Seven Days' battles.[172] The bloody campaign cost the Confederates 20,141 men[173] versus 15,849 for the Federals.[174] Richmond was saved, yet Lee was far from satisfied. "Under ordinary circumstances the Federal Army should have been destroyed," he would later write in his official report.[175] During the Seven Days' campaign, though, the circumstances were far from ordinary. This was Lee's first major command. His unfamiliarity with the capabilities and limitations of his subordinates resulted in a crippling lack of coordination, which was compounded by poor staff work, inadequate maps, and the inexplicably miserable performance of Stonewall Jackson.

After the war James Longstreet wrote that "Jackson was a very skillful man against such men as Shields, Banks, and Fremont, but when pitted against the best of the Federal commanders, he did not appear so well." Longstreet also implied that had Jackson participated in Magruder's affair on June 29 at Savage Station, there would have been no Frayser's Farm.[176] D. H. Hill then added had Jackson supported Longstreet and A. P. Hill at

171. Freeman, *R. E. Lee,* 2:218; Lamb, "Malvern Hill—July 1, 1862," 217.

172. For battle reports and important correspondence relating to the Seven Days' battles, see *Official Records,* ser. 1, vol. 11, pt. 2, 19–994. Important testimony relating to the Union effort in the Seven Days' can be found in the *Report of the Joint Committee on the Conduct of the War.* See also *Battles and Leaders of the Civil War,* 2:313–427, as well as the numerous accounts of participants published in the *Confederate Veteran, Southern Historical Society Papers* and the *Papers of the Military Order of the Loyal Legion of the United States.*

173. Alexander, *Military Memoirs of a Confederate,* 171.

174. Organization of Troops and Return of Casualties in the Army of the Potomac during the Operations before Richmond, Va., June 25–July 2, 1862, inclusive, recapitulation. *Official Records,* ser. 1, vol. 11, pt. 2, 37.

175. Lee's Report, March 6, 1863, ibid., 497.

176. Longstreet, "'Seven Days,' Including Frayser's Farm," in *Battles and Leaders of the Civil War,* 2:405.

Frayser's Farm, there would have been no Malvern Hill.[177] Robert Chilton, who faulted nearly everyone except himself, stated that Jackson ought to have been shot for his failures during the Seven Days.[178] Indeed, within Lee's army the blame for the failure to defeat McClellan centered on Jackson.[179] And yet, as Porter Alexander pointed out, because Jackson had performed so brilliantly earlier in the Shenandoah Valley, he received remarkably little criticism from either the southern people or the press corps following the Seven Days' campaign.[180] For the most part the public criticism that missed Stonewall Jackson found its target in Prince John Magruder.[181]

On the evening of July 1 diarist John B. Jones wrote, "To-day Gen Magruder led his divisions into action at Malvern Hill, it is said, contrary to the judgment of other commanders . . . and fearful was the slaughter."[182] Thomas J. Goree of Longstreet's staff, unaware of the commands that Magruder had received from Lee via Chilton, stated in a letter to his mother: "Genl. Magruder, contrary to orders had attacked them [the entrenched Federals]. The result was that Magruder having engaged his Division, others had to come to his support and very soon the Divisions of Huger, D. H. Hill, & Jackson were also engaged." Under the circumstances, as he understood them, Goree blamed Huger and Magruder for "our failure to render the victory as decisive as could be wished."[183] Likewise, Mary Chesnut wrote, "Public opinion is hot against Huger and Magruder for McClellan's escape."[184] And Thomas R. R. Cobb, who had briefly served under Magruder at Yorktown,

177. Hill, "McClellan's Change of Base and Malvern Hill," in *Battles and Leaders of the Civil War,* 2:389.

178. Alexander to Colston, April 7, 1898. Campbell-Colston Family Papers, Southern Historical Collection, University of North Carolina, Chapel Hill. Frederick Colston recalled Chilton's remarks in written comments on the back of the April 7, 1898 letter from Porter Alexander.

179. Wert, *General James Longstreet,* 151.

180. Alexander, *Fighting for the Confederacy,* 96.

181. Gallagher, "Undoing of an Early Confederate Hero," 134. Gallagher described Magruder as "the prime villain."

182. Jones, *Rebel War Clerk's Diary,* 87.

183. Thomas Jewett Goree to Sarah Williams Kittrell Goree, July 21, 1862, in Thomas J. Goree, *Longstreet's Aide: The Civil War Letters of Major Thomas J. Goree,* ed. Thomas W. Cutrer (Charlottesville: University Press of Virginia, 1995), 91, 96.

184. Chesnut, *Diary from Dixie,* 266. Diarist Sallie Putnam expressed very similar sentiments, writing: "Public opinion reflected rather severely on General Magruder and General Huger. It was said if Magruder had been less rash, and Huger less tardy, the Federal army [would have] never reached the security of their gunboats." See Putnam, *Richmond during the Civil War,* 149.

conceded not long after the fighting had ended at Malvern Hill that "Old Magruder made no reputation in this battle. He lost rather than gained. He was depressed, and I fear was drinking."[185]

Magruder's departure for service in the Trans-Mississippi on July 12, 1862, sparked additional controversy.[186] Many, including Judith McGuire, who wrote in her diary on July 15 that "General Magruder is relieved, and sent to take command in the West,"[187] believed the transfer was a demotion precipitated by a poor performance at Malvern Hill, when in fact the initial assignment had been made on May 23, over a month before the Seven Days' battles began. The orders had been temporarily suspended by Secretary of War Randolph on May 26, in view of the military crisis then at hand. As soon as the crisis passed, Magruder, on July 2, informed Randolph that he was ready to assume command of the Trans-Mississippi Department, as per his original orders.[188] On the following day Robert Chilton issued special field orders, stating, "Maj. Gen. J. B. Magruder, having been ordered upon special service in the West (temporarily suspended), will now proceed to carry out that order, [the] circumstances causing its suspension having been removed."[189] Afterward, however, Chilton, perhaps influenced by the rumors then swirling around Richmond, began having second thoughts about the wisdom of the assignment. On July 11 he wrote Adjutant and Inspector General Samuel Cooper, urging him to rescind Magruder's transfer to the Trans-Mississippi, calling Prince John a "marplot" and claiming that he was "incompetent to command." Chilton declared, "The more I have thought upon the subject of Magruder's Mission, the more strongly convinced I am of the sad injustice to be inflicted upon the people of the South West by sending one so utterly incompetent and deficient as is Magruder." He also claimed that "General Lee concurs in my belief of his [Magruder's] incompetency," and D. R. Jones "charges him with something worse than incompetency." Chilton did not specify what "something worse than incompetency" meant. Nevertheless,

185. Cobb, "Extracts from Letters to His Wife, February 3, 1861–December 10, 1862," 293. In a letter to his wife, July 5, 1862.

186. Kenneth H. Williams, "Prince without a Kingdom: The Recall of John Bankhead Magruder," *Civil War History* 41, no. 1 (March 1995): 5n.

187. Judith McGuire, *Diary of a Southern Refugee, during the War* (New York: E. W. Hale and Son, 1867), 127.

188. Magruder to Randolph, July 2, 1862, *Official Records*, ser. 1, vol. 11, pt. 3, 630.

189. Special Field Orders No. ___, July 3, 1862, ibid.

he was so sure of his allegations that he invited an official court of inquiry to prove their validity.[190]

Samuel Cooper immediately forwarded Chilton's letter to President Davis, along with an accompanying note of his own. Interestingly, although Chilton made no mention of any alcoholic impropriety when he charged Prince John with incompetency, Cooper, who had long been a Magruder detractor,[191] wrote that the colonel's letter served to remind him of his former convictions, "that no reliance can be placed in the assumed information of one who is addicted to the vice of intemperance. As far as my observations have gone," stated Cooper, "I am satisfied that the partially reformed drunkard will as surely return to his cup as 'the dog to his vomit.'"[192] Because no one, Chilton included, had officially charged that Magruder had been under the influence of alcohol at any time during the Seven Days' battles, Cooper's unsolicited assertion that the general could not be counted on was based solely on his long-standing personal belief that Prince John was an alcoholic. Nevertheless, because Jefferson Davis held Samuel Cooper in high regard and valued his judgment, Cooper's endorsement of Chilton's charges was taken seriously. On July 13, immediately after receiving General Cooper's warning, Davis recalled Magruder, via telegraph, to address all concerns regarding his fitness to command the Trans-Mississippi Department.[193] Then, before Magruder could return to Richmond to defend himself, the president, on July 16, appointed Theophilus Holmes to command the Trans-Mississippi in his stead.[194]

While Confederate bureaucrats were conspiring against him in Richmond, Magruder was making his way toward what he thought was to be his new command. The general and his staff reached Columbia, South Carolina, on July 14, where they took lodgings at the Congaree House. On the following

190. Chilton to Cooper, July 11, 1862, Board of Proceedings in the Case of Colonel Robert H. Chilton, Confederate States Army, War Department Collection of Confederate Records, National Archives.

191. Only once did Samuel Cooper ever recommend Magruder—on June 21, 1862, when he suggested that Magruder succeed John C. Pemberton in command in South Carolina. Even then, he made the recommendation to Davis "with much reluctance." Cooper to Davis, June 21, 1862, *Official Records*, ser. 1, 14:670.

192. Cooper to Davis, July 12, 1862. Dearborn Collection, Harvard University.

193. Davis to French, July 13, 1862, *Official Records*, ser. 1, vol. 11, pt. 3, 641; Randolph to Duncan, July 13, 1862, National Archives.

194. Special Orders, No. 164, July 16, 1862, *Official Records*, ser. 1, 13:855.

day the *Columbia Guardian* noted, "In response to the call of a large number of our citizens, and to the compliment of music by the Fort Sumter band, General Magruder expressed his gratification and thanks in a few soldierly words." He assured his audience that McClellan had been defeated in the recent fighting around Richmond and that the Federal change of base from the Chickahominy to the James was the result of military necessity rather than choice. Magruder's comments brought "loud cheering" from the crowd. And observer Susan Matilda Middleton judged that the speech overall "seemed to give great satisfaction."[195] After the speech the *Guardian* reported, "General Magruder looks the brave leader that we knew him to be." The newspaper also stated that the general was soon to depart for east Tennessee on his way to his new assignment.[196] Instead, after receiving Davis's telegram, the general and his entourage immediately headed back to Richmond.

On July 19, in a personal interview with the president, Magruder was informed of the reason for his recall,[197] and was shown Robert Chilton's accusatory letter.[198] Although he must have been shocked that such charges were levied by an officer of inferior rank, Prince John did not challenge his accuser to a duel, nor did he bluster publicly. He took the charges seriously and endeavored to refute each of them as thoroughly and as professionally as possible, with strict adherence to military procedure.[199] During the next month after his recall Magruder expanded his original brief report of 225 words into a document of approximately 10,000 words, to which was added 26 attachments, including sworn statements from each of the guides involved in the Quaker Road mix-up; Chilton's orders, which directed the ill-fated attack into the teeth of the Federal artillery at Malvern Hill; and an eyewitness report that refuted the tales of drunkenness that circulated throughout the army and in Richmond following the Seven Days' battles.

195. Isabella Middleton Leland, ed., "Middleton Correspondence, 1861–1865," *South Carolina Historical Magazine* 63 (July 1962): 167. In a letter, Susan Matilda Middleton to her cousin, Harriott Middleton, July 19, 1862. Susan Middleton, the wife of a wealthy South Carolina planter, stated that Magruder was "a rather rowdy looking man in very shabby gray clothes" who looked much more dissipated and seedy than he used to at Fort Adams when in command, superintending the movements of his troops on the parade ground.

196. *Columbia Guardian*, July 15, 1862.

197. Magruder to Davis, August 13, 1862, *Official Records*, ser. 1, vol. 11, pt. 2, 687.

198. Testimony of Allan B. Magruder, Board of Proceedings in the Case of Colonel Robert H. Chilton, Confederate States Army, War Department Collection of Confederate Records, National Archives.

199. Freeman, *Lee's Lieutenants*, 1:608.

The charge of having been "under the intoxicating influence of ardent spirits"[200] while in command of his troops was particularly galling to Magruder. That charge, though unsubstantiated, was simultaneously the most damaging of the various allegations and the most difficult to dispel. Rumors of intoxication emerged following the general's unusual behavior on June 30, even though, as Major Brent pointed out, the nontypical deportment was caused by illness and a lack of sleep, not drunkenness. The morphine added to Magruder's prescribed medication also worsened his condition so that the casual observer might have thought him to have been alcoholically impaired. One such observer was Captain Greenlee Davidson, commander of the Letcher Artillery. When Davidson chanced upon General Magruder on the afternoon of the first, he stated that Magruder "seemed to be laboring under the most terrible excitement. The wild expression in his eyes and his excited manner impressed me at once with the belief that he was under the influence of some powerful stimulant."[201] On the other hand, neither Brent nor anyone else close to the general reported that he had been drinking at any time during the Seven Days' battles.

Over a year earlier Magruder had given Jefferson Davis his word of honor that he would remain sober for the entire war, and he had kept his promise. To support his claim of sobriety, Magruder included in his official report the testimony of Surgeon E. J. Eldridge of the 16th Georgia Regiment. Eldridge, who had been with the general twice during the fighting at Malvern Hill and again immediately afterward, declared, "I can say most positively that if he was under the influence of liquor, I failed entirely to see it, and from my knowledge of his usual appearance and manner (having been in his command for eight months and seen him very frequently during that time), had he been laboring under such influences, I must have noticed it."[202] Additionally, Benjamin Stoddert Ewell, Jefferson C. Phillips, and the Reverend L. W.

200. Putnam, *Richmond during the Civil War,* 148.

201. Davidson to Hill, April 23, 1863, in Greenlee Davidson, *Captain Greenlee Davidson, C.S.A.: Diary and Letters, 1851–1863,* ed. Charles W. Turner (Verona, Va.: McClure Press, 1975), 71.

202. Report of E. J. Eldridge, August 4, 1862, Enclosure No. 13 in Magruder's Report, August 12, 1862, *Official Records,* ser. 1, vol. 11, pt. 2, 683. Surgeon Eldridge also reported that Magruder's "manner betrayed to me no excitement or want to self-possession beyond the ordinary excitement of the battle-field. I saw no disposition on his part to screen himself from the enemy's fire. On the contrary, heard remarks about his fearlessness" (682). Freeman implied that Eldridge's statements had been made to counter charges that Magruder had "shown the white feather" when, in fact, no such charges of cowardice were made at all. According to the *Richmond Whig,*

Allen offered corroborating written testimony denying that Magruder had been drinking.[203] Nevertheless, the rumors persisted. Over a third of a century after the fighting at Malvern Hill, soldiers who had served under Prince John were still trying to put to rest the notion that their commander had been drunk. "General Magruder was perfectly sober that whole day," insisted John Lamb in an 1897 article that appeared in the *Southern Historical Society Papers*.[204] Likewise, John Baytop Cary stated in a speech to the Lee Camp of Confederate Veterans on September 11, 1897: "I solemnly affirm that I never once, saw him touch a drop of liquor, nor do I believe he had any about his person. Perish then the vile slander, and let the foul charge never again be uttered by mortal lips!"[205] The efforts by Lamb and Cary were noble but not entirely successful. Neither their testimony nor that of others who served under the general and swore to his sobriety totally succeeded in expunging the false perception of Magruder as an irresponsible commander who was drunk while leading his troops into battle at Malvern Hill.

Fortunately for Magruder, Robert Chilton's overstated charges were much easier to refute. The colonel had written his July 11 letter to Samuel Cooper in confidence, never intending for it to have been circulated. Because the communiqué was not marked "private," however, Cooper sent it directly to President Davis. Davis then recalled Magruder based on Chilton's letter, and suddenly Chilton found himself boiling in a caldron of controversy. He had been both bold and careless when first stating his accusations to General Cooper. But as soon as he realized that he would have to substantiate the

---

if Magruder was to be faulted, it was because he "too rashly exposed himself and [his] command in the vain endeavor to recover that which had been lost by another." See Freeman, *Lee's Lieutenants*, 1:607; and *Richmond Whig*, August 25, 1862.

203. Ewell and Phillips to Magruder, August 1862; sworn statement of L. W. Allen, July 26, 1862, J. B. Magruder file, Confederate Papers Relating to Citizens or Business Firms, National Archives. Reverend Allen reported "on Wednesday morning, July 2, when very wet & cold his [Magruder's] Quarter Master proposed to him [Magruder] to take a drink of brandy & bitters, which he did & then remarked to me 'Mr. Allen this is the first drink I have taken for a year.'"

204. Lamb, "Malvern Hill—July 1, 1862," 217. Lamb reported that he did not leave Magruder's side, except to carry an order.

205. Remarks of John B. Cary in delivering a portrait of General John Bankhead Magruder to the Lee Camp of Confederate Veterans in Richmond, September 11, 1897, Virginia Historical Society, Richmond. Cary reported having been with or near Magruder from 1:00 a.m. until 10:00 p.m. on July 1, 1862. The Magruder portrait, painted by John P. Walker, is in the possession of the Virginia Historical Society, Richmond.

charges, he began retreating. Chilton apologetically told the president that the July 11 letter "was a matter entirely between Genl C & myself" and "was not intended for your eyes." He also admitted that he had written the letter without Lee's knowledge or approval and that the use of the general's name was conjectural. Chilton in fact conceded that Lee did not even know of the letter's existence at the time that it was written.[206]

The mistake-prone colonel likewise erred in presuming D. R. Jones's condemnation of Magruder. His statement that Jones had charged his commander "with something worse than incompetency" was based on secondhand information from Jones's assistant adjutant general, Captain Ashbury Coward,[207] and not from any direct communication with Jones. Chilton so regretted having involved Jones that when he sent Magruder a revised copy of the original letter to Samuel Cooper, he made no mention of Jones's alleged accusation.[208] Later, when taken to task for the omission, Chilton stated, "I omitted General Jones' name (from the letter to Magruder) because I had no right to involve him in any differences which might arise between Genl Magruder and myself."[209]

The omission undermined Chilton's credibility but did not handicap Magruder. He was already aware of the allegations attributed to D. R. Jones, as President Davis had shown him the unexpurgated text of Chilton's accusatory letter during their meeting in Richmond on July 19. Immediately afterward, Magruder asked General Jones for an explanation, and on the twentieth Jones quickly replied: "I cannot understand Col. Chilton's meaning in using the term 'something worse,' nor can I understand his use of my name in connection with the support of so vague a charge not being aware of having, at any time expressed an opinion, of my own knowledge or observation, likely to originate such a charge."[210] In short, Robert Chilton's accusations were based on his own conclusions, without any corroborating

206. Chilton to Davis, July 20, 1862, Board of Proceedings in the Case of Colonel Robert H. Chilton, Confederate States Army, War Department Collection of Confederate Records, National Archives.

207. Testimony of Colonel Ashbury Coward, ibid. Coward was a captain during the Seven Days' battles but a colonel by the time he testified on behalf of Chilton in May 1863.

208. Chilton to Magruder, July 21, 1862, ibid.

209. Chilton to Sparrow, March 22, 1863, ibid.

210. Jones to Magruder, July 20, 1862, J. B. Magruder file, Confederate Papers Relating to Citizens or Business Firms, National Archives.

support from D. R. Jones, Robert E. Lee, or anyone else of authority close to Magruder. Under the circumstances Chilton's request for a court of inquiry to prove his charges against Magruder was denied.[211]

Magruder, in the meantime, completed his expanded report on August 12, 1862, and on the following day sent copies to Robert E. Lee and Jefferson Davis. He assumed no responsibility for the Quaker Road mix-up, nor did he shoulder any blame for the losses he sustained after sending his men into battle piecemeal against the enemy at Malvern Hill.[212] Truly, Lee had failed to coordinate the movements of his right with his left and center. But as Magruder commanded on the right, he was immediately responsible for directing the movements of his forces there. Unfortunately, he failed to coordinate his advances. He simply sent his men into battle as soon as they became available, per instructions from Lee's headquarters to "advance rapidly." Magruder made no apology for his actions. He genuinely believed, given the direct orders he had received from his superiors, that he had done all he could do.[213]

General Lee gave Magruder's report a "cursory examination," noting a handful of minor exceptions in an August 14 letter to Secretary of War Randolph. More important, he lent no support to either the charges of intoxication or incompetency. In assessing Magruder's performance during the Seven Days' battles, Lee succinctly stated: "General Magruder appears to have greatly exerted himself to accomplish the duty devolved on him, and I can bear testimony to the uniform alacrity he displayed in its execution. He

211. Sparrow to Chilton, April 22, 1863; Determination of Court Procedure, n.d., Board of Proceedings in the Case of Colonel Robert H. Chilton, Confederate States Army, War Department Collection of Confederate Records, National Archives. Magruder later moved to Texas and won the Battle of Galveston on January 1, 1863. The victory effectively dismissed the charge of incompetency and further discredited Chilton. Afterward, Magruder's supporters in Congress, led by Edward Sparrow, chairman of the Military Affairs Committee, blocked Chilton's promotion to brigadier general, charging that the infamous July 11 letter to Samuel Cooper was "an attempt to injure Genl Magruder in a covert and unfair manner." An outraged Robert Chilton, on March 18, 1863, demanded a court of inquiry to disprove the charge that he had maliciously and wrongfully impugned the character of a fellow officer. The court eventually met in mid-May 1863 and concluded that the colonel had acted out of "no unworthy motive." Nevertheless, his promotion was delayed until February 16, 1864.

212. Magruder's Report, August 12, 1862, plus enclosures, *Official Records*, ser. 1, vol. 11, pt. 2, 660–88.

213. Magruder to the Adjutant General of General R. E. Lee, n.d., ibid., 674; Brent, *Memoirs of the War between the States*, 222. Brent wrote that Magruder had been "issued orders impossible of intelligent execution." In the end he judged the Battle of Malvern Hill to have been "a lamentable series of successive errors, misconceptions and sacrifices" (203).

had many difficulties to contend with, I know. I regretted at the time, and still regret, that they could not have been more readily overcome. I feel assured, however, that General Magruder intentionally omitted nothing that he could do to insure success."[214]

When Lee's letter effectively cleared Magruder of Chilton's charges, Magruder's focus immediately returned to the Trans-Mississippi. In his report Prince John had complained to Davis that his recall had "given rise to many unfounded rumors" and suggested that, if his report was found to be satisfactory, a speedy restoration to the command of the Trans-Mississippi Department would be the most equitable way to repair the injustice that had been done him.[215] During a meeting with the president at the Confederate White House, Magruder told Davis that General Holmes had not wanted the assignment. The president countered by saying that Holmes was reluctant to accept command of the Trans-Mississippi only because the department was so large. Magruder then stated that the Missouri delegates in Congress wanted him, rather than Holmes, to command the department. "Yes," answered the president, "because you assured them you would not interfere with [Sterling] Price, but, would give him his own way. They care nothing for you, general, it is Price they wish for."[216] As Davis intensely disliked Price, whom he called "the vainest man he had ever met,"[217] he was not at all interested in giving Magruder a command wherein he would give Price free rein. In truth Jefferson Davis did not know what to do with Magruder. He could not return him to Lee's army because of Chilton's presence there, nor would he recall his friend Theophilus Holmes from the Trans-Mississippi in order to restore Magruder to his originally assigned position. So, for the time being the president put off making any decision on the assignment, explaining that he was too busy with other important matters.[218]

214. Lee to Randolph, August 14, 1862, Enclosure No. 10 in Magruder's Report, August 12, 1862, *Official Records*, ser. 1, vol. 11, pt. 2, 679–80. Seemingly, Lee's summary missed Jefferson Davis altogether but his exceptions did not. Davis's only comments after reading Lee's letter to Randolph on August 14, 1862, were, "The objections to the report of General Magruder indicate that General Lee will give a different aspect to the affairs noted in this report." Davis's comments appear as an endorsement at the end of Lee's remarks on Magruder's report (680).

215. Magruder to Davis, August 13, 1862, ibid., 687.

216. William Preston Johnston to Rosa D. Johnston, August 15, 1862, Mrs. Mason Barret Collection of Albert S. and William P. Johnston Papers, Tulane University.

217. Thomas C. Reynolds, "Gen. Sterling Price and the Confederacy," MS, Missouri Historical Society, St. Louis, 44.

218. Williams, "Prince without a Kingdom," 19.

In the interim Davis at least gave Magruder permission to have his report published and distributed, perhaps in order to gauge the public's reaction to it. The forty-six-page report was published at Magruder's expense by Charles H. Wynne, Printer, in Richmond.[219] When distributed, the pamphlet won immediate support for Prince John in the capital city, particularly from the local press. The *Richmond Whig,* on August 28, stated: "Rumors, preposterous in their character, and highly derogatory to this gallant and meritorious officer, were freely circulated, and, for a time, obtained easy credence . . . It is sincerely to be hoped that they have found the oblivion they deserve." The *Whig* also facetiously noted how remarkable it was that Magruder's alleged incompetency for command was not discovered until over a year after he had successfully defended the peninsular approach to Richmond against a vastly superior foe.[220] Three weeks later, on September 18, the *Whig* urged the Confederate Congress to pass a resolution recognizing Magruder for his effort against his enemy on the Peninsula. "If anybody deserves thanks," stated the *Whig,* "surely Gen. Magruder deserves them. To him, as much as to any other man, the safety of Richmond, and of all eastern Virginia, is due."[221] On the following day the Confederate Congress officially recognized Magruder and his men "for their gallantry and distinguished services in the first battle of the war at Bethel, and in the protracted defense of the Peninsula for many months against the overwhelming numbers and boundless resources of the enemy."[222]

Though impressive, the editorials and congratulatory resolutions had no discernible effect on Jefferson Davis, who stubbornly refused to restore Magruder to command in the Trans-Mississippi. There being no solution in sight, Prince John finally broke the impasse when he sent Davis a compromise proposal, protecting Holmes, that the president could accept. Magruder suggested that Davis send him to Texas, where he had many friends and supporters. In a September 29 letter he stated:

> Judge Hart, a friend of mine, and many influential Texans, have expressed their wish to have me in command of the troops in Texas and of a district to be composed of that state and the territories of New Mexico and Arizona. I think this can be done without injustice to anyone and I would accept the command with pleasure subject to the orders of Major General Holmes or

219. Thomas Robson Hay, "General John B. Magruder and the Trans-Mississippi," Hay Papers.
220. *Richmond Whig,* August 28, 1862.
221. Ibid., September 18, 1862.
222. *Journal of the Congress of the Confederate States of America, 1861–1865,* 5:404.

not as you might deem best. My remaining in my present state of activity gives encouragement to many idle rumors prejudicial and unjust to me. I confess I am restive under these, for while I wish to avoid being the cause of any embarrassment to you . . . I would rather die, even on the scaffold as a gentleman than to have to face the slightest taint attached to my name or reputation.[223]

Finally, on October 10, 1862, President Davis, through Secretary of War Randolph, assigned Magruder to command the District of Texas, New Mexico, and Arizona, under Theophilus Holmes.[224] The assignment was somewhat less than Magruder had hoped for, yet after spending nearly three unproductive months in Richmond, he was eager to put the Chilton controversy to rest and resume command in the field. He knew that in Texas he would face long odds with limited resources, but at least there, over twelve hundred miles away from the Confederate capital and disencumbered from the suffocating clutches of Jefferson Davis and Samuel Cooper, he could finally find the freedom to be his own man.

223. Magruder to Davis, September 29, 1862, Samuel W. Ritchie Confederate Collection, Miami University, Oxford, Ohio.
224. Special Orders No. 237, October 10, 1862, *Official Records,* ser. 1, 15:826.

7

HIGH TIDE, LOW TIDE, IN TEXAS

Texas was in a highly vulnerable position from the outset of the Civil War. Besides having a thousand-mile frontier open to Indian attack, it had over six hundred miles of defenseless coastline that lay open to a possible Federal naval attack or invasion. Coastal fortifications were desperately needed, yet sandbags and driftwood constituted the only readily available building material, and slaves, borrowed from owners throughout the state, provided the only form of labor. There also existed a great scarcity of lead, powder, and ammunition,[1] and other than small arms, the only artillery pieces available were a few cannon that John S. "Rip" Ford and Ebenezer B. Nichols had captured from the Federals at Brazos Santiago on February 21 and Brownsville on March 3, 1861, before the war had officially begun.[2] When General Paul O. Hebert assumed command of the District of Texas in mid-September 1861, he surveyed the Texas coast and immediately informed his superiors in Richmond, "I regret to say that I find this coast in almost a defenseless state, and in the almost total want of proper works and armaments; the task of defending successfully any point against an attack of any magnitude amounts to a military impossibility."[3] A month later, after it became apparent that materials, supplies, and weapons were nowhere available, Hebert's anxiety turned to grim resignation. To Secretary of War Judah P. Benjamin he wrote: "As an

1. Dudley G. Wooten, ed., *A Comprehensive History of Texas, 1685–1897,* 2 vols. (Dallas: William G. Scarff, 1898), vol. 2, pt. 5, chap. 1, 526.

2. Ernest W. Winkler, ed., *Journal of the Secession Convention of Texas* (Austin: Austin Printing Co., 1912), 324–48.

3. Hebert to secretary of war, September 27, 1861, *Official Records,* ser. 1, 4:112.

engineer, I can but too well appreciate the defenseless state of the sea-coast, see plainly what is needed generally, but of course can only deplore my inability to remedy the evil. I much fear that I have brought my little military reputation to an early grave."[4]

That which Paul Hebert feared most occurred on October 4, 1862, when Commander William B. Renshaw brought his Federal blockading squadron, consisting of the *Harriet Lane, Owasco, Clifton,* and flagship *Westfield* into Galveston harbor and demanded unconditional surrender of the city, Texas's second largest. Galveston was also one of the busiest ports on the entire Gulf of Mexico. Because of its obvious importance to the Confederacy, five thousand troops were stationed in and around Galveston, yet Hebert chose not to fight, declaring it "folly to attempt resistance."[5] On October 9, after a brief truce expired, Renshaw ceremoniously raised Old Glory over Galveston's customhouse to indicate official possession of the city.[6] He was forced to restrict his men to their ships and the adjacent wharves, however, because he did not have the necessary troop strength to secure complete possession of the town. Conversely, the Confederates did not possess the necessary long-range artillery to contest the Federal fleet and were forced to withdraw to the town to protect civilian property. Galveston was thus controlled neither by the Federals for lack of manpower nor by the Confederates for lack of firepower. To remedy this awkward situation, Renshaw requested that troops be sent to Galveston to maintain Federal control over the city. Rear Admiral David G. Farragut, commander of the West Gulf Blockading Squadron, sent assurances that General Benjamin F. Butler was sending aid immediately,[7] but nearly two months passed before the first contingent of the promised reinforcements arrived.

In the meantime, owing to a series of misfortunes, the Federal fleet was having difficulty maintaining itself. In November a cutter from the *Owasco* suffered the loss of its entire crew when it was attacked by Confederate cavalry on Bolivar Peninsula, on the mainland across from Fort Point.[8] Shortly afterward, on November 20, several seamen from the schooner *Henry Janes*

---

4. Hebert to Benjamin, October 31, 1861, ibid., 130–31.

5. Hebert to Cook, May 19, 1862, ibid., 712.

6. Philip C. Tucker III, "The United States Gunboat *Harriet Lane*," *Southwestern Historical Quarterly* 21 (April 1918): 362.

7. Farragut to Renshaw, October 28, 1862, *Official Records of Navies,* ser. 1, 19:319.

8. Abstract log from the USS *Owasco,* November 14, 1862, ibid., 345.

suffered a similar fate when they went ashore in search of beef, and in December the entire fleet was ravaged by yellow fever.[9] Renshaw was so discouraged that he seriously considered abandoning his position in Galveston harbor.[10] On December 24, however, the first group of the long-awaited reinforcements arrived aboard the *Saxon* from New Orleans. The troops consisted of three companies of the 42nd Massachusetts Volunteer Infantry Regiment, commanded by Colonel Isaac S. Burrell. These troops were put ashore on the morning of the twenty-fifth and immediately assumed sentry positions on Kuhn's Wharf.[11] Nevertheless, Commander Renshaw feared his position would not be secure from a possible attack until the remainder of the regiment, totaling approximately a thousand men, had arrived in Galveston.[12]

Meanwhile, in response to a petition signed by hundreds of impatient Texans, Hebert was removed from command and Magruder designated to be his successor. Observer Thomas North reported that Prince John was precisely the kind of man that "suited Texas."[13] It was widely believed that his advent "was equal to the addition of 50,000 men to the forces of Texas."[14]

9. Abstract log of the U.S. schooner *Henry Janes,* November 1–24, 1862, ibid., 361; Pennington to Renshaw, December 1, 1862, ibid., 360–61; Report of Xavier B. Debray, November 25, 1862, ibid., 361.

10. Farragut was furious when he learned that Renshaw was considering withdrawing from Galveston and sent the following message, "The gunboats must hold Galveston until the army arrives, and I have no doubt that when you are attacked you will make a defense that will do credit to the Navy as well as to yourselves." Farragut to Renshaw, December 12, 1862, *Official Records of Navies,* ser. 1, 14, ibid., 19:404.

11. Davis to Schouler, January 10, 1863, ibid., 457.

12. "All December, 1862, the United States Naval forces lay at Galveston anticipating an attack. Letters published in the Northern papers from Commodore Renshaw, and Captain Wainwright of the *Harriet Lane,* show this apprehension; so that when the attack came in January, 1863, they could not claim to have been unprepared." Scharf, *History of the Confederate States Navy,* 505.

13. Thomas North, *Five Years in Texas; or, What You Did Not Hear during the War from January 1861 to January 1866. A Narrative of His Travels, Experiences, and Observations in Texas and Mexico* (Cincinnati: Elm Street Printing Co., 1871), 105–8. North explained that Texans did not like General Hebert because "he proved to be a man of no military force or practical genius, though a West Pointer, and had enjoyed the advantages of military associations in Europe, the reflex of which appeared rather to damage his usefulness than otherwise. He brought with him so much European red-tapism, and being a constitutional ape, that he preferred red-top boots, and a greased rat-tail moustache, with a fine equipage, and a suite of waiters, to the use of good, practical common sense . . . Everybody became tired and disgusted with the General and his policy. He was too much of a military coxcomb to suit the ideas and ways of a pioneer country; besides, he was suspected of cowardice."

14. John Salmon Ford, *Rip Ford's Texas,* ed. Stephen B. Oates (Austin: University of Texas Press, 1963), 343.

When he arrived in Houston, the entire populace honored him with a parade that ended in front of a platform erected at the corner of Main and Congress streets. On stage were thirteen beautiful girls, representing the states of the Confederacy, each carrying a handsome sword crowned with a laurel wreath. Magruder took the stage, graciously acknowledged the young ladies, and briefly addressed the crowd before adjourning to a grand ball in Perkins Hall.[15] When the entertaining came to an end, however, Texans made it perfectly clear to their new commander that they expected him to retrieve the disgraceful loss of Galveston.[16]

Magruder realized that he would have to strike quickly before the remainder of the Federal reinforcements arrived from New Orleans. He immediately began to devise a plan, making several visits under cover of darkness to Galveston, where he carefully observed the strength and position of the enemy.[17] He planned to move a large force of men and artillery into the port city at night for the purpose of securing strategic positions from which he could fire upon the decks of the enemy vessels in the harbor at a close range. After the battle started and the Federal ships were occupied repelling the land assault, there was to be a surprise naval attack forcing the Federals to oppose the Confederates on two fronts.[18]

15. William Norris Scrapbook, Norris Family Papers. Alderman Library Archives, University of Virginia.

16. Francis R. Lubbock, *Six Decades in Texas or Memoirs of Francis Richard Lubbock: A Personal Experience in Business, War, and Politics*, ed. C. W. Raines (Austin: Ben C. Jones and Co., Printers, 1900), 424; North, *Five Years in Texas*, 108; *New Orleans Times*, March 19, 1871.

17. Magruder to Cooper, February 26, 1863, *Official Records*, ser. 1, 15:212; Wooten, *Comprehensive History of Texas*, 2:531.

18. Magruder to Cooper, February 26, 1863, *Official Records*, ser. 1, 15:212–14; Charles Waldo Hayes, "The Island and City of Galveston," MS in the Rosenberg Library, Galveston, Tex., 549–50. Hayes wrote that Colonel A. C. McKeen claimed to have originated the plan for the recapture of Galveston. It is more likely, however, that the daring scheme was authored by consulting engineer Caleb G. Forshey because he and Magruder discussed retaking Galveston during their journey from Virginia to Texas and then continued corresponding on the subject after he arrived. During the early discussions, when one of Magruder's staff officers questioned whether retaking the port city should even be considered in view of the obstacles involved, Major Forshey immediately turned to his commander and said, "General, I think the best plan is to resolve to retake Galveston . . . and then canvass the difficulties." Pollard, *Lee and His Lieutenants*, 845. For a discussion of Major Forshey's role in formulating the plan to recapture Galveston, see Edward T. Cotham Jr., "The Origin of the Confederate Battle Plan to Recapture Galveston," paper presented to the Texas State Historical Association at its annual meeting in Austin, March 3, 2000.

To execute this bold plan, General Magruder commissioned Captain Leon Smith to command the naval part of the expedition, which consisted of the river steamers *Neptune* and *Bayou City.*[19] Each vessel carried a small complement of artillerymen and a force of 150 riflemen, most of whom were armed with new Enfield rifles that Magruder had brought with him from Virginia.[20] As the river steamers possessed very little armor, Captain Smith ordered cotton bales to be stacked on the boiler and hurricane decks to protect both the sharpshooters and the vital machinery from the shot and shell of the enemy.[21] Hence, these vessels were referred to as "cotton clads."

Magruder's task was a difficult one, as the Federals enjoyed a decided advantage in manpower, firepower, and naval strength. The Federal fleet included the *Harriet Lane,* mounting four heavy guns and two twenty-four-pound howitzers; the flagship *Westfield,* carrying eight heavy guns; the *Owasco,* which also carried eight heavy guns; the *Clifton,* a steam propeller with four heavy guns; the *Sachem,* a similar vessel armed with four guns; two armed transports; two large barks; and an armed schooner. In addition to the naval forces, Colonel Burrell commanded the Massachusetts infantrymen on Kuhn's Wharf. Two lines of barricades impeded the land approaches to the wharf, and communication with the shore was cut off by the removal of large portions of the wharf planking in front of the barricades.[22]

After Magruder and Smith reached agreement on all of the details of the battle plan, the Confederate forces began their coordinated advance toward Galveston on the night of December 31, 1862. Captain Smith cautiously moved his fleet to a point about ten miles above Galveston to wait for the land forces to begin the battle, while at the same time Magruder silently led his army across the railroad bridge that connected Galveston with the mainland.[23] As soon as his troops were safely behind cover and the artillery positioned where it would be most effective, Prince John fired the first cannon

19. Magruder had known Smith in California and judged him to be of "great experience in steamboat management." Magruder to Cooper, February 26, 1863, *Official Records,* ser. 1, 15:212.

20. Ibid., 213; Magruder to Anderson, December 15, 1862, ibid., 901.

21. Hayes, "Island and City of Galveston," 550.

22. Magruder to Cooper, February 26, 1863, *Official Records,* ser. 1, 15:213.

23. In addition to being used by General Magruder, the bridge connecting Galveston with the mainland was used by Confederate scouts who maintained a continuous watch on the Union fleet anchored in Galveston Bay. The bridge had not been destroyed by the Federals because there had been several reports that an invasion of Texas would be launched from Galveston, and in such a case the bridge would have been a strategic necessity.

and reportedly shouted to his men: "I've done my duty as a private. Now I will attend to my duties as a general."[24]

Magruder's opening shot received prompt response along the entire twenty-two-gun Confederate line. Shortly thereafter, the guns of the Union fleet were returning a similarly devastating volley in an exchange that Confederate naval historian J. Thomas Scharf described as "one of the most terrific on record."[25] In the midst of the artillery duel five hundred Confederate troops led by Colonel Joseph J. Cook plunged into chest-deep water with fifty cumbersome scaling ladders and advanced toward the Federal infantrymen on the end of the wharf. Simultaneously, Confederate sharpshooters deployed on either side of the wharf opened with a lethal supporting fire. Cook's men made a valiant and determined attack, but upon reaching the end of the wharf, much to their chagrin, they found the scaling ladders too short to accomplish their mission and were forced to retreat.[26]

The battle for the wharf a failure, the artillery duel at best a standoff, and Captain Smith and his steamers nowhere in sight Magruder at daybreak on January 1, 1863, ordered his men to fall back from the wharf area into the city. Just before these orders were executed, however, the *Bayou City* and the *Neptune* arrived and engaged the *Harriet Lane,* the nearest of the Union vessels as well as one of the best prizes in the bay.[27] The *Bayou City* opened fire on the *Lane* and struck it a damaging blow near its wheelhouse. On the third round, however, the *Bayou City*'s thirty-two-pounder exploded, leaving the ship void of artillery.[28] Leon Smith, who was on the *Bayou City,* reacted quickly and ordered his pilot, Captain Michael McCormick, to ram the *Harriet Lane* to facilitate boarding by the sharpshooters. McCormick steamed for the *Lane* but, due to a strong ebb tide, struck it only a glancing blow in which he lost his port wheelhouse. Meanwhile, the *Neptune* rammed the *Lane* on the starboard side, causing it to leak badly. Shortly afterward, from the opposite direction, the partially crippled *Bayou City* returned to the attack and, under a full head of steam, smashed into the *Harriet Lane* aft of the port wheelhouse with such force that its iron prow remained firmly embedded in the Federal vessel and the two ships stuck fast together. With the badly damaged

24. Frank X. Tolbert, *Dick Dowling at Sabine Pass* (New York: McGraw-Hill, 1962), 42–43; Hayes, "Island and City of Galveston," 553.

25. Scharf, *History of the Confederate States Navy,* 506.

26. Magruder to Cooper, February 26, 1863, *Official Records,* ser. 1, 15:214.

27. Ibid., 214–15.

28. Scharf, *History of the Confederate States Navy,* 507.

Lane now immobilized, riflemen aboard both Confederate cotton clads poured a deadly, close-range fire into its crew. Simultaneously, Leon Smith led troops aboard the *Harriet Lane* from the *Bayou City*.[29] Smith's boarding party met a stubborn resistance led by Lieutenant Edward Lea, the *Lane*'s executive officer, and the ship's commander, Captain Jonathan Wainwright. But after Lea was mortally wounded on the main deck and Wainwright was killed on his ship's bridge, the fighting aboard the *Harriet Lane* lasted only a few more minutes,[30] until the last resistance was quashed and the Confederates were in control of the ship.

Leon Smith followed up his victory by sending Henry S. Lubbock,[31] captain of the *Bayou City,* to demand the surrender of the remainder of the Federal fleet. Lubbock and his crew rowed, under a flag of truce, to the *Clifton,* where they confronted Captain Richard L. Law with the demand. Lubbock stated that all Federal ships except one were to be surrendered and all crews of the surrendered vessels were to be allowed to withdraw on the one remaining ship.[32] The alternative would be an immediate resumption of the battle, in which, Captain Lubbock declared, the only possible result would be the complete destruction of the Federal fleet.[33] Law secured a three-hour truce from Lubbock and proceeded to the *Westfield,* which had accidentally run aground and consequently had been kept out of action, to present the terms of the surrender to Commander Renshaw.[34]

During the truce Magruder sent Brigadier General William R. Scurry to demand the surrender of the Federal troops on Kuhn's Wharf. Colonel Burrell

29. Statement of Captain McCormick concerning the naval battle at Galveston, published in the *Houston Telegraph,* January 5, 1863.

30. *Galveston Daily News,* July 30, 1922; Hayes, "Island and City of Galveston," 557, 572.

31. Captain Henry S. Lubbock was the brother of Francis R. Lubbock (governor of Texas, 1861–63), William M. Lubbock, Thomas S. Lubbock, and John B. Lubbock, prominent Texans of the Civil War era. Two of the Lubbock brothers, Henry and William, fought in the Battle of Galveston.

32. Testimony of Henry S. Lubbock before Philip C. Tucker, commissioner of prize. "In the matter of the Confederate States of America vs. the Gunboat Steamship called the *Harriet Lane.* Evidence taken before the Commissioner of Prize, for the Eastern District of Texas, at Galveston; in obedience to an order of the Honorable District Court, of the Confederate States for said District sitting in Admiralty on the 12th day of September, A.D., 1863." Certified MS of the original, Rosenberg Library.

33. Charles C. Cumberland, "The Confederate Loss and Recapture of Galveston, 1862–1863," *Southwestern Historical Quarterly* 51 (October 1947): 125.

34. Report of Court of Inquiry to Farragut, January 12, 1863, *Official Records of Navies,* ser. 1, 19:449.

asked for a three-hour truce to coincide with that which was granted to Captain Law, but as he was refused and faced an immediate resumption of action without the support of the fleet, he had no choice but to surrender.[35] Magruder left General Scurry in charge of the captured Massachusetts infantrymen and hurried to Labadie's Wharf, where the wounded and dead were being removed from the *Harriet Lane*. One of the first of Magruder's staff to arrive was his old West Point companion Major Albert M. Lea, who found his mortally wounded son dying. As Major Lea comforted his son, the boy whispered: "You have seen that I have done my duty to the last and have died fighting for my country. Tell them at home that I love them." Those were his last words. He died in his father's arms.[36]

Meanwhile, Commander Renshaw had decided not to surrender but to withdraw his remaining ships from the harbor. He ordered his commanders, through Law, to abandon their positions in the bay and to destroy their ships should they be in danger of capture by the Confederates.[37] And in order to keep his own ship, the grounded *Westfield*, from being taken by his enemy, Renshaw decided to scuttle the vessel. He evacuated his crew to the transport *Mary Boardman*, then poured turpentine over his flagship's magazine and set it afire with his own hand. But as he prepared to depart the doomed *Westfield*, the magazine exploded prematurely with such a tremendous force that it ripped the forward half of the ship apart, killing Renshaw and the crew members who were standing by to row him to safety.[38] The noise of the blast was heard fifty miles from the coast. No trace was ever found of Commander Renshaw or the sailors who were at his side.[39]

The deaths of Renshaw and Wainwright left Richard Law as the senior naval officer in charge of the Federal vessels at Galveston. His first command decision came near the end of the truce, after Captain Lubbock had returned

35. Statement of Colonel Isaac S. Burrell in relation to the surrender of a portion of the 42nd Massachusetts Infantry Regiment, at Galveston, on the morning of January 1, 1863, *Official Records*, ser. 1, 15:226; see also Magruder's note in relation to Burrell's statement, ibid., 227.

36. *Galveston Daily News*, July 30, 1922; *Houston Post*, December 30, 1962; Ben C. Stuart, *Galveston Daily News*, December 12, 1909, in *Stuart Book: A Series of Articles of Historic Interest Relating to Galveston and Texas, Published in Galveston "News" during the Years 1906 to 1911*, 149–50. The *Stuart Book* was compiled in 1913 and is presently in the Rosenberg Library.

37. Cumberland, "Confederate Loss and Recapture of Galveston, 1862–1863," 126.

38. Burt to Banks, n.d., *Official Records*, ser. 1, 15:203; Long to Houston, January 10, 1863, ibid., 209; testimony of Daniel Phillips before Philip C. Tucker, commissioner of prize. "In the matter of the Confederate States of America vs. the Gunboat Steamship called the *Harriet Lane*."

39. Stuart, *Galveston Daily News*, January 2, 1910, in *Stuart Book*, 150.

to the *Clifton* to ascertain whether his earlier demands would be met. But Law, like Renshaw, would have no part of a surrender. Instead, by his order the *Owasco, Sachem, Saxon, Mary Boardman,* as well as the *Clifton,* began suddenly and simultaneously steaming out of the harbor, still flying their flags of truce. When Lubbock angrily charged Law with breach of faith, the latter countered by asserting that he was obligated to follow the directives that he had received from Renshaw and refused to give orders to the contrary. He stopped his ship only long enough to permit Lubbock to depart in a rowboat, then immediately resumed full steam as he and his fellow commanders departed Galveston for New Orleans.[40]

When Magruder observed the flight of the Federal vessels, he sent "a swift express on horseback to General Scurry, directing him to open fire on them."[41] Scurry was quick to get his shore batteries into operation, but they were of insufficient caliber to reach the rapidly retreating enemy ships. Simultaneously, an effort was being made to bring the heavy guns of the *Harriet Lane* into action, but the *Lane* was listing so badly that it was impossible to maneuver its guns into the proper firing position. This having failed, Leon Smith issued an urgent plea for volunteers to board the *John F. Carr.* Instantly, 150 men joined Smith and pursued the Federals to the bar at the entrance to Galveston Harbor, where the *Carr,* a small tender, came very close to being swamped by breakers. Captain Smith was forced to abandon the chase but while returning captured the barks *Cavallo* and *Elias Pike* and the pilot schooner *Lecompte.* The barks were laden with seven hundred tons of coal, six hundred barrels of Irish potatoes, and a considerable quantity of military supplies.[42] Smith placed a guard over these prizes and then made his way to the *Harriet Lane,* where he and Magruder assessed the damages it had sustained in the battle. They hoped that the vessel could soon be used by the Confederacy,[43] but it was not to be. The *Bayou City* had driven its prow into the wheel of the *Lane* with such force as to careen the ship and break

---

40. A year later Law was court-martialed and found guilty of "leaving his station, in time of war, before regularly relieved" and "not doing his utmost to capture or destroy a vessel which it was his duty to encounter." The court dismissed him from the navy, but in view of the gallantry displayed in his attack on the Confederate shore batteries during the battle, the sentence was commuted to a three-year suspension from the U.S. Navy. General Orders No. 28 signed by Gideon Welles, secretary of the navy, January 7, 1864, *Official Records of Navies,* ser. 1, 19:463–64.

41. Magruder to Cooper, February 26, 1863, *Official Records,* ser. 1, 15:216.

42. Hayes, "Island and City of Galveston," 565–66.

43. Magruder to Cooper, February 26, 1863, *Official Records,* ser. 1, 15:219.

the flanges of the iron wheel. When the *Lane* recovered from the shock, its weight settled down on the broken flanges, crushed them through the prow of the *Bayou City*, and fastened the ship so securely that a part of its bow had to be cut away to get it out. It turned out that the wheel of the *Harriet Lane* was so badly damaged that the ship was unseaworthy and would be useless until extensive repairs were made.[44]

Despite the escape of a major portion of the enemy's fleet, Magruder had won a stunning victory, in which the Confederates lost only 26 killed and 117 wounded. In his official report Prince John generously credited Leon Smith, Henry Lubbock, Michael McCormick, General Scurry, and Colonel Cook for their heroic efforts during the battle.[45] In return Magruder's men united "in ascribing to the General commanding the chief honor and glory of this brilliant and decisive victory."[46] Magruder indeed had planned the high-risk attack. He then superintended the fighting and won in decisive fashion a rare land-sea battle that few of his contemporaries would have dared to fight. The victory at Galveston no doubt eased the lingering disappointment of Malvern Hill.[47] And one can only imagine the immense satisfaction that

44. Hayes, "Island and City of Galveston," 566. Repairs on the *Harriet Lane* were not completed until early 1864, when, due to the desperate need for supplies, it was used as a blockade-runner rather than a cruiser. On the night of April 30, 1864, it successfully evaded the Federal blockaders and subsequently reached Havana, where it sold its cargo of cotton. But because no arms or munitions were available for purchase at that port, the *Lane* remained in Havana until the end of the war, when it was turned over to United States authorities.

45. In addition to the aforementioned, Magruder credits several others who distinguished themselves during the battle. Magruder to Cooper, February 26, 1863, *Official Records*, ser. 1, 15:216–17.

46. Hayes, "Island and City of Galveston," 575.

47. For battle reports and important correspondence relating to the Battle of Galveston, see *Official Records of Navies*, ser. 1, 19:437–77; and *Official Records*, ser. 1, 15:199–227. Because the Battle of Galveston involved both land and sea forces, some of the reports and correspondence were published in both the army and navy records. For additional information, see Magruder to Jefferson Davis, January 6, 1863, Jefferson Davis Collection of the Robert W. Woodruff Library, Emory University, Atlanta; statement of Captain McCormick concerning the naval battle at Galveston, published in the Houston *Telegraph*, January 5, 1863; X. B. Debray, "A Sketch of Debray's Twenty-sixth Regiment of Texas Cavalry," *Southern Historical Society Papers* 12 (1884): 547–54; and Franklin, *Story of the Battle of Galveston* (1911). Following the Battle of Galveston, Magruder was initially disinclined to grant a military funeral, with full honors, to his adversary, Wainwright. However, Major Philip C. Tucker, who superintended the funeral arrangements, reminded Magruder that such a burial had already been given by Federal officials to a Texas officer who had been killed at Corinth, Mississippi, on October 4, 1862. The major then said to his commander, "It is said that you are never to be outdone in courtesy by friend or enemy."

Magruder must have felt when he penned the following summary to Samuel Cooper: "We thus captured one fine steamship, two barks, and one schooner. We ran ashore the flagship of the commodore, drove off two war steamers and sunk another . . . and took 300 or 400 prisoners. The number of guns captured was fifteen and . . . a large quantity of stores, coal, and other material was also taken."[48] Within a few days after the battle, Magruder officially reopened the port to foreign commerce in a proclamation that read:

> Whereas the undersigned has succeeded in capturing and destroying a portion of the enemy's fleet and in driving the remainder out of Galveston harbor and beyond the neighboring waters and thus raising the blockade virtually, he therefore proclaims to all concerned that the harbor of Galveston is open for trade to all friendly nations, and their merchants are invited to resume their usual intercourse with this port.
>
> Done at Galveston this fifth day of January, eighteen hundred and sixty-three.
>
> J. BANKHEAD MAGRUDER
> Major-General, Commanding[49]

Magruder so completely removed the blockade from Galveston waters that when the Union transport *Cambria* arrived off the bar with the remainder of the 42nd Massachusetts Infantry Regiment, there was no Federal vessel to warn it that the port had been recaptured by the Confederates. Anticipating such an event, Magruder had ordered the United States flag to remain flying over the customhouse and at the mastheads of the ships in the harbor.[50] Thus, completely unaware that the Confederates possessed the town, the captain of the *Cambria* signaled for a pilot, but receiving none, dispatched a boat containing the notorious Thomas "Nicaragua" Smith and

---

Magruder immediately replied, "Not by a damned sight!" The following day Wainwright and his executive officer, Lea, were buried in the same service, with honors. Wainwright's remains were later exhumed and interred in the cemetery at the Naval Academy at Annapolis. Lea's family, on the other hand, preferred to have the body of the gallant lieutenant remain on the spot where he had died in the line of duty. Edward Lea is the only Federal officer falling at the Battle of Galveston whose remains rest on the island. His grave is located close to Magruder's, in Galveston's Trinity Episcopal Cemetery. Stuart, *Galveston Daily News*, December 12, 1909, in *Stuart Book*, 149–50.

48. Magruder to Cooper, February 26, 1863, *Official Records*, ser. 1, 15:216.

49. Proclamation of Major General J. Bankhead Magruder announcing the raising of the blockade of Galveston, January 5, 1863, *Official Records of Navies*, ser. 1, 19:465.

50. Magruder to Cooper, February 26, 1863, *Official Records*, ser. 1, 15:219.

five of his crew to secure instructions for entering the port. When the boat reached shore, Smith and the five sailors were immediately made prisoners by the Confederates. Smith, who had defected to the Federals on August 5, 1862, after leaving his duty post at Pelican Spit in Galveston Harbor, was court-martialed immediately after his capture. On the following day he was executed by a firing squad.[51]

In the meantime Magruder learned that the *Cambria* carried heavy siege guns, railroad flatcars, and two locomotives, in addition to the remainder of the 42nd Massachusetts Regiment and a small number of the 1st (Union) Texas Cavalry, commanded by Colonel Edmund J. Davis.[52] Because the *Harriet Lane* was badly damaged and the cotton clads were not sturdy enough to venture into the rough seas beyond the bar, Magruder decided to capture the *Cambria* by trickery. Accordingly, a call for volunteers was made and was quickly answered by Captain John Payne, a well-known and skilled river captain who held a Confederate commission as captain of a gunboat on the Sabine River.[53] Captain Payne and a small crew boarded the recently captured pilot schooner *Lecompte* and departed for the *Cambria*. When the *Lecompte* reached the Union transport, Payne volunteered to guide the vessel ashore. But at this point some of the Texans of the 1st Cavalry Regiment recognized him. Payne boarded the transport, nervously attempting to carry out his bluff, but when he was told that he must pilot the vessel in safely or "his brains would be blown out upon the spot," he confessed that Galveston had been recaptured by the Confederates.[54] The crew of the *Cambria* immediately demanded that Payne be hanged. Payne replied that he expected

51. "Blockades and Battles, 1861–1865," 71. MS, Rosenberg Library; Stuart, *Galveston Daily News*, January 2, 1910, in *Stuart Book*, 22. Smith, described as "one of the worst desperadoes ever known in [Texas]" (North, *Five Years in Texas*, 116), had been with William Walker on his filibustering expedition against Nicaragua in 1856, hence the nickname. He is reported to have set fire to Galveston on several occasions, and Magruder confirmed that "he was dreaded by everyone." After deserting his post in August 1862, he was taken aboard the USS *Santee* to New Orleans, where he subsequently joined the Union army. When captured, he was returning to Galveston to serve as Federal provost marshal. Magruder to Cooper, February 26, 1863, *Official Records*, ser. 1, 15:219.

52. Magruder to Cooper, February 26, 1863, *Official Records*, ser. 1, 15:219–20; Bach to Banks, January 7, 1863, ibid., 205–6; Joseph Osterman Dyer, *Dyer Scrap Book: Articles on Galveston and Texas History, Mostly from Galveston "News," December 14, 1919, to September 19, 1926*, 105. The *Dyer Scrap Book* was compiled in 1932 and is presently in the Rosenberg Library.

53. Stuart, *Galveston Daily News*, December 30, 1906, in *Stuart Book*, 19.

54. Scharf, *History of the Confederate States Navy*, 514–15.

them to shoot him as soon as they discovered that they were being made prisoners through him. But at the same time he reminded the irate Federal sailors that there were six hundred of their own men, captured in the battle, who would receive the same punishment.[55] Upon hearing this, Colonel Davis stepped forward and said, "When you get us into your power, you hang us; but when we get you into our power, we are not savages, we treat you better." Thus, Captain Payne's life was spared. He was subsequently sent to New Orleans, where he was questioned by Union naval authorities regarding the fate of the prisoners taken during the Galveston battle.

The New Orleans sojourn ultimately proved to be an interesting experience for Payne, who became somewhat of a celebrity during the time of his interrogation. The ladies of the Crescent City regularly entertained him in their homes and provided him with clothes, money, and anything else he could possibly need. He reported that he was never so well treated in his life as he was by the ladies of New Orleans. Later, after Payne was released, he made his way back to Texas, reentered the Confederate navy, and served in Galveston until the end of the war.[56]

Meanwhile, when Admiral Farragut learned of the Union disaster at Galveston, he exploded into a rage and described the defeat as "the most shameful [and] unfortunate thing that ever happened to the Navy."[57] He had no intention of allowing the city to remain in Magruder's hands and on January 3, 1863, issued orders to Commodore Henry H. Bell, commanding the USS *Brooklyn,* to recapture Galveston.[58] Farragut also expressed hope that Bell could retake the *Harriet Lane* because he feared that if the ship successfully eluded the blockade, "she would be a most formidable cruiser . . . on account of her speed and battery."[59]

55. Payne obviously exaggerated. Magruder listed the Federal prisoners as between three or four hundred in his official report to the adjutant general.

56. Stuart, *Galveston Daily News,* December 30, 1906, in *Stuart Book,* 19; January 2, 1910, ibid., 150. To the day that he died, Captain Payne remained a close friend of E. J. Davis and repeatedly stated that he was indebted to Davis for saving his life from the angry crowd aboard the *Cambria.*

57. Farragut to Bailey, April 22, 1863, *Official Records of Navies,* ser. 1, 20:157. Rear Admiral Samuel Francis Du Pont of the Atlantic Blockading Squadron suggested that the recapture of Galveston had been accomplished while "John Magruder and his party were drunk." Du Pont to wife, February 1, 1863, in *Samuel Francis Du Pont: A Selection from His Civil War Letters,* ed. John D. Hayes, 3 vols. (Ithaca, N.Y.: Cornell University Press, 1969), 2:410.

58. Farragut to Bell, January 3, 1863, *Official Records of Navies,* ser. 1, 19:479.

59. Farragut to Welles, January 3, 1863, ibid., 481.

Bell arrived off Galveston on the morning of January 7 and reestablished the Federal blockade. Soon the fleet, larger and more powerful than that commanded by Renshaw, was at full strength and consisted of the flagship *Brooklyn* and the gunboats *Cayuga, Hatteras, New London, Owasco, Sciota, Katahadin,* and the *Itasca.* The masts of the *Harriet Lane,* clearly visible to the entire fleet, served only to antagonize the blockaders. A correspondent aboard the USS *New London* wrote in a letter, "Galveston is a doomed town; the disgrace attending the capture of the *Harriet Lane* must be wiped out, and vengeance upon its butchers and captors will be awful."[60] On January 10 Commodore Bell fired 107 rounds into the city to test his enemy's defenses. Several of the shells exploded near Confederate batteries along the beach, but very little damage was done, other than causing a stampede among local citizens during which "two of the Negroes, in their terror, ran into the sea and drowned."[61]

Immediately after the bombardment, Magruder dispatched a boat with a letter, signed by the foreign consuls, protesting the bombardment. Bell was reminded that hospitals containing both Union and Confederate wounded were within range of the Federal guns, as were innocent women, children, and foreign noncombatants. Furthermore, the Confederate government had declared Galveston a free port, and it was the opinion of the consuls that the blockade was in fact broken and therefore could not be legally reestablished until communication with their respective governments occurred.[62] Commodore Bell ceased firing but kept his vessels stationed outside of the harbor, and on January 20 he issued a proclamation:

U.S. Steamship Brooklyn
Off Galveston, January 20, 1863

Whereas, Major General J. Bankhead Magruder declared the port of Galveston open for trade with all friendly nations . . . The undersigned hereby warns all concerned that the port of Galveston . . . as well as the whole coast of Texas, are under an actual blockade by a sufficient force of United States vessels, and any merchant vessel appearing off the aforesaid ports, or attempt-

60. Frederick Thompson to Joseph Thompson (father), January 10, 1863, ibid., 505. Thompson apparently believed the widespread rumor that the entire crew of the *Harriet Lane* had been massacred.

61. Lieutenant Colonel Arthur Fremantle, *Three Months in the Southern States: April–June, 1863* (New York: John Bradburn, 1864), 73.

62. Scharf, *History of the Confederate States Navy,* 515.

ing to pass out . . . under any pretext whatever, will be captured . . . and sent into an open port of the United States for adjudication.

H. H. BELL
Commodore, commanding U.S. Forces
off Galveston and the Coast of Texas[63]

Shortly after Commodore Bell reestablished the blockade, the Confederate steam cruiser *Alabama,* commanded by the intrepid Raphael Semmes, appeared south of Galveston. Captain Semmes had learned through captured northern newspapers that a Federal expedition consisting of not less than thirty thousand men commanded by General Nathaniel P. Banks was to arrive in Galveston on or about January 10. To transport such an army, a large number of heavy transports would be required, and given that there was only twelve feet of water at the bar, the fleet would have to anchor in the open sea. Semmes planned to "surprise this fleet by a night attack, and if possible destroy it, or at least greatly cripple it."[64]

When he arrived off Galveston, however, the *Alabama*'s lookout reported sighting not transports but five steamers that resembled ships of war.[65] Captain Semmes realized what had happened when he observed a shell, fired by one of the steamers, bursting over the city: "'Ah, ha!' exclaimed I, to the officer of the deck who was standing by me, 'there has been a change of programme here. The enemy would not be firing into his own people, and we must have recaptured Galveston, since our last advices . . .' What was best to be done in this changed condition of affairs? I certainly had not come all the way into the Gulf of Mexico to fight five ships of war, the least of which was probably my equal. And yet, how could I very well run away, in the face of promises I had given my crew?"[66]

At the very instant that Semmes was pondering the question, his lookout shouted, "One of the steamers, sir, is coming out in chase of us." Captain Semmes

63. Proclamation of Commodore Henry H. Bell, announcing the re-establishment of the blockade of the coast of Texas including Galveston, January 20, 1863, *Official Records of Navies,* ser. 1, 19:451–52.

64. Raphael Semmes, *Memoirs of Service Afloat during the War between the States* (Baltimore: Kelly, Piet and Co., 1869), 519–20.

65. After the Confederates had recaptured Galveston on January 1, 1863, Banks's expedition disembarked at New Orleans, from whence General Banks later attempted the invasion of Texas via Sabine Pass.

66. Semmes, *Memoirs of Service Afloat during the War between the States,* 541–42.

took full advantage of the situation by luring the pursuing vessel into the open sea while simultaneously preparing his ship for combat. When the vessels were about twenty miles from Galveston, Semmes wheeled his ship about to meet the pursuer, the USS *Hatteras,* which was now within hailing distance. A lieutenant aboard the *Alabama* gave a vivid account of the ensuing action:

> The enemy has now come up. We have been standing inshore while awaiting her, but now our head is turned off shore again. Then comes the hail, "What ship is that?" "This is her Britannic Majesty's steamer *Petrel,*" is the reply. The two vessels are now nearly motionless, and both of course at quarters. Our men are wild with excitement and expectation. In the darkness it is impossible to make out her class except that she is a side-wheeler. Our crew have lock-strings in hand, keeping the guns trained on her and awaiting the command to fire. The two vessels are so near that conversation in ordinary tones can be easily heard from one to the other. For a time the *Hatteras* people seem to be consulting. Finally they hailed again, "If you please, I'll send a boat on board of you," to which our executive officer replied, "Certainly, we shall be pleased to receive your boat." The boat was soon lowered from the davits and began pulling toward us. All occasion for subterfuge being now at end, word was immediately passed to the divisions that the signal to fire would be "Alabama." When the boat was about half-way between the two vessels, Lieutenant Kell hailed, "This is the Confederate States steamer, *Alabama!*" The last words had barely passed his lips when the sky and waters are lighted up by the flash of our broadside, instantly followed as it seemed by that of the enemy. A running fight was now kept up, the *Alabama* fighting her starboard and the *Hatteras* her port battery, both vessels gathering headway rapidly. Never did a crew handle a battery more deftly than ours. About six broadsides were fired by us. The enemy replied irregularly, and the action only lasted thirteen minutes. It was evident to us from the trifling nature of the wounds to our hull and rigging that the *Hatteras* was being whipped. A crash amongst her machinery soon settled the business. Then she fired a lee gun, and we heard the quick, sharp hail of surrender, accompanied by the request that our boats be sent to her immediately as she was sinking. The whole thing had passed so quickly that it seemed to us like a dream.[67]

Commodore Bell, having seen the flashes of gunfire on the horizon, ordered the *Cayuga* and *Sciota* along with his flagship, the *Brooklyn,* to proceed southward under full steam to assist the *Hatteras.* The three vessels searched

67. Arthur Sinclair, *Two Years on the "Alabama"* (Boston: Lee and Shepard, 1895), 68–69.

the entire night but found no trace of their sister ship. The following morning, after having given up the search and returning toward Galveston, the *Brooklyn* discovered the skeletal remains of the *Hatteras*. Its mastheads were standing upright out of the water, tops and gaffs awash, the hurricane deck adrift, and a U.S. naval pennant flying from the main mast.[68] Bell gazed sadly upon the wreckage and then returned to the blockade, where he found the boat crew from the *Hatteras*, who told him the grim details of their encounter with the *Alabama*.[69]

The *Hatteras* incident had a pronounced psychological effect on Bell's blockading fleet. For more than a year after the sinking, Admiral Farragut received reports that the *Alabama* had been "sighted" in Texas waters.[70] The false sightings caused considerable alarm and confusion among the blockaders, allowing Magruder additional time to strengthen Galveston's defenses by placing the undamaged heavy guns from the *Westfield* and *Harriet Lane* in key defensive positions near the harbor. Each day that the Federals delayed their attempt to recapture Galveston, the more difficult the task became. Finally, Commodore Bell conceded the island to the Confederates and devoted his efforts solely toward the business of preventing blockade-running.

Meanwhile, on the Confederate side Prince John Magruder became the toast of Texas. The *Galveston News* called the city's recapture "the most exciting military event in Texas since the Battle of San Jacinto."[71] Governor Lubbock concurred when he stated that "this month's campaign (January, 1863)

68. Reports of Henry H. Bell, January 12, 1863, *Official Records of Navies*, ser. 1, 19:507; January 13, 1863, ibid., 508.

69. For battle reports and important correspondence relating to the naval battle between the *Hatteras* and *Alabama*, see the *Official Records of Navies*, ser. 1, 2:18–23, 683–85, 721–24; 19:506–10. The following sources also contain excellent firsthand accounts of the duel between the *Hatteras* and *Alabama*: Semmes, *Memoirs of Service Afloat during the War between the States;* Sinclair, *Two Years on the "Alabama";* and John McIntosh Kell, *Recollections of a Naval Life, Including the Cruises of the Confederate States Steamers "Sumter" and "Alabama"* (Washington, D.C.: Neale Co., 1900).

70. Tolbert, *Dick Dowling at Sabine Pass,* 48. After sinking the *Hatteras*, Captain Semmes headed his vessel for Jamaica, never to return to Texas waters.

71. Stanley E. Babb, "A History of the *Galveston Daily News*," bound MS in the Rosenberg Library, 31. The *Galveston News,* dating back to 1842, is the oldest newspaper still being published in Texas. The newspaper's masthead listed it as either the *Galveston Daily News, Tri-Weekly News,* or the *Weekly News.* The official name of the publication, however, was the *Galveston News.* The terms *daily, tri-weekly,* and *weekly* simply specified the frequency of the publication of a particular edition of the *News.*

is the most brilliant in the annals of Texas."[72] And when the first report of Galveston's recapture reached Richmond, John B. Jones, the famous diarist, termed it "cheering news" and predicted "if this be Magruder's work, it will make him famous."[73] Few believed that such glorious results could be obtained by men handicapped by insufficient resources, even when sustained by the highest courage and noblest spirit. Magruder received congratulatory letters from Jefferson Davis,[74] Sam Houston,[75] Governor Lubbock,[76] and many generals[77] and prominent citizens of the Confederacy.[78] Both the Texas State Legislature[79] and the Confederate Congress[80] passed resolutions praising Magruder and his men for their heroism and patriotism. Clearly, the successes at Galveston stirred the hearts of people throughout the Confederacy.

With Galveston safely under Confederate control, General Magruder, on February 13, 1863, turned affairs there over to Colonel Xavier B. Debray,[81] and retired to his headquarters in Houston to concentrate on administrative matters within the District of Texas, New Mexico, and Arizona. His most pressing problem was a shortage of arms, munitions, and military supplies, and because the Confederacy lacked specie, he intended to supply that want through the purchasing power of "King Cotton."

72. Lubbock, *Six Decades in Texas*, 462.

73. Jones, *Rebel War Clerk's Diary*, 149. Preliminary reports about the recapture of Galveston reached Richmond on January 9, 1863. On the following day Jones wrote: "To-day we have official intelligence confirming the brilliant achievement at Galveston; and it was Magruder's work. He has men under him fitted for desperate enterprises; and he has always had a penchant for desperate work."

74. Davis to Magruder, January 28, 1863, *Official Records*, ser. 1, 15:211.

75. Houston to Magruder, January 7, 1863, in *The Writings of Sam Houston, 1813–1863*, ed. Amelia W. Williams and Eugene C. Barker, 8 vols. (Austin: University of Texas Press, 1938–43), 8:324. This was among the last of the letters written by Sam Houston; he died on July 26, 1863.

76. Lubbock, *Six Decades in Texas*, 453.

77. Among these was a letter from Lieutenant General Theophilus H. Holmes, Magruder's immediate superior, who was then in command of the Trans-Mississippi Department. Anderson to Magruder, February 7, 1863, *Official Records*, ser. 1, 15:220–21.

78. One such congratulatory letter was from St. George S. Lee, a prominent citizen of Cuero, Texas. Lee to Magruder, January 1863. Original draft owned by Margaret Hutchings, Houston.

79. Joint Resolution of thanks to General J. B. Magruder and others, March 6, 1863, *Official Records*, ser. 1, 15:221.

80. *Journal of the Congress of the Confederate States of America, 1861–1865*, 3:76, 77, 80, 101, 112; *Official Records*, ser. 1, 53:849.

81. General Orders No. 24, February 13, 1863, *Official Records*, ser. 1, 15:979.

From the outset of the war private citizens had been granted military exemptions to purchase cotton, transport it to the border, and exchange it for military supplies for the government. Many disregarded their contracts, however, and exchanged the cotton in Brownsville for specie, with which they purchased Confederate currency at about 30 percent of the face value, and then returned to the interior to buy more cotton at par. The speculators made immense profits and drove down the value of Confederate currency in the process.[82] In the fall of 1862 Trans-Mississippi Department commander general Theophilus H. Holmes struck at the speculation problem by issuing General Orders No. 25, which declared in part that "the exportation of cotton from the District of Texas is prohibited, except by authorized agents of the government and by persons known to the commanding general to be engaged through the medium of traffic in cotton, in providing for the actual necessities of the people and army."[83]

General Hamilton P. Bee, commanding the Western Subdistrict of Texas, which was engaged in operations along the Mexican border, was required to carry this order into effect. He restricted cotton exportation to three classes of people: those who purchased supplies for the army were allowed to export to the value of the invoice; those who gave bond with security to import army supplies; and planters who made affidavit that they exported in order to purchase family supplies and necessities not used for speculation or resale.[84] Magruder further instructed General Bee to seize all unauthorized cotton shipments and to enroll into service anyone hauling cotton who came under the conscript act, unless they agreed to use their teams for government service.[85] Such orders reduced speculation and improved the critical transportation problem, but it soon became obvious that private citizens alone could not adequately supply the army.

On November 14, 1862, the Confederate War Department assigned Major Simeon Hart, a prominent citizen of El Paso, to "purchase army supplies from Mexico." His letter of appointment outlined further instructions: "You will be furnished with money, which you can deposit with the public depository in San Antonio, and draw as your necessities may require. You will probably find it advantageous to make your payments in cotton. Should this be the case, you will purchase and transport the cotton to the most favorable

82. *Galveston Daily News,* January 26, 1863.

83. Seddon to Holmes, January 28, 1863, *Official Records,* ser. 1, 53:845.

84. Ibid.

85. Magruder to Anderson, December 15, 1862, ibid., 15:900.

points on the Mexican frontier. You will call on the general commanding the District of Texas for such assistance as you may require."[86] Hart confined his operations to west and north Texas, while Major Andrew W. McKee, the cotton-purchasing agent of the Treasury Department, worked eastern Texas and Louisiana.[87] But they were not alone. Quartermasters in each of the subdistricts bought cotton from the beginning of the war to meet their immediate military needs, and in February 1862 the state of Texas had appointed sixteen purchasing agents who operated primarily in the heavy cotton-producing regions in the southeastern part of the state.[88]

By mid-December 1862, less than three weeks after arriving in Texas, Magruder had gathered statistical proof indicating that competition between the government purchasing agents increased the price of cotton by twenty-five cents per pound. He insisted that the agents, whether appointed by the War Department, the Treasury Department, the state, General Holmes, or any other authority, know each other and act in unison. Magruder then nominated Major Hart, whom he judged "more likely than anyone I know to bring order out of the chaos I find the cotton trade in here," to coordinate the purchasing operations of all authorized agents in the field.[89]

Two months later, on February 22, 1863, Magruder issued General Orders No. 28, setting forth comprehensive guidelines to be followed by government agents and private citizens alike in relation to cotton exportation. General Bee's restrictions remained in effect, and Major Hart was designated the only official authorized to make contracts based on cotton. The various disbursing officers were to furnish him with lists of needed items for their respective departments. All previous contracts were to be transmitted with the permits and passes to Brigadier General William R. Scurry at Houston, Colonel Smith Pyne Bankhead at San Antonio,[90] or Lieutenant Colonel Augustus Bu-

86. Randolph to Hart, November 14, 1862, ibid., 866.

87. Agnes Louise Lambie, "Confederate Control of Cotton in the Trans-Mississippi Department" (master's thesis, University of Texas, 1915), 7.

88. Charles W. Ramsdell, "The Texas State Military Board, 1862–1865," *Southwestern Historical Quarterly 27* (April 1924): 262.

89. Magruder to Anderson, December 15, 1862, *Official Records,* ser. 1, 15:900–901.

90. Smith Pyne Bankhead, Magruder's first cousin, was one of six children of General James Bankhead and his wife, Anne Pyne. Four of the six were boys. The oldest of the Bankhead children, James Monroe, died in 1855, before the Civil War began. Each of the three remaining sons, however, played important roles in the war. John Pyne, the third born, commanded the *Monitor* when it foundered off Cape Hatteras on December 31, 1862. Smith Pyne, the fourth born, and Henry Cary, the sixth, both became generals during the war. Smith Pyne served the South,

chel at Brownsville for examination. Contracts carried out in good faith were to be respected; otherwise, the contracts were voided, and the unauthorized cotton was to be seized at the border by General Bee's agents.[91]

Individuals involved in Texas cotton transactions viewed Magruder's regulations favorably,[92] but authorities in Richmond, ignorant of military necessities in Holmes's department, became concerned over the legality of the cotton restrictions. Secretary of War James A. Seddon reminded General Holmes that "no law of the Confederate states impose[d] any restraint upon the exportation of cotton through Mexico." And because Congress alone had the "power to regulate commerce with foreign nations and to lay restraints upon foreign intercourse," Seddon judged Holmes and Magruder to have transcended their authority, forcing him to revoke their restrictions on the cotton trade.[93]

Seddon's order was specifically aimed at Holmes's October 1862 General Orders No. 25 and the directives that Magruder issued shortly afterward in December. The revocation order, of course, did not target Magruder's General Orders No. 28, which was not issued until February 22, 1863, over three weeks after Seddon had sent his January 28 order to General Holmes. When Magruder issued the General Orders No. 28, he was unaware of Seddon's position. Nevertheless, because his orders simply supplemented Holmes's General Orders No. 25, which Secretary Seddon struck down, Seddon's order effectively nullified Magruder's February 22 restrictions on the cotton trade before they ever went into effect.

When, on March 31, 1862, Magruder received a copy of Seddon's directive to Holmes, he immediately wrote Adjutant and Inspector General Samuel Cooper, warning that the secretary's instructions might force him to "fall back from the Rio Grande and give up that frontier to the enemy from the difficulty of supplying the troops there except through the means of cotton." Impressment seemed the only alternative, but Magruder opposed such

---

Henry Cary the North. Reportedly, they once served in the same theater against each other. On one occasion, according to notes in the Bankhead family genealogy, the servant of General Smith Pyne Bankhead was captured and brought before his brother, who recognized him and had him returned. See Warren, "Bankhead Family," *William and Mary College Quarterly Historical Magazine* 9, ser. 2 (1929): 303–14.

91. General Orders No. 28, February 22, 1863, *Official Records,* ser. 1, 15:986–88.
92. Magruder to Cooper, March 31, 1863, ibid., 1031.
93. Seddon to Holmes, January 28, 1863, ibid., 53:845–46; Campbell to Hitchcock, February 14, 1863, ibid., ser. 4, 2:399–400.

a drastic step because of the public dissatisfaction it would cause. Instead, he reiterated that his restrictions were giving "general satisfaction" and that they did not conflict with the Confederate constitution. "As the object of the law allowing the exportation of cotton by the Mexican frontier seems to have been to cause the importation of supplies," wrote Magruder, "I presume[d] that any means made necessary to support my army and . . . the law without injuring any class, except speculators, would . . . be permitted."[94] In short he argued that General Orders No. 28 was perfectly legal, absolutely necessary, and acceptable to those it affected.

Simeon Hart wrote a more vehement letter of protest to the secretary of war in which he angrily charged "that the effect of your order to take off all restrictions on the export of cotton to Mexico has produced a state of things disastrous to the public service." He complained that at commercial points and in most of the urban districts of the state those holding cotton refused to sell except for specie, which was paid to them by speculators. The disgruntled major predicted that when the mania for speculation reached the more remote districts, the price of cotton would increase from fifteen to sixteen cents per pound to forty or fifty cents in currency until ultimately holders would refuse to sell for paper at all. Hart further stated that very little of his cotton had reached the Rio Grande, owing to the difficulty in getting transportation, and he believed that unless the government took all of the cotton in the state and controlled the transportation required to get it to the border, the army could not be supplied. "I see no alternative," he declared. "It is a question of supply or no supply, and I do not see how the Government can hesitate."[95] But Seddon, his actions having been approved by Jefferson Davis and Secretary of the Treasury Christopher Memminger,[96] stood firm on his revocation order.

Hart had little money, and General Edmund Kirby Smith, who had succeeded Holmes in the command of the Trans-Mississippi, on February 9, 1863,[97] refused to give him funds from public depositories until he had received authority from Richmond.[98] It became ever more apparent that it would be necessary to impress, yet Magruder remained hesitant. He doubted

94. Magruder to Cooper, March 31, 1863, *Official Records,* ser. 1, 15:1030–31; June 8, 1863, ibid., vol. 26, pt. 2, 62.

95. Hart to Seddon, May 16, 1863, *Official Records,* ser. 1, 53:867–68.

96. Third and fourth endorsements of Hart's May 16 letter to Seddon, ibid., 869.

97. Special Orders No. 33, February 9, 1863, ibid., vol. 22, pt. 2, 787.

98. Boggs to Magruder, May 29, 1863, ibid., vol. 26, pt. 2, 20.

the right of seizing cotton under the Impressment Act and consequently declined to give Major Hart or any other officer such authority without specific instructions from his new commander, Kirby Smith.[99]

On June 11 Major Charles Russell, Bee's quartermaster, wrote from Fort Brown that Hart possessed only seventy-five bales of cotton, yet two English ships laden with army supplies had been at anchor in the mouth of the Rio Grande for three weeks, and four others were expected within hours. Hart had previously contracted for the supplies, but because he could not pay for them, the ships' captains decided to sail for Nassau to dispose of their cargoes as best they could. The supply of Magruder's army as well as the credit of the Confederacy, lamented Russell, were hanging perilously in the balance.[100]

Magruder urged General Smith to decide on the impressment question "at the very earliest convenient moment, and send the result to me by swift express."[101] Before Smith's affirmative reply arrived,[102] however, Magruder unilaterally authorized General Bee to impress cotton held by government contractors and speculators according to the provisions of the military emergency clause of the Impressment Act.[103] Even then, nearly a month elapsed before sufficient cotton could be collected to pay for the supplies.[104]

It became obvious to Magruder that the contract system, under Major Hart's guidance, had failed. Magruder had afforded him every facility in his power, even to the extent of punishing as deserters conscript teamsters who had left his service without being released.[105] But he finally admitted that he had overrated Hart's abilities. The major was honest, reported Magruder, but he also demonstrated "a great want of energy, a great want of foresight, and a great want of ability in the management of his department."[106]

The job was too big for Hart, as it may well have been for any man given that subsequent efforts to solve the supply problem also failed. On April 26,

99. Magruder to Anderson, June 17, 1863, ibid., 89; Magruder to Boggs, June 22, 1863, ibid., 89–90.

100. Russell to Bloomfield, June 11, 1863, *Official Records,* ser. 1, vol. 26, pt. 2, 93–94; Russell to Pendleton, June 10, 1863, ibid., 92–93.

101. Magruder to Boggs, June 22, 1863, *Official Records,* ser. 1, vol. 26, pt. 2, 90.

102. Smith to Magruder, June 27, 1863, ibid., 95.

103. Yancey to Bee, June 22, 1863, ibid., 75–76; July 2, 1863, ibid., 100–101.

104. Bee to Turner, August 17, 1863, *Official Records,* ser. 1, 53:892.

105. *Galveston Tri-Weekly News,* January 8, 1864.

106. Magruder to Boggs, June 25, 1863, *Official Records,* ser. 1, vol. 26, pt. 2, 92; Magruder to Cooper, June 8, 1863, ibid., 63.

1864, a committee appointed by General Smith to examine the cotton business in Texas concluded that the supply problem could have been solved if Secretary Seddon had not revoked Magruder's General Orders No. 28.[107] Without control of cotton, as Hart had warned, there was little chance for an adequate supply.

Without sufficient provisioning, troops inevitably suffered in the Trans-Mississippi Department. They often went without pay and constantly lacked even basic supplies, particularly food. John Simmons, a volunteer in the 22nd Texas Infantry reported from Arkansas on January 7, 1863, "This country is nearly et-out here."[108] Two months later he told his wife, "I can't think of anything to write, for I am thinking all the time of my empty stomach and when I can get some meat to eat." Simmons described living conditions as "horrible" and reported that men were deserting daily. "We are mad all the time," he declared, "and the cause is we are hungry, and the government won't feed us."[109] One soldier, as a remedy, reportedly ate green plums directly from the

---

107. Report of the Commission appointed to investigate the cotton business in Texas, April 26, 1864, National Archives. The commission, headed by Colonel Alexander Watkins Terrell and Judge Thomas J. Devine, concluded that

> Had Order No. 28 continued in force, though Maj. Hart might have failed, the army would have been supplied through other channels. But unfortunately for the Trans-Mississippi Department the necessities which embarrassed it, and the mysteries of its cotton interests, were not, and could not be understood beyond its borders, and Order No. 28, and every other order, having for its object the procurement of supplies, by imposing restrictions on the exportation of cotton, was annulled in obedience to the requirements of a letter addressed by the Hon. Secretary of War to the Commandant of the Department.
>
> The letter of the Secretary of War in effect declared that the military authorities should do no act to prevent the unrestricted exportation of cotton to Mexico, through its coterminous boundary. This clearly announced the law, but could that able functionary have witnessed the spectacle of capital in the hands of speculators, aliens and traitors, seeking investment abroad through the medium of cotton, thus draining the country of its resources, without any benefit to the army or people, he would have recognized the existence of a military necessity paramount to every other consideration.
>
> It is our firm conviction that Order No. 28, in which Gen. Magruder sought to the extent of his power to thwart the efforts of unscrupulous enterprise, would have accomplished its object, *had it not been revoked.*

108. Jon P. Harrison, ed., "The Confederate Letters of John Simmons," *Chronicles of Smith County, Texas* 14 (Summer 1975): 30. Letter, Simmons to his wife, January 7, 1863.

109. Ibid., 32. In a letter, Simmons to his wife, March 4, 1863.

tree. He explained that doing so pulled his mouth together just small enough to accommodate his shrinking rations.[110]

Hunger was also a growing problem for Magruder's men in Texas. Their meager diet consisted of beef, molasses, and cornmeal, the latter being "sour, dirty, weevil-eaten, and filled with ants and worms."[111] Several of the soldiers became sick because of the wretched food, and most of the others complained about military life in general. Morale was low, dissatisfaction high, and on August 10, 1863, the 3rd Regiment of Texas Infantry mutinied when they were ordered to drill.[112] Discontent spread rapidly. On the following day the miners and sappers refused to work, claiming they were owed six months' pay. Then Colonel Joseph J. Cook's Heavy Artillery Regiment refused to leave the batteries. So few men remained loyal that no force could be found to guard the armory.[113]

Magruder was "deeply mortified" to hear of the mutiny and responded by sending General Philip N. Luckett to thoroughly investigate the causes of the dissatisfaction. Luckett reported that the complaints were just and that he had found no real disloyalty existing among the troops. He consequently issued an order suspending further drills until better provisions could be obtained. As far as he was concerned, once the troops recognized that they had been expressing their grievances improperly and were ashamed of their rash behavior, the mutiny was over.[114]

Declining morale and disciplinary breakdowns were directly related to the failure of the contract system to provide Trans-Mississippi soldiers with decent food and adequate supplies. Magruder recommended,[115] and Kirby Smith created, a new system—a bureau to centralize cotton purchasing operations for the entire Trans-Mississippi Department.[116] The Cotton Bureau, headed by Colonel W. A. Broadwell, was to pay for cotton with certificates pledging the government for the payment of an agreed-upon price, in 6 per-

---

110. Getulius Kellersberger, *Memoirs of an Engineer in the Confederate Army in Texas,* trans. Helen S. Sundstrom (n.p.: n.p., 1957), 35.

111. Report of Edward F. Gray, August 4, 1863, *Official Records,* ser. 1, vol. 26, pt. 1, 241.

112. Report of Xavier B. Debray, August 11, 1863, ibid., 242.

113. DeBray to Turner, August 12, 1863, ibid., 243.

114. Report of Philip N. Luckett, August 13, 1863, ibid., 245–46.

115. Magruder to Allen, May 20, 1864, ibid., vol. 34, pt. 2, 835; Magruder to Boggs, January 6, 1864, ibid., pt. 3, 831.

116. General Orders No. 35, August 3, 1863, *Official Records,* ser. 1, vol. 22, pt. 2, 953.

cent coupon bonds, the interest to be paid semi-annually in specie.[117] These bonds were preferable to highly inflated Treasury notes, and if successful the purchasing program would eliminate the need for impressment.

While Broadwell studied the cotton situation and organized purchasing and transportation operations from his headquarters in Shreveport, the military situation worsened. On August 28 General Smith ordered Magruder to concentrate all available forces near the Red River in preparation for a threatened Federal attack.[118] Lacking alternatives, Magruder obeyed Smith's hastily prepared order, but he dispatched a letter to his commander on September 4 in which he voiced his disapproval and questioned the relative importance of the different sections of Texas to be defended. Magruder complained that removing troops from their positions along the coast left vital points almost destitute of the means of defense. Furthermore, he warned Kirby Smith, "should the enemy succeed in forcing the Sabine, or Galveston, or the Brazos, he will . . . virtually be master of Texas."[119]

Subsequent events proved Magruder's fears well-founded. When he reached Millican, a short distance south of present-day Bryan, Texas, and then the northernmost station of the Houston and Texas Central Railroad, he received the dreaded news of a massive Federal landing attempt at Sabine Pass. Magruder immediately halted the movement of his troops toward the Red River and rushed all available forces to Beaumont, where he hoped to thwart the Federals.[120] When he arrived, however, he was astonished to learn that the Federal invasion force, consisting of four gunboats and eighteen transports with over five thousand troops aboard, had been defeated by Lieutenant Richard W. Dowling and his forty-seven-man garrison at Fort Griffin.

The Federals, in order to clear the way for a large-scale troop landing, attempted to silence the guns of the Confederate mud fort by a direct naval assault. The gunboats *Clifton* and *Sachem* led the ill-fated attack, with the remaining gunboats and transports held in reserve. When the enemy vessels closed to within twelve hundred yards, the Confederate artillerymen in the

117. Proceedings of the Marshall, Tex., Conference called by General Edmund Kirby Smith in relation to the critical status of the Trans-Mississippi Department after the fall of Vicksburg, ibid., 1008–9.

118. Boggs to Magruder, August 28, 1863, ibid., 982.

119. Magruder to Boggs, September 4, 1863, ibid., vol. 26, pt. 2, 203–4.

120. Magruder to Boggs, September 9, 1863, ibid., vol. 26, pt. 1, 302–3; Yancey to Boggs, September 9, 1863, ibid., vol. 26, pt. 2, 215–16.

fort opened fire with their four thirty-two-pounders and two twenty-four-pounders. The *Sachem* soon suffered a direct hit in its steam drum, rendering it helpless. This enabled Lieutenant Dowling to concentrate his artillery on the *Clifton*, which attacked at full speed with all guns firing. The oncoming vessel fought gallantly until a damaged steering tiller caused the ship to run aground in such a position that it could use only three of its guns against the fort. The *Clifton* had grounded within easy range of the Confederate artillery and soon suffered a direct hit that struck its boiler, completely disabling it, thus forcing it to surrender. The remaining vessels, fearing a similar fate, abandoned the invasion attempt and fled back to New Orleans.[121]

Dowling captured two gunboats with a full supply of ordnance stores, eighteen heavy guns, and two hundred prisoners. Fifty Union soldiers were also killed and wounded. There were no battle casualties on the Confederate side.[122] Magruder was unrestrained in his praise for Lieutenant Dowling and his men and called their victory "the most extraordinary feat of the war."[123] At the same time, however, he was apprehensive that with so large a force still intact, the Federals would make another invasion attempt on the weakly defended Texas coast.

When the remnants of the Sabine Pass expedition returned to New Orleans, General Nathaniel P. Banks attempted to invade Texas by an overland troop movement across southern Louisiana. This plan proved highly impracticable, however, because of a lack of water and supplies in the area of the attack.[124] Banks withdrew his troops but soon developed plans for another water-borne expedition. He intended to gain a foothold in the Rio Grande region of South Texas and then move northward along the coast until all important passes and ports on the Texas coast were under Federal control. General Banks personally organized the expedition, which departed New Orleans on October 26, 1863, and arrived at Brazos Santiago in early November. The Federals succeeded in capturing Brazos Santiago, Brownsville, Port Isabel, Aransas Pass, and Fort Esperanza until the only important coastal

121. For battle reports and important correspondence relating to the Battle of Sabine Pass, see *Official Records of Navies,* ser. 1, 20:517–63; and *Official Records,* ser. 1, vol. 26, pt. 1, 285–312; vol. 26, pt. 2, 218. Because the Battle of Sabine Pass, like the Battle of Galveston, involved both land and sea forces, some of the reports and correspondence were published in both the army and navy records.

122. Magruder to Boggs, September 10, 1863, *Official Records,* ser. 1, vol. 26, pt. 1, 303.

123. Magruder to Cooper, September 27, 1863, ibid., 305–6.

124. Banks to Stanton, April 6, 1865, ibid., 19–20; Banks to "The President of the United States," October 22, 1863, ibid., 292.

positions remaining in the hands of the Confederates were the works at the mouth of the Brazos River, Galveston, and Fort Griffin.[125]

Immediately after Banks made his initial landing, General Magruder ordered that the government cotton at Brownsville be destroyed and all cotton in the surrounding area be removed to Eagle Pass, 275 miles up the Rio Grande, to prevent its capture.[126] This order, though issued entirely because of military necessity, drew Magruder into a heated jurisdictional dispute with Lieutenant Colonel William J. Hutchins, chief of the newly established Texas Cotton Office, which was headquartered in Houston. Magruder deemed it his duty, under the threatening circumstances, to oversee temporarily all operations involving cotton and suggested that Hutchins devote his efforts solely to procuring weaponry. "We can exist without other things," wrote Magruder, "but cannot without arms."[127]

General Magruder also assumed it was his responsibility to collect sufficient cotton to meet contractual requirements, which had been agreed upon prior to the establishment of the Texas Cotton Office. One such contract with E. B. Nichols and Nelson Clements was for the importation of military supplies from Europe, including a large number of new Enfield rifles. Magruder required his chief quartermaster, Major Benjamin Bloomfield, to round up all of the cotton he could find, but then Kirby Smith stepped in and ordered all 1,150 collected bales to be turned over to Hutchins,[128] declaring all unfilled contracts null and void. Unfortunately, this decision caused further delay at a time when thousands of Magruder's men lacked military supplies and thousands of others were entirely unarmed.[129]

Magruder was so incensed that he asked "to be relieved from all connection with the cotton business,"[130] and to his utter dismay Kirby Smith agreed. Without mincing words Smith informed Magruder that "the operations of the Cotton Office are independent of your control . . . You have no further connection with that subject other than to render such military assistance as may be needed by Colonel Hutchins for carrying out the object for which [his] office was created."[131]

125. Banks to Stanton, April 6, 1865, *Official Records,* ser. 1, vol. 26, pt. 1, 20–21.

126. Magruder to Boggs, December 1, 1863, ibid., vol. 26, pt. 2, 466; *Galveston Tri-Weekly News,* December 23, 1863.

127. Magruder to Sorley, December 21, 1863, *Official Records,* ser. 1, vol. 26, pt. 2, 520–21.

128. Magruder to Boggs, November 29, 1863, ibid., 457.

129. Magruder to Sorley, December 21, 1863, ibid., 521; Turner to Bee, October 14, 1863, ibid, 316.

130. Magruder to Boggs, November 29, 1863, *Official Records,* ser. 1, vol. 26, pt. 2, 457.

131. West to Magruder, December 26, 1863, ibid., 538–39.

Suddenly realizing that his commander was losing confidence in him,[132] Magruder defended his actions at great length, explaining that his orders, which appeared to run counter to those from headquarters, had been issued before he knew that those powers had been assigned to the Texas Cotton Office.[133] His sole aim, he explained, was to supply his troops with desperately needed arms.[134] But no matter what Magruder said, Kirby Smith stood firm. Magruder was to have nothing else to do with cotton for the remainder of the war, except to support Broadwell and Hutchins.

When Magruder's men realized their commander was stripped of his ability to furnish them with food and essential military supplies, many began fending for themselves. Texans were tough, rugged, and independent. Most obeyed the law only as long as it did not inconvenience them, and they had a notorious tendency to do as they pleased, especially in times of privation.[135] They held such an open disregard for discipline and regimentation that General Richard Taylor wrote in disgust, "[Texans] had no more conception of military gradations than of the celestial hierarchy of the poets."[136] The hardships of frontier living imparted to Texans a rocklike individualism. It hardened their spirit, left them with an indomitable will to survive, and made them resourceful in the face of all obstacles. They refused to stand idly by and starve, nor would they fight an enemy without weaponry. If the Confederacy could not furnish them with their essentials, they would simply provide for themselves by stealing. At the same time, Magruder permitted his subdistrict commanders to draw up impressment schedules that allowed soldiers to take livestock, weapons, and other supplies without proper compensation.[137] Toward the latter stages of the war many of the ranchers, farmers, and planters of Texas actually feared their own troops more than they did the enemy.[138]

From the time John Magruder arrived in Texas, he found himself in the middle of the controversy that pitted military against civilian authority, a

132. Magruder to Boggs, January 6, 1864, ibid., vol. 34, pt. 3, 830.

133. *Galveston Tri-Weekly News,* December 30, 1863.

134. Magruder to Allen, May 20, 1864, *Official Records,* ser. 1, vol. 34, pt. 2, 831–36.

135. Stephen B. Oates, "Texas under the Secessionists," *Southwestern Historical Quarterly* 67 (October 1963): 191–94.

136. Richard Taylor, *Destruction and Reconstruction: Personal Experience of the Late War,* ed. Richard B. Harwell (New York: Longmans, Green and Co., 1955), 150.

137. Oates, "Texas under the Secessionists," 196.

138. Ibid., 193; Stephen B. Oates, *Confederate Cavalry West of the River* (Austin: University of Texas Press, 1961), 81–82.

problem that was compounded when the states' rights issue was thrown into the mix. The multitude of cotton purchasing agents exemplified the problem. Additionally, the state of Texas had its own troops, while others were directly under Confederate control. Generally, the state troops patrolled the frontier, but who would protect citizens from Indian attacks if the ranger companies were ordered into Confederate service in an emergency? Were lawbreakers to be tried in civil or military courts? Did the Impressment and Conscription Acts violate the rights of private citizens? These questions would result in considerable controversy and ill will in the course of the war.

As there was no clear dividing line between military versus civilian authority or Confederate versus state authority, General Magruder let military necessity dictate his actions. He had to have troops and supplies. And he had to maintain control of his district. He instructed his subdistrict commanders to enforce the draft strenuously, including in the Texas hill country counties of Bexar, Comal, Gillespie, Kendall, Kerr and Medina, in which lived a large concentration of pro-Union, antislavery citizens of German ancestry, and along the Red River in northeast Texas, an area that had opposed secession.[139] In Cooke, Wise, Denton, and other counties in the northern subdistrict, armed gangs of draft dodgers, deserters, and Unionists so often harassed both loyal southern citizens, as well as General Henry S. McCulloch's troops,[140] that Kirby Smith in October 1863 wrote, "The question is whether they or we shall control."[141]

Magruder authorized McCulloch to shoot deserters "without hesitation or mercy,"[142] and both men agreed that if there was any question regarding civilian or military judicial jurisdiction, defendants were to be court-martialed.[143] Magruder's commanders in the field ruled their subdistricts with dictatorial powers. They suspended habeas corpus whenever necessary and dealt severely with dissidents.[144] General Magruder in effect turned Texas

139. Oates, "Texas under the Secessionists," 198–99.

140. McCulloch to Magruder, January 23, 1864, with enclosures, Bourland to McCulloch, January 21, 1864, and Hale to Bourland, January 11, 1864, *Official Records*, ser. 1, vol. 34, pt. 2, 908–11.

141. Smith to McCulloch, October 2, 1863, ibid., vol. 26, pt. 2, 285.

142. Magruder to McCulloch, January 29, 1864. ibid., vol. 34, pt. 2, 926.

143. McCulloch to Turner, February 15, 1864, ibid., 969. When the question of civilian versus military courts arose, Edmund Turner, Magruder's assistant adjutant general, instructed McCulloch in the letter's endorsement: "Order a court-martial. Those subject to military service can be tried, and those who are not can be, as spies attempting to carry across our lines information to the enemy."

144. Oates, "Texas under the Secessionists," 196–200.

into "a great military camp, subject to military rules."[145] Francis R. Lubbock had supported Magruder while he had been governor, but Lubbock's successor, Pendleton Murrah, a staunch states' rightist, condemned Magruder for trying to run Texas like a tyrant. And Kirby Smith agreed, asserting that Magruder had "an utter disregard for law."[146] Perhaps so, because in John Magruder's mind necessity always prevailed over legality.

Kirby Smith respected Magruder as a fighter with ability and great energy. However, in a January 15, 1864, letter to Senator Robert Ward Johnson of Arkansas, Smith complained that "no reliance could be placed upon his obedience to an order unless it chimed in with his own plans and fancies." Magruder, on the other hand, believed that his commander, like Secretary of War Seddon, was more concerned with legality than reality. Smith was also very slow to act, and waiting for his orders compounded the problem. Quite often, when General Smith's authorization arrived, it was too late—the opportunity had been lost. Under the circumstances Magruder acted as his judgment and military exigencies dictated. In Smith's opinion, however, such actions were not the result of necessity but of impulse.[147]

General Smith also wrote that Magruder "has no faculty for drawing around him good men, and his selection of agents is almost always unfortunate."[148] Clearly, the nomination of Simeon Hart to coordinate cotton purchasing operations in Texas was regrettable, and it was a mistake that Magruder acknowledged. Otherwise, the record throughout the entire course of the war indicates that Magruder performed an exemplary job of recognizing and then employing talented administrators. In Virginia he selected his nephew George A. Magruder Jr. and Hugh M. Stanard as his personal assistants. They were young, bright, gentlemanlike, and handsome.[149] More important, they were hardworking and loyal and would serve with Prince John to the very end.

Early in the war General Magruder also saw excellent potential in both George Wythe Randolph and Joseph Lancaster Brent. They were lawyers by profession. Neither man had anything in common with their flamboyant commander, but they were very talented men who were intensely loyal to

---

145. Oran M. Roberts, "The Political, Legislative, and Judicial History of Texas for Its Fifty Years of Statehood, 1845–1895," in Wooten, *Comprehensive History of Texas,* 2:145.

146. Smith to Johnson, January 15, 1864, *Official Records,* ser. 1, vol. 34, pt. 2, 870.

147. Ibid.

148. Ibid.

149. Fremantle, *Fremantle Diary,* 28.

Magruder. When detractors attempted to undermine the general's reputation, both Randolph and Brent wrote spirited rebuttals in defense of their commander. Randolph would become Magruder's chief of artillery and later the Confederate secretary of war. Brent would return to his native Louisiana and do a commendable job as Richard Taylor's chief of artillery and ordnance. Following the war Taylor wrote in his memoirs, "The *esprit de corps* of Brent's artillery was admirable, and its conduct and efficiency in action unsurpassed."[150]

Whether Magruder's staff members came with him from Virginia or were newly selected in Texas, they were chosen with the same intuitive skill, and they worked productively together in remarkable harmony. To a man Magruder's principal administrators were loyal and efficient. Benjamin Bloomfield and Edward C. Wharton displayed great energy and resourcefulness, administering to their duties as quartermasters in spite of the insurmountable odds that they faced. Engineers Valery Sulakowski and Getulius Kellersberger were well educated, experienced, and highly respected.[151] Good friend and fellow West Pointer Albert Miller Lea had been chief engineer of the State of Tennessee before the war and Professor Caleb Forshey the architect of Magruder's defenses earlier on the Peninsula in Virginia. These men personified professionalism. Their skilled work kept Galveston and the upper Texas coast safely in Confederate control until the war ended, a task that Magruder's predecessor Paul O. Hebert, himself a professional engineer, had deemed impossible. And finally, Magruder's adjutant general and staff officers Oscar M. Watkins, A. G. Dickinson, Alexander C. Jones, E. B. Pendleton, Edmund P. Turner, and Stephen D. Yancey performed quality service

150. Taylor, *Destruction and Reconstruction,* 140.

151. Before the American Civil War, Polish-born Valery Sulakowski had served as an officer in the Austrian army; Getulius (Julius) Kellersberger had been director of the iron works at Wiener-Neustadt. In the early 1850s Kellersberger came to California, where he surveyed and laid out the City of Oakland, then worked as a railroad engineer in Mexico. Sulakowski had been with Magruder in Virginia; Kellersberger joined the staff in Texas. Together they did a marvelous job fortifying Galveston after its recapture. On March 12, 1864, the mayor and aldermen of Galveston unanimously passed a resolution thanking "Colonel V. Sulakowski and Colonel G. Kellersberger, the two distinguished engineers who have displayed so much scientific and military skill in erecting defenses around the city and other vulnerable points on the gulf coast, which stand in bold defiance now complete, to resist any force which our common enemy can bring to bear against us." August Raymond Ogden, "A Blockaded Seaport, Galveston, Texas, CSA" (master's thesis, St. Mary's University, 1939), 136; Hayes, "Island and the City of Galveston," 593; and Kellersberger, *Memoirs of an Engineer in the Confederate Army in Texas,* i, ii, 27, 29.

for their commander and remained loyal to him until the day he died. Edward T. Cotham Jr., who authored the excellent study *Battle on the Bay: The Civil War Struggle for Galveston,* judged that "General Magruder assembled the best administrative staff in the Trans-Mississippi, and arguably, one of the best in the entire army."[152]

Magruder philosophized that "Texas is virtually the Trans-Mississippi Department, and the railroads of Galveston and Houston are virtually Texas."[153] He therefore opposed the Federal army's march up the coast of Texas with only token resistance until it neared Galveston. But there he dug in and determined to stop the advance. The Confederates nervously waited for months, but the expected enemy assault never materialized. Finally, there resulted a virtual standoff wherein the Federals held the lower coast of Texas and Magruder the upper coast (the southeastern portion of the state), with neither side anxious to advance upon the other.

Signs of nervous tension, mental fatigue, and physical exhaustion were evident among Magruder's soldiers as a result of the endless waiting. The wearing effects of inactivity were compounded by the Cotton Bureau's inability to obtain sufficient supplies and the fact that the troops were not paid regularly. A soldier wrote from Galveston that he had received no pay for eight months,[154] and another complained that because of inflation "a Confederate soldier here, cannot buy his tobacco with his wages."[155] Additionally, food was of a disgracefully wretched quality. H. C. Medford, a Confederate soldier stationed opposite Galveston, at Virginia Point, wrote in his diary: "Our rations are very scanty. The beeves that we eat here are so poor that they can scarcely stand. It is an outrage that Confederate soldiers should be compelled to live upon what we live upon . . . We have not drawn anything but poor beef in the way of meat since we have been in the state . . . I am the last one to mutiny or desert; but if there are any justifiable causes for such things, it is here in our army."[156]

About one month after Medford complained of the substandard food and living conditions, the ladies of Galveston held a supper and ball in honor of General Magruder and other ranking officers of his command. When the

152. Cotham to Settles, March 17, 2000, letter in possession of author.

153. Magruder to Smith, September 26, 1863, *Official Records,* ser. 1, vol. 26, pt. 2, 260–62.

154. *Houston Telegraph,* May 6, 1864.

155. Rebecca W. Smith and Marion Mullins, eds., "Diary of H. C. Medford, Confederate Soldier, 1864," *Southwestern Historical Quarterly* 34 (October 1930): 121.

156. Ibid., 120–21.

party reached its "acme of jocularly," about five hundred armed soldiers appeared and threatened to burn the house to the ground if General Magruder did not come forth and listen to their demands. The soldiers protested that it was no time for "feasting, fiddling and dancing" because they were starving and the Confederacy was "bleeding at every pore." Magruder sympathized with their grievances, promising more food of a higher quality and better living conditions. Finally, however, when the mob of angry soldiers dispersed, Prince John returned to the party, where he rallied the frightened participants and continued the ball in a grand manner.[157]

Although the military situation in southeastern Texas had become calm enough in mid-1864 to permit General Magruder to attend an occasional party, the situation elsewhere remained desperate. General Robert E. Lee was hard-pressed by Grant at Petersburg. Jubal Early, operating in the valley of Virginia, faced a numerically superior adversary and needed every available man. And in northern Georgia, Sherman advanced upon Joseph E. Johnston's battered Army of Tennessee. West of the Mississippi River, General Nathaniel P. Banks and Admiral David Porter organized a huge Federal land-and-water enterprise whose main objective was to proceed up the Red River, enter Texas, and establish Union control over the state. Banks left General Napoleon J. T. Dana in command of Union troops on the Texas coast. General Banks hoped that by forcing the Confederates defending the state to oppose the Federals on two fronts, the Red River and on the coast, he could divide their forces sufficiently to overpower them and seize control of the state. But the Red River expedition—lasting from March 10 to May 22, 1864—proved to be a costly fiasco for the Federals. General Richard Taylor defeated the Federals at Mansfield, Louisiana, on April 8, 1864, forcing Banks to begin a general withdrawal without having accomplished any of his objectives.

Kirby Smith decided to follow up Taylor's victory by attacking General Frederick Steele in Arkansas. Taylor was to have led the expedition but asked for reassignment elsewhere after having an argument with his commander over the conduct of the Red River campaign.[158] Magruder seemed the logical choice to succeed Taylor. In July, however, Smith received orders from Jefferson Davis, via Stephen D. Lee and Braxton Bragg, directing him to transfer Taylor and the infantry of his corps from Louisiana, east of the Mississippi

---

157. Ibid., 128–29.

158. Thorough but contrasting accounts of the Taylor-Smith feud can be found in Taylor, *Destruction and Reconstruction*, 213–34; and Joseph Howard Parks, *General Edmund Kirby Smith, C.S.A.* (Baton Rouge: Louisiana State University Press, 1954), 381–82, 403–31.

to protect Mobile and to create a diversion in support of the Army of Tennessee, now operating in northern Georgia under the command of General John Bell Hood.[159] As the first part of the order deprived Smith of a significant portion of his infantry, he canceled his proposed offensive, ordered Magruder from Texas to Arkansas to occupy Steele, and sent the popular but inept Sterling Price on a diversionary raid into his native state of Missouri.[160]

General Smith hoped Price could recruit successfully in Missouri, sweeping the countryside clean of horses, mules, cattle, and military supplies as he progressed. If successful, the raid was certain to ease the pressure on Hood by forcing the Federals to divert reinforcements to Missouri that normally would have been sent to Sherman in Georgia.[161] In addition, Smith intended for Price to gain control of Missouri for the Confederacy by holding new elections for a governor and a legislature.[162]

Magruder arrived to take command of the District of Arkansas in early September, a few days after Price had begun his march into Missouri. He reported that Steele had received nine thousand reinforcements in addition to his extant twelve thousand–man force. Magruder conjectured that the Federals would attack neither Texas nor Louisiana, but in view of the troop concentrations under Steele, they would attempt to seize the remainder of Arkansas, thus isolating both Missouri and Price, rendering the latter's expedition useless. Magruder called for immediate reinforcements from Texas and Louisiana with which to oppose the Federals. Then, if Steele sent a sizable portion of his army after Price, Magruder would crush those who remained behind.[163]

Smith declined to send Magruder the requested reinforcements. He could not afford them, nor did he expect Steele to attack unless Price failed in Missouri. For the present time Kirby Smith suggested that Magruder simply keep a careful watch on the enemy line.[164]

159. Lee to Smith, July 9, 1864, *Official Records,* ser. 1, vol. 41, pt. 1, 89; July 16, 1864, ibid.; Bragg to Lee, July 22, 1864, ibid., 90; Smith to Davis, November 21, 1864, ibid., pt. 4, 1068–69.

160. General Orders No. 60, August 4, 1864, *Official Records,* ser. 1, vol. 41, pt. 2, 1039; Boggs to Magruder, ibid.; Boggs to Price, ibid., 1040–41.

161. Boggs to Price, August 4, 1864, *Official Records,* ser. 1, vol. 41, pt. 2, 1040–41.

162. Albert Castel, *General Sterling Price and the Civil War in the West* (Baton Rouge: Louisiana State University Press, 1968), 202.

163. Magruder to Boggs, September 10, 1864, *Official Records,* ser. 1, vol. 41, pt. 3, 917–18; September 11, 1864, ibid., 922; September 15, 1864, ibid., 932–34; September 17, 1864, ibid., 938–39.

164. Smith to Magruder, September 22, 1864, *Official Records,* ser. 1, vol. 41, pt. 3, 950; October 3, 1864, ibid., 978–79.

It was difficult to predict Frederick Steele's moves. His was a much larger army than Magruder's, but he had shown no inclination to take the offensive. By the end of October Magruder had become convinced, along with General Smith, that Steele would move rapidly from Little Rock to Fort Smith against Sterling Price in the event that Price returned from Missouri in a weakened or disorganized condition. Magruder requested permission to move his forces northwest of Little Rock to prevent a Federal offensive against Price.[165] But before such a maneuver could be undertaken, Price's totally demoralized army began straggling back into Arkansas.[166]

The Army of Missouri had traveled 1,434 miles; fought forty-three battles and skirmishes; captured and paroled over three thousand Federal officers and men; seized eighteen pieces of artillery, three thousand stand of small arms, large numbers of horses, wagons, teams and vast quantities of military supplies, including blankets, shoes, and uniforms. They also destroyed miles of railroad track, diverted troops en route to Sherman's army, and secured a large number of new recruits.[167] Kirby Smith enthusiastically termed the expedition a success in a letter dated November 21, 1864, to President Davis,[168] but he was unaware that General Price had lost approximately two-thirds of his original force—half from fighting and sickness, half from desertions and "furloughs." As late as December 15, Price had only thirty-five hundred troops "in hand," of whom no more than a third possessed weapons. Moreover, they were so exhausted, disorganized, and demoralized that in Magruder's judgment they were "not in a fit condition to fight any body of men."[169] Fortunately for them, General Steele had crossed the Mississippi to support George H. Thomas against Hood, who had moved into Tennessee.[170]

When Steele moved east, Secretary of War Seddon concluded that the Federals had abandoned their military designs west of the river.[171] Yet after Thomas defeated Hood decisively at Nashville on December 15–16, 1864, they began concentrating their troops at New Orleans, again threatening the

165. Magruder to Boggs, October 30, 1864, *Official Records*, ser. 1, vol. 41, pt. 4, 1020.

166. Maxey to Boggs, November 17, 1864, ibid., 1058–59.

167. Price to Boggs, December 28, 1864, ibid., pt. 1, 640.

168. Smith to Davis, November 21, 1864, ibid., pt. 4, 1068–69.

169. Magruder to Smith, December 15, 1864, ibid., 1112; Price to Magruder, November 24, 1864, ibid., 1076–77; Magruder to Boggs, ibid., 1075–76.

170. Beauregard to Smith, December 2, 1864, *Official Records*, ser. 1, vol. 45, pt. 2, 639–40; Seddon to Smith, December 7, 1864, ibid., vol. 41, pt. 1, 123.

171. Seddon to Smith, December 7, 1864, *Official Records*, ser. 1, vol. 41, pt. 1, 123.

Trans-Mississippi Department. Kirby Smith immediately placed his men on alert and then awaited further enemy action,[172] while in the east Sherman marched from Georgia into the Carolinas, and Grant pounded against the stubborn Lee at Petersburg.

On March 7 Smith received an urgent warning from General John G. Walker, who was given command in Texas when Magruder was sent to Arkansas, that enemy troops commanded by General Edward R. S. Canby were making final preparations for an invasion of the Texas coast. The intelligence had come from Catholic archbishop John Odin in New Orleans, who estimated the Federal strength at forty thousand men.[173] General Smith immediately ordered Magruder back to Texas,[174] but when he arrived on the coast he learned that Canby's expedition had been canceled. The Federals needed no invasion; the Confederacy was crumbling.

The impending sense of doom and the uncertainties of the future wore heavily upon the souls of those who had supported the southern cause throughout the long years of the war. On April 6, 1865, in Magruder's newly established headquarters at the Fannin Hotel in Houston, the tension sparked a violent argument between two of his officers, Major General John A. Wharton and Colonel George W. Baylor. Magruder went upstairs and ordered the men to end their disagreement. Yet when he returned downstairs to his office, the argument resumed. Wharton reportedly called Baylor a liar and slapped him, whereupon Baylor drew his pistol and killed the unarmed Wharton. The following day General Magruder orchestrated a military funeral with full honors. He personally led the procession down Main Street to Houston's Central Railroad Depot, where the casket bearing General Wharton's body was dispatched to his widow in Hempstead.[175]

172. Belton to Greer, January 21, 1865, ibid., vol. 48, pt. 1, 1336; Anderson to Forney, ibid., 1336–37; Belton to Wharton, ibid., 1337; Belton to Forney, January 22, 1865, ibid; Boggs to Magruder, ibid., 1338; Boggs to Churchill, ibid; Boggs to Maxey, ibid; Smith to Walker, ibid., 1338–39; Belton to Walker, ibid., 1339; Special Orders No. 18, January 23, 1865, ibid., 1340; Boggs to Maxey, ibid.; Churchill to Hawthorn, ibid.

173. Walker to Smith, March 7, 1865, *Official Records,* ser. 1, vol. 48, pt. 1, 1412.

174. Boggs to Magruder, March 8, 1865, ibid., 1416; General Orders No. 30, March 31, 1865, ibid., 1455.

175. *Galveston Daily News,* April 7, 8, and 9, 1865. Wharton's obituary was in the *News* on April 9, 1865. *Galveston Tri-Weekly News,* April 7, 10, and 12, 1865. The obituary was published in the April 10, 1865, edition; a memorial to General Wharton was published on April 12, 1865. *Dallas Herald,* April 20, 1865. Besides Magruder, the pallbearers were General James E. Harrison, Major Xavier B. DeBray, and colonels Edward Waller and D. S. Terry.

Wharton's tragic death and the nearly simultaneous surrender of Lee's Army to Grant on April 9, 1865, at Appomattox had a devastating effect on Magruder's men. "The cloud of dark seems to be hovering over us at this time," wrote John Simmons to his family on April 13.[176] Several days later he reported, "The soldiers are getting very restless, and some talk of breaking up and going home."[177]

Generals Kirby Smith and Magruder tried to counter the creeping defeatism by issuing stirring addresses urging their men to continue the struggle. On April 21 Smith implored the soldiers of the Trans-Mississippi Department to stand by their colors. "Prove to the world that your hearts have not failed in the hour of disaster," he urged, "and that at the last moment you will sustain the holy cause which has been so gloriously battled for by your brethren east of the Mississippi."[178] Two days later Magruder likewise encouraged his men "to set an example of devotion, bravery, and patriotism, worthy of the holy cause of liberty and independence," and to meet the enemy "at the water's edge, and let him pay dearly for every inch of territory he may acquire."[179] Throughout Texas General Magruder's subdistrict commanders made similar pleas. The soldiers listened, but few believed. In the end reality prevailed over rhetoric. The men knew that with the surrender of generals Lee and Johnston in the east, the war had in actuality come to an end.

Kirby Smith rejected demands for the unconditional surrender of the Trans-Mississippi Department on May 9,[180] hoping to obtain more liberal terms for his men. The troops, however, did not care about the terms. The important item was that they had lost, and accepting this, they began leaving their units "by tens and twenties a night."[181] Texans were not quitters, but they were not fools either. When it became obvious that the demise of the Confederacy was imminent, war-weary soldiers simply wanted to go home. Those who remained were merely "waiting for what they [considered] the inevitable result, viz, surrender." Commanders agreed that their troops were unmanageable and even conjectured that the men would "lay down their

---

176. Harrison, "Confederate Letters of John Simmons," 50. Letter to "My dear Companion and children," April 13, 1865.

177. Ibid., 52. In a letter to "My dear Nancy," April 25, 1865.

178. Smith to the "Soldiers of the Trans-Mississippi Army," April 21, 1865, *Official Records*, ser. 1, vol. 48, pt. 2, 1284.

179. General Orders No. 20, April 23, 1865, ibid., 1285; Harrison, "Confederate Letters of John Simmons," 52. In a letter to "Dear Companion," April 29, 1865.

180. Smith to Pope, May 9, 1865, *Official Records*, ser. 1, vol. 48, pt. 1, 189.

181. Magruder to Boggs, April 29, 1865, ibid., pt. 2, 1291.

arms at the first appearance of the enemy."[182] Four hundred Galveston-based troops attempted to desert with their weapons on the night of May 14, and although Magruder persuaded them to stay, he reported that it was impossible "to induce them to preserve their organization."[183]

Two days later, on May 16, Magruder reported that he had done all that he could do "to instill a spirit of resistance into the men, but in vain." He judged that he was now making himself antagonistic to his army and was becoming "an object of their displeasure." The time had come to divide the government property and send the men to their homes and families "with as little damage to the community as possible." As it was likely that any additional delay would result in the total collapse of discipline, lawlessness, and perhaps even anarchy, an obviously exasperated Magruder begged his commander, "For God's sake, act or let me act."[184] The frantic dispatch was the last communiqué that John Magruder sent to Kirby Smith during the war.

Facing no alternative in view of the desperate military situation within his department, Smith sent his chief of staff, General Simon Bolivar Buckner, as commissioner to General E.R.S. Canby, commanding the Federal force at New Orleans, to take up again the question of terms of surrender.[185] While these negotiations were pending, Magruder dispatched Colonel Ashbel Smith and William Pitt Ballinger to New Orleans "for the purpose of opening negotiations with the proper authorities of the United States for the pacification of the State of Texas."[186] Smith and Ballinger had hoped to prevent the establishment of a Federal military government in Texas, but when they arrived in New Orleans, they learned that General Buckner had completed preliminary negotiations for the surrender of the Trans-Mississippi Department; thus, their action on the subject was concluded.[187] A few days later, on June 2, Generals Smith and Magruder signed the Canby-Buckner Convention aboard the USS *Fort Jackson* outside of Galveston Bay,[188] bringing the war in the Trans-Mississippi west to an official close.

182. Walker to Smith, May 16, 1865, ibid., 1308–9.

183. Magruder to Smith, May 16, 1865, ibid., 1308.

184. Ibid.

185. Charles W. Ramsdell, "Texas from the Fall of the Confederacy to the Beginning of Reconstruction," *Quarterly of the Texas State Historical Association* 11 (January 1908): 204.

186. Proclamation of Major-General Magruder of an armistice pending negotiations of peace commissioners at New Orleans, May 26, 1865, *Official Records of Navies*, ser. 1, 22:272.

187. Smith and Ballinger to Canby, May 30, 1865, *Official Records*, ser. 1, vol. 48,, pt. 2, 675–76.

188. Report of H. K. Thatcher, June 8, 1865, *Official Records of Navies*, ser. 1, 22:216.

8

POSTWAR ODYSSEY

It must have been extremely difficult for so proud a man as John Bankhead Magruder to have signed the articles surrendering the Trans-Mississippi Department. But when the Federals began arresting and imprisoning high Confederate officials, he resolutely refused to submit to such personal humiliation. He was not eligible for the amnesty proclaimed by President Lincoln on December 8, 1863,[1] or that proclaimed by Andrew Johnson on May 29, 1865,[2] so he determined instead to join the Confederate exodus to Mexico. Magruder and "three or four [officers of his] staff and fifteen gallant young soldiers" departed Houston on June 11, on horseback with three accompanying pack mules carrying their only possessions. On the eighteenth they arrived in San Antonio and checked into the Menger Hotel.[3] This now-famous landmark was the point of rendezvous for those Confederates wishing to journey across the border. Governors Thomas O. Moore and Henry Watkins Allen of Louisiana, Edward Clark and Pendleton Murrah of Texas, Trusten Polk and Thomas C. Reynolds of Missouri, and Charles S. Morehead of Kentucky went there, as did generals Kirby Smith, Sterling Price, Jo Shelby, Cadmus M. Wilcox, Hamilton P. Bee, James M. Hawes, Thomas C. Hindman,

---

1. Proclamation of Amnesty and Reconstruction, December 8, 1863, in *The Collected Works of Abraham Lincoln,* ed. Roy P. Basler, 8 vols. (New Brunswick, N.J.: Rutgers University Press, 1953), 7:53–56.

2. Proclamation of Andrew Johnson, May 29, 1865, *Official Records,* ser. 2, 8:578–80.

3. "Our Mexican Problem as Viewed Fifty Years Ago by the Emperor Maximilian: Hitherto Unpublished Narrative by Famous Confederate General Magruder, of Timely Interest Today," *New York Times Magazine,* April 2, 1916 (hereafter cited as "Magruder Narrative," *New York Times Magazine*); *New York Times,* August 20, 1865.

Danville Leadbetter, William P. Hardeman, William Preston, John B. Clark, and many of their devout followers.[4] Some had been bitter military rivals during the war, yet these men set their grievances aside, planned the Mexican venture, serenaded one another, and spent many delightful hours exchanging reminiscences while sampling the fine wares kept behind William A. Menger's Honduran mahogany bar.[5]

The frolicking ended on June 20, 1865, and the exodus to Mexico began. Magruder, Kirby Smith, Wilcox, Bee, and about twenty other officers moved slightly ahead of the main body of troops led by General Shelby as they "had business with certain French and Mexican officers at Piedras Negras."[6] Shelby caught up to them on the morning of the twenty-sixth on the banks of the Rio Grande, where he ceremoniously buried his battle flags, signifying the death of the cause for which his men had so desperately fought. Major John N. Edwards, Shelby's adjutant, described the proceedings: "With bare, bowed heads [the] soldiers gathered around the dear old banner. It had been all to them and they worshipped it . . . the sun shone out broad and good upon the upturned faces of those engaged in silent prayer—and, at last, with not a dry eye among all these five hundred stern soldiers, the Battle Flag of Shelby's division was lowered slowly and sadly beneath the water."[7]

Later in the day Magruder and his traveling entourage led the first of several small groups to leave Piedras Negras for Monterrey. His companions included Edmund P. Turner, Oscar Watkins, Leon Smith, and A. C. Jones. The heat was scorching, the terrain rugged, and the countryside filled with Mexican bandits, but they appear to have made the trip without incident, arriving on the twenty-ninth. Judge Alexander Watkins Terrell, who arrived the previous day, reported that Magruder rode up in an ambulance given to

4. A list of the Confederates who immigrated to Mexico can be found in W. C. Nunn, *Escape from Reconstruction* (Fort Worth: Texas Christian University, 1956), 129–36, appendix. For additional information, see Sarah Anne Dorsey, ed., *Recollections of Henry Watkins Allen, Brigadier-General Confederate States Army, Ex-Governor of Louisiana* (New York: M. Doolady, 1866), 325–26; Luther Edward Chandler, "The Career of Henry Watkins Allen" (Ph.D. diss., Louisiana State University, 1940), 233–34; Jennie Edwards, comp., *John N. Edwards: Biography, Memoirs, Reminiscences and Recollections* (Kansas City, Mo.: Jennie Edwards, 1889), 247–56. The latter work contains a reprint of John N. Edwards, *Shelby's Expedition to Mexico*.

5. Daniel O'Flaherty, *General Jo Shelby: Undefeated Rebel* (Chapel Hill: University of North Carolina Press, 1954), 241–43. O'Flaherty incorrectly identified the Menger's proprietor as Otto.

6. Edwards, *John N. Edwards,* 260.

7. John N. Edwards, *Shelby and His Men; or, The War in the West* (Cincinnati: Miami Printing and Publishing Co., 1867), 545–46.

him by Colonel George Giddings of San Antonio. Two small mules were at the wheel, and in the lead were two fine saddle horses that Magruder had ridden at Big Bethel and later during the Seven Days' battles. "No razor had touched the General's face for ten days," noted Terrell, "and his snow white beard looked strange on a face, until then cleanly-shaven, except for moustache and side-whiskers which were blackened."[8]

The Confederates were cordially received by French colonel, soon to be general, Pierre Jean Joseph Jeanningros, who gave a banquet in their honor. According to Magruder: "The light of gastronomic civilization broke upon us in all its glory . . . Battalions of inviting French dishes, regiments of bottles of the most exquisite French wines, and barricades of boxes of the most fragrant Havanas were placed, as it were, in battle array before us."[9] Prince John "was in his happiest mood," still a master of merrymaking, despite the hardships and disappointments that had befallen him. "His joyous temperament," wrote Judge Terrell, "could never be depressed"; thus, he was able to cheer those who were with him "who had no flag and nothing but hope to sustain them."[10]

Soon after the banquet, Magruder departed Monterrey for Mexico City to treat with Maximilian on the subject of Confederate colonization. Apparently short of money, he sold his ambulance and team to a Texas cattle buyer at San Luis Potosí.[11] He then completed the remainder of his journey by stage, arriving in Mexico City on July 24.[12] Magruder checked into a room on the first floor of the fashionable Iturbide Hotel,[13] and there he received several distinguished visitors, including Matthew Fontaine Maury and his old friend

8. Alexander Watkins Terrell, *From Texas to Mexico and the Court of Maximilian in 1865* (Dallas: Book Club of Texas, 1933), 18. Alexander Watkins Terrell, born in Virginia and raised in Missouri, came to Texas in 1852 with his wife and two children. He served as a judge in central and southern Texas before the war, rose to the rank of brigadier general during the war, and following the flight to Mexico, returned to Texas and served in both houses of the state legislature. He authored numerous important pieces of legislation, including the bill organizing the still powerful Texas Railroad Commission, and coauthored another that created the University of Texas. For a number of years he served on the university's board of regents and at the time of his death was president of the Texas State Historical Association. Terrell died in 1912 at the age of eighty-five.

9. "Magruder Narrative," *New York Times Magazine.*

10. Terrell, *From Texas to Mexico and the Court of Maximilian in 1865*, 19–20.

11. Ibid., 37–38.

12. Padgett, "Life of Alfred Mordecai in Mexico," *North Carolina Historical Review* 22 (April 1945): 222. In a letter, Mordecai to his wife, July 24, 1865. The Mexico City *Mexican Times*, September 30, 1865, incorrectly reported that Magruder reached the City of Mexico on August 5.

13. Terrell, *From Texas to Mexico and the Court of Maximilian in 1865*, 45.

Marshal François-Achille Bazaine, now in command of the imperial forces in Mexico. He also met the British minister to Mexico, Sir Peter Campbell Scarlett, whose nephew, Lord Abinger, had married Magruder's niece, Helen Magruder, in Montreal several years earlier.

After a few days' rest, Magruder obtained an appointment with Emperor Maximilian and his consort, Empress Carlotta. He exchanged his nearly worn out uniform for "a cut-a-way suit of salt and pepper color, with a tall dove-colored hat and patent leather boots,"[14] and then went to the palace of Montezuma, which Scott's army had victoriously occupied eighteen years earlier. Magruder found the emperor to be about thirty-four years of age. He was tall and commanding in stature, and his face reflected strength and firmness. His wife was "beautifully formed, and graceful in the highest degree. Her dark brown hair, and long, black eyelashes, veiling lustrous eyes of gray, seemed to deepen the melancholy expression of her face. Her features were clearly defined, and classic in the extreme."[15]

When Magruder was comfortably seated, Carlotta asked him "if any obstacle existed in the United States to the recognition of the Imperial Government." The question was one that Prince John had hoped not to discuss because he could offer his young French hosts no hope. So he made light of the subject by answering playfully:

> "Yes, your Majesty, I will tell you frankly there does exist in the United States an obstacle to the recognition of the Empire."
>
> "And what is it?" she asked.
>
> "Why, your Majesty, it was born of timidity, but I fear it is now the child of arrogance. It is also a thing of air, for it is used by the contending political parties in the United States as a shuttlecock, the politicians being the performers, the people the spectators, and it is kept up with surprising skill and pertinacity, least it fall to the ground and the losers of the game thus displease the audience."
>
> "What can it be?" she inquired.
>
> "Your Majesty, that is the Monroe Doctrine, the shuttlecock of politicians.'"[16]

The tone of conversation became more serious when Maximilian expressed concern about the political activities of the Confederates in Mexico.

14. Ibid.; "Magruder Narrative," *New York Times Magazine.*
15. "Magruder Narrative," *New York Times Magazine.*
16. Ibid.

Magruder, however, assured him, as he had Jeanningros earlier, that "under no circumstances would we accept military service with either of the contending parties in Mexico, and that unlike other political refugees we [would] abstain from plotting against our own country."[17] The former Confederates were no longer interested in fighting. On the contrary, those who went to Mexico went with the expectation of acquiring land by purchase or gift from Maximilian for the purpose of colonization. Matthew Maury, soon to be appointed imperial commissioner of colonization, discussed these plans with the emperor, and Magruder volunteered to aid "in any capacity in which he might be deemed useful. The emperor expressed his satisfaction and said that at an early day he would avail himself of his services." The interview ended with Magruder having charmed Carlotta and won over the trust of Maximilian. He obviously impressed him in other ways too because the next time they saw each other, the emperor was wearing a dove-colored top hat and a salt-and-pepper cutaway.[18]

When Magruder left Texas for Mexico, he was accused of having taken the proceeds from the sale of Confederate cotton under his jurisdiction in Texas during the war. The *New Orleans Era* charged that "it is a well-known fact that not two-thirds of the enormous sums of money derived from the seizure and sale of cotton by General Magruder and his emissaries was ever used for the benefit of the rebel government, but was invested in sterling bills and foreign loans for the benefit of Magruder and the men connected with him in the swindling transactions."[19] The preponderance of evidence, however, indicates that Magruder had very little money when he crossed into Mexico, and even less when he left the country sixteen months later.

Kirby Smith's biographer Joseph Howard Parks wrote that Smith divided the seventeen hundred dollars he had left on hand after the surrender in Texas among five general officers, including Magruder, "as part of the pay due them."[20] Furthermore, when General Magruder left Houston for Mexico via San Antonio, Charles R. Benton, who had formerly headed Magruder's artillery office, wrote that his commander had "barely enough gold or money

17. Ibid.; Magruder to T. L. Snead, June 17, 1866, Historical Society of Pennsylvania, Philadelphia. Magruder never served as a major general in Maximilian's army, as is reported in the *Dictionary of American Biography*.

18. Terrell, *From Texas to Mexico and the Court of Maximilian in 1865*, 45, 52.

19. House Executive Documents, Diplomatic Correspondence, pt. 3, 39th Cong., 1st sess., 498.

20. Parks, *General Edmund Kirby Smith*, 479.

to carry him to the frontier."[21] The exact amount of money will probably never be known, but all of those close to the old general agreed that the amount was relatively insignificant. Judge Terrell scoffed at those "who believed that Magruder left Texas loaded with gold!" He further reported that whatever money General Magruder possessed, he divided with his staff the day after arriving in Monterrey. "My recollection," wrote Terrell years later, in his book *From Texas to Mexico and the Court of Maximilian in 1865,* "is that the share of each officer was less than two hundred dollars."[22]

Perhaps the most reliable commentary on Magruder's financial status at the time of his exodus from Texas to Mexico is that of General Hamilton P. Bee, who, as a Confederate officer in Texas during the war, was well aware of the government's dealings in cotton. From Havana on March 3, 1866, General Bee wrote to his friend Colonel Walter L. Mann in Galveston:

> Mrs. Bee says she heard you say that the proof existed that Magruder had made a great deal of money by his connections with Texas. I assure you that I know what I saw when I tell you that all the money he had on leaving Texas was given to him by his friends—and that if Gen. [James E.] Slaughter had not sent him five hundred dollars after he got to Mexico—the old man would not have had a dollar . . . You will be doing the man simple justice who did more for Texas than any man in it—by examining for yourself the proofs— and giving his friends a chance to refute them. The only man Walter, who got public money was Gen. Walker—he and his wife drew seven thousand dollars in gold here, for cotton sold by the Confederacy—and he never said divide to any of his fellow exiles—the proofs of that transaction are here in black and white.
>
> It is said that you received an order from Walker to prevent the passing of Magruder to Galveston, that he might sail on the Blockade runner to Havana—and that if Magruder could have got to Havana, he could as Comdg. general of the District of Texas, have disposed of the money, although the said cotton was shipped while Walker was in command, and hence some see a motive in Walker's anxiety to prevent Magruder getting there ahead of

21. Charles R. Benton to "Dear Major" (Edward Clifton Wharton), March 29, 1886, in Edward Clifton Wharton and Family Papers, Louisiana State University, Baton Rouge. Benton, who was with Magruder and Kirby Smith at the time of the surrender, wrote in his letter to Wharton: "Gen. M. never accepted a single dollar from those whose fortunes he made—he was *too high* for that. He was *every inch* Prince John Magruder, as brave and skillful a soldier as any, but broken-hearted."

22. Terrell, *From Texas to Mexico and the Court of Maximilian in 1865,* 20.

him—at all events Walker got the money—and his wife drew four thousand dollars in person before he got here—and so goes the world.[23]

General Bee's statement is independently corroborated by a correspondent of the *New Orleans Times,* who wrote from Galveston on June 13, 1865, that "there is not a word of truth" to the charges "that Gens. Smith and Magruder engaged extensively in cotton speculations, and made a heap of money, which they took with them when they fled to Mexico." He further stated that Magruder

> came to Texas without any money in his pocket, and left the state with less than two hundred dollars, and this his friends in Houston loaned him to pay his expenses to Mexico . . . This general has his strong and weak points. He would spurn a bribe, knowing it to be intended as such, as soon as any upright man, and yet a presentation of a few choice liquors or cigars were too apt to gain his favor, and induce him, in his unsuspecting way, to grant privileges to designing men in search of fat contracts. In this manner he might have given others a chance to speculate, but [he never did so himself] to the extent of a dollar while in Texas . . . This correspondent can have no interest in stating [such facts], but he deems it his duty to do so as a simple act of justice to injured parties.[24]

The assembled evidence indicates that Magruder did not have a large sum of money when he left Texas. He probably started with the three or four hundred dollars back pay that Kirby Smith had given him and later received the five hundred dollar loan from General Slaughter. No doubt he could have borrowed various amounts from Bazaine or Scarlett once he was in Mexico City, but it does not appear that he had either a large amount of money with him or that any hidden depositories existed. If so, he would not have had to sell his team and wagon even before completing the trip to Mexico City, nor would he have been penniless upon his return to the United States.

On September 17, 1865, after having become a naturalized Mexican citizen,[25] Magruder was appointed chief of the Land Office of Colonization at an annual salary of $3,000. He was allowed $150 for office furniture, $1,200

23. Bee to Mann, March 3, 1866. San Jacinto Museum of History, Houston.

24. *New York Times,* July 29, 1865.

25. Sara Y. Stevenson, "How an Austrian Archduke Ruled an American Empire," *Century Magazine* 55 (February 1898): 610.

a year for office rent, $500 for general expenses, and $300 for a private messenger. He was authorized to estimate the number of engineers and surveyors needed to carry on the work of his office and the appropriations needed for salaries. There were no guidelines to follow. The land of Mexico had not previously been surveyed, and there had never been a land office.[26]

While Maury sent agents to the United States to attract southerners to Mexico, Magruder dispatched others to survey and inspect possible colonization locations. Sterling Price, Isham G. Harris, and Judge John Perkins went to the Córdoba region; William P. Hardeman and Judge Oran M. Roberts to Guadalajara; William M. Anderson and John G. Lux to Monterrey; George W. Clarke to Durango; Alonzo Ridley to Mazatlán; John Henry Brown to Mérida; and Z. P. Cropesa to Vera Cruz.[27]

When the inspection reports were received from these groups, Magruder and Maury recommended to Maximilian a series of colonies to be established along the railroad between Vera Cruz and Mexico City.[28] Their first settlement, which they named Carlotta in honor of the empress, was to be located near Córdoba, approximately seventy miles west of Vera Cruz, on lands that Maximilian had claimed after Juárez had expropriated them from the Catholic Church. He offered 640 acres to each head of a family and 320 acres to any single person free or at a nominal cost. Three classes of lands were available to the colonists: improved public lands that had been confiscated or had escheated to the government; unimproved parts of the public domain; and private lands that the owners would agree to sell on liberal terms. The confiscated, improved lands could be purchased at a dollar per acre at 6 percent interest payable in five equal annual installments, and the government usually gave unimproved lots to the immigrants but reserved every alternate section for the public domain. Private lands brought slightly higher prices but were a bargain nonetheless.[29]

The Mexican soil was fertile, rainfall moderate, and the climate excellent. Maury judged the land suitable for raising an infinite variety of crops, including cotton, corn, olives, grapes, tobacco, coffee, sugarcane, cocoa, rice, indigo, cochineal, pimento, India rubber, and henequen. He also estimated

---

26. *Mexican Times*, October 14, 1865; *New York Herald*, October 24, 1865; House Executive Documents, Diplomatic Correspondence, pt. 3, 39th Cong., 2nd sess., 212.

27. Carl Coke Rister, "Carlotta, a Confederate Colony in Mexico," *Journal of Southern History* 11 (February 1945): 40–41.

28. House Executive Documents, Diplomatic Correspondence, pt. 3, 39th Cong., 2nd sess., 205.

29. Ibid., 208–9; *Mexican Times*, December 2, 1865.

that the land value might rise as high as one hundred dollars per acre,[30] and another optimistic settler predicted that in a short time Carlotta "will be as large as Richmond or New Orleans."[31]

Among the hundreds of new immigrants who streamed into Mexico were Magruder's wife, his youngest daughter, Kate Elizabeth, and son, Henry. They had sailed on an English packet from London to Vera Cruz via Havana, finally reaching their destination in early March 1866.[32] Magruder had not seen any of his family for over five years and would not see his eldest daughter, Isabella, who lived in Baltimore with her husband, Dr. Riggin Buckler, for several more months. Shortly after Henrietta and the children disembarked, Magruder brought them from Vera Cruz to Mexico City, where they occupied a "roomy and comfortable house" a short distance from the land office. Theirs was "an uncomfortable and tedious journey," wrote Major Alfred Mordecai, a West Point graduate and prominent railroad engineer then working in Mexico City. Mrs. Magruder was ill; consequently, Mordecai reported having seen only the children, both of whom made "favorable impression[s], especially the daughter, quite [*sic*] and lady like tho' not at all handsome."[33] After Henrietta regained her strength, the Magruders hosted a ball in their newly furnished home.[34] Major Mordecai wrote that both of the Magruder children were "very good musicians."[35] And another guest, former governor Henry Watkins Allen of Louisiana, declared that Kate Elizabeth "has the finest voice out of Italy": "She is a prodigy, and sings better than any Prima Donna I ever heard."[36] Young Henry became an admirer of Maximilian and distinguished himself by becoming a *chevalier de l'ordre de guadaloupe* in the

30. House Executive Documents, Diplomatic Correspondence, pt. 3, 39th Cong., 2nd sess., 209–12; Charles Lee Lewis, *Matthew Fontaine Maury: The Pathfinder of the Seas* (Annapolis: U.S. Naval Institute, 1927), 198.

31. *New York Herald*, January 17, 1866.

32. Bee to Mann, March 3, 1866, San Jacinto Museum of History.

33. Padgett, "Life of Alfred Mordecai in Mexico," *North Carolina Historical Review* 23 (January 1946): 85. In a letter, Mordecai to his wife, March 15, 1866.

34. Ibid., 95. Letter, Mordecai to his sister, April 20, 1866.

35. Ibid., 93. Letter, Mordecai to his sister, April 18, 1866.

36. Allen to Mrs. Sarah A. Dorsey, April 2 and 7, 1866, in Dorsey, *Recollections of Henry Watkins Allen,* 354–55. Allen, former governor of Louisiana and a close friend of Magruder's, edited the *Mexican Times,* an English-language newspaper subsidized by the imperial government. After Allen died, on April 22, 1866, Magruder, Beverly Tucker, and John N. Edwards continued publication operations. Magruder wrote several editorials and reportedly displayed "much aptitude for his new profession" (*New York Herald*, July 10, 1866), but Edwards eventually took over all of the paper's operations until it was sold in late November 1866 to E. C. Barksdale.

emperor's service. Although the Magruders were most accomplished people, Mordecai surmised that they were "not the sort of people to enjoy the novelties of Mexico," and he did not predict a lengthy stay for them.[37]

None of the former Confederates were destined to remain long in Mexico. On April 10, 1866, Richard L. Maury, who was acting commissioner of colonization while his father was in England, reported that Federal authorities had refused to permit Mexican colonization agents to operate in the United States,[38] and while the government was discreetly prohibiting any advertising or recruiting, the press of both the North and South was distinctly hostile. The January 19, 1866, *New York Times* contained a report entitled "Interview with Seedy Southern Exiles—Failure of Southern Emigration Scheme," in which a correspondent wrote:

> At Cordova we had a look at some of those great and mighty Southerners who have sold four thousand Southern families to the empire. The Emperor, however, begins to smell a rat, and begins to see that Maury, Price, and Magruder have humbugged him. The four thousand families have not been delivered according to bargain—not even one thousand, not even one hundred, not even fifty. The poor fellows looked seedy enough and I could not help pitying them as they in turn mounted a poor down-trodden pony. They had one horse between four. Indeed the ways of a sinner are hard.[39]

Even Jefferson Davis reportedly spoke out against his countrymen who fled reconstruction.[40] He encouraged them, instead, to accept the results of the war as a fait accompli and to apply for their pardons following the example of Robert E. Lee.

In the face of such opposition it became increasingly difficult to attract southerners into Mexico, while at the same time many of the earlier colonists, having become disillusioned, were returning to their former homes. Those who remained, determined to make their settlements successful, were

---

37. Padgett, "Life of Alfred Mordecai in Mexico," *North Carolina Historical Review* 23 (January 1946): 85. In a letter, Mordecai to his wife, March 15, 1866. A month later, on April 18, 1866, Major Mordecai observed in a letter to his sister that "the ladies & young Henry, who have lived almost always, in Europe are not at all charmed with Mex[ico]." Ibid., 93.

38. Maury to O'Neal, April 10, 1866, House Executive Documents, Diplomatic correspondence, Mexican Affairs, 39th Cong., 2nd sess., 527–28.

39. *New York Times,* January 19, 1866.

40. John J. Craven, *Prison Life of Jefferson Davis Embracing Details and Incidents of His Captivity, Particulars Concerning His Health and Habits, Together with Many Conversations on Topics of Great Public Interest* (New York: Carleton, 1866), 200–201.

to be victimized by the decision of Napoleon III to withdraw French support of Maximilian's government. When Napoleon signed the order, under pressure from Secretary of State Seward, Magruder grimly judged that he had "affixed a stain upon the honor of France which will remain there through all time." Within a short time "internal improvements, colonization, public schools, and charities were all given up . . . Bands of men appeared in all parts of the country, who captured poor native Indians at the plow, and hurried them into the ranks of the Liberal Party. Each robber chief or Liberal Captain left his guitar, fandango, and monte table and hastened toward a common centre, to be in at the death and to get his share of the spoils and power. Backed thus by the United States, Juárez, who up to this moment was a mere cipher, became a formidable power."[41]

Maximilian was forced "by motives of economy" to close the Imperial Commission of Colonization on April 19, 1866.[42] Magruder was out of a job, and Confederate colonization was ended. But as late as June 17 Magruder wrote to a friend that his relations with the emperor were cordial and that he considered himself "under obligations to him for doing kindness to me, to my family, and to my countrymen."[43] The government continued to deteriorate, however, particularly after Napoleon III began withdrawing French troops. Within a short time Magruder's attitude changed radically. "The Imperial Government has gone to hell," he declared, "and we have got to be away from here."[44]

Shortly before Magruder departed Mexico City, on November 1, 1866, Marshal Bazaine induced him to treat with President Andrew Johnson regarding the transition of power from Maximilian to the Juáristas. Bazaine said that "the moral influence wielded by the government of the United States has destroyed this empire" and that it was their responsibility to ensure that the new government "shall secure the protection of life and property, and the tranquility of this people." He further stated that someone had to protect the foreigners who remained and suggested that "ten or fifteen thousand United States troops, properly distributed in the northern States, and a similar number of French troops in the southern States, cooperating with each other could accomplish this."[45]

41. "Magruder Narrative," *New York Times Magazine.*

42. Maximilian to Maury, April 19, 1866, vol. 25 in Maury Papers, Library of Cong., 51 vols.

43. Magruder to Snead, June 17, 1866, Historical Society of Pennsylvania, Philadelphia.

44. *New Orleans Picayune,* July 4, 1866; *New York Herald,* July 4, 1866.

45. Campbell to Seward, November 21, 1866, House Executive Doc. 30, 40th Cong., 1st sess., 11–12.

Magruder reached Havana with his family on November 17 and there gave Bazaine's message to Lewis D. Campbell, a representative of the U.S. government who was on his way to Mexico with General William T. Sherman to establish contact with Benito Juárez. Immediately after the interview with Magruder, Campbell relayed the confidential message to Seward. He closed it by stating that Magruder "was sincere, and . . . desired in good faith to serve the interests of the government," but that he could not then journey to Washington personally because of the death of his attorney, John Van Buren, and for "other causes" that might detain him "for some time."[46]

Van Buren's death no doubt delayed Magruder's obtaining a pardon. The "other causes" refer, however, to his difficulty in working out a satisfactory modus vivendi with his wife, who desired to return to Europe. But Magruder, not wishing another exile, refused to go. Instead, he remained in Cuba for several weeks,[47] visiting Bee and other friends, while Henrietta, Kate Elizabeth, and Henry returned to the Continent in November 1866, living first in Paris, then in Rome and Florence. He never saw them again.

John Magruder returned to the United States early in 1867. He visited briefly with his married daughter, Isabella, in Baltimore and then moved to New York City, where he opened a law practice.[48] He received a cold welcome. On August 19 the *New York Times* reported that Magruder had been treated roughly at the New York Stock Exchange—and justifiably so. The paper blasted him for trying to "fire the Southern heart anew" in speeches to his men after Lee and others had surrendered in the East and for fleeing to Mexico "to live under the yoke of a foreign usurpation rather than as a citizen of the old Republic." The *Times* concluded, "General Magruder's own record is the reason for his unpopularity here."[49]

The article received Magruder's immediate reply. He deemed the criticism unwarranted and angrily charged that some of the allegations were completely false:

> So many misrepresentations have been made lately regarding me, that I deem it right to say that I was not at the Stock Exchange . . . that I do not know where that institution is; that I did my duty in attempting to keep up the spirit of the troops under my command until my commanding officer had decided

46. Ibid., 12.
47. *New York Herald,* December 13, 1866.
48. *New York Times,* February 13, 1867.
49. Ibid., August 19, 1867.

on surrender [and] by the terms of that surrender, the commissioned officers of the Trans Mississippi department were allowed to select their residence within or without the limits of the United States.

I will further state that upon the surrender of the Trans Mississippi department, I published an order—probably the last of the war—condemning in the strongest terms the formation of guerrilla parties, and urging all to support the laws and obey the orders of the United States' authorities with an honest, zealous and loyal spirit.[50]

When on January 17, 1868, Magruder voluntarily presented himself in the clerk's office of the U.S. District Court and swore his allegiance to the government,[51] the critics were silenced.

Several months later General Magruder journeyed to White Sulphur Springs, West Virginia, where Lee and other leading former Confederate soldiers and politicians occasionally gathered during the summer months. There, along with Lee, he found Alexander H. Stephens, P. G. T. Beauregard, former governor John Letcher of Virginia, James Lyons of Richmond, and others of greater or less renown. In the last week of August, General William S. Rosecrans, former commander of the Union Army of the Cumberland but now a politician, arrived seeking the endorsement of prominent southerners for Horatio Seymour, the Democratic presidential aspirant. Rosecrans consulted with Lee, who called a meeting of those present to discuss and consider support of a statement to the effect that the South accepted the results of the war and emancipation but opposed the exercise of political power by freedmen. A statement was prepared and signed by Lee and thirty-one others, but Magruder's name does not appear among the signatories,[52] probably because of a desire to steer clear of potentially controversial political involvements.[53]

Magruder, however, seemed to attract both attention and controversy regardless of his intentions. After returning to New York City, he and another

50. "Card from General J. B. Magruder [to the editor]," ibid., August 20, 1867.

51. *New York Herald*, January 18, 1868.

52. The statement with signators was published in the *New York Times*, September 5, 1868. The statement, without signators, is in Alexander F. Robertson, *Alexander Hugh Holmes Stuart, 1807–1891* (Richmond: William Byrd Press, 1925), 261–63; and Freeman, *R. E. Lee*, 4:375–77. Magruder's presence in White Sulphur Springs is established by his appearance in an often-reproduced photograph, which can be found in Roy Meredith, *The Faces of Robert E. Lee in Life and in Legend* (New York: Charles Scribner's Sons, 1947), 84–85.

53. Magruder to editor, *Philadelphia Evening Telegraph*, May 8, 1870, in *New York Times*, May 23, 1870; *Army and Navy Journal* 7 (June 1870): 663.

former Confederate, General Edward Higgins, were arrested on October 23 for disturbing the peace in a store at 677 Broadway. The two spent the night in jail and early the next morning were brought to the Jefferson Market Police Court for a formal hearing. The store manager, Elisha H. Wildey, charged that they had "conducted themselves in a manner decidedly ungentlemanly, insulting the lady attendants and preventing by disparaging remarks the sale of goods on exhibition." The complainant testified further that when he confronted them, Higgins had indignantly asked if he knew to whom he was talking—that "his companion was General Magruder." Higgins "raised his cane and threatened to annihilate" Wildey when Officer Rae arrived, arrested the two troublemaking southerners, and jailed them at the Fifteenth Precinct Station House. In court Magruder steadfastly denied all charges and vowed to Judge Ledwith that he and his companion were visiting the store on legitimate business. He acknowledged having addressed the ladies present about several articles of Bohemian origin on sale but assured the judge that "nothing was said that could offend the most refined and fastidious lady alive." Ledwith listened patiently but ruled for the plaintiff, Wildey. Magruder and Higgins were put under bonds of three hundred dollars each "to keep the peace for six months." As there was no one in court to enter the assessed payment, both men were remanded to their cells until bondsmen arrived later in the morning. Shortly before noon, Mrs. Rose Andrews entered the court and gave the required surety for General Higgins, and soon afterward Daniel Mabens paid for Magruder. Not long after Magruder was released from jail, he left New York and never returned.[54]

Magruder established himself in New Orleans at Camp and Gravier streets in an office provided to him by Captain Edward C. Wharton, who had formerly served as his assistant quartermaster in the Trans-Mississippi Department. The general then embarked on a lecture tour, and Wharton, the proprietor of a news agency, served as his agent. On February 10, 1869, Magruder wrote to a friend in New Orleans, sending "complimentary tickets to my lecture tomorrow night." He added, "Though I have rheumatism or gout, my head is clear and my spirit good and I hope I may be able to compensate those who do me the honor to attend."[55] The subject of this lecture,

54. *New York Herald,* October 25, 1868. The store was located in the Southern Hotel, a popular postwar rendezvous for many former Confederates.

55. Magruder to Mrs. Maltby, February 10, 1869, in Edward Clifton Wharton and Family Papers, Louisiana State University.

subsequently repeated in Boston, Baltimore, Richmond, Mobile, Galveston, Houston, and perhaps elsewhere, was "Maximilian and Carlotta." An "unpublished narrative" of the subject by Magruder appeared in the *New York Times Magazine,* April 2, 1916, at about the height of the Mexican border troubles of that period. General Magruder spoke kindly of the well-intentioned emperor and his ambitious wife and judged that they were genuinely concerned about the welfare of Mexico and its people. He also spent considerable time at the lectern chronicling the financial commitments, economic accomplishments, and sociopolitical reforms that Maximilian's regime had championed. In summary, Magruder surmised, "could Maximilian have maintained his Government within ten years Mexico . . . would have completely regenerated. He would have aided in giving her a republican form of government suited to her interests. She would have enjoyed real liberty and prosperity, and would have become either a valuable neighbor to the United States or an integral part of the Union."[56]

On the lecture circuit John Magruder returned to familiar ground. Armed with a classical education, a superb command of the English language, and keen political acumen, he was a natural at the podium. His speech was powerful and compelling when necessary, yet on other occasions it reflected unusual gentility and sensitivity. As one observer put it, "To the sting of the bee he added the honey of the clover."[57] Even the lisp, a liability for most orators, became an asset for Magruder as it lingered over its puns, caressed its rhetoric, and emphasized points of importance.[58] He had studied French in Paris, Italian in Rome, and Spanish in the halls of the Montezumas and was well versed in international affairs. Caleb Forshey claimed that his former commander "could deal with princes, potentates and governments . . . with the hand of a master." Magruder's foreign experience and political expertise, combined with his oratorical talents, resulted in lectures that were, in Forshey's opinion, "matchless."[59] Indeed, Prince John Magruder became the "darling of the lecture platform."[60]

The inaugural lecture in New Orleans on February 11, 1869, was well attended and generously applauded, as might have been expected when the

56. "Magruder Narrative," *New York Times Magazine.*

57. "John Bankhead Magruder," vertical file, Center for the Study of American History, University of Texas, Austin.

58. Edwards, *Shelby's Expedition to Mexico,* 20.

59. *New Orleans Times,* March 19, 1871.

60. O'Flaherty, *General Jo Shelby,* 229.

speaker was a colorful, well-known former Confederate general lecturing in a southern venue less than four years after the Civil War came to an end. However, the real magnitude of John Magruder's oratorical magic was revealed less than a month after the New Orleans address, when he journeyed to Boston and spoke to an understandably less receptive crowd. A local reporter who covered the event wrote that those in attendance greeted the rebel general with "a hospitable amount of applause," but many were skeptical. They came with "half-formed prejudices," expecting to hear a "bombastic" speech full of "oratorical extravagances and absurdities" from a defiant, unreformed southern fire-eater. Instead, General Magruder charmed his audience by making "very graceful reference to the time before the war when he was stationed in Boston." Then he eased into his lecture, shifting the focus to Maximilian and Carlotta. In the end those who heard him were unanimously "impressed with his simplicity, dignity, and sense."[61]

While in Boston, Magruder was approached by Isaac Burrell, commander of the 42nd Massachusetts Infantrymen during the Battle of Galveston. As he was still being criticized for the loss of his position and surrender of his men, Burrell asked Magruder for a written vindication of his actions.[62] The always gracious Magruder complied with the request, assuring his former prisoner that "no military man of whatever rank or experience could have made better arrangements and displayed more ability and courage than you and your troops did in the face of the most trying and embarrassing situations that I have ever seen officers and men placed in."[63] In a reciprocal show of respect and gratitude Colonel Burrell and his men treated Magruder with such courtesy while in Boston that he later reported "the fighting element in the North was ready and anxious to forget past differences, and had extended to him the right hand of fellowship on all occasions."[64]

After the successful tour stop in Boston, Magruder accepted an invitation to lecture in Baltimore on March 20, 1869.[65] More important, the trip to Baltimore allowed him the opportunity to visit his eldest daughter, Isabella,

61. William Norris Scrapbook, Norris Family Papers, Alderman Library Archives, University of Virginia.

62. Edward T. Cotham Jr., *Battle on the Bay: The Civil War Struggle for Galveston* (Austin: University of Texas Press, 1998), 187.

63. Magruder to Isaac Burrell, Boston, October 24, 1869, Autograph Collection, MOLLUS—Massachusetts Commandery Collection, 3:214, U.S. Military History Institute, Carlisle Barracks, Pa.

64. *Galveston Tri-Weekly News,* May 11, 1870.

65. *Baltimore American and Commercial Advertiser,* March 16 and 20, 1869; William Norris Scrapbook, Norris Family Papers, Alderman Library Archives, University of Virginia.

her husband, Dr. Riggin Buckler, and their five young children, Lilly, Nelly, Isabel, Matilda, and Thomas. Because neither Kate Elizabeth nor Henry ever married, these were Magruder's only grandchildren. Unfortunately, during the visit Isabella, who had often been ill in the past, again fell victim to deteriorating health. Dr. Buckler, General Magruder, and the Buckler children comforted and encouraged Isabella but to no avail. She died on July 20, 1869, at thirty-five years of age.[66]

The loss of Isabella, the absence of his wife and two remaining children, and Magruder's own fragile health seemed to have a debilitating effect on the general, as he did not return to his lectures until early 1870. On March 2, 1870, he spoke in New Orleans and in Mobile three weeks later, on March 23.[67] When news of the resurrected lecture tour reached Galveston through the newspapers, several prominent Texans, his good friend and former governor Francis R. Lubbock among them, and other old comrades, including Xavier Debray, Oscar Watkins, Sydney Fontaine, and Caleb Forshey, invited Magruder to return to speak in the city that he had once saved "from the desolations of invading armies." The twelve signatories of the flowery invitational letter stated, "We would be most happy . . . to receive you in the spirit with which we served in your command." When Magruder was assured that everywhere in the Lone Star State "you would find friends and welcome,"[68] he put his affairs in order, packed his few belongings, and gleefully headed for Texas.

On Thursday, May 5, 1870, the *Galveston Daily News* reported that General Magruder "arrived in the city this morning, looking in excellent health and spirits."[69] After receiving countless friends and visitors at his temporary residence in the Exchange Hotel, Prince John announced through the local newspapers that he would deliver his lecture on "Mexico, Maximilian and Carlotta" at Casino Hall on the evening of May 9. The *News* informed its readers that "the general has appeared in the capacity of lecturer before some of the most critical audiences in the country, and the verdict invariably has

66. *Baltimore American and Commercial Advertiser,* July 23, 1869.

67. Magruder to Wharton, February 20, 1870, Edward Clifton Wharton and Family Papers, Louisiana State University.

68. Lubbock et al. to Magruder, February 26, 1870. Edward Clifton Wharton and Family Papers, Louisiana State University; *Galveston Daily News,* March 11, 1870. The page containing the Magruder material is incorrectly dated Friday, March 10, 1870, when the date was actually Friday, March 11, 1870. Magruder accepted the invitation to return to Galveston in a letter dated March 6, 1870. Both the letter of invitation and the letter of acceptance appear in the *Galveston Daily News,* March 11, 1870.

69. *Galveston Daily News,* May 5, 1870.

been most complimentary. Here, where he has so many friends and admirers, his success is not a matter of doubt."[70] A later edition of the newspaper predicted that "the hall will certainly be crowded" and warned that "those who expect favorable locations will have to put in an early appearance."[71]

Casino Hall was indeed packed to capacity. Among the attendees were many who had earlier been a part of Magruder's military family in Texas: generals Xavier DeBray and Sidney Sherman, Colonel Thomas Jack, and majors Oscar Watkins and E. B. Pendleton. Magruder was so pleased with the reception that he revealed to the audience his intentions of becoming a citizen of Texas and to reside within its borders for the remainder of his existence. Then he delivered his often repeated lecture in a fashion that the *Galveston Tri-Weekly News* described as "masterly."[72] A week later, on May 16, 1870, General Magruder lectured in Houston and was similarly acclaimed.[73]

On June 14 sixteen leading Galvestonians sent Magruder a letter asking him to repeat his lecture in their city, declaring that "many of those who heard your recent lecture desire to hear it again, and many who were prevented, from various causes, from attending then, are anxious to have the opportunity of hearing it."[74] Magruder graciously accepted and once again did not disappoint. Following the speech the *Galveston Tri-Weekly News* wrote, "Either Gen. Magruder is personally popular beyond all precedent or his story of 'Mexico, Maximilian and Carlotta' is one of intense interest [because] Turner Hall was well filled, and no audience ever left a lecture room better pleased with the entertainment served out to them."[75] The June 17, 1870, lecture was Magruder's last. He then triumphantly departed Galveston for Houston, just as he had seven years earlier after winning his last battle.

In Houston General Magruder moved into the luxurious Hutchins House as the honored guest of the owner, Captain Edmund P. Turner, who had formerly been his adjutant in Texas and later followed him to Mexico. The four-story brick structure ranked as "one of the best hotels in the South."[76]

70. Ibid., May 6, 1870.

71. Ibid., May 8, 1870.

72. *Galveston Tri-Weekly News*, May 11, 1870.

73. Ibid., May 18, 1870.

74. *Galveston Daily News*, June 15, 1870.

75. *Galveston Tri-Weekly News*, June 19, 1870.

76. *The Industrial Advantages of Houston, Texas and Environs, Also a Series of Comprehensive Sketches of the City's Representative Business Enterprises* (Houston: Akehurst Publishing Co., 1894), 87.

The *Galveston Tri-Weekly News* described the Hutchins House as "magnificent."[77] Another publication reported every accommodation that administered to the comfort and convenience of guests was provided, and the house was thoroughly equipped and furnished in first-class style. There were richly appointed parlors; reading, billiard, and bar rooms; excellent cuisine; plus, "the most elegant Turkish and Russian baths in the South are in this hotel."[78] The Hutchins House was also "made famous by the fact that most of the State associations, societies, and many of the large commercial enterprises had their inception in its parlors."[79] It was precisely the type of venue where John Magruder, the prince of society, would have reigned supreme.

Unfortunately, Magruder was destined to reside in the comforts of the Hutchins House for only a short time. As the seasons changed and the weather worsened, his health began steadily to decline. On February 17 he told his attendant, "I don't think I am long for this world." Later in the evening Major W. B. Cobb, who had served under Magruder in Virginia, stopped by to see his former commander before retiring but found him speechless and breathing heavily. Cobb immediately alerted Captain Turner and went in search of Dr. Louis A. Bryan. Magruder did not speak a word after Turner's arrival, although the attendant said that he had been talking unintelligibly for several hours. In a short time his breathing grew easy, and it was believed that he was sleeping. But it was the sleep of death—Magruder died early in the morning of February 18, 1871, and his burial followed immediately afterward, on Sunday, February 19.[80]

There was no display at the funeral. Magruder was arrayed in plain black clothing without the insignia of military rank. The Reverend Mr. Trader performed the funeral solemnities at the Episcopal church, after which a string of carriages escorted the body to the old Masonic Cemetery in Houston, then

77. *Galveston Tri-Weekly News*, June 13, 1870.

78. *Industrial Advantages of Houston, Texas*, 87.

79. Dr. S. O. Young, *A Thumb-Nail History of the City of Houston, Texas from Its Founding in 1836 to the Year 1912* (Houston: Rein and Sons Press, 1912), 50. Among the associations formed in Houston at about the time that Magruder relocated there was the Texas State Historical Society. It was organized on May 20, 1870, and almost all of its officers had served under Magruder when he was commander in Texas during the Civil War. The original officers were Colonel Ashbel Smith, president; General Sidney Sherman, first vice president; P. W. Gray, registrar; Captain Farmer, recording secretary; Captain Edmund P. Turner, corresponding secretary; and Major Benjamin A. Botts, treasurer. *Galveston Tri-Weekly News*, May 25, 1870.

80. *Galveston Daily News*, February 21 and 24, 1871; *Houston Telegraph*, February 19, 1871; *New York Herald*, February 20 and 21, 1871; *New York Times*, February 20, 1871.

located between the junction of Bagby and McKinney streets and Buffalo Bayou. At journey's end, pallbearers Major Benjamin A. Botts, Dr. Bryan, Colonel L. Lorgescope, Colonel E. H. Cushing, E. W. Burke, Colonel [?] Shannon, John Shean, Robert Brewster, and Captain Turner brought their charge to a lot jointly owned by Captain Fritz Mohl and the late Colonel T. B. J. Hadley. In Captain Mohl's half of the lot, Prince John Magruder was laid to rest in a fine metallic coffin.[81]

Journalistic inaccuracy and controversy unfortunately followed Magruder to his grave. The *Houston Telegraph,* in its Sunday, February 19, edition, implied that the general had "died alone and neglected in the garret of the Hutchins House."[82] Two days later the *New York Herald* repeated the misinformation in an article entitled "The Late General Magruder—Magruder's Last Hours—A Sad Scene—Alone with Death—His Demise Unexpected." Both newspapers incorrectly reported that Magruder was buried in Houston's Episcopal Cemetery.[83] Aurelia H. Mohl, the wife of Fritz Mohl, wrote to the *Telegraph* and identified the Masonic Cemetery as the correct burial site, and such was noted by the *Telegraph* in its Tuesday, February 21, 1871, edition.[84] More important, the *Galveston News* endeavored to correct the erroneous information that the *Telegraph* had published indicating Magruder had died under pitiful circumstances.

On February 24, in an article entitled "How General Magruder Died," the *News* reported that one of its correspondents had personally been in Houston at the Hutchins House "at the time of the General's death, and for a long time previous to the sad event." Far from being neglected, Magruder had lived in "one of the best gentleman's apartments" in the Hutchins House and had been treated with as much consideration as any guest in the hotel. The *News* correspondent also stated that Dr. Bryan, as well as several of the employees of the hotel, had regularly attended to Magruder in his room.[85] And Captain Turner, who reportedly loved his former commander "as a son should his father," was with Prince John to the bitter end.[86]

81. Obituaries in *Galveston Daily News,* February 21, 1871; *New York Herald,* February 21, 1871; *Virginia Herald,* February 23, 1871.

82. *Galveston Daily News,* February 24, 1871; *Houston Telegraph,* February 19, 1871.

83. *New York Herald,* February 21, 1871; *Houston Telegraph,* February 19, 1871.

84. *Houston Telegraph,* February 21, 1871.

85. *Galveston Daily News,* February 24, 1871.

86. Ibid., February 21, 1871. In Texas the *Galveston News* did an admirable job of informing its readers that General Magruder had died comfortably, with dignity, and in the presence of

On March 2, 1871, the *Galveston News* again came to General Magruder's defense after the *New York Tribune* slandered him and defiled his memory in the obituary notice that it published on February 20, 1871.[87] The *News* reprinted the entire obituary as it had appeared in the *Tribune* and termed it "low-flung and hateful . . . revengeful and spiteful."[88]

The *New York Tribune* obituary painted Magruder as a traitor. The *Tribune* reported that after declaring his fidelity to President Lincoln, he defected to Richmond as soon as he received all of the money due him. The piece credited Magruder for having held Yorktown "with a ridiculously inferior force" but then stated that "he was thrashed soundly by Hooker and Kearney nearly all the way from Yorktown to Williamsburg." Afterward, according to the *Tribune,* the rebel general appeared only at intervals in the records of the rebellion. There was no mention of Magruder's recapture of Galveston or of any other service in Texas. Instead, the obituary abruptly ended by stating, "Soon after the war closed he was arrested for disturbance in this city, and was committed to Ludlow Street Jail."[89]

The editorial staff of the *Galveston News* was outraged. The *News* termed the *Tribune*'s article "an indecent obituary" and charged that through "petty meanness and womanish spitefulness" the *Tribune* had failed to chronicle either Magruder's heroism in the Mexican War or his faithful service in the Federal army. Furthermore, the *News* rhetorically asked, "Where is the evidence that General Magruder ever protested fidelity to President Lincoln?" It answered that there was not an ounce of testimony showing that he ever induced Mr. Lincoln to suppose that he would remain committed to the Union if his native state, Virginia, seceded. The *News* also pointed out that Magruder's command was not engaged with Hooker, Kearney, or anyone else after the evacuation of Yorktown until the Battle of Fair Oaks, and consequently he was not "soundly thrashed all the way from Yorktown to Williamsburg." Finally, the *News* referred to the report of Magruder's arrest in New York as "abominable." "He was arrested and confined for a few hours,"

---

friends. But elsewhere the report that the general had died under unenviable circumstances was more widely circulated and accepted as fact. From Richmond John F. Lee, cousin of Robert E. Lee, wrote to a friend, "When I read the account of his [Magruder's] solitary neglected death in a tavern in Texas—'in the worst inn's worst room' . . . I could feel but sad." J. F. Lee to unknown (1871?), Lee Family Papers, Virginia Historical Society Library.

87. *New York Tribune,* February 20, 1871.
88. *Galveston Daily News,* March 2, 1871.
89. *New York Tribune,* February 20, 1871.

said the *News,* when, in fact, "General Magruder did nothing but resent an affront offered to a friend."[90]

The *Galveston News* defended Magruder as a gentleman of honor, nobility, and integrity: "When a great journal like the *Tribune,* when a great editor like Mr. Greeley, infuses into the obituary notice of a dead general such spleen and such venom, we may well hide our faces for the disgrace of journalism . . . any living ass can kick the dead lion." The journalistic misdeeds of the *New York Tribune* were classless and callused. Contrariwise, the *News* declared, "There is not in all Texas a single reputable Democratic journal that will attack a dead man's memory, much less throw nasty filth upon his grave."[91]

Shortly after Magruder's death and burial in Houston, the citizens of Galveston, "mindful of [his] splendid military achievements . . . and grateful for the courage and genius displayed by him in saving their soil from invasion and their property from pillage," initiated a campaign to have the body returned to the island, reburied, and memorialized by a grand monument.[92] Major Oscar M. Watkins chaired the subcommittee that corresponded with Mrs. Magruder and her two surviving children, Katherine Elizabeth and Henry. Once Watkins had procured their blessings to have the general's remains removed to Galveston, he journeyed to Houston and showed the correspondence to the Mohl family, who readily agreed and courteously complied with the specified wishes of Mrs. Magruder and her children.[93]

On Friday morning, January 7, 1876, James Sorley, chairman of the Executive Committee, traveled from Galveston to Houston to supervise the removal of General Magruder's remains. At 11:00 a.m. the body was disinterred. At 6:00 p.m. there was a procession through Houston's Main Street. Then the remains were brought to Galveston on the 8:25 p.m. train, escorted by Chairman Sorley; C. C. Beavens, Galveston's assistant fire chief; and a detail of the Lone Star Rifles under the command of Lieutenant Hurxthall. When the train arrived, at midnight, General X. B. Debray, chairman of the Committee on Arrangements, and Captain Weekes of the Lone Star Rifles

90. *Galveston Daily News,* March 2, 1871.

91. Ibid.

92. Circular letter from the Magruder Monumental Association to the Citizens of Texas, January 1, 1876, ibid., January 8, 1876.

93. Ibid., January 6, 1876; Debray, "Sketch of Debray's Twenty-sixth Regiment of Texas Cavalry," 552–53.

escorted the casket to the Galveston Artillery Armory, where a guard of honor was posted for the night.[94]

Shortly after 11:00 a.m. on Monday, January 10, the procession moved from the armory along Avenue I to Tremont Street, onto Broadway, then to the corner of Bath Avenue, where a large stand had been erected for the ceremony. Former Texas governor Francis R. Lubbock organized and supervised the procession, which included mounted policemen, 150 uniformed firemen, the Lone Star Band, Lone Star Rifles, Island City Rifles, Cadet Brass Band, the mayor and members of the Board of Aldermen, and other city officials, judges of the Supreme Court, attorney general, clerks of the Supreme Court, members of the Executive Committee, various additional state and federal governmental officials, and a huge crowd of local citizens. Among Magruder's pallbearers were such prominent military figures as generals Braxton Bragg, Xavier B. Debray, Felix Robertson, Thomas N. Waul, William P. Hardeman, Mathew D. Ector, Jerome B. Robertson, John S. "Rip" Ford, and leading Galvestonians, including Robert G. Street, Thomas M. Jack, Mart H. Royston, Henry W. Rhodes, William H. Nichols, M. C. McLemore, Leslie Thompson, and J. Maynard Smith.[95]

When the procession reached its destination, distinguished guests, including the orator, Lieutenant Governor (later Governor) Richard B. Hubbard, the Reverend Doctor Robert F. Bunting, and Reverend Stephen M. Bird, were escorted to the stand. Dr. Bunting delivered the opening prayer. Hubbard then meticulously recalled the deeds and accomplishments of John Magruder to an admiring, appreciative audience, many of whom had known the general well. Lieutenant Governor Hubbard made it clear that his intention was not to perpetuate sectional strife or rekindle any bitter feelings of the past but, rather, "to pay our respects as citizens of a great and glorious nation to the memory of one whom we have loved and revered in the past." The respects were paid with such passion and eloquence that observers, some weeping, others rejoicing, frequently interrupted Hubbard's address with spontaneous, heartfelt applause.[96]

At the conclusion of Hubbard's oration, the processional line was reestablished and advanced to the Episcopal Cemetery where the remains were

94. *Galveston Daily News*, January 7 and 11, 1876.

95. Ibid., January 11, 1876.

96. Ibid.

taken from the hearse and placed in a private vault. The coffin was covered with flags, bouquets of flowers, and a beautiful shield of white silk on which was worked with evergreens and flowers the words "Virginia's Gallant Son, Our Texas Hero." Reverend Bird pronounced the benediction, and the processioners returned to their site of origination at the armory.[97]

The ceremony marking the final return of John Magruder to Galveston was well organized and flawlessly executed. However, the final chapter, erecting the monument to memorialize forever the deeds of the gallant general, took quite some time to materialize. For eighteen years Magruder's body lay in a temporary vault in Cahill's Mortuary, "begging for a grave,"[98] while solicitors sought funds for the purchase of a cemetery plot and monument for the gravesite. One fund-raiser, sponsored by the Magruder United Confederate Veterans Post No. 105, netted only $33.85.[99] Fortunately, others were more fruitful. Memorial fund organizers eventually bought a lot in Galveston's Trinity Episcopal Cemetery and commissioned the Ott Monument Works to produce a fitting memorial.[100]

Charles Sebastian Ott designed the monument, but his talented seventeen-year-old son, John, was its sculptor. The base was carved from eastern gray granite, the die from American marble, and the eighteen-foot-high superstructure from Italian marble. The elder Ott incorporated elements of size, strength, and elegance into his design, all reflective of the qualities of General Magruder. On each of the sides of the plinth were exquisitely carved representations of the four branches of the service—cavalry, artillery, infantry, and navy. And an ornately sculpted Confederate flag, whose stars and bars were easily discernible, was draped over the top of the spire.[101]

The ceremony to dedicate the monument took place on Saturday, April 7, 1894. A procession at Tremont and Post Office streets began at 2:30 p.m. and marched from Tremont to Broadway and then to the Episcopal Cemetery—

97. Ibid.

98. Debray, "Sketch of Debray's Twenty-sixth Regiment of Texas Cavalry," 553.

99. Thomas G. Rice, "Man Who Beat Yank Navy Finally Got His Gravestone," *Galveston Daily News*, April 5, 1959.

100. When Kate Elizabeth Magruder died in Italy on April 26, 1896, she designated in her will that five hundred dollars be allotted to pay for her father's tombstone, unaware of the fact that the citizens of Galveston had properly honored him with a handsome memorial two years earlier.

101. *Galveston Daily News*, April 8, 1894. The Magruder monument is located in lot no. 7, sec. no. 2, near the intersection of 40th Street and Avenue K. Its only flaw is that the general's birth date is incorrectly reported as 1808. Magruder was born on May 1, 1807.

a twenty-two-block march, one and seven-tenths miles long. In addition to those in the procession, some five hundred to six hundred people were waiting at the cemetery when the procession arrived. The same Reverend Bird who had delivered the benediction eighteen years earlier offered the opening prayer, and General Thomas N. Waul delivered the featured speech, the entire text of which was published in the *Galveston Daily News* on Sunday, April 8, 1894. Waul said in part: "With joy do we hail the dedication of this monument. We glory in the rectitude of the cause and exult in the valor and knightly qualities of the hero, John Bankhead Magruder . . . as gallant a soldier and as intrepid a hero as ever drew sword in liberty's cause. Educated to arms, stately in person, with distinguished presence and princely bearing, courtly in manner, chivalric in action, he was every inch a soldier of the truest type." At the appropriate moment Miss Lilian Walker unveiled the monument. According to the *News*, "A great hush came over those assembled . . . and heads were bowed and hats were lifted in humble tribute of love and respect."[102]

Near the end of the ceremony, Colonel Robert G. Street followed General Waul at the speaker's stand. He reminded spectators of Galveston's role in the Civil War. Street pointed out that on August 21, 1861, the ladies of Galveston had presented the men of the Lone Star Rifles with a silk battle flag to carry with them into Virginia. At that time the Lone Star Rifles were 120 strong. "Of this number," said Colonel Street reverently, "there are today only three who survive." Street then unfurled the very flag that those gallant young soldiers had carried with them—a flag that Galvestonians had not seen since it left the island city a third of a century before. The crowd broke into wild applause. "This silken banner sings a requiem. Not loud, but it strikes deeply to the hearts of us all," Colonel Street somberly told the crowd of teary-eyed mourners. "The war is over and the dead sleep; pray for them," he urged, "and think of the living for whom they fought": "The bloody fields and noble souls are no more, but our cherished bit of silken kindness is here to remind us of them."[103]

Immediately following the closing prayer, memorial committee members bearing flowers scattered them in every direction. They were spontaneously joined by citizens and ladies who had lost husbands, fathers, brothers, or lovers. They heaped wreaths, garlands, and flowers of all kinds and colors— roses, lilies, pansies, violets, and daisies—upon the graves of all of those who

102. Ibid.
103. Ibid.

had served the Confederate cause, from General Magruder to the lowliest of soldiers.[104] At least for one glorious moment in time, Magruder and his comrades would sleep peacefully together beneath the soft burden of the lovely blossoms that were produced in the very soil that they had fought and died for many years earlier.

Not even Prince John Magruder could have scripted a more perfect ending.

104. Ibid.

BIBLIOGRAPHY

DIARIES, MANUSCRIPTS, AND PAPERS

Bee to Mann Letter. San Jacinto Museum of History, Houston, Tex.

Thomas Bragg Diary. Southern Historical Collection, University of North Carolina.

Joseph L. Brent Papers. Tulane University.

Campbell-Colston Family Papers. Southern Historical Collection, University of North Carolina.

Howell Cobb Collection. University of Georgia.

Thomas R. R. Cobb Collection. University of Georgia.

Cave Johnson Couts Papers. Huntington Library, San Marino, Calif.

Jefferson Davis Collection. Woodruff Library, Emory University.

William H. Emory Papers. San Diego Historical Society.

Benjamin Stoddert Ewell Papers. Library of Congress.

Caleb G. Forshey Papers. Rosenberg Library, Galveston, Tex.

Thomas Jewett Goree Diary and Papers. Louisiana State University.

Thomas Robson Hay Papers. Central Rappahannock Heritage Center, Fredericksburg, Va.

Samuel P. Heintzelman Diary. Library of Congress.

D. H. Hill Papers. United States Military History Institute, Carlisle Barracks, Pa.

Ethan Allen Hitchcock Papers. Library of Congress.

Mrs. Mason Barret Collection. Collection of Albert S. and William P. Johnston Papers. Tulane University.

George H. S. King Papers. Virginia Historical Society.

Lee Family Papers. Virginia Historical Society Library.

Lee-Magruder Letters. New York Public Library.

James Longstreet Papers. Perkins Library, Duke University.

Papers of Governor F. R. Lubbock. Texas State Archives.

George B. McClellan Papers. Library of Congress.

Lafayette McLaws Papers. Southern Historical Collection, University of North Carolina.

John Bankhead Magruder Papers, Aztec Club Archives. U.S. Military History Institute, Carlisle Barracks, Pa.

John Bankhead Magruder Papers. Brockenbrough Library, Museum of the Confederacy, Richmond, Va.

John Bankhead Magruder Papers. Chicago Historical Society Library.

John Bankhead Magruder Papers. Perkins Library, Duke University.

John Bankhead Magruder Papers. Rosenberg Library, Galveston, Tex.

John Bankhead Magruder, Vertical File, Center for the Study of American History, University of Texas, Austin.

Magruder to Burrell Letter. Autograph Collection, MOLLUS—Massachusetts Commandery Collection, U.S. Army Military History Institute, Carlisle Barracks, Pa.

Magruder to Carlisle Letter. In possession of Brian Green of Kernersville, N.C.

Magruder to Markoe Letter. New York Public Library.

Magruder to Snead Letter. Historical Society of Pennsylvania, Philadelphia.

Matthew Fontaine Maury Papers. Library of Congress.

William Norris Scrapbook, Norris Family Papers. Alderman Library Archives, University of Virginia.

Robb-Bernard Papers. Swem Library, College of William and Mary.

St. George S. Lee to Magruder Letter. Original draft owned by Margaret Hutchings of Houston, Texas.

J. E. B. Stuart Collection. Huntington Library, San Marino, Calif.

von Kapff Family Bible. Bible in possession Ellinor Wilson Poultney of Garrison, Md.

Edward Clifton Wharton and Family Papers. Louisiana State University.

NEWSPAPERS

American Star

Baltimore American

Baltimore American and Commercial Advertiser

Baltimore Gazette

Baltimore Republican and Commercial Advertiser

Baltimore Sun

Columbia (S.C.) *Guardian*

Corpus Christi Gazette

Dallas Herald

Fredericksburg (Va.) *News*

Galveston News

Houston Post

Houston Telegraph

Los Angeles Star
Memphis Daily Appeal
Mexican Times
New Orleans Delta
New Orleans Era
New Orleans Picayune
New Orleans Times
New York Herald
New York Illustrated News
New York Sun
New York Times
New York Times Magazine
New York Tribune
Philadelphia Evening Telegraph
Political Arena (Fredericksburg, Va.)
Raleigh Weekly Register and North Carolina Gazette
Richmond Dispatch
Richmond Examiner
Richmond Whig
San Antonio Light
San Antonio Texan
San Diego Herald
San Diego Union
Virginia Herald (Fredericksburg)
Wilmington (N.C.) *Daily Journal*

GOVERNMENT DOCUMENTS

Board of Proceedings in the Case of Colonel Robert H. Chilton. Confederate States Army, War Department Collection of Confederate Records. National Archives.

The Centennial of the United States Military Academy at West Point, New York. 2 vols. Washington, D.C.: Government Printing Office, 1904.

Congressional Globe. 41st Cong., 2nd sess.

J. B. Magruder file. Confederate Papers Relating to Citizens or Business Firms. National Archives.

Journal of the Congress of the Confederate States of America, 1861–1865. 7 vols. Washington, D.C.: Government Printing Office, 1904–5.

Letters Received by the Office of the Adjutant General, 1822–60. National Archives.

Letters Received, Secretary of War, National Archives.

Letters Sent, Secretary of War, National Archives.

Letters Sent by the Office of the Adjutant General, 1800–1890. National Archives.

Magruder, John Bankhead. "Plan for Organizing the Batteries of Light Artillery into One or More Battalions." National Archives.

———. "Project for Organizing into a Battalion the Batteries of Light Artillery, Now Authorized by the Acts of Congress of 1821 and 1847." National Archives.

Official Records of the Union and Confederate Navies in the War of the Rebellion. 30 vols. Washington, D.C.: Government Printing Office, 1894–1922.

Official Return of the First Artillery, November 1846–January 1847. National Archives.

Post Orders, United States Military Academy, 1827–30. U.S. Military Academy Archives.

Records of the Tenth Military Department, 1846–51, Letters Received. National Archives.

Records of the Tenth Military Department, 1846–51, Letters Sent. National Archives.

"Regulations of the United States Military Academy at West Point—Extract from the General Regulations of the Army—Article 78." *American State Papers, Military Affairs.* 7 vols. Washington, D.C.: Gales and Seaton, 1832–61.

Report of the Commission Appointed to Investigate the Cotton Business in Texas, April 26, 1864. National Archives.

Report of the Joint Committee on the Conduct of War. 8 vols. Washington, D.C.: Government Printing Office, 1863–66.

Report of the U.S. Census Bureau, 1810, for Caroline County, Va.

Report of the U.S. Census Bureau, 1820, for Caroline County, Va.

Returns from U.S. Military Posts, 1800–1916. National Archives.

Richardson, James D. *A Compilation of the Messages and Papers of the Presidents, 1789–1812.* 11 vols. New York: Bureau of National Literature and Art, 1907.

Statutes at Large and Treaties of the United States of America from December 1, 1845, to March 3, 1851. Boston: Little, Brown, 1851.

Testimony of Henry S. Lubbock before Philip C. Tucker, Commissioner of Prize. "In the matter of the Confederate States of America vs. the Gunboat Steamship called the *Harriet Lane.* Evidence taken before the Commissioner of Prize, for the Eastern District of Texas, at Galveston; in obedience to an order of the Honorable District Court, of the Confederate States for said District sitting in Admiralty on the 12th day of September, A. D., 1863." Certified MS of the original in the Rosenberg Library, Galveston, Tex.

U.S. Congress. House Executive Doc. 41, 30th Cong., 1st sess.

———. House Executive Doc. 60, 30th Cong., 1st sess.

———. House Executive Doc. 1, 30th Cong., 2nd sess.

———. House Executive Doc. 24, 31st Cong., 1st sess.

———. House Executive Docs., Diplomatic Correspondence, 39th Cong., 1st sess.

———. House Executive Docs., Diplomatic Correspondence, 39th Cong., 2nd sess.

———. House Executive Doc. 30, 40th Cong., 1st sess.

———. Senate Executive Doc. 1, 29th Cong., 1st sess.

———. Senate Executive Doc. 388, 29th Cong., 1st sess.

———. Senate Executive Doc. 1, 30th Cong., 1st sess.

————. Senate Executive Doc. 65, 30th Cong., 1st sess.

U.S. Military Academy Cadet Application Papers, 1805–66. National Archives.

U.S. Military Academy Register of Merit, 1817–35. U.S. Military Academy Archives.

U.S. War Department, Rebel Records, "Correspondence of the Department of the Peninsula." National Archives.

The War of the Rebellion: A Compilation of the Official Records of the Union and Confederate Armies. 128 vols. Washington, D.C.: Government Printing Office, 1880–1901.

BOOKS

Alcaraz, Ramón. *The Other Side; or, Notes for the History of the War between Mexico and the United States.* Translated by Albert C. Ramsey. New York: J. Wiley, 1850.

Alexander, Edward Porter. *Fighting for the Confederacy: The Personal Recollections of General Edward Porter Alexander.* Edited by Gary W. Gallagher. Chapel Hill: University of North Carolina Press, 1989.

————. *Military Memoirs of a Confederate.* New York: Scribners, 1907.

Allan, William. *The Army of Northern Virginia in 1862.* Boston: Houghton, Mifflin, 1892.

Ambrose, Stephen E. *Duty, Honor, Country: A History of West Point.* Baltimore: Johns Hopkins Press, 1966.

Anderson, Robert. *An Artillery Officer in the Mexican War, 1846–7.* New York: G. P. Putnam's Sons, 1911.

Arnold, Thomas Jackson, *Early Life and Letters of General Thomas J. Jackson.* New York: Fleming H. Revell Co., 1916.

Ballentine, George. *Autobiography of an English Soldier in the United States Army, Comprising Observations and Adventures in the States and Mexico.* New York: Stringer and Townsend, 1853.

Bancroft, Hubert Howe. *History of California.* 7 vols. San Francisco: History Co., 1884–90.

Barbour, Philip Nordbourne. *Journals of the Late Brevet Major Philip Nordbourne Barbour, Captain in the 3rd Regiment, United States Infantry.* Edited by Rhoda van Bibber Tanner Doubleday. New York: G. P. Putnam's Sons, 1936.

Barnard, John G. *The Peninsular Campaign.* New York: D. Van Nostrand, 1864.

Bartlett, John Russell. *Personal Narrative of Explorations and Incidents in Texas, New Mexico, California, Sonora, and Chihuahua, Connected with the United States and Mexican Boundary Commission during the Years 1850, '51, '52, and '53.* 2 vols. New York: D. Appleton, 1854.

Basler, Roy P., ed. *The Collected Works of Abraham Lincoln.* 8 vols. New Brunswick, N.J.: Rutgers University Press, 1953.

Bauer, K. Jack. *The Mexican War, 1846–1848.* New York: Macmillan, 1974.

————. *Zachary Taylor: Soldier, Planter, Statesman of the Old Southwest.* Baton Rouge: Louisiana State University Press, 1985.

Bell, Horace. *On the Old West Coast.* Edited by Lanier Bartlett. New York: William Morrow, 1930.

———. *Reminiscences of a Ranger: or, Early Times in Southern California.* Los Angeles: Yarnell, Caystile, and Mathis, 1881.

Bill, Alfred Hoyt. *Rehearsal for Conflict: The War with Mexico, 1846–1848.* New York: Alfred A. Knopf, 1947.

Blackwood, Emma Jerome, ed. *To Mexico with Scott: Letters of Captain E. Kirby Smith to His Wife.* Cambridge: Harvard University Press, 1917.

Boney, F. N. *John Letcher of Virginia: The Story of Virginia's Civil War Governor.* Tuscaloosa: University of Alabama Press, 1966.

Bosson, Charles P. *History of the Forty-Second Regiment Infantry, Massachusetts Volunteers, 1862, 1863, 1864.* Boston: Mills, Knight and Co. Printers, 1886.

Bowie, Effie Gwynn. *Across the Years in Prince George's County.* Richmond, Va.: Garrett and Massie, 1947.

Brandes, Ray, and James R. Moriarty III. *New Town, San Diego.* San Diego: San Diego Science Foundation, 1985.

Brent, Joseph Lancaster. *Memoirs of the War Between the States.* New Orleans: Fontana Printing Co., 1940.

Bridges, Hal. *Lee's Maverick General: Daniel Harvey Hill.* New York: McGraw-Hill, 1961.

Bruce, Philip Alexander. *History of the University of Virginia, 1819–1919.* 4 vols. New York: Macmillan, 1920.

Burton, Brian K. *Extraordinary Circumstances: The Seven Days Battles.* Bloomington: Indiana University Press, 2001.

Butler, Benjamin F. *Butler's Book: Autobiography and Personal Reminiscences.* Boston: A. M. Thayer and Co., 1892.

Casdorph, Paul D. *Prince John Magruder: His Life and Campaigns.* New York: John Wiley and Sons, 1996.

Castel, Albert. *General Sterling Price and the Civil War in the West.* Baton Rouge: Louisiana State University Press, 1968.

Chambers, Lenoir. *Stonewall Jackson.* 2 vols. New York: William Morrow, 1959.

Chapman, Craig S. *More Terrible Than Victory: North Carolina's Bloody Bethel Regiment, 1861–1865.* Washington, D.C.: Brassey's, 1998.

Chesnut, Mary Boykin. *A Diary from Dixie,* Edited by Ben Ames Williams. Boston: Houghton Mifflin, 1949.

Conner, Philip Syng Physick. *The Home Squadron under Commodore Conner in the War with Mexico.* Philadelphia: n.p., 1896.

Constitution of the Aztec Club of 1847 and List of Members. London: Hanbury, Tomsett and Co., 1928.

Cotham, Edward T., Jr. *Battle on the Bay: The Civil War Struggle for Galveston.* Austin: University of Texas Press, 1998.

Craven, John J. *Prison Life of Jefferson Davis Embracing Details and Incidents of His Captivity, Particulars Concerning His Health and Habits, Together with Many Conversations on Topics of Great Public Interest.* New York: Carleton, 1866.

Crist, Lynda Lasswell, and Mary Seaton Dix, eds. *The Papers of Jefferson Davis.* 12 vols. to date. Baton Rouge: Louisiana State University Press, 1971–.

Cullum, George Washington. *Biographical Register of the Officers and Graduates of the U.S. Military Academy at West Point, New York, from Its Establishment, March 16, 1802, to the Army Reorganization of 1866–67.* 2 vols. New York: D. Van Nostrand, 1868.

Cunz, Dieter. *The Maryland Germans: A History.* Princeton, N.J.: Princeton University Press, 1948.

Davidson, Greenlee. *Captain Greenlee Davidson, C.S.A.: Diary and Letters, 1851–1863.* Edited by Charles W. Turner. Verona, Va.: McClure Press, 1975.

Davis, Burke. *Jeb Stuart: The Last Cavalier.* New York: Rinehart and Co., 1957.

Davis, Jefferson. *The Rise and Fall of the Confederate Government.* 2 vols. New York: D. Appleton and Co., 1881.

Davis, Varina Howell. *Jefferson Davis: Ex-President of the Confederate States of America, a Memoir by His Wife.* 2 vols. New York: Belford Publishers, 1890.

Davis, William C. *Jefferson Davis: The Man and His Hour.* New York: HarperCollins, 1991.

Davis, William Heath. *Seventy-five Years in California.* Edited by Harold A. Small. San Francisco: John Howell Books, 1967.

de Voto, Bernard. *The Year of Decision: 1846.* Boston: Little, Brown, 1943.

Dorsey, Sarah Anne, ed. *Recollections of Henry Watkins Allen, Brigadier-General Confederate States Army, Ex-Governor of Louisiana.* New York: M. Doolady, 1866.

Dowdey, Clifford. *Lee.* Boston: Little, Brown, 1965.

———. *The Seven Days: The Emergence of Lee.* Boston: Little, Brown, 1964.

Downey, Fairfax. *Sound of the Guns: The Story of American Artillery from the Ancient and Honorable Company to the Atom Cannon and Guided Missile.* New York: David McKay Co., 1955.

Dufour, Charles L. *Gentle Tiger: The Gallant Life of Roberdeau Wheat.* Baton Rouge: Louisiana State University Press, 1957.

Dupuy, R. Ernest. *Where They Have Trod: The West Point Tradition in American Life.* New York: Frederick A. Stokes Co., 1940.

Early, Jubal Anderson. *War Memoirs: Autobiographical Sketch and Narrative of the War between the States.* Philadelphia: J. B. Lippincott, 1912.

Eaton, Clement. *A History of the Southern Confederacy.* New York: Free Press, 1954.

Eckenrode, H. J., and Bryan Conrad. *George B. McClellan: The Man Who Saved the Union.* Chapel Hill: University of North Carolina Press, 1941.

Edwards, Jennie, comp. *John N. Edwards: Biography, Memoirs, Reminiscences and Recollections.* Kansas City, Mo.: Jennie Edwards, 1889.

Edwards, John N. *Shelby and His Men; or, The War in the West.* Cincinnati: Miami Printing and Publishing Co., 1867.

———. *Shelby's Expedition to Mexico: An Unwritten Leaf of the War.* Kansas City, Mo.: Kansas City Times Steam Book and Job Printing House, 1872.

Ellett, Mrs. E. P. *Court Circles of the Republic.* Philadelphia: Philadelphia Publishing Co., n.d.

Elliott, Charles Winslow. *Winfield Scott: The Soldier and the Man.* New York: Macmillan, 1937.

Fall, Ralph Emmett. *Hidden Village, Port Royal, Virginia, 1744–1981.* Verona, Va.: McClure Printing Co., 1982.

Ford, John Salmon. *Rip Ford's Texas.* Edited by Stephen B. Oates. Austin: University of Texas Press, 1963.

Freeman, Douglas Southall. *Lee's Lieutenants: A Study in Command.* 3 vols. New York: Charles Scribner's Sons, 1942.

———. *R. E. Lee.* 4 vols. New York: Charles Scribner's Sons, 1934.

Fremantle, Arthur James Lyon. *The Fremantle Diary: Being the Journal of Lieutenant-Colonel Arthur James Lyon Fremantle, Coldstream Guards, on His Three Months in the Southern States.* Edited by Walter Lord. Boston: Little, Brown, 1954.

———. *Three Months in the Southern States: April–June, 1863.* New York: John Bradburn, 1864.

French, Samuel G. *Two Wars: An Autobiography of Gen. Samuel G. French.* Nashville, Tenn.: Confederate Veteran, 1901.

Fry, James B. *The History and Legal Effect of Brevets in the Armies of Great Britain and the United States from Their Origin in 1692 to the Present Time.* New York: D. Van Nostrand, 1877.

Furber, George C. *The Twelve Months Volunteer; or, Journal of a Private in the Tennessee Regiment of Cavalry, in the Campaign, in Mexico, 1846–1847.* Cincinnati: J. A. and U. P. James, 1849.

Goree, Thomas J. *Longstreet's Aide: The Civil War Letters of Major Thomas J. Goree.* Edited by Thomas W. Cutrer. Charlottesville: University Press of Virginia, 1995.

Gorgas, Josiah. *The Journals of Josiah Gorgas, 1857–1878.* Edited by Sarah Woolfolk Wiggins. Tuscaloosa: University of Alabama Press, 1995.

Gouverneur, Marian. *As I Remember: Recollections of American Society during the Nineteenth Century.* New York: D. Appleton and Co., 1911.

Grant, Ulysses S. *Personal Memoirs of U.S. Grant.* 2 vols. New York: Charles L. Webster and Co., 1885.

Haecker, Charles M., and Jeffrey G. Mauck. *On the Prairie of Palo Alto.* College Station: Texas A&M University Press, 1997.

Hamilton, Holamn. *Zachary Taylor: Soldier in the White House.* Indianapolis: Bobbs-Merrill, 1951.

———. *Zachary Taylor: Soldier of the Republic.* Indianapolis: Bobbs-Merrill, 1941.

Haskin, William L. *The History of the First Regiment of Artillery from Its Organization in 1821, to January 1, 1876.* Portland, Maine: B. Thurston and Co., 1879.

Hayden, Rev. Horace Edwin. *Virginia Genealogies: A Genealogy of the Glassell Family of Scotland and Virginia, Also of the Families of Ball, Brown, Bryan, Conway, Daniel, Ewell, Holladay, Lewis, Littlepage, Moncure, Peyton, Robinson, Scott, Taylor, Wallace, and Others, of Virginia and Maryland.* Baltimore: Genealogical Publishing Co., 1973.

Hayes, John D., ed. *Samuel Francis Du Pont: A Selection from His Civil War Letters.* 3 vols. Ithaca, N.Y.: Cornell University Press, 1969.

Henderson, G. F. R. *Stonewall Jackson and the American Civil War.* New York: David McKay, 1961.

Henry, Robert Selph. *The Story of the Confederacy.* Indianapolis: Bobbs-Merrill, 1931.

———. *The Story of the Mexican War.* Indianapolis: Bobbs-Merrill, 1950.

Henry, W. S. *Campaign Sketches of the War with Mexico.* New York: Harper and Bros., 1847.

Hitchcock, Ethan Allen. *Fifty Years in Camp and Field: Diary of Major-General Ethan Allen Hitchcock, U.S.A.* Edited by W. A. Croffut. New York: G. P. Putnam's Sons, 1909.

Holzman, Robert. *Stormy Ben Butler.* New York: Macmillan, 1954.

Hood, John Bell. *Advance and Retreat: Personal Experiences in the United States and Confederate Armies.* New Orleans: Hood Orphan Memorial Fund, 1880.

Hughes, Robert M. *General Johnston.* New York: D. Appleton and Co., 1897.

Hummel, Jeffrey Rogers. *Emancipating Slaves, Enslaving Free Men.* Chicago: Open Court, 1996.

Johnson, Timothy D. *Winfield Scott: The Quest for Military Glory.* Lawrence: University Press of Kansas, 1998.

Jones, John B. *A Rebel War Clerk's Diary.* Edited by Earl Schenck Miers. New York: Sagamore Press, 1958.

Kane, Harnett C. *Gentlemen, Swords, and Pistols.* New York: William Morrow, 1951.

Kearny, Thomas. *General Philip Kearny: Battle Soldier of Five Wars.* New York: G. P. Putnam's Sons, 1937.

Kell, John McIntosh. *Recollections of a Naval Life, Including the Cruises of the Confederate States Steamers "Sumter" and "Alabama."* Washington, D.C.: Neale Co., 1900.

Kellersberger, Getulius. *Memoirs of an Engineer in the Confederate Army in Texas.* Translated by Helen S. Sundstrom. N.p.: n.p., 1957.

Kerby, Robert L. *Kirby Smith's Confederacy: The Trans-Mississippi South, 1863–1865.* New York: Columbia University Press, 1972.

Keyes, E. D. *Fifty Years' Observation of Men and Events.* New York: Charles Scribner's Sons, 1884.

Lane, Lydia Spencer. *I Married a Soldier; or, Old Days in the Old Army.* Philadelphia: J. B. Lippincott, 1893.

Lee, Susan P. *Memoirs of William Nelson Pendleton.* Philadelphia: J. B. Lippincott, 1893.

Leech, Margaret. *Reveille In Washington, 1860–1865*. New York: Harper and Bros., 1941.

Lewis, Lloyd. *Captain Sam Grant*. Boston: Little, Brown, 1950.

Lomax, Elizabeth Lindsay. *Leaves from an Old Washington Diary, 1854–1863*. Edited by Lindsay Lomax Wood. New York: E. P. Dutton, 1943.

Longstreet, James. *From Manassas to Appomattox: Memoirs of the Civil War in America*. Philadelphia: J. B. Lippincott, 1896.

Lubbock, Francis R. *Six Decades in Texas or Memoirs of Francis Richard Lubbock: A Personal Experience in Business, War, and Politics*. Edited by C. W. Raines. Austin: Ben C. Jones and Co., Printers, 1900.

Magruder, Egbert Watson, ed. *Yearbook of the American Clan Gregor Society, 1913*. Richmond, Va.: Ware and Duke Printers, 1914.

Mahon, John K. *History of the Second Seminole War, 1835-1842*. Gainesville: University of Florida Press, 1967.

Marshall, Charles. *An Aide-de-Camp of Lee*. Edited by Sir Frederick Maurice. Boston: Little, Brown, 1927.

McCash, William B. *Thomas R. R. Cobb: The Making of a Southern Nationalist*. Macon, Ga.: Mercer University Press, 1983.

McClellan, George B. *McClellan's Own Story*. New York: Charles L. Webster and Co., 1887.

Meade, Bishop William. *Old Churches, Ministers and Families of Virginia*. 2 vols. Baltimore: Genealogical Publishing Co., 1978.

Meade, George. *The Life and Letters of George Gordon Meade, Major General, United States Army*. Edited by George Gordon Meade. 2 vols. New York: Charles Scribner's Sons, 1913.

Meade, Robert Douthat. *Judah P. Benjamin: Confederate Statesman*. New York: Oxford University Press, 1943.

Meredith, Roy. *The Faces of Robert E. Lee in Life and in Legend*. New York: Charles Scribner's Sons, 1947.

Mosby, John S. *The Memoirs of Colonel John S. Mosby*. Edited by Charles Wells Russell. Boston: Little, Brown, 1917.

Motte, Jacob Rhett. *Journey into Wilderness: An Army Surgeon's Account of Life in Camp and Field during the Creek and Seminole Wars, 1836–1838*. Edited by James F. Sunderman. Gainesville: University of Florida Press, 1953.

Myers, William Starr. *General George Brinton McClellan*. New York: D. Appleton–Century, 1934.

Nichols, James L. *The Confederate Quartermaster in the Trans-Mississippi*. Austin: University of Texas Press, 1964.

Nicolay, John G., and John Hay. *Abraham Lincoln: A History*. 10 vols. New York: Century Co., 1890.

North, Thomas. *Five Years in Texas; or, What You Did Not Hear during the War from January 1861 to January 1866. A Narrative of His Travels, Experiences, and Observations in Texas and Mexico*. Cincinnati: Elm Street Printing Co., 1871.

Nunn, W. C. *Escape from Reconstruction.* Fort Worth: Texas Christian University Press, 1956.

Oates, Stephen B. *Confederate Cavalry West of the River.* Austin: University of Texas Press, 1961.

O'Flaherty, Daniel. *General Jo Shelby: Undefeated Rebel.* Chapel Hill: University of North Carolina Press, 1954.

Oswandel, J. Jacob. *Notes of the Mexican War.* Philadelphia: n.p., 1885.

Parks, Joseph Howard. *General Edmund Kirby Smith, C.S.A.* Baton Rouge: Louisiana State University Press, 1954.

Parrish, T. Michael. *Richard Taylor: Soldier Prince of Dixie.* Chapel Hill: University of North Carolina Press, 1992.

Parton, James. *General Butler in New Orleans.* New York: Mason Bros., 1864.

Pletcher, David M. *The Diplomacy of Annexation: Texas, Oregon, and the Mexican War.* Columbia: University of Missouri Press, 1973.

Polk, William M. *Leonidas Polk: Bishop and General.* 2 vols. New York: Longmans, Green and Co., 1915.

Pollard, Edward A. *Lee and His Lieutenants: Comprising the Early Life, Public Services, and Campaigns of General Robert E. Lee and His Companions in Arms, with a Record of Their Campaigns and Heroic Deeds.* New York: E. B. Treat and Co., 1867.

Poore, Ben Perley. *Perley's Reminiscences of Sixty Years in the National Metropolis.* 2 vols. Philadelphia: Hubbard Bros., 1886.

Pourade, Richard F. *The History of San Diego: The Silver Dons.* San Diego: Union-Tribune Publishing Co., 1963.

———. *The History of San Diego: Time of the Bells.* San Diego: Union-Tribune Publishing Co., 1961.

Powell, H. M. T. *The Santa Fe Trail to California, 1849–1852: The Journal and Drawings of H. M. T. Powell.* Edited by Douglas S. Watson. San Francisco: Book Club of California, 1931.

Putnam, Sallie. *Richmond during the War: Four Years of Personal Observation.* New York: G. W. Carleton and Co., 1867.

Quaife, Milo Milton, ed. *The Diary of James K. Polk during His Presidency, 1845 to 1849.* 4 vols. Chicago: A. C. McClurg and Co., 1910.

Ratchford, J. W. *Some Reminiscences of Persons and Incidents of the Civil War.* Richmond: Whittet and Shepperson, 1909.

Raymond, Henry J. *The Life and Public Serves of Abraham Lincoln.* New York: Derby and Miller, 1865.

Reagan, John H. *Memoirs.* Austin: Pemberton Press, 1968.

Rhoades, Jeffrey L. *Scapegoat General: The Story of Major General Benjamin Huger, C.S.A.* Hamden, Conn.: Anchor Books, 1985.

Rives, George Lockhart. *The United States and Mexico, 1821–1848: A History of the Relations between the Two Countries from the Independence of Mexico to the Close of the War with the United States.* 2 vols. New York: Charles Scribner's Sons, 1913.

Robertson, Alexander F. *Alexander Hugh Holmes Stuart, 1807–1891.* Richmond, Va.: William Byrd Press, 1925.

Robertson, James I., Jr. *Stonewall Jackson: The Man, the Soldier, the Legend.* New York: Macmillan, 1997.

Roland, Charles P. *Albert Sidney Johnston: Soldier of Three Republics.* Austin: University of Texas Press, 1964.

Rolle, Andrew F. *The Lost Cause: The Confederate Exodus to Mexico.* Norman: University of Oklahoma Press, 1965.

Rowland, Dunbar, ed. *Jefferson Davis, Constitutionalist: His Letters, Papers, and Speeches.* 10 vols. Jackson: Mississippi Department of Archives and History, 1923.

Scharf, John Thomas. *Chronicles of Baltimore: Being a Complete History of "Baltimore Town" and Baltimore City from the Earliest Period to the Present Time.* Baltimore: Turnbull Bros., 1874.

———. *History of the Confederate States Navy from Its Organization to the Surrender of Its Last Vessel.* New York: Rogers and Sherwood, 1887.

Scott, Ed. *San Diego County: Soldier-Pioneers, 1846–1866.* National City, Calif.: Crest Printing Co., 1976.

Scott, Winfield. *Memoirs of Lieutenant-General Scott, LLD.* 2 vols. New York: Sheldon and Co., 1864.

Sears, Stephen W. *George B. McClellan: The Young Napoleon.* New York: Ticknor and Fields, 1988.

———. *To the Gates of Richmond: The Peninsula Campaign.* New York: Ticknor and Fields, 1992.

Seitz, Don C. *Braxton Bragg: General of the Confederacy.* Columbia, S.C.: State Co., 1924.

Semmes, Raphael. *Memoirs of Service Afloat during the War between the States.* Baltimore: Kelly, Piet and Co., 1869.

———. *Service Afloat and Ashore during the Mexican War.* Cincinnati: William H. Moore, 1851.

Shackleford, George. *George Wythe Randolph and the Confederate Elite.* Athens: University of Georgia Press, 1988.

Shalhope, Robert E. *Sterling Price: Portrait of a Southerner.* Columbia: University of Missouri Press, 1971.

Sinclair, Arthur. *Two Years on the "Alabama."* Boston: Lee and Shepard, 1895.

Singletary, Otis A. *The Mexican War.* Chicago: University of Chicago Press, 1960.

Smith, Arthur D. Howden. *Old Fuss and Feathers: The Life and Exploits of Lt. General Winfield Scott.* New York: Greystone Press, 1937.

Smith, David Paul. *Frontier Defense in the Civil War: Texas' Rangers and Rebels.* College Station: Texas A&M University Press, 1992.

Smith, Gustavus W. *The Battle of Seven Pines.* New York: C. G. Crawford, 1891.

Smith, Justin H. *The Annexation of Texas.* New York: Baker and Taylor Co., 1911.

————. *The War with Mexico.* 2 vols. New York: Macmillan, 1919.

Smythe, William E. *History of San Diego, 1542–1908.* San Diego: History Co., 1908.

Sorrel, G. Moxley. *Recollections of a Confederate Staff Officer.* Edited by Bell Irvin Wiley. Jackson, Tenn.: McCowat-Mercer Press, 1958.

Stewart, George R. *John Phoenix, Esq., the Squibob, a Life of Captain George H. Derby, U.S.A.* New York: Henry Holt, 1937.

Swinton, William. *Campaigns of the Army of the Potomac: A Critical History of Operations in Virginia, Maryland, and Pennsylvania from the Commencement to the Close of the War, 1861–5.* New York: Charles B. Richardson, 1866.

Taylor, Richard. *Destruction and Reconstruction: Personal Experience of the Late War.* Edited by Richard B. Harwell. New York: Longmans, Green and Co., 1955.

Taylor, Walter H. *General Lee: His Campaigns in Virginia, 1861–1865.* Brooklyn, N.Y.: Braunworth and Co., 1906.

Terrell, Alexander Watkins. *From Texas to Mexico and the Court of Maximilian in 1865.* Dallas: Book Club of Texas, 1933.

The Industrial Advantages of Houston, Texas and Environs, Also a Series of Comprehensive Sketches of the City's Representative Business Enterprises. Houston: Akehurst Publishing Co., 1894.

Tolbert, Frank X. *Dick Dowling at Sabine Pass.* New York: McGraw-Hill, 1962.

Tyler, Ronnie C. *Santiago Vidaurri and the Southern Confederacy.* Austin: Texas State Historical Association, 1973.

Utley, Robert M. *Frontiersmen in Blue: The United States Army and the Indian, 1845–1865.* New York: Macmillan, 1967.

Vandiver, Frank. *Mighty Stonewall.* New York: McGraw-Hill, 1957.

————. *Rebel Brass: The Confederate Command System.* Baton Rouge: Louisiana State University Press, 1956.

Wallace, Edward S. *General William Jenkins Worth: Monterey's Forgotten Hero.* Dallas: Southern Methodist University Press, 1953.

Warner, Ezra J. *Generals in Gray.* Baton Rouge: Louisiana State University Press, 1959.

Webb, Alexander S. *The Peninsula: McClellan's Campaign of 1862.* New York: Charles Scribner's Sons, 1881.

Werlich, Robert. *"Beast" Butler: The Incredible Career of Major General Benjamin Franklin Butler.* Washington, D.C.: Quaker Press, 1962.

Wert, Jeffrey D. *General James Longstreet: The Confederacy's Most Controversial Soldier—A Biography.* New York: Simon and Schuster, 1993.

West, George Benjamin. *When the Yankees Came: Civil War and Reconstruction on the Virginia Peninsula.* Edited by Parker Rouse Jr. Richmond, Va.: Dietz Press, 1977.

Wilcox, Cadmus M. *History of the Mexican War.* Edited by Mary Rachel Wilcox. Washington, D.C.: Church News Publishing Co., 1892.

Williams, Amelia W., and Eugene C. Barker, eds. *The Writings of Sam Houston, 1813–1863.* 8 vols. Austin: University of Texas Press, 1938–43.

Williams, Frances Leigh. *Matthew Fontaine Maury, Scientist of the Sea.* New Brunswick, N.J.: Rutgers University Press, 1963.

Winkler, Ernest W., ed. *Journal of the Secession Convention of Texas.* Austin: Austin Printing Co., 1912.

Wise, Jennings Cropper. *The Long Arm of Lee or the History of the Artillery of the Army of Northern Virginia.* 2 vols. Lynchburg, Va.: J. P. Bell Co., 1915.

Wood, Oliver E., ed. *The West Point Scrap Book: A Collection of Stories, Songs and Legends of the United States Military Academy.* New York: D. Van Nostrand, 1871.

Woodworth, Steven E. *Davis and Lee at War.* Lawrence: University Press of Kansas, 1995.

Wooten, Dudley G., ed. *A Comprehensive History of Texas, 1685–1897.* 2 vols. Dallas: William G. Scarff, 1898.

Wright, Marcus J. *General Officers of the Confederate Army.* New York: Neale Publishing Co., 1911.

Young, Dr. S. O. *A Thumb-Nail History of the City of Houston, Texas from Its Founding in 1836 to the Year 1912.* Houston: Rein and Sons Press, 1912.

ARTICLES AND ESSAYS

Armistead, Drury L. "The Battle in Which General Johnston Was Wounded." *Southern Historical Society Papers* 18 (1890).

"Blockades and Battles, 1861–1865." MS in the Rosenberg Library, Galveston, Tex.

Bohannon, Keith S. "One Solid Unbroken Roar of Thunder: Union and Confederate Artillery at the Battle of Malvern Hill." In *The Richmond Campaign of 1862: The Peninsula and the Seven Days.* Edited by Gary W. Gallagher. Chapel Hill: University of North Carolina Press, 2000.

"Cadet Life before the Mexican War." Bulletin No. 1, the Library, U.S. Military Academy. New York: U.S. Military Academy Printing Office, 1945.

Carmichael, Peter S. "The Great Paragon of Virtue and Sobriety: John Bankhead Magruder and the Seven Days." In *The Richmond Campaign of 1862: The Peninsula and the Seven Days.* Edited by Gary W. Gallagher. Chapel Hill: University of North Carolina Press, 2000.

Carr, Joseph B. "Operations of 1861 about Fort Monroe." *Battles and Leaders of the Civil War.* Edited by Robert U. Johnson and Clarence C. Buel. Vol. 2. New York: Century Co., 1887–88.

Cobb, Thomas R. R. "Extracts from Letters to His Wife, February 3, 1861–December 10, 1862." *Southern Historical Society Papers* 28 (1900).

Cumberland, Charles C. "The Confederate Loss and Recapture of Galveston, 1862–1863." *Southwestern Historical Quarterly* 51 (October 1947).

Dabney, R. L. "Memoir of a Narrative Received of Colonel John B. Baldwin, of Staunton, Touching the Origin of the War." *Southern Historical Society Papers* 1 (1876).

Darkis, Fred, Jr. "Alexander Keith McClung (1811–1855)." *Journal of Mississippi History* 40 (November 1978).

Debray, X. B. "A Sketch of Debray's Twenty-sixth Regiment of Texas Cavalry." *Southern Historical Society Papers* 12 (1884).

Douglas, Hugh Thomas. "A Famous Army and Its Commander: Sketch of the Army of the Peninsula and General Magruder." *Southern Historical Society Papers* 42 (1917).

"The First Regiment (N.C.) Volunteers." *Southern Historical Society Papers* 19 (1891).

Franklin, William B. "Rear-Guard Fighting during the Change of Base." *Battles and Leaders of the Civil War.* Edited by Robert U. Johnson and Clarence C. Buel. Vol. 2. New York: Century Co. 1887–88.

Frazer, Robert W. "Military Posts in San Diego, 1852." *Journal of San Diego History* 20 (Summer 1974).

"F. W. Brune & Sons." *Biographical Sketches* from the Maryland Historical Society.

Gallagher, Gary W. "The Undoing of an Early Confederate Hero: John Bankhead Magruder at the Seven Days." In *Lee and His Generals in War and Memory.* Edited by Gary W. Gallagher. Baton Rouge: Louisiana State University Press, 1998.

Grimsley, Mark. "Inside a Beleaguered City: A Commander and Actor, Prince John Magruder." *Civil War Times Illustrated* 21 (September 1982).

Hale, Edward J. "The Bethel Regiment, the First North Carolina Volunteers." *Histories of Several Regiments and Battalions from North Carolina in the Great War, 1861–65.* Edited by Walter Clark. 5 vols. Raleigh: State of North Carolina, 1901.

Harrington, Fred. "A Royal Tour." *South Atlantic Quarterly* 38 (July 1939).

Harrison, Jon P., ed. "The Confederate Letters of John Simmons." *Chronicles of Smith County, Texas* 14 (Summer 1975).

Hay, Thomas Robson. "General John B. Magruder and the Trans-Mississippi." Hay Papers.

Hill, Daniel H. "Lee's Attacks North of the Chickahominy." *Battles and Leaders of the Civil War.* Edited by Robert U. Johnson and Clarence C. Buel. Vol. 2. New York: Century Co., 1887–88.

———. "McClellan's Change of Base and Malvern Hill." *Battles and Leaders of the Civil War.* Edited by Robert U. Johnson and Clarence C. Buel. Vol. 2. New York: Century Co., 1887–88.

———. "The Real Stonewall Jackson." *Century* 47 (1893–94).

Huske, Benjamin. "More Terrible than Victory." Edited by Walter Brown Jr. *Civil War Times Illustrated* (October 1981).

"John Magruder." *Army and Navy Journal* 18 (September 1880).

Johnston, Joseph E. "Manassas to Seven Pines." *Battles and Leaders of the Civil War.* Edited by Robert U. Johnson and Clarence C. Buel. Vol. 2. New York: Century Co., 1887–88.

Lamb, John. "Malvern Hill—July 1, 1862." *Southern Historical Society Papers* 25 (1897).

Lea, Albert Miller. Autobiographical sketch in the *Iowa Historical Record* 8 (1892).

Lee, Baker P. "Magruder's Peninsula Campaign in 1862." *Southern Historical Society Papers* 19 (1891).

Leland, Isabella Middleton, ed. "Middleton Correspondence, 1861–1865." *South Carolina Historical Magazine* 63 (July 1962).

Longstreet, James. "'The Seven Days,' Including Frayser's Farm." *Battles and Leaders of the Civil War.* Edited by Robert U. Johnson and Clarence C. Buel. Vol. 2. New York: Century Co., 1887–88.

MacMullen, Jerry. "Selim Woodworth: A Heel or Hero?" *San Diego Union,* September 3, 1961.

Magruder, Allan B. "A Piece of Secret History: President Lincoln and the Virginia Convention of 1861." *Atlantic Monthly* 35 (April 1875).

Magruder, John B. "The First Battle of the War: Big Bethel." In *Battles and Leaders of the Civil War.* Edited by Peter Cozzens. Vol. 5. Urbana: University of Illinois Press, 2002.

McRae, D. K. "The Battle of Williamsburg—Reply to Colonel Bratton." *Southern Historical Society Papers* 7 (1879).

Nelson, Bernard. "Confederate Slave Impressment Legislation, 1861–1865." *Journal of Negro History* 31 (October 1946).

Oates, Stephen B. "Texas under the Secessionists." *Southwestern Historical Quarterly* 67 (October 1963).

"Opposing Forces at Seven Pines, May 31–June 1, 1862." *Battles and Leaders of the Civil War.* Edited by Robert U. Johnson and Clarence C. Buel. Vol. 2. New York: Century Co., 1887–88.

"Our Mexican Problem as Viewed Fifty Years Ago by the Emperor Maximilian: Hitherto Unpublished Narrative by Famous Confederate General Magruder, of Timely Interest Today." *New York Times Magazine,* April 2, 1916; *New York Times,* August 20, 1865.

Padgett, James A., ed. "Life of Alfred Mordecai in Mexico 1865–1866, as Told in His Letters to His Family." *North Carolina Historical Review* 22 (April 1945).

———, ed. "Life of Alfred Mordecai in Mexico, 1865–1866, as Told in His Letters to His Family." *North Carolina Historical Review* 23 (January 1946).

Pierce, Edward L. "The Contrabands at Fortress Monroe." *Atlantic Monthly* 8 (1861).

Ramsdell, Charles W. "Texas from the Fall of the Confederacy to the Beginning of Reconstruction." *Quarterly of the Texas State Historical Association* 11 (January 1908).

———. "The Texas State Military Board, 1862–1865." *Southwestern Historical Quarterly* 27 (April 1924).

"Recollections of Cadet Life." *Army and Navy Journal* 4 (August 1867).

Reynolds, Thomas C. "Gen. Sterling Price and the Confederacy." MS in the Missouri Historical Society, St. Louis.

Rister, Carl Coke. "Carlotta, a Confederate Colony in Mexico." *Journal of Southern History* 11 (February 1945).

Roberts, Oran M. "The Political, Legislative, and Judicial History of Texas for Its Fifty Years of Statehood, 1845–1895." In *A Comprehensive History of Texas, 1685–1897.* Vol. 2. Edited by Dudley G. Wooten. Dallas: William G. Scarff, 1898.

Smith, Rebecca W., and Marion Mullins, eds. "Diary of H. C. Medford, Confederate Soldier, 1864." *Southwestern Historical Quarterly* 34 (October 1930).

"The Soldiers' Temperance Union." *Army and Navy Journal* 21 (October 1883).

Spraggins, Tinsley Lee. "Mobilization of Negro Labor for the Department of Virginia and North Carolina, 1861–1865." *North Carolina Historical Review* 24 (April 1947).

Stevenson, Sara Y. "How an Austrian Archduke Ruled an American Empire." *Century Magazine* 55 (February 1898).

"Strength of General Lee's Army in the Seven Days Battles around Richmond." *Southern Historical Society Papers* 1 (1876).

Strother, D. H. "Personal Recollections of the War." *Harper's Magazine* 33 (October 1866).

Trexler, Harrison A. "The Opposition of Planters to the Employment of Slaves as Laborers by the Confederacy." *Mississippi Valley Historical Review: A Journal of American History* 27 (1940).

Tucker, Philip C., III. "The United States Gunboat *Harriet Lane*." *Southwestern Historical Quarterly* 21 (April 1918).

Warren, Mrs. J. E. "Bankhead Family." *William and Mary Quarterly* 9, ser. 2 (1929).

THESES AND DISSERTATIONS

Chandler, Luther Edward. "The Career of Henry Watkins Allen." Ph.D. diss. Louisiana State University, 1940.

Lambie, Agnes Louise. "Confederate Control of Cotton in the Trans-Mississippi Department." Master's thesis. University of Texas, 1915.

Milota, Robert Stephen. "John Bankhead Magruder: The California Years." Master's thesis. University of San Diego, 1990.

Ogden, August Raymond. "A Blockaded Seaport: Galveston, Texas, CSA." Master's thesis. St. Mary's University, 1939.

Riedel, Leonard W., Jr. "John Bankhead Magruder and the Defense of the Virginia Peninsula, 1861–1862." Master's thesis. Old Dominion University, 1991.

Settles, Thomas M. "The Military Career of John Bankhead Magruder." Ph.D. diss. Texas Christian University, 1972.

———. "The Port of Galveston during the Civil War." Master's thesis. Trinity University, 1968.

Spell, Timothy D. "John Bankhead Magruder: Defender of the Texas Coast, 1863." Master's thesis. Lamar University, 1981.

MISCELLANEOUS SOURCES

Assessed Land Valuations, 1872. San Diego County.

Babb, Stanley E. "A History of the *Galveston Daily News.*" Bound MS in the Rosenberg Library.

Bankhead v. Miller. Fredericksburg, Va., Circuit Court Clerk's Auxiliary Office. Ended year 1818.

Bankhead & Gray v. Miller's Executors. Fredericksburg, Virginia Circuit Court Clerk's Auxiliary Office. Ended year 1823.

Calendar of Virginia State Papers. 11 vols. Vol. 11. New York: Kraus Reprint Corp., 1968.

Caroline County Order Book, 1822–24.

Caroline County Personal Property Tax Lists, 1794–1811.

Caroline County, Virginia Land Tax List, 1817–26.

Cotham, Edward T., Jr. "The Origin of the Confederate Battle Plan to Recapture Galveston." Paper presented to the Texas State Historical Association at its annual meeting in Austin, Tex., March 3, 2000.

Davis, Emma-Jo. "Mulberry Island and the Civil War, April, 1861–May, 1862." MS in the Fort Eustis Historical and Archaeological Association, Fort Eustis, Va.

Delinquent Taxes, 1861. San Diego County.

Dyer, Joseph Osterman. *Dyer Scrap Book: Articles on Galveston and Texas History, Mostly from Galveston "News," December 14, 1919, to September 19, 1926.* The *Dyer Scrap Book* was compiled in 1932 and is presently in the Rosenberg Library, Galveston, Tex.

Faculty Records, 1825–26, University of Virginia. Alderman Library, University of Virginia.

Franklin, Robert M. *The Battle of Galveston, January 1st, 1863.* [Galveston, Tex.: Galveston News, 1911].

Hayes, Charles Waldo. "The Island and City of Galveston." MS in the Rosenberg Library, Galveston, Tex.

Index of Deeds. San Diego County.

Johnson, Allen, and Dumas Malone, eds. *Dictionary of American Biography.* 31 vols. New York: Charles Scribner's Sons, 1936.

Last Will and Testament of Henrietta H. Magruder. Will on file with the Register of Wills, Baltimore, Md.

Last Will and Testament of Henry R. Magruder. Will on file with the Register of Wills, Baltimore, Md.

Last Will and Testament of Kate Elizabeth Magruder. Will on file with the Register of Wills, Baltimore, Md.

Magruder v. Anderson. Caroline County, Va., Circuit Court Record Room. Ended Papers, 1848–49.

Magruder v. Miller. Fredericksburg, Va., Circuit Court Clerk's Auxiliary Office. Ended year 1818.

Matriculation Register of the University of Virginia. Alderman Library, University of Virginia.

New Catholic Encyclopedia. 15 vols. New York: McGraw-Hill, 1967.

Presidential Contest of 1856, in Three Letters by Col. J. Bankhead Magruder of the United States Army. San Antonio: Printed by the *San Antonio Texan,* 1856.

Stuart, Ben C. *Galveston Daily News,* December 12, 1909, *Stuart Book: A Series of Articles of Historic Interest Relating to Galveston and Texas, Published in Galveston "News" during the Years 1906 to 1911.* The *Stuart Book* was compiled in 1913 and is presently in the Rosenberg Library, Galveston, Tex.

Will for George Frazer Magruder with Executor's Final Accounting, Benjamin Murdock, acting executor. Frederick County, Wills, in the Maryland State Archives.

Wills for Samuel Magruder and Sarah Magruder. Prince George's County, Md., Wills, in the Maryland State Archives.

Wills for William Magruder and Mary Magruder. Prince George's County, Md., Wills, in the Maryland State Archives.

INDEX

Abinger, Lord, 284

Alabama, 58, 256–58

Albert Edward, Prince of Wales, 109

Alcohol drinking: and El Dorado saloon in Los Angeles, 95–96; by Magruder, 26–29, 96, 98, 98*n*91, 236*n*203; Magruder's cautions of soldiers against, 33–34, 85; prohibition of, during Virginia Peninsula campaign, 164, 164*n*29; rumors and allegations of Magruder's drunkenness, 28, 97, 131–32, 139*n*90, 141–43, 233–36, 254*n*57; by U.S. soldiers in Corpus Christi, 40

Alexander, Porter, 200–201, 201*n*32, 209, 210, 211*n*77, 229, 231

Allen, Augustus Albert, 12–13, 13*n*52

Allen, Henry Watkins, 281, 289*n*36

Allen, John J., 118

Allen, Rev. L. W., 28, 217–18, 235–36, 236*n*203

Ames, J. Judson, 93, 98

Ampudia, Pedro de, 44

Anderson, George T. ("Tige"), 193, 204, 227–28

Anderson, William M., 288

Andrews, Major, 85–86

Andrews, Rose, 294

Archer, James, 193

Arguello, Santiaguito, 91

Arista, Mariano, 44–51, 45*n*41

Arkansas District, 275–77

Armistead, Lewis, 218, 224–25, 227–28

Army of Missouri, 277

Army of Northern Virginia: Lee as commander of, 190, 191–92, 191*n*158; Magruder as division commander in, 193; organization of, 193–94; size of, 194, 194*n*182, 196, 196*n*5, 205–6, 205*n*52, 209, 211, 215. *See also* Johnston, Joseph E.; Lee, Robert E.; Seven Days' battles

Army of Tennessee, 275, 276

Army of the Peninsula. *See* Virginia Peninsula campaign

Army of the Potomac: McClellan as commander of, 157–61, 158*n*1; organization of, 186; size of, 157, 160, 172, 174, 177, 186–87, 188*n*143, 196, 196*n*6, 196*n*8, 202, 205, 211, 216. *See also* McClellan, George B.; Virginia Peninsula campaign

Aroostook (gunboat), 213

Artillery schools, 24–25, 111–12, 140

Ashby, Richard and Turner, 124

August, Thomas P., 127

Aztec Club, 80–81, 80–81*n*5

Baldwin, John B., 113–14

Ballentine, George, 54*n*87, 56, 59–63, 64*n*137, 66*n*151, 70–72, 73*n*185

Ballinger, William Pitt, 280

Baltimore, Md., 19–23, 19*n*84, 25, 36, 52, 82, 104, 292, 296–97

Bancroft, Hubert Howe, 88*n*41

Bankhead, James, 5, 8, 26–27, 36, 101*n*98, 261*n*90

Bankhead, Smith Pyne, 261, 261–62*n*90
Banks, Nathaniel P., 186, 256, 268–69, 275
Barbour, John and Alfred, 124
Barbour, Philip, 50*n*65
Barksdale, William, 204, 206–7, 226
Barnard, John G.: on McClellan's mistakes, 160*n*7, 163, 163*n*18; on Norfolk as strategic position, 161*n*12; and Seven Days' battles, 216; and Virginia Peninsula campaign, 163, 163*n*18, 171, 177; and Washington, D.C., defenses, 120
Barron, Samuel, 124
Barry, James E., 204
Barry, William F., 54, 160*n*7
Bartlett, John R., 93, 99–100, 99–100*n*94
Bartlett, William H. C., 16
Baton Rouge, La., 108
Baylor, George W., 278
Bayou City, 246, 247–48, 250–51
Bazaine, François-Achille, 104, 112, 284, 287, 291, 292
Beall, Lloyd J., 13
Beauregard, P. G. T., 293
Beavens, C. C., 302
Bee, Barnard E., 76, 76*n*200
Bee, Hamilton P., 260–62, 264, 281–82, 286–87, 292
Belknap, William G., 45
Bell, Henry H., 254–58
Bell, Horace, 95
Beltzhoover, Daniel M., 92, 97–98, 99
Bendix, John E., 132*n*58
Benjamin, Judah P.: and call-up of Virginia militiamen by Magruder, 147, 147*n*126; and construction of Virginia Peninsula defensive works, 151–54, 167–68; criticisms of, for Confederate military setbacks, 154–56, 156*n*178; and Hebert in Texas, 242–43; and Stonewall Jackson, 154; legal career of, 157; Magruder's difficulties with generally, xi, 151; personality of, 157; resignation of, 155; and Roanoke Island defenses, 156, 157; and Virginia Peninsula campaign, 151–57, 155*n*172, 167–68
Benton, Charles R., 285–86, 286*n*21
Benton, Thomas Hart, 42, 52*n*79

Berard, Claudius, 16
Big Bethel, Battle of, x–xi, 132–36, 132*n*58, 135*n*70, 138–39, 141, 240
Bird, Rev. Stephen M., 303, 304, 305
Blaettermann, George, 9, 10
Bland, Rev. Adam, 96
Bledsoe, Albert T., viii, 28, 142–43, 150
Bloomfield, Benjamin, 152, 152*n*154, 273
Bocanegra, José María de, 80
Bohannon, Keith, 227
Boney, F. N., 146
Bosson, Charles P., 29
Boswell, James K., 206
Botts, Benjamin A., 300
Boykin, Hamilton, 177
Boynton, Edward C., 81
Bragg, Braxton, 28, 275, 303
Bragg, Mrs. Braxton, 136
Bragg, Thomas, 156
Bravo, Nicolás, 75
Breckenridge, Clifton Rodes, 157*n*180
Breckenridge, John C., 157*n*180
Brent, Joseph Lancaster: in California, 94–95*n*75, 212; on headquarters of Magruder, 192*n*165; and Lee's plans before Seven Days' battles, 196–97; on Lee's stress and fatigue, 221–22; in Louisiana as chief of artillery and ordnance, 273; loyalty of, to Magruder, 272–73; and Magruder's disoriented movements during Seven Days' battles, 211–12, 235; on Magruder's drinking behavior, 28, 235; and Malvern Hill Battle, 219, 219*n*113, 225, 238*n*213; and Seven Days' battles, 205, 205*n*52, 208*n*65, 211–13; and Virginia Peninsula campaign, 168, 182, 187, 188*n*143
Brewster, Robert, 300
Bridges, Hal, x, 135*n*70, 178*n*99
Broadwell, W. A., 266–67
USS *Brooklyn*, 254–58
Brown, J. Thompson, 223
Brown, John Henry, 288
Bruce, Philip Alexander, 8–9, 9*n*31
Bryan, Henry, 212, 226
Bryan, Louis A., 299, 300
Buchanan, James, 107, 108–9
Buchel, Augustus, 261–62

Buckler, Isabella Magruder. *See* Magruder, Isabella

Buckler, Riggin, 23, 23*n*100, 104, 289, 297

Buckner, Richard, Jr., 101*n*98

Buckner, Simon Bolivar, 280

Buena Vista, Battle of, 60, 139

Bull Run, Battles of, 123, 158

Bunting, Rev. Dr. Robert F., 303

Burke, E. W., 300

Burke, Martin J., 71

Burnside, Ambrose E., 156

Burrell, Isaac S., 244, 246, 248–49, 296

Burton, Brian, 194*n*182, 216

Burton, Henry S., 103

Butler, Benjamin Franklin: and Big Bethel Battle, 134–35; at Fort Monroe at beginning of Civil War, 127–30, 128*n*39; lack of military training and experience of, 130–31, 130*n*47; Lincoln's lack of confidence in, 135, 138; personality and ambition of, 130–31; physical appearance of, 128; and prisoners of war during Virginia Peninsula campaign, 136–38; rank of, at beginning of Civil War, 131; and reinforcements for Renshaw in Galveston, 243; release of, from command at Fort Monroe, 138; Richmond as goal of, 131, 131*n*52; on slaves, 130, 149, 149–50*n*143; and Virginia Peninsula campaign, 127–30, 128*n*39, 134–38; on Washington, D.C., defenses, 122*n*11

Butler, William O., 52*n*79

Byrd, William, 182

Cadwalader, George, 70

Calhoun, John C., 8

California: American soldiers quartered in Mission San Diego, 92–93; Beltzhoover's accusations against Magruder over misuse of horses, 97; court-martial trials in, 94, 96, 100, 103; Craig murder case in, 100; description of San Diego, 90–92; deserters in, 95, 100; disagreements between Magruder and Jones regarding San Diego command, 85–87, 97, 99; El Dorado saloon in Los Angeles, 95–96; fist fight between Magruder and Franklin in, 97; Garra Insurrection in,

97–98; gold rush in, 89–90; land purchases by Magruder in, 93–94; law practice of Magruder in, 29, 94; leave of absence for Magruder from, 102–3; Magruder's command of San Diego post, 88–93, 96–100; Magruder's housing in, 92; Magruder's military assignment in, 29, 84–103; Magruder's personal papers destroyed in San Francisco fire, vii, 32–33, 88, 103–4; McCall's inspection of San Diego military facilities, 99; military execution in, 100; Mission San Diego in, 92–93; orders to Magruder for military assignment in, 86; Pacific Pioneer Yacht Club in, 98; pay controversy involving Magruder's Company I going to, 85–86; railroad in, 102, 103; social life in, 91–92, 94–95, 98–100; statehood for, 89; travel from San Francisco to San Diego, 89; travel to and from East Coast, 84–87, 87*n*38, 103. *See also specific cities*

Callender, Franklin D., 69, 162*n*17

Cambria, 252–54

Cameron, Simon, 114–15, 149, 149–50*n*143

Campbell, Archibald, 140

Campbell, Kimberly C., 5*n*17

Campbell, Lewis D., 292

Canby, Edward R. S., 1–2, 278, 280

Capron, Erastus A., 71–72

Carey, Wilson Miles, 10

Carlisle, J. Mandeville, 19*n*84

Carlotta, Empress, 284, 288, 295–98

Carmichael, Peter S., 27

Carroll, John Alexander, vii

Carter, Hill, 150

Carter, Private, 136, 138

Cary, John Baytop, 28, 128–30, 236, 236*n*205

Casdorph, Paul D., 27

Casey, Silas, 186

Cedar Mountain, Battle of, 201*n*32

Cerro Gordo, Battle of, 63–66, 64*n*137, 81

Chancellorsville, Battle of, 123

Chandler, Zachariah, 160

Chapultepec, Battle of, 74–77, 81

Chesnut, James, 136

Chesnut, Mary Boykin, 136, 173, 177, 231

Chickahominy River, 187–89, 196

Childs, Thomas: at Fort McHenry, 84; in Mexican War, 39, 39n8, 45, 47, 49, 60, 65–67, 66n151

Chilton, Robert H.: on alleged incompetence of Magruder in Seven Days' battles, viii, 2, 232–34, 236–38, 238n211; on divisional organization of Army of Northern Virginia, 193n171; on Jackson's mistakes during Seven Days' battles, 231; and Lee's battle plan for Malvern Hill, 221; on Magruder's "incompetence" generally, 2, 232–33; and Magruder's orders during Seven Days' battles, 210, 213, 215, 224, 231, 234; and Magruder's transfer to Trans-Mississippi Department, 232–33; and Malvern Hill Battle, 224, 227; mistakes of, during Seven Days' battles, ix, 210, 215–16, 221, 237; promotion of, to brigadier general, 238n211

Church, Albert E., 16

Churchill, William H., 45, 47, 49

Churubusco, Battle of, 71–72

Civil War: and Arkansas District, 275–77; casualties during, 132n58, 133–34, 156n178, 166n37, 174, 182–83, 183n121, 184n122, 195, 195n1, 199, 201, 204, 207, 229, 230; Confederate problem of lost opportunities during, 124; defective weapons and ammunition for Confederate army during, 143–44; deserters during, 170, 218, 264, 265, 271, 275, 277, 279–80; end of, 279–80, 292–93; explosives used in, 166n37; labor shortages for Confederate army during, 147–52; and Lincoln on defense of Washington, D.C., 122n11, 171–72; Magruder appointed as colonel in Confederate Army, 118; Magruder as division commander in Army of Northern Virginia, 193; Magruder's assignment and later recall as commander of Trans-Mississippi Department, 185–86, 232–34, 239, 240; Magruder's assignments in Richmond at beginning of, 124, 125; Magruder's headquarters during, 126, 127, 129, 143, 192, 192n165, 259, 278; Magruder's letters to superiors during, 120–21, 142, 145, 146, 152–54, 152n154, 156n174, 164n29, 185, 187–88, 262; Magruder's proposal for capture of Washington, D.C.,
at beginning of, 119–24; Magruder's staff during, 272–74; navies of U.S. and Confederacy during, 58, 159–61, 160n5, 161n12, 180, 243–58, 267–68; Pawnee scare and threat to Richmond at beginning of, 119, 119n4, 125; press coverage of generally, 139n90; prisoners of war during, 136–38, 156n178, 252–54, 254n55; selection of officers for Virginia military forces at beginning of, 118, 124; slave labor for construction of Confederate defensive works during, 127, 148–54, 167–68; slaves' defection to Union Army during, 130, 149–50; supply and troop shortages for Confederate army during, 126–27, 128, 143–47, 145n116; transfer of Virginia's forces to Confederate control, 141, 145–46, 146n118. See also Army of Northern Virginia; Army of the Potomac; Seven Days' battles; Texas in Civil War; Virginia Peninsula campaign; specific battles; and specific generals

Clark, Edward, 281

Clark, Henry T., 156, 157

Clark, John B., 282

Clarke, George W., 288

Clay, Henry, 100

Clifton, 243, 246, 248–50, 267–68

Cobb, Howell, 28, 165, 193, 206, 226, 227

Cobb, Thomas R. R., 28, 164, 164–65n32, 167, 190n157, 231–33

Cobb, W. B., 299

Columbia Guardian, 234

Condon, John, 100

Confederacy. See Civil War; Davis, Jefferson; Secession; Seven Days' battles; Texas in Civil War; Virginia Peninsula campaign; and specific battles and generals

Connor, David, 56, 58

Conrad, Bryan, 202–3

Conrad, Charles M., 102–3

Contreras, Battle of, 69–72, 71n176, 72n179, 78, 98, 162n17

Cook, Joseph J., 247, 251, 266

Cooper, Samuel: as Adjutant and Inspector General of Confederate army, 120; and allegations of Magruder's alcohol drinking, 233; and Battle of Galveston, 252; and

Benjamin-Magruder relationship, 154; and call-up of Virginia militiamen by Magruder, 146; and construction of defensive works for Virginia Peninsula campaign, 152, 154; and cotton sales for military supplies in Texas, 262; and Davis, 233; and European fact-finding mission by Magruder, 112–13; and International Boundary Commission's survey team in Texas, 104–6; and Magruder on Company I's California mission, 87*n*38; Magruder recommended by, for command in South Carolina, 233*n*191; Magruder's problems with, 121, 140–41, 143, 233; and Magruder's transfer to and recall from Trans-Mississippi Department, 232–33, 236–37; on shortage of troops for Confederate army, 147; and shortages of needed items for Confederate army, 144, 145; and slave labor used by Confederate army, 152–53, 152*n*154; and uniforms, 111; and Virginia Peninsula campaign, 144, 145, 152*n*154

Cornwallis, Lord, 179

Corpus Christi, Tex., 38, 40–42, 40*n*14

Cortéz, Hernán, 60

Cos, Martín Perfecto de, 54–55

Cotham, Edward T., Jr., 274

Cotton sales for military supplies during Civil War, 259–67, 265*n*107, 269–71

Couch, Darius, 186, 216

Couts, Cave, 97

Coward, Ashbury, 237, 237*n*207

Crabb, Henry A., 96

Craig, Lewis S., 99–100

Cropesa, Z. P., 288

Cuba, 251*n*44, 292

Curtin, Andrew Gregg, 122*n*11

Cushing, E. H., 300

Cuyler, John M., 129

Dabney, Robert L., 209

Davidson, Greenlee, 235

Davies, Charles, 16

Davis, Burke, 115

Davis, Edmund J., 253, 254, 254*n*56

Davis, Jefferson: and alleged incompetence of Magruder in Seven Days' battles, viii; and Army of Missouri, 277; and Battle of Galveston, 259; and Benjamin-Magruder relationship, 154; and call-up of Virginia militiamen by Magruder, 146; Chesnut as aide to, 136; and Cooper, 233; criticism of, 28; and flight of Confederate troops near Malvern Hill, 213; and Griffith's dying, 204*n*47; and Holmes as commander of Trans-Mississippi Department, 233, 239, 240; and Johnston, 175, 175*n*84, 193; Lee's relationship with, 192–93; and Magruder as commander of District of Texas, New Mexico, and Arizona, 241; and Magruder's proposal for capture of Washington, D.C. at beginning of Civil War, 120–21, 122*n*11; Magruder's relationship with, 139–43, 175–76; and Magruder's report refuting charges of incompetence, 238, 239*n*214; and martial law on Virginia Peninsula, 164*n*29; on Mexican colonization by former Confederates, 290; in Mexican War, 139, 140*n*93, 204, 204*n*47; military experience of, 139–40, 140*n*93; on Mobile, 275–76; and Quitman, 185; and recall of Magruder from Trans-Mississippi Department, 233, 234, 236, 239; and rumors of Magruder's drunkenness, 141, 142, 143, 235; as secretary of war in Pierce administration, 104, 112, 140; and Gustavus Smith, 190; and transfer of Virginia's forces to Confederate control, 141, 145–46; and Virginia Peninsula campaign, 175–79; at West Point, 139

Davis, Joseph R., 115

Davis, William Heath, 91–92

De la Vega, Rómulo Díaz, 44, 50, 50*n*65

De Voto, Bernard, 51

Debray, Xavier B., 259, 278*n*175, 297, 298, 302, 303

Democratic Party, 102, 106–7, 118, 128, 135, 185

Derby, George H. (John Phoenix), 81, 101

DeRussy, Lewis G., 54–55

Deserters: in California, 95, 100; during Civil War, 170, 218, 264, 265, 271, 275, 277, 279–80; during Mexican War, 40, 44

Devine, Thomas J., 265*n*107

Dickinson, A. G., 224

Douglas, David B., 16

Douglas, Hugh T., 179, 181
Dowdey, Clifford, 180, 208n65
Dowling, Richard W., 267–68
Drunkenness. *See* Alcohol drinking
Du Pont, Samuel Francis, 254n57
Dueling, 7, 13, 13n52, 67, 100–102, 101n98, 138, 228
Dummer, Samuel R., 94–96
Duncan, James, 45, 47, 68, 83–84
Dusenberry, Samuel B., 86–87
Dysentery, 40, 66

Early, Jubal, 175, 183, 183n121, 196n5, 275
Eaton, Clement, 123
Eckenrode, H. J., 202–3
Ector, Mathew D., 303
Edwards, John N., 282, 289n36
Eldridge, E. J., 28, 235, 235n202
Elgin, Lord, 109
Emmet, John P., 9
Emory, William H., 90, 105
Europe: Magruder in, 23, 102–4, 112–13, 140; Magruder's family in, 19–23, 102–4, 113, 292; military fact-finding missions to, 104, 111–13, 121, 140
Ewell, Benjamin Stoddert, 9n29, 11, 28, 145n116, 235–36
Ewell, Richard Stoddert, 118, 124, 193

Farragut, David G., 243, 244n10, 254
Farrow, Private, 30
Ferrell, William C., 94
Fitzgerald, Major, 97
Florida, 31–33, 36
Floyd, John B., 111, 112
Fontaine, Sydney, 297
Ford, John S. "Rip," 242, 303
Forshey, Caleb G., 20, 121–22n9, 245n18, 273, 295, 297
Fort Adams, R.I., 108, 109–10, 234n195
Fort Bliss, Tex., 105
Fort Brown, 264
Fort Clark, Tex., 105–6
Fort Donelson, 154
Fort Gibson Treaty, 30–31
Fort Henry, 154
Fort Johnston, N.C., 29

Fort Leavenworth, Kans., 110–12, 140
Fort Macon, N.C., 29
Fort Magruder, Va., 182–84
Fort McHenry, Md., 25–26, 29, 82–84
Fort Monroe, Va.: at border of Magruder's command on Virginia Peninsula during Civil War, 125; Butler's command of, during beginning of Civil War, 127–30, 128n39; Butler's release from command of, 138; Magruder at artillery school at, 24–25; Magruder's reports of Federal troop build-up at, 155–57, 155nn171–172; and McClellan's plan for capture of Richmond, 159; runaway slaves at, 149; Wool's command of, at beginning of Civil War, 138
Fort Pierce, Fla., 32
Fort Texas, 43–45, 166
Fort Washington, Md., 29–30
Fox, Gustavus V., 160n5, 161n12
Franklin, Lewis A., 97
Franklin, William B.: and Gaines's Mill Battle, 200; Malvern Hill position of, 216; number of Federal troops under, 196n6; position of, after Seven Pines Battle, 195; position of, following Gaines's Mill Battle, 203; position of (June 29), 205; and Savage Station Battle, 207; and Sumner's opposition to Federal retreat, 209n66; and threat against Richmond, 197; and Virginia Peninsula campaign, 186–87, 186n136
Frayser's Farm (or Glendale), Battle of, 213–16, 218, 230–31
Fredericksburg, Battle of, 123, 201n32
Freeman, Constant, 8
Freeman, Douglas Southall: on alleged incompetence of Magruder during Seven Days' battles, 216, 235n202; bias of, against Magruder generally, vii; on Big Bethel Battle, 139; and factual errors about Magruder, viii–ix; on Frayser's Farm Battle, 215; on Jackson's mistakes during Seven Days' battles, 214–16; on Lee at West Point, 16n65; on Magruder's correspondence with War Department, 156n174; on Magruder's skills as artillerist, 111; on Magruder's social life, 2; on Malvern Hill, 217, 220; on Seven Days'

battles, 200*n*28, 214–15; on Seven Pines
Battle, 189; on Virginia Peninsula campaign,
169, 189
Fremantle, Arthur Lyon, 21
Fremont, John C., 107, 186
French, Samuel G., 50*n*65
French, William H., 22, 200
Fugitive Slave Law, 130
Funston, Oliver, 124

Gaines, John P., 84
Gaines's Mill, Battle of, 199–201, 200*n*28, 209
Galena (gunboat), 213
Galveston News, 258, 297, 298–302, 300–
301*n*86, 305
Galveston, Tex.: battle of, 24, 28–29, 238*n*211,
246–52, 251*n*47, 259*n*73, 296; Bell's attempt
to recapture, for Union, 254–58; capture of
Cambria at, 252–54; casualties during battle
of, 248, 249, 251; Federal blockade of, 243,
255, 258; as free port reopened by Confed-
erates, 252, 255–56; Magruder's lecture in,
297–98; Magruder's plan for recapture of,
245–46, 245*n*18; monument to Magruder
in, 304–6, 305*n*101; prisoners of war in, 252,
253, 254, 254*n*55; reburial of Magruder in,
302–4; unconditional surrender of, to Fed-
eral blockading squadron, 243
Gambling, 40, 80
Garibaldi, Giuseppe, 113
Garland, John, 76
Garnett, James, 198, 202
Garnett, Robert S., 5*n*17, 8, 8*n*26, 124
Garra Insurrection, 97–98
Gatewood, L. T., 219
Gettysburg, Battle of, 115, 188
Giddings, George, 283
Gimbrede, Thomas, 16
Glendale (or Frayser's Farm), Battle of, 213–16,
218, 230–31
Goldsborough, Louis M., 161, 161*n*12
Goree, Thomas J., 231
Gorgas, Josiah, 143, 180
Grant, Ulysses S., 41, 47, 61–62, 74–75, 275, 278, 279
Gray, Andrew B., 90, 91
Grayson, John B., 80

Greble, John T., 133, 133–34*n*63
Greeley, Horace, 302
Griffith, Richard, 193, 204, 204*n*47
Grimsley, Mark, 181
Gwin, William, 110

Hadley, T. B. J., 300
Hale, Edward, 135*n*70
Hampton, Wade, 177, 193
Hancock, Winfield Scott, 182–83, 202
Hancock Barracks, Maine, 35–36
Hardee, William J., 45
Hardeman, William P., 282, 288, 303
Harman, John, 124
Harney, William S., 62, 63, 65, 67
Harper's Ferry, Battle of, 201*n*32
Harper's Ferry, Va., 120
Harriet Lane, 243, 244*n*12, 246, 249–51,
251*n*44, 253, 255, 255*n*60, 258
Harris, Ira, 171
Harris, Isham G., 288
Harrison, James E., 278*n*175
Hart, Simeon, 240, 260–65, 265*n*107, 272
Haskin, William L., 58, 72*n*179
USS *Hatteras,* 255, 257–58
Hawes, James M., 281
Hay, John, 160*n*7
Hay, Thomas Robson, vii, ix
Hayden, Horace Edwin, 5*n*17
Hayes, Charles Waldo, 245*n*18
Hayes, William, 100
Hebert, Paul O., 242–44, 244*n*13, 273
Heintzelman, Samuel P.: and Gaines's Mill
Battle, 200; on Magruder's drunkenness,
98*n*91; on Magruder's travel to California
military assignment, 87*n*38; Malvern Hill
position of, 216; number of troops under,
196*n*6; position of, before Seven Days' bat-
tles, 195; position of, following Gaines's Mill
Battle, 203; position of (June 29), 205; in San
Diego, 91; and threat against Richmond,
197; and Virginia Peninsula campaign,
169–70, 186–89, 188*n*143
Henry, Robert Selph, 229
Henry, William S., 39*n*7, 40, 50*n*65
Heth, Henry, 118

Heyward, William C., 13

Heywood, William C., 13*n*53

Higgins, Edward, 294

Hill, A. P.: and Battle of Frayser's Farm (or Glendale), 218, 230–31; and Battle of Gettysburg, 115; and Battle of Seven Pines, 188, 189; as division commander in Army of Northern Virginia, 193; and Gaines's Mill Battle, 199–201, 209; and Lee's plans before Seven Days' battles, 196; and Mechanicsville Battle, 197–98, 198*n*15, 209; position of, during Malvern Hill Battle, 218; position of (June 30), 211, 212; pursuit of McClellan's troops during Seven Days' battles, 203–4

Hill, D. H.: and Battle of Seven Pines, 188, 189, 209; and Big Bethel Battle, x–xi, 133, 135, 135*n*70; as division commander in Army of Northern Virginia, 194; on drinking behavior of Magruder, 28, 131–32; on Fort Magruder Battle, 183; and Gaines's Mill Battle, 199; on Jackson's mistakes during Seven Days' battles, 230–31; and Lee as commander of army of Northern Virginia, 192; Magruder's relationship with, 190*n*157; and Malvern Hill Battle, 222, 223, 227–29, 227*n*157, 231; and Malvern Hill position of Federal troops, 217–18; and Mechanicsville Battle, 197–98; in Mexican War, 76, 76*n*200; and retreat from Virginia Peninsula, 181; and Seven Days' battles, viii, 196, 203, 215; and Virginia Peninsula campaign, 127, 131–33, 135, 145, 178*n*99, 181, 183, 188, 189

Hindman, Thomas C., 281–82

Hitchcock, Ethan Allen, 12, 39–40, 42, 46, 64, 73, 97

Hoffman, Saterlee, 71

Holmes, Theophilus: in Army of Northern Virginia, 194, 194*n*179, 196*n*5; and Battle of Galveston, 259*n*77; as commander of Trans-Mississippi Department, 233, 239–41; and cotton sales for military supplies for Texas, 259–67; and Seven Days' battles, 204, 211–13, 215–16, 218

Hood, John Bell, 127, 149, 193, 276, 277

Hooker, Joe, 182–83, 186

Houston, Sam, 259

Houston, Tex., 245, 259, 278, 298–300

Houston Telegraph, 300

Hubbard, Richard B., 303

Huger, Benjamin: and Battle of Seven Pines, 188–89, 209, 225; Benjamin's transfer of troops to, 155, 156, 167; as division commander in Army of Northern Virginia, 193, 194, 194*n*179; and Gaines's Mill Battle, 199, 200; and Malvern Hill Battle, 218, 225–26, 231, 231*n*184; mistakes of, during Seven Days' battles, 216; movements of (June 30), 211, 212, 214; at Norfolk, 169, 177; number of troops under, 188*n*144, 196*n*5; seniority of, over Longstreet and Magruder, 224*n*146, 225–26; and Seven Days' battles, ix, 196, 203–6, 205*n*49, 209, 229; withdrawal of, from Virginia Peninsula, 180

Hughes, John H., 96

Hughes, Archbishop John Joseph, 96

Hughes, Robert M., 162, 182*n*116

Hummel, Jeffrey Rogers, 123

Hunt, Henry J., 216

Hunter, Robert M. T., 36

Hurxthall, Lieutenant, 302

Huske, Benjamin, 135*n*70

Imboden, John, 124

Impressment Act, 262–64, 270–71

Indians: and Craig murder case, 100; and Garra Insurrection, 97–98; Jackson's removal policy on, 30–31; and Magruder's assignment in Texas with International Boundary Commission, 105–6; and Second Seminole War, 31–33, 41

International Boundary Commission, 22, 23, 90, 93, 99, 99–100*n*94, 104–6, 140

Irons, Joseph S., 71

Jack, Thomas M., 298, 303

Jackson, Andrew, 30–31, 51, 100

Jackson, Thomas Jonathan (Stonewall): Benjamin's relationship with, 154; criticism of, 28; friendship between Magruder and, 67; and Gaines's Mill Battle, 200–201; and Lee's plans before Seven Days' battles, 196; on Magruder's relationships with women, 22;

and Malvern Hill Battle, 218, 219*n*113, 223, 231; and Mechanicsville Battle, 197–98; in Mexican War, 67, 70, 75–77, 162*n*17; military successes of, 201*n*32; mistakes of, during Seven Days' battles, viii, ix, 197–98, 198*n*15, 200–201, 201*n*32, 205–10, 209*n*68, 214–16, 230–31; pursuit of McClellan's troops during Seven Days' battles, 203, 209–11; and Savage Station Battle, 205–10, 208*n*65, 209*n*68; and Shenandoah Valley campaign, 186, 193, 231; and Virginia Peninsula campaign during Civil War, 67

James River, 125–26, 161*n*12, 167, 171, 177, 178, 180, 192, 213, 217, 230

Jeanningros, Pierre Jean Joseph, 283, 285

Jefferson, Thomas, 9–10, 135

Jesup, Thomas, 32–33, 36

Johnson, Andrew, 281, 291

Johnson, Robert Ward, 272

Johnston, Joseph E.: appointment of, as major general of Virginia volunteers, 118; army of, in northern Virginia, 158, 159, 159*n*3, 169; and Army of Tennessee, 275, 276; and Battle of Seven Pines, 188–90, 189*n*148; and Battle of Williamsburg, 182–84; and cautious, low-risk approach to war, 175*n*84, 179; compared with Magruder, 176–77, 190; Davis's opinion of, 175, 175*n*84, 193; family background of, 177; on indefensibility of Virginia Peninsula, 175–78, 178*n*99; and Lee on proposed Washington, D.C., attack, 123*n*12; Magruder's disagreements with, xi, 190–91; and McClellan's plan for capture of Richmond, 158, 159, 159*n*3; personality of, 176–77, 191; and Second Seminole War, 31; and selection of Virginia officers at beginning of Civil War, 124; and Virginia Peninsula campaign, 175–84, 188–90; Washington, D.C., temporary assignment for, 110; withdrawal of, from Virginia Peninsula, 179–86; wounds of, in Battle of Seven Pines, 189–90

Johnston, Robert, 143, 149

Johnstone, John P., 62, 71–72, 71*n*169, 162*n*17

Jones, A. C., 282

Jones, David R., 182, 184, 193, 204–6, 227, 232–33, 237

Jones, John B., 231, 259, 259*n*73

Jones, Roger, xi, 83–87, 97, 99, 106, 121, 141, 191

Jones, Wilson, 100

Juárez, Benito, 291, 292

Kearny, Philip, 112, 186

Keating, J. P., 98

Kellersberger, Getulius, 273, 273*n*151

Ker, Croghan, 45, 46

Kershaw, Joseph B., 193, 205, 207, 228

Key, Thomas Hewett, 9, 10

Keyes, Erasmus D.: and Gaines's Mill Battle, 200; Malvern Hill position of, 216; and threat against Richmond, 197; and Virginia Peninsula campaign, 169–71, 186–89, 188*n*143, 195; at West Point, 25; and withdrawal of Federal troops following Gaines's Mill Battle, 203

Know-Nothing Party, 106

La Atalaya, Battle of, 62–63

Lamb, John, 28, 219*n*112, 236

Lane, Harriet, 108

Law, Richard L., 248–50

Lawton, Alexander, 193

Lea, Albert Miller, 24, 249, 273

Lea, Edward, 248, 249

Leach, Richard, 22

Leadbetter, Danville, 282

Ledwith, Judge, 294

Lee, Custis, 115

Lee, John Fitzgerald, 24, 301*n*86

Lee, Robert E.: appointment of, as major general of Virginia military forces, 118; on attack on Washington, D.C., by Joe Johnston, 123*n*12; as commander of Army of Northern Virginia, 190, 191–92, 191*n*158; and construction of fortifications, 192; criticism of, 28; as Davis's military coordinator, 168–69; Davis's relationship with, 192–93; on labor shortage for defensive works around Richmond, 147; Longstreet's misgivings about, 191; and Magruder's proposal for capture of Washington, D.C., 119, 122–24, 123*n*12; and Magruder's report refuting charges of incompetence, 238–39; in Mexican War, 61,

Lee, Robert E. (*continued*):
69; and organization of Army of Northern
Virginia, 193–94; pardon for, 290; at Petersburg, 275, 278; protection of Richmond as
goal of, 194; and questions of Magruder's
competence, 232; reassignment of, to western Virginia and South Carolina, 151, 168;
and rumors of Magruder's drunkenness,
141–43; surrender of, at Appomattox, 279;
and Virginia Peninsula campaign, 145, 151,
169, 172*n*66, 173, 175, 177–78; at West Point,
16*n*65, 191; and White Sulphur Springs statement, 293
—Seven Days' battles: end of, 230; frustrations during, 207–8, 214, 215, 230; Gaines's
Mill Battle, 199–201; Magruder's need for
reinforcements during, 205, 209; Magruder's reprimands during, 207–8, 224–25,
229–30; Malvern Hill Battle, 217–32, 219*n*113;
Malvern Hill position of Federal troops,
217–18; Mechanicsville Battle, 197–98,
198*n*15; mistakes of Lee during, viii, 219–24,
229, 238; plans before, 196–97; plans for
June 30 actions, 211–14; Porter's retreat following Gaines's Mill Battle, 201–2; problem
of inadequate maps, 201, 220–21, 224*n*114,
230; Savage Station Battle, 209, 224–25, 230;
stress and fatigue of Lee during, 221–22. *See
also* Army of Northern Virginia
Lee, St. George S., 259*n*78
Lee, Stephen D., 198, 199, 275
Lee, Susan P., 10, 13*n*53
Lee, Sydney Smith, 124
Leech, Margaret, 115–16, 122*n*11
Lee's Mill, Va., 168, 170, 171, 174, 181
Letcher, John, 118, 119, 124, 125, 141, 145–46,
146*n*118, 155, 293
Lincoln, Abraham: and amnesty for former
Confederates, 281; and Butler, 135, 138; and
defense of Washington, D.C., 122*n*11, 171–72;
and Magruder's resignation, 114–17; and
McClellan, 158, 160, 160*n*7, 172–73, 186; and
secession of Virginia, 113–17
Lockahatchee, Battle of, 32
Lomax, Elizabeth Lindsay, 110
Lomax, John Tayloe, 3

Long, George, 9
Longstreet, James: and Army Theater Troupe,
41; and Battle of Frayser's Farm (or Glendale), 213–15, 218, 230–31; and Battle of
Seven Pines, 188–89, 209, 225; on commissioning of Gustavus Smith and Lovell,
185*n*126; as division commander in Army
of Northern Virginia, 193; on explosives not
to be used in Civil War, 166*n*37; on Jackson's mistakes during Seven Days' battles,
209*n*68, 215, 230; on Lee as commander of
Army of Northern Virginia, 191; Lee's meeting with, 192; and Lee's plans before Seven
Days' battles, 196; and Malvern Hill Battle,
221–23; and Malvern Hill position of Federal troops, 217–18; and Mechanicsville Bat-
tle, 197–98; position of, during Malvern Hill
Battle, 218; position of (June 30–July 1), 211,
212; pursuit of McClellan's troops during
Seven Days' battles, 203–4; and withdrawal
from Virginia Peninsula, 181–83
Lorgescope, L., 300
Los Angeles, Calif., 94–96, 100–101
Louisiana, 108, 275. *See also* New Orleans, La.
Lovell, Mansfield, 184–85, 185*n*126
Lowe, Thaddeus S., 199–200
Lubbock, Francis R., 248*n*31, 272, 297, 303
Lubbock, Henry S., 248–51, 248*n*31, 258–59
Lubbock, John B., 248*n*31
Lubbock, William M., 248*n*31
Lux, John G., 288
Lyon, Nathaniel, 91, 92
Lyons, James, 106–8, 122–23, 293

Mabens, Daniel, 294
Mackenzie, William Lyon, 33
Macrae, Nathaniel C., 110
Madison, James, 9
Magruder, Alexander, 4
Magruder, Allan B., 5, 6*n*17, 102–3, 113
Magruder, Eleanor Bowie, 5
Magruder, Elizabeth Bankhead, 5–7, 7*n*24
Magruder, Esther Henrietta von Kapff: in
Baltimore, 19–20, 19*n*84, 22, 23, 36, 82, 104;
birth date of, 18; children of, 19, 19*nn*83–84,
following p. 194; death of, 23; in Europe,

19–23, 102–4, 113, 292; given name of, 18n80; health problems of, 21–22, 23, 289; inheritance of, 18n80; marriage of, viii, 2n6, 7, 18–24, 19n81, 82, 113, 289, 292; in Mexico, 20, 289–90; miniature of, *following p. 194*; physical appearance of, 18; and reburial of Magruder in Galveston, 302; siblings of, 18n79, 19n84

Magruder, George A., Jr., 127, 272

Magruder, George Allan, 5, 5–6n17, 113

Magruder, George Frazer, 4–5

Magruder, Helen, 284

Magruder, Henry R.: in Baltimore, 82, 104; in Europe, 19, 23, 104, 292; death of, 23; inheritance of father's sword by, 23, 78n211; in Mexico, 20, 289–90; parents of, viii; portrait of, *following p. 194*; and reburial of Magruder in Galveston, 302

Magruder, Isabella: in Baltimore, 82, 292, 296–97; children of, 23n100, 297; death of, 297; in Europe, 19, 23, 102–3; health problems of, 19, 23, 102–3, 297; Magruder's visits with, after her marriage, 292, 296–97; marriage of, 23, 23n100, 104, 289, 292, 296–97; and money for father's tombstone, 23, 304n100; parents of, viii

Magruder, John Bankhead: accusations against, of taking money from Confederate cotton sale to Mexico, 285–87; and alcohol drinking, 26–29, 96, 97, 98, 98n91, 131–32, 139n90, 141–43, 233–36, 236n203, 254n57; arrest of, in New York City for disturbing the peace, 293–94, 301–2; birth date and place of, viii, 2, 2n6, 176, 305n101; at Buchanan inauguration and inaugural ball, 108–9; business failures of, 95–96; business of, in Los Angeles owned by, 95–96; children of, viii, 19, 19nn83–84, *following p. 194*; death, funeral, and burial of, 299–300, 300–301n86; and dueling, 7, 13, 67, 100–102, 138; education of, 8–18; estate of, 94; in Europe, 23, 102–4, 112–13, 140; factual errors and misunderstandings about generally, vii–ix, 114–16, 292–93, 300–302; family history of, 2–8, 9n29, 177; father of, compared with, 7–8; finances of, xi, 1, 7, 20, 34n150, 285–87;

fist fight with Franklin in San Diego, 97; grandchildren of, 23n100, 297; health problems of, 31, 35–36, 81–82, 180–82, 211–12, 214, 235, 294, 297, 299; land purchases by, in California, 93–94; law practice of, 29, 94, 292; lecture tour and speeches by, 103, 234, 294–98; lisp of, 11, 295; marriage and family relations of, viii, 2n6, 7, 18–24, 19n81, 82, 113, 289, 292; in Mexico after Civil War, 20, 23, 281–91; moniker of, as "Prince John," 20; monument to, in Galveston, 304–6, 305n101; New Orleans home of, 294; in New York City, 103, 292–94; obituaries of, 301–2; pardon for, 292, 293; personal papers destroyed in San Francisco fire, vii, 32–33, 88, 103–4; personality of, xi; photographs and portrait of, *following p. 194*, 236n205; physical appearance of, 11, 21, 234n195; and political parties, 53, 106–8; reburial of, in Galveston, 302–4; siblings of, 5, 5–6n17; social life of, 1, 2, 3, 7, 20–21, 25, 34–35, 80–81, 92, 94–95, 98–100, 106, 108–10, 245, 274–75; on states' rights, 107; tombstone for, 23, 304n100; at West Point, xi, 1, 8, 10–18, 17n73, 39, 139; women's relationships with, 21, 22, 110; yachting by, 98–99; youth of, 3

—military career: assessment of Magruder's military strategy, 1–2, 121–22, 121–22n9; Baton Rouge, La., temporary assignment, 108; California assignment, 29, 84–103; disagreements between Magruder and his superiors, xi, 83–87, 97, 99; dismounting/remounting of Company I, 1st Artillery, 83–84, 97, 105–6, 109, 140; dissatisfactions with, 35–36, 52; as draftsman in Ordnance Department in Washington, D.C., 31; European military fact-finding mission, 112–13, 140; Fort Adams, R.I., 108, 109–10; Fort Johnston, N.C., 29; Fort Leavenworth, Kans., 110–12, 140; Fort Macon, N.C., 29; Fort McHenry, Md., 25–26, 29, 82–84; Fort Monroe artillery school, 24–25; Fort Washington, Md., 29–30; Hancock Barracks, Maine, garrison duty, 35–36; honors for, 23, 77–78; knowledge of light artillery, 82–83, 111; letters to superiors during, 36, 83–84, 86,

—military career (*continued*):
104, 105, 112, 120–21, 142, 145, 146, 152–54,
152n154, 156n174, 164n29, 185, 187–88, 262;
in Plattsburg, N.Y., along Canadian border,
33–35; and promotions, 14, 36, 39, 42, 65,
77, 81, 105, 141–42; recruiting assignments,
35, 36, 52; resignation from U.S. Army following Virginia's secession, 114–17; salary
for military service, 34, 34n150; San Diego
command, 88–93, 96–100; Second Seminole
War in Florida, 31–33, 36; in Texas with International Boundary Commission, 22, 23,
104–6, 140; and uniforms, 81, 111; Washington, D.C., temporary assignment, 110. *See
also* California; Civil War; Mexican War;
Seven Days' battles; Texas in Civil War; Virginia Peninsula campaign
Magruder, Katherine Elizabeth: in Baltimore,
82, 104; death and will of, 23, 304n100; in
Europe, 19, 23, 104, 292; in Mexico, 20, 289;
parents of, viii; portrait of, *following p. 194*;
and reburial of Magruder in Galveston, 302
Magruder, Samuel and Sarah, 4
Magruder, Thomas, 2–8, 3n7, 7n24, 8n27,
101n98, *following p. 194*
Magruder, William and Mary Frazer, 4
Magruder, William T., 115–16
Mahone, Billy, 193–94, 194n179, 218, 225–27
Malaria, 180–82
Mallory, Charles K., 130
Malvern Hill: artillery not ready for, 222–23;
battle of, 224–32; criticisms of Magruder
at, 229–32, 231n184; description of, 217–18;
Federal position at, 216–17, 217n103; flight of
Confederate troops during skirmish near,
213; Lee's battle plan (July 1) for, 218–24;
Lee's mistakes at, 219–24, 238; Magruder
and Quaker Road mix-up before battle of,
218–19, 219nn112–113, 234, 238; Magruder at,
224–25, 229–32, 231n184, 234, 238, 238n213;
McClellan's withdrawal from, 230
Manassas, Second Battle of, 201n32
Mann, Walter L., 286–87
Mansfield, Jared, 16
Mansfield, La., Battle, 275
Marcy, Randolph, 170

Marcy, William L., 41–42, 64
Marshall, James, 89
Martinez, Dr., 81–82
Mathew, Theobald, 28, 28–29n124
Maury, Dabney H., xi
Maury, Matthew Fontaine, 118, 283, 288–90
Maverick, Samuel A., 108
Maximilian, Emperor, 283–85, 285n17, 288–91,
295–98
May, Charles A., 45, 49–50, 50n65
McCall, George A., 99, 196n8
McClellan, George B.: and Battle of Seven
Pines, 188–90, 189n148; and capture of
Yorktown, 161, 172, 174; and cautious,
slow approach to war, 160, 160n7, 174, 186,
199–200, 202–3; as commander of Army
of the Potomac, 157–61, 158n1; criticisms of
and mistakes by, 160–61, 160n7, 161–63, 172,
175; and Gaines's Mill Battle, 200; headquarters of, at White House, 186, 195; inaccurate
information and inadequate maps for,
161–63, 163nn18–19, 170, 189, 199–200, 203;
and Johnston's retreat from Virginia Peninsula, 180; Lee's plans against, before Seven
Days' battles, 195–97; and Lincoln, 158, 160,
160n7, 172–73, 186; Magruder's deceptive
ploys against, 173–74, 198–200, 199n20,
200n28; Magruder's plan for defense of
Virginia Peninsula against, 126–27, 131,
166–68, 172–75, 178; Magruder's plan of attack against, in Virginia Peninsula, 178–79;
in Mexican War, 69, 162n17; movement of,
toward Richmond, 169–72, 186–87, 195–96;
and organization of Army of the Potomac,
186; plans of, for capture of Richmond, 158–
63, 160n7, 161n14; and Seven Days' battles,
198–99; and Urbanna plan, 158–59, 162; and
withdrawal of Federal troops during Seven
Days' battles, 202–4, 205n49, 206, 209–13,
230. *See also* Army of the Potomac
McClung, Alexander Keith, 13n52
McClure, Alexander K., 122n11
McCormick, Michael, 247, 251
McCoy, James, 93–94
McCulloch, Henry S., 271, 271n143
McDowell, Irvin, 159, 171–72, 186

McGuire, Judith, 232

McIntosh, James S., 39

McKee, Andrew W., 261

McKeen, A. C., 245n18

McKinstry, Justus, 98

McLane, George, 102

McLaughlin, John T., 31

McLaws, Lafayette: as division commander in Army of Northern Virginia, 193; and Seven Days' battles, 204–7, 214n85, 228; and Virginia Peninsula campaign, 165, 166, 177, 186n134, 190

McLemore, M. C., 303

McRae, Duncan K., 183, 183n121

Meagher, Thomas F., 200, 228

Mechanicsville, Battle of, 197–99, 198n15, 199n20, 209

Medford, H. C., 274

Mejía, Francisco, 44

Melton, Samuel W., 185

Menger, Otto, 282n

USS Merrimack, 159

Mexican Times, 289n36

Mexican War: Arista's retreat after Battle of Palo Alto, 48–49; armistice during, after U.S. victory at Monterrey, 51n72; and Aztec Club, 80–81, 80–81n5; Battle of Buena Vista, 60, 139; Battle of Cerro Gordo, 63–66, 64n137, 81; Battle of Chapultepec, 74–77, 81; Battle of Contreras, 69–71, 71n176, 72, 72n179, 78, 98, 162n7; Battle of La Atalaya, 62–63; Battle of Molino del Rey, 72–75; Battle of Monterrey, 51n72, 74; Battle of Palo Alto, 46–48, 47n54, 51, 166; Battle of Resaca de la Palma, 48–51, 166; beginning of, 44–45; Carricitos Ranch skirmish, 44–45; casualties of, 44, 47–48, 48n58, 50, 59, 59n115, 64, 64n137, 65, 69–74, 70n169, 73n185, 76, 77, 162n7; cease-fire during, granted by Scott, 72–73; Churubusco assault, 71–72; competency of U.S. officers during, 39–40; Connor's blockading fleet during, 56; Jefferson Davis in, 139–40, 140n93, 204, 204n47; defense of Mexico City during, 68–69; DeRussy's Louisiana volunteers' avoidance of capture, 54–55; deserters during, 40, 44;

and Fort Texas, 43–45, 166; Lobos Islands as staging ground for Vera Cruz expedition, 55–56; Magruder's battlefield experiences during, 45–48, 62–67, 69–70, 73–78, 81, 162n7; Magruder's orders and assignment for, 37, 39; Magruder's wounds during, 76, 77; morale of U.S. soldiers in Texas before, 40; movement of U.S. Army from Corpus Christi to mouth of Rio Grande, 42–44; movement of U.S. Army from Plan de Río around La Atalaya, 61–62; movement of U.S. Army from Vera Cruz to Plan del Río, 60–61, 61n120; Padierna Ranch assault, 69–71, 71n176, 72; praise for Magruder and his promotions during, 39, 65, 77–78, 81; prisoners of war during, 44–45, 64, 70, 70n169, 71; provisions for U.S. Army during, 45, 66; Puebla encampment for U.S. Army, 66–67, 66n151; Scott's advance on Mexico City, 66–77; Scott's command during, 52–77, 165; size of U.S. Army in, 38–39, 53, 61, 66–67; Tampico encampment for U.S. Army during, 53–54; Taylor's command during, 37–39, 38n4, 39n8, 41–52, 51n72, 165; and U.S. annexation of Texas, 37, 38; U.S. Army in Texas before, 38–44; U.S. occupation of Mexico City during, 77, 79–81, 80–81n5; Vera Cruz expedition, 52, 55–60, 58n110, 59n115

Mexico: agriculture in, 288; Confederate colonization of, 281–91; Emperor Maximilian and Empress Carlotta in, 283–85, 285n17, 288–91, 295–98; Land Office of Colonization in, 287–91; land values in, 288–89; Magruder and Mexican Times in, 289n36; Magruder as Mexican citizen, 287; Magruder family in, 20, 289–90; Magruder in, after Civil War, 20, 23, 281–91; railroad in, 288; Slidell mission to, 38, 42; social life in, 283; travel to, 282–83. See also Mexican War

Mexico City, 68–69, 77, 79–81, 283–85, 287–91

Meyers, Gunner, 91–92

Michler, Nathaniel, 105

Middleton, Susan Matilda, 234, 234n195

Military uniforms. See Uniforms

Militias, 146–47

Minor, John, 3
Mission San Diego, 92–93
Missouri, 276–77
Mohl, Aurelia H., 300
Mohl, Fritz, 300
Molino del Rey, Battle of, 72–75
USS *Monitor*, 159–60, 160*n*5
Monroe, James, 9
Monterrey, Battle of, 51*n*72, 74
Moore, Thomas O., 281
Morales, Juan, 57, 58
Mordecai, Alfred, 289–90, 290*n*37
Morehead, Charles S., 281
Morell, George, 186, 216
Mosby, John S., 123*n*12
Murrah, Pendleton, 272, 281
Myers, Abraham C., 152, 152*n*154

Napier, Lady, 110
Napoleon I, 202–203
Napoleon III, 291
Nashville, Battle of, 156, 277
Navies during Civil War, 58, 159–61, 160*n*5,
    161*n*12, 180, 243–58, 267–68
Neptune, 246, 247–48
New Orleans, Battle of, 51
New Orleans, La., 254, 277–78, 280, 294–97
New Orleans Delta, 165–66, 166*n*36
New Orleans Era, 285
New York City, 103, 292–94, 301–2
New York Herald, 1, 300
New York Times, 89, 287, 290, 292, 293*n*52
New York Times Magazine, 295
New York Tribune, 149, 301–2
Newcastle, Duke of, 109
Newport News, Va., 128, 129, 155*n*171
Newport, R.I., 110
Newspapers. *See specific newspapers*
Nichols, William H., 303
Nicolay, John G., 160*n*7
Norfolk, Va., 159, 161, 161*n*12, 169, 172, 177–78, 180
Norris, William, 155*n*171
North, Thomas, 244*n*13

Odin, John, 278
Oliver, William, 98

Osborn, William, 100–101, 101*n*97
Ott, Charles Sebastian, 304
Ott, John, 304
Owasco, 243, 250, 255
Owsley, Lady, 110

Padierna Ranch, Battle of, 69–71, 71*n*176, 72
Page, John, 47
Palo Alto, Battle of, 46–48, 47*n*54, 51, 166
Parks, Joseph Howard, 285
Parton, James, 136
Partridge, Alden, 12
Paschal, I. A., 108
Patterson, Francis E., 92
Patterson, Robert, 52*n*79, 53–56, 60–61
Pawnee scare, 119, 119*n*4, 125
Payne, John, 253–54, 254*nn*55–56
Payne's Landing Treaty, 30–31
Pegram, Robert, 124
Pemberton, John C., 233*n*191
Pender, Dorsey, 193
Pendleton, Eugene B., 93, 298
Pendleton, William Nelson, 10, 13, 17, 202*n*37,
    223
Perkins, John, 288
Petersburg, Battle of, 275, 278
Phillips, Jefferson C., 28, 235–36
Pierce, Benjamin K., 31, 32, 36
Pierce, Ebenezer, 132, 134
Pierce, Franklin: and Aztec Club in Mexico
    City, 80, 80*n*5; Davis as secretary of war
    for, 104, 112, 140; and dueling, 67, 102; in
    Mexican War, 70; as presidential candidate
    (1852), 53, 102
Pillow, Gideon J., 63, 67, 69, 72*n*179, 73, 75, 77
Pinkerton, Allan, 162, 203, 203*n*41
Political parties. *See specific political parties*
Polk, James K., 42, 46*n*48, 51*n*72, 52*n*79, 53, 84
Polk, Leonidas, 15
Polk, Trusten, 281
Pollard, E. A., 175
Poore, Ben Perley, 108–9
Porter, David, 41, 275
Porter, Fitz John: as commander of 5th Corps
    of Army of the Potomac, 186, 186*n*136; and
    Gaines's Mill Battle, 199–201; Lee's plans

against before Seven Days' battles, 196; Malvern Hill position of, 213, 216, 217n103; and Mechanicsville Battle, 197–99; number of troops under, 196, 196n8; position of, before Seven Days' battles, 187, 195; retreat of, following Gaines's Mill Battle, 201–2; and withdrawal of Federal troops following Gaines's Mill Battle, 203

Porter, Theodoric, 41

Powell, H. M. T., 90

Power, William, 36

Preston, William, 282

Price, Sterling, 239, 276, 277, 281, 288

Prime, Frederick E., 120

Prisoners of war: in Civil War, 136–38, 156n178, 252–54, 254n55; in Mexican War, 44–45, 64, 70, 70n169, 71

Prostitutes, 40, 80

Putnam, Sallie, 133n60, 231n184

Quitman, John A., 67, 76, 80, 80n5, 185

Railroads: in California, 102, 103; in Mexico, 288; in Texas, 274; in Virginia, 119, 120, 159. See also Transportation and travel

Rains, Gabriel James, 166, 166n37

Randolph, George Wythe: biography of, viii; and call-up of Virginia militiamen by Magruder, 146; as Confederate secretary of war, 155n171, 169, 273; loyalty of, to Magruder, 272–73; and Magruder's assignment as commander of Trans-Mississippi Department, 185–86, 232; and Magruder's report refuting charges of incompetence, 238; and Magruder's reports of Federal troop build-up in Virginia Peninsula, 155n171; on rumors of Magruder's drunkenness, 28, 142–43; on Virginia Peninsula, 162; and Virginia Peninsula campaign, 131, 132, 135, 177–78

Ransom, Robert, 194, 194n179, 218, 225–26, 228–29

Ransom, Trueman B., 70

Red River expedition, 267, 275

Renshaw, William B., 243–44, 244n10, 244n12, 249, 250

Republican Party, 107, 122n11

Resaca de la Palma, Battle of, 48–51, 166

Revolutionary War, 165, 179

Reynolds, Thomas C., 281

Rhode Island, 109–10

Rhodes, Henry W., 303

Richardson, Israel, 186

Richardson, William H., 147n126

Richmond Dispatch, 139

Richmond Enquirer, 108

Richmond Examiner, 136

Richmond Whig, 133, 133n60, 149–50n143, 166n36, 235–36n202, 240

Ridgley, Randolph, 47, 49

Ridley, Alonzo, 288

Riley, Bennett, 60, 70

Ringgold, Samuel, 42–43, 45, 47, 49

Ripley, Roswell, 194

Roanoke Island, 154, 156, 156n178, 157

Roberts, Oran M., 288

Robertson, Felix, 303

Robertson, James I., Jr., 76n200, 221

Robertson, Jerome B., 303

Robinson, James W., 94

Rosecrans, William, 293

Royston, Mart H., 303

Runaway slaves. See Slaves

Russell, Charles, 264

Sabine Pass expedition, 267–68

Sachem, 246, 250, 267–68

San Antonio, Tex., 281–82

San Diego, Calif., 29, 84, 88–100, 90n49, 102

San Diego Herald, 97–98, 102

San Francisco, Calif., vii, 32–33, 88, 88n41, 90

Santa Anna, General, 60–61, 63, 64, 68–72, 75, 77, 79

Savage Station, Battle of, 205–10, 208n65, 209n68, 224–25, 230

Scarlett, Sir Peter Campbell, 284, 287

Scharf, J. Thomas, 180, 247

Scott, Ed, 98

Scott, Winfield: and Big Bethel Battle during Civil War, 134–35; and Butler, 130; education of, 52; and Mackenzie's abortive attempt to overthrow Canadian government, 33; and

Scott, Winfield (*continued*):
Magruder, 53, 121; and Mexican War, 42, 52–77, 52*n*79, 61*n*120, 165; military effectiveness of, 53, 61; nickname of, 53; occupation of Mexico City by, 77, 79–81; orders to Magruder from, to return from European trip, 113; physical appearance of, 52; presidential candidate (1852), 52*n*79, 53, 102; and Second Seminole War, 31; on Washington, D.C., as not defensible at beginning of Civil War, 122*n*11; and Whig Party, 52*n*79

Scurry, William R., 248–51, 261

Sears, Stephen, 121, 176, 194*n*182, 221

Secession, 113–18, 130

Second Seminole War, 31–33, 41

Seddon, James A., 262, 265, 272, 277

Sedgwick, John, 186, 189

Semmes, Paul J., 193, 207, 228–29

Semmes, Raphael, 58, 58*n*110, 256–58

Serra, Junípero, 92

Seven Days' battles: of Allen's farm, 204, 207; casualties in, 199, 201, 204, 204*n*47, 207, 229, 230; Davis's visit during, 213; end of, 230; of Frayser's Farm (or Glendale), 213–16, 218, 230–31; of Gaines's Mill, 199–201, 200*n*28, 209; Huger's movements (June 30), 211, 212, 214; at James Garnett's farm, 202; and "Land Merrimack" (armor-plated mobile gun), 204; Lee's frustrations during, 207–8, 214, 215, 230; Lee's plan before, 196–97; Lee's plan for June 30 actions, 211–14; Lee's problems with inadequate maps during, 201, 220–21, 224*n*114, 230; Lee's stress and fatigue during, 221–22; of Malvern Hill, 219–32, 231*n*184, 238*n*213; McClellan's lack of accurate information during, 199–200, 203; of Mechanicsville, 197–99, 198*n*15, 199*n*20, 209; mistakes by Chilton during, ix, 210, 215–16, 237; mistakes by Lee in, viii, 219–24, 229, 238; mistakes by Stonewall Jackson in, viii, ix, 197–98, 198*n*15, 200–201, 201*n*32, 205–10, 209*n*68, 214–16, 230–31; Porter's retreat following Gaines's Mill Battle, 201–2; pursuit of McClellan's troops by Confederates, 203–4, 209–11; of Savage Station, 205–10, 208*n*65, 209*n*68, 224–25, 230; size of Army

of Northern Virginia during, 196, 196*n*5, 205–6, 205*n*52, 209, 211, 215; size of Army of the Potomac during, 196*n*6, 196*n*8, 202, 205, 211, 216; supplies for Federal troops during, 203; withdrawal of McClellan's troops during, 202–4, 205*n*49, 206, 209–13, 230; wounded and sick Union troops left behind during Federal retreat, 207
—Magruder in: alleged incompetence of Magruder, viii–ix, 200*n*28, 205*n*49, 207–10, 216, 229–34, 236–38; and deceptive ploys, 198–200, 199*n*20, 200*n*28; health problems of Magruder, 211–12, 214; June 28 night position, 202; June 29 position, 204–6; June 30–31 disoriented movements, 211–14, 235; Lee's reprimands of Magruder during, 207–8, 224–25, 229–30; Malvern Hill Battle, 224–25, 229–32, 231*n*184, 234, 238, 238*n*213; need for reinforcements, 205, 209; position during Frayser's Farm battle (June 30), 213–16; Quaker Road mix-up before Malvern Hill Battle, 218–19, 219*nn*112–113, 234, 238; report by Magruder refuting charges of incompetence, 234–40

Seven Pines, Battle of, 188–90, 189*n*148, 209, 225

Seward, William H., 291

Seymour, Horatio, 293

Shackleford, George, viii

Shannon, Colonel, 300

Sharpsburg, Battle of, 201*n*32

Shean, John, 300

Shelby, Jo, 281–82

Shenandoah Valley campaign, 186, 193, 231

Sherman, Sidney, 298

Sherman, William T., 275, 276, 278, 292

Shields, James, 53, 186

Simmons, John, 279

Slaughter, James E., 286, 287

Slaves: construction of Confederate defensive works by, 127, 148–54, 167–68; defection of, to Union Army, 130, 149–50; Fugitive Slave Law, 130; lack of information by, for Union plans, 163*n*19; and Magruder family, 7, 107; Whig Party on slavery, 106

Slemmer, Adam, 92

Slidell, John, 38, 42

Slocum, Henry W., 186, 200

Smith, Ashbel, 280

Smith, Charles F., 80

Smith, Edmund Kirby: and Army of Missouri, 277; and back pay for Magruder after surrender in Texas, 285, 287; and Canby's proposed invasion of Texas coast, 278; as commander of Trans-Mississippi Department, 263; and conscription in Texas, 271; and Cotton Bureau, 266, 269–70; and cotton sales for military supplies in Texas, 263, 264, 266, 269–70; on Magruder, 272; and Magruder in Arkansas District, 275–76; Magruder's view of, 272; in Mexico, 281–82; and Red River expedition, 267; surrender of Trans-Mississippi Department by, 279–80

Smith, Francis H., 118

Smith, Gustavus W.: and Battle of Seven Pines, 188, 190; as commander of Army of Northern Virginia, 190; commissioning of, as major general, 184–85, 185n126; and conversion hysteria, 190n156; Davis's removal of, as commander of Army of Northern Virginia, 190, 191; dismissal of, by Lee, 193; Magruder's disagreements with, xi, 184; withdrawal of, from Virginia Peninsula, 181

Smith, J. Maynard, 303

Smith, Justin H., x, 50n65

Smith, Leon, 246–48, 246n19, 250, 251, 282

Smith, Persifor F., 60, 62, 70, 88

Smith, Thomas "Nicaragua," 252–53, 253n51

Smith, William F., 186, 205, 207

Social life: Aztec Club in Mexico City, 80–81, 80–81n5; in Baltimore, 25; Buchanan's inaugural ball, 108–9; in California, 91–92, 94–95, 98–100; dinner for British military officers in Plattsburg, N.Y., 34; Grand Military Banquet in New York City, 103; Magruder's enjoyment of and talent for, 2, 20–21, 25, 274–75; of Magruder's father, 7; and Magruder's lack of funds, 1, 7; and Magruder's moniker of "Prince John," 20; in Magruder's youth in Virginia, 3; in Mexico, 283; in Newport, R.I., 110; San Diego dance, 91–92; sleigh race on Lake Champlain, 34–35; in Tampico, Mexico, 54; in Texas,

106, 245, 274–75; in Washington, D.C., 110; women's relationships with Magruder, 21, 22, 110; and yachting in California, 98–99

Sorley, James, 302

Sorrell, G. Moxley, 197–98

Sparrow, Edward, 238n211

Stanard, Hugh, 127, 272

Stanton, Edwin M., 195

States' rights, 106, 271–72

Stearns, Don Able, 95

Steele, Frederick, 275–77

Steiner, Josephus M., 81–82

Stephens, Alexander H., 293

Stevens, Walter, 192

Stevenson, Carter, 3

Stinnecke, H. A., 29–30, 30n135

Stoneman, George, 92

Street, Robert G., 303, 305

Strother, David H., 1, 121

Stuart, Jeb, 28, 181, 210, 221

Stuart, William D., 131

Sturgis, Samuel D., 115

Sulakowski, Valery, 273, 273n151

Sumner, Edwin V. "Bull": and Allen's Farm Battle, 204, 207; and Gaines's Mill Battle, 200; and Malvern Hill Battle, 224, 228; Malvern Hill position of, 216; number of Federal troops under, 196n6; opposition of, to Federal retreat during Seven Days' battles, 208–9, 209n66; position of, after Seven Pines Battle, 195; position of, following Gaines's Mill Battle, 203; position of (June 29), 205; and Savage Station Battle, 207, 208–9; and threat against Richmond, 197; and Virginia Peninsula campaign, 169–70, 186–89

Sutherland, Thomas W., 94

Sweeney, S. B., 219

Sweeny, Thomas W., 91

Swift, Alexander J., 14, 17

Swift, Joseph G., 17

Swinton, William, 222

Sykes, George, 186, 216

Talcott, Andrew, 125–26

Tampico, Mexico, 53–54

Tatnall, Josiah, 180

Taylor, Richard, 270, 273, 275–76

Taylor, Walter, 174, 210

Taylor, Zachary: death of, 97; and Mexican War, 37–39, 38*n*4, 39*n*8, 41–52, 51*n*72, 52*n*79, 139, 165; and remounting of Company I, 1st Artillery, 84; shortcomings of, 46–47, 46*n*48, 51*n*72, 52*n*79; uniform of, 46

Tebbetts, George P. "Two-Bits," 101

Terrell, Alexander Watkins, 265*n*107, 282–83, 283*n*8, 286

Terry, D. S., 278*n*175

Texas: annexation of, U.S., 37, 38; Hutchins House in Houston, 298–300; individualism of Texans, 270; International Boundary Commission survey team in, escorted by Magruder's Company I, 22, 23, 104–6, 140; railroads in, 274; social life in, 106, 245, 274–75; U.S. Army in, before Mexican War, 38–44. *See also* Texas in Civil War; *and specific cities*

Texas in Civil War: Banks's attempted invasion of, 268–69; casualties during Civil War in, 248, 249, 251, 268; civilian versus military authority in, 270–72, 271*n*143; conscription during, 271; and Cotton Bureau, 266–67, 269–70, 274; cotton sales for military supplies for, 259–67, 265*n*107, 269–71; fatal argument between Wharton and Baylor at Magruder's headquarters, 278–79; Federal troops along coast of, 267–68, 274, 278; food shortages in, 265–66, 274–75; Magruder as commander of District of Texas, New Mexico, and Arizona, 241, 244–45, 272; Magruder's communication with troops before surrender of, 279, 292–93; Magruder's headquarters in, 259, 278; Magruder's staff in, 273–74, 273*n*151; mutiny of 3rd Regiment of Texas Infantry, 266; pay owed to soldiers in, 265, 266, 274; praise for Magruder in, 244–45, 251, 258–59, 259*n*73; prisoners of war in, 252, 253, 254, 254*n*55; Red River expedition, 267, 275; Sabine Pass expedition, 267–68; shortage of arms, munitions, and military supplies in, 259, 265; surrender of, 279–80, 292–93; vulnerable position of,

242–43; Walker as commander in, 278. *See also* Galveston, Tex.

Thayer, Sylvanus, 11–12, 14–17

Theater, 40–41, 54, 80

Thomas, George H., 277

Thomas, Lorenzo, 171–72

Thompson, Frederick, 255*n*60

Thompson, Leslie, 303

Thornton, Seth B., 44–45

Thorton, George A., 127

Toombs, Robert, 192, 193, 202, 227–28

Torrejón, Anastacio, 44, 47

Townsend, Frederick, 132*n*58

Trader, Rev. Mr., 299

Trans-Mississippi Department: Cotton Bureau in, 266–67, 269–70, 274; cotton sales for military supplies in Texas, 259–67, 265*n*107, 269–71; Holmes's assignment as commander of, 233, 239–41; Kirby Smith as commander of, 263; Magruder's assignment as commander of, 185–86, 232–34; Magruder's request for reinstatement of appointment to, 239, 240; recall of Magruder from, 232–34, 236, 239; surrender of, 279–80, 292–93. *See also* Texas in Civil War

Transportation and travel: between Baltimore and Washington, D.C., 25–26; between California and East Coast, 84–87, 103; and difficulties of travel, 19; to Mexico, 282–83; from San Francisco to San Diego, 89; in Texas, 105; to West Point, 10. *See also* Railroads

Trousdale, William, 75–76

Trumbull, Lyman, 160

Tucker, Beverly, 289*n*36

Tucker, George, 9

Tucker, Philip C., 251–52*n*47

Tunnell, Hannah, 132, 132*n*57

Turner, Edmund P., 271*n*143, 273–74, 282, 298, 299, 300

Twiggs, David E., 39, 41–43, 45, 53–69, 61*n*120, 74

Tyler, John, 150

Uniforms, 46, 81, 111

U.S. Military Academy. *See* West Point

University of Virginia, 8–10, 16

Valencia, Gabriel, 69–71

Van Buren, John, 292

Van Buren, Martin, 33

Vandiver, Frank, 140, 140*n*93

Vera Cruz expedition, 5*n*115, 52, 55–60, 58*n*110

Vernon, S. F. Gay de, 14

Victor Emmanuel II, King, 113

CSS *Virginia*, 159–61, 160*n*5, 161*n*12, 167, 172, 180

Virginia: borders of, 118–19; *Pawnee* scare and threat to Richmond at beginning of Civil War, 119, 119*n*4, 125; railroads in, 119, 120, 159; secession of, 113–14, 116–18, 130. *See also* Civil War; Fort Monroe, Va.; Seven Days' battles; Virginia Peninsula campaign

Virginia Peninsula: boundaries of Magruder's command in, 125; topography of Virginia Peninsula, 162, 170, 182*n*116, 195–96; weather conditions of, 170, 174, 187–89, 195–96, 195*n*3

Virginia Peninsula campaign: Battle of Big Bethel, x–xi, 132–36, 132*n*58, 135*n*70, 138–39, 141, 240; Battle of Lee's Mill, 174; Battle of Seven Pines, 188–90, 189*n*148, 225; Battle of Williamsburg, 182–84, 183*n*121; Benjamin's mishandling of, 155–57; and Butler, 127–30, 128*n*39, 134–35; call-ups of Virginia militiamen by Magruder, 146–47; care of wounded and burial of dead during, 134; casualties in, 132*n*58, 133–34, 166*n*37, 174, 182–83, 183*n*121, 184*n*122; command of, by Magruder, 125; Confederate reinforcements needed for, 172–73, 172*n*66; deceptive ploys by Magruder against McClellan, 173–74; and defective weapons and ammunition, 144; defensive fortifications and defensive lines for, 127, 148–52, 163*n*18, 166–68, 170–71, 177, 178*n*99, 183, 184, 184*n*122; and divisions of Army of the Peninsula, 166; and eight-brigade arrangement of Army of the Peninsula, 166*n*38; and exodus of pro-Confederate Virginians from Newport News, 129–30, 129*n*43; explosives used during, 166*n*37; and Federal occupation of Newport News, 128–29; and Fort Magruder, 182–84; and Hill, 127, 131–33, 135; horses needed for, 144; T. J. Jackson's tardiness during, 67; Johnston's arrival with reinforcements for, 174, 178;

Johnston's withdrawal from, 179–86; labor shortage for defensive works for, 147–52; Magruder's army under Gustavus Smith during, 184–86; Magruder's attack plans for, 178–79; Magruder's battlefield experiences during, 133, 133*n*60, 135*n*70, 166, 189; Magruder's plans for defense of Virginia Peninsula, 126–27, 131, 166–68, 172–75, 178; Magruder's preparations for McClellan's advance, 163–68, 164*n*29, 164–65*n*32, 166*n*36, 172–75; Magruder's prohibition of alcohol during, 164, 164*n*29; Magruder's reports of Federal troop build-up in Virginia Peninsula, 155–57, 155*nn*171–172; Magruder's staff for, 127; malaria contracted by Magruder during, 180–82; and McClellan's headquarters at White House, 186, 195; McClellan's inaccurate information and inadequate maps during, 161–63, 163*nn*18–19, 170, 189; McClellan's movement toward Richmond, 169–72, 186–87; and McClellan's plan for capture of Richmond, 158–63, 161*n*14; and McClellan's plans for capture of Yorktown, 161, 172, 174; number of Confederate troops under Magruder, 126, 135, 157, 167, 174, 181; praise for Magruder and his promotion during, 138–39, 141–42, 174–75, 197, 240; prisoners of war from, 136–38; razing of Hampton ordered by Magruder, 149, 149–50*n*143; roads on Virginia Peninsula, 161–62, 161*n*14, 170; rumors of Magruder's drunkenness during, 28; rumors of Magruder's womanizing during, 22; and shortages of supplies and troops for Confederate army, 126–27, 128, 143–47, 145*n*116; size of Army of the Potomac in, 157, 160, 172, 174, 177, 186–87, 188*n*143; slave labor for construction of defensive works for, 127, 148–54; success of Magruder's defense of Virginia Peninsula before Johnston's arrival, 174–75, 197, 240

Von Kapff, Bernard Johann, 18, 18*n*78

Von Kapff, Esther Henrietta. *See* Magruder, Esther Henrietta von Kapff

Wade, Ben, 160

Waggaman, Eugene, 228–29

Wainwright, Jonathan, 244*n*12, 248, 251–52*n*47

Walker, John G., 278

Walker, John P., 236*n*205

Walker, Leroy Pope, 145, 151

Walker, Lilian, 305

Walker, William, 253*n*51

Waller, Edward, 278*n*175

War with Mexico. *See* Mexican War

Ward, Sam, 25, 25*n*113

Warner, Ezra J., 166*n*37

Warren, Mrs. J. E., 5*n*17

Warwick River, 170–71

Washington, George, 179

Washington, D.C.: defenses for, 122*n*11, 158, 172–73; Magruder as draftsman in Ordnance Department in, 31; Magruder's proposal for capture of, at beginning of Civil War, 119–24; Magruder's travel to, after night of drinking, 26; social life of, 110

Watkins, Charles, 219

Watkins, Oscar, 273–74, 282, 297, 298, 302

Waul, Thomas N., 303, 305

Webb, Alexander, 160*n*7, 161*n*12

Webster, Daniel, 100

Weekes, Captain, 302

Wellington, Duke of, 68

Werlich, Robert, 130*n*47

West, George Benjamin, 129

West, Parker, 129

West Point: Butler's opinion of graduates of, 130–31; Lee at, 16*n*65, 191; Magruder at, xi, 1, 8, 8*n*26, 10–18, 17*n*73, 39, 116, 139; other graduates of, 81, 127, 133, 143*n*107, 166, 177, 244*n*13, 289

Westfield, 243, 246, 248, 249, 258

Wharton, Edward Clifton, 273, 286*n*21

Wharton, John A., 278–79, 278*n*175

Wheat, Roberdeau, 113

Whig Party, 52*n*79, 53, 106, 118

Whistler, William, 39, 42

Whitcomb, Thomas, 35

White Sulphur Springs, W.Va., 293

Whiting, Jasper S., 190*n*156

Whiting, Levi, 53, 60

Whiting, Mr., 137

Whiting, William H. C., 188, 189, 192, 193, 224

Wilcox, Cadmus M., 39*n*7, 80*n*5, 183*n*121, 281–82

Wildey, Elisha H., 294

Williams, Isaac, 3

Williams, J. B., 208

Williamsburg, Battle of, 182–84, 183*n*121

Wilmington Daily Journal, 137, 138

Winthrop, Theodore, 133–34, 134*n*63

Wise, Henry A., 124, 156, 156*n*178, 157

Wise, Obadiah Jennings, 156*n*178

Woodworth, Steven E., 175*n*84

Wool, John E., 138, 150

Worth, William Jenkins: in Mexican War, 39, 40*n*14, 41–44, 55, 56, 59–60, 66–69, 71, 73, 76, 77; as supporter of Magruder, 36; at West Point, 12

Wright, Ambrose Ransom ("Rans"), 218, 225–28

Wyatt, Henry Lawson, 133

Wynne, Charles H., 240

Yachting, 98–99

Yancey, Stephen D., 273–74

Yellow fever, 57, 244

York River, 125–26, 161, 161*n*12, 167, 177, 178

Yorktown, Va.: care for wounded Union soldiers in, 134; Confederate defenses at, 125, 148, 161, 167, 171, 172, 178; Confederate weapons and supplies left at, after Johnston's retreat, 180; gun carriages at, 143; Hill on defense of, 178*n*99; importance of, for defense of Richmond, 145*n*116; and Magruder's call-up of militiamen, 146; Magruder's headquarters at, 126, 127, 129, 143; and McClellan's advance toward Richmond, 169–72; McClellan's plans for capture of, 161, 172, 174; Rains's 1st Division at, 166; refugees from Newport News at, 129; and Revolutionary War, 165, 179